Study Guide

MW01205170

Understanding Abnormal Behavior

NINTH EDITION

David Sue
Western Washington University

Derald Wing Sue
Teachers College, Columbia University

Stanley Sue
University of California, Davis

Prepared by

Fred W. Whitford
Montana State University

WADSWORTH
CENGAGE Learning™

Australia • Brazil • Japan • Korea • Mexico • Singapore • Spain • United Kingdom • United States

ISBN-13: 978-0-547-17102-9
ISBN-10: 0-547-17102-1

Wadsworth
10 Davis Drive
Belmont, CA 94002-3098
USA

Cengage Learning is a leading provider of customized learning solutions with office locations around the globe, including Singapore, the United Kingdom, Australia, Mexico, Brazil, and Japan. Locate your local office at: **www.cengage.com/international**

Cengage Learning products are represented in Canada by Nelson Education, Ltd.

To learn more about Wadsworth, visit **www.cengage.com/wadsworth**

Purchase any of our products at your local college store or at our preferred online store **www.ichapters.com**

Printed in Canada
1 2 3 4 5 6 7 12 11 10 09 08

Contents

To the Student

This *Study Guide* was designed to help you master the material in the Ninth Edition of *Understanding Abnormal Behavior* by Sue/Sue/Sue. The *Study Guide* supplements the text but does not replace it. If used properly, it should help you to understand and master key facts, concepts, and issues discussed in the text.

ORGANIZATION OF THE *STUDY GUIDE*

Each *Study Guide* chapter corresponds to a text chapter and is divided into the following sections: Chapter Outline, Learning Objectives, Key Terms Review, and Multiple-Choice Questions.

- *Table of Contents* This material is directly from the textbook and included to help remember where the material occurs in the chapter.

- *Learning Objectives* The learning objectives guide your mastery of the material by focusing your attention on the key ideas and concepts in each chapter. Page numbers corresponding to the objectives have been identified to encourage you to use the text and Study Guide interactively for maximum benefit.

- *Chapter Outlines* The outlines present the major ideas and topics in each chapter. Key terms are defined. The outlines are condensed overviews of chapter material and are excellent review mechanisms. But they cannot and should not be used as substitutes for reading the chapter.

- *Key Terms Review* Key terms appearing at the end of each chapter in the text are also defined in the chapter outlines. To further reinforce your mastery of these terms, we provide fill-in-the-blank quizzes. This three-pronged approach to learning should strengthen your command of the terminology common to abnormal psychology.

- *Multiple-Choice Questions* Once you have read the text and worked your way through the first three sections of the Study Guide, you will be ready to test your knowledge of the material covered. Three sets of multiple-choice questions are provided. First, *Factual Multiple-Choice Questions* quiz your basic recall of key points in the chapter. *Conceptual Multiple-Choice Questions* add a degree of challenge by assessing your understanding of abnormal psychology concepts. These questions typically involve comparisons and contrasts, and the use of cognitive skills at a level somewhat higher than simple factual recall. Last, *Application Multiple-Choice Questions* present situations in which you will assess, diagnose, or treat the problem at hand. These application questions pose situations faced by practitioners or researchers, and challenge you to reason like a psychologist. In order to improve your understanding of the material, answers to the questions are provided with corresponding textbook page numbers referenced. In addition, a justification is provided for the incorrect answers. Don't be a passive learner. Study the reasons why you made an incorrect response. The feedback will help you sharpen your analytical skills in this class and also in other classes where similar assessment methods are used.

- *Objectives Defined* This short review defines the learning objective from earlier in each chapter. These are a good summary for studying the learning objectives.

- *Margin Definitions* Are definitions for all the key terms from earlier in the chapters. These definitions are an excellent study source.

STUDY SKILLS

Although each student may have his or her preferred way to study a subject, research shows that many students use ineffective learning methods. Educational psychologists have studied various techniques that result in improved academic performance. Check with your professor to see whether or not your college has a learning assistance center. Typically, these centers have services to help students improve their academic success. In addition to workshops that may be offered by your college learning assistance center, an excellent printed resource is Pauk's (2005) *How to Succeed in College*. This book is recommended for all college students in any discipline and has excellent material on time management, note taking, learning from textbooks, and test-taking strategies. One method discussed in the book is SQ3R, a method designed to help students read and study textbooks effectively.

The SQ3R method was developed by Francis P. Robinson, a psychologist at Ohio State University. Professor Robinson's research demonstrated that students' understanding and performance in academic courses increased by using the SQ3R method. SQ3R stands for: Survey, Question, Read, Recite, Review, and the method is outlined below.

- *Survey*. Page through the chapter, looking at the main headings and the organization of the chapter. Read the final summary of the chapter. Try to get a *gestalt* of the chapter—an overall picture of how the chapter is organized and what's to come. Why is this important? Scanning a chapter helps you develop a cognitive schema of the chapter. When you begin to read the chapter, you will have a better idea of how ideas are linked to one another, and you will organize the information you encounter more efficiently.

- *Question*. Based on your survey of the chapter, formulate some questions about the material. One way to develop questions is to turn the chapter headings into questions. Another strategy is to read the Learning Objectives in the *Study Guide* prior to reading the text material. Why is this important? When we have a question in mind, we seek to resolve the question. Presumably, this strategy makes us more active readers.

- *Read*. Actively read the chapter. Have your *Study Guide* nearby so that you can look periodically at the Chapter Outline. Break your reading into smaller segments. Don't read the entire chapter in one sitting, since there is too much material to absorb. While reading, take small breaks in between major sections of the chapter. During your break (e.g., while jogging) actively reflect on what you've read. See if you can answer the question(s) you formulated. After you have read several sections, and certainly before you quit your studying, review the Chapter Outline.

- *Recite*. Looking away from the book, briefly recite out loud the main points of the section you've read. Try to create an original example that would illustrate the concept under discussion. If a research study is discussed, summarize the main points of the research study. Another recitation strategy is to use the Key Terms Review in the *Study Guide*.

- *Review*. The Chapter Outlines in the *Study Guide* serve as a useful tool for review prior to an examination. Again, be active in your review. Look at the major headings but try to actively recite the subpoints under the heading.

A big thanks for all the authors' contributions from earlier editions of this manual. You are about to embark on a fascinating journey into the world of abnormal behavior. I hope you find this *Study Guide* a helpful resource as you commence your study.

Fred Whitford

Montana State University

whitford@montana.edu

References

Pauk, W. and Owens, R. *(2005). How to Succeed in College.* Boston: Houghton Mifflin Company (ISBN-0-618-37972X).

Robinson, F. P. *(1970). Effective study* (4th ed.). New York: Harper & Row.

CHAPTER 1

Abnormal Behavior

TABLE OF CONTENTS

LEARNING OBJECTIVES

1.   Define abnormal psychology.

2.   Understand the criteria used to determine normal or abnormal behaviors.

3.   Discuss how the role of context and cultural differences affect definitions of abnormality.

4.   Determine how common mental disorders are.

5.   Define some common misconceptions of the mentally disturbed.

6.   Discuss how explanations of abnormal behavior have changed over time.

7.   Discuss early viewpoints of the causes of mental disorders.

8.   Define some of contemporary trends in abnormal psychology.

CHAPTER OUTLINE

I.   **The concerns of abnormal psychology.** *Abnormal psychology* seeks to describe, explain, predict, and control those behaviors that are considered strange. In describing disorders, psychologists develop a *psychodiagnosis*. Diagnosis is a useful first step in treatment but, because of labeling, may sometimes have harmful consequences. Explanations about the causes of abnormal behavior differ depending on the psychologist's theoretical orientation. The prediction of future behavior is difficult; for instance, psychologists tend to overpredict future violent behavior. *Therapy* is the method by which psychologists try to control behavior. A growing number of individuals have entered clinical psychology and related mental health professions. There are an increasing number of mental health professionals in the United States. Clinical psychologists have Ph.D. or Psy.D. degrees and are trained to assess and treat people with serious disorders. Counseling psychologists are trained in much the same way as clinical psychologists, but they traditionally treat less serious problems. Marriage and family counseling look at the family as a unit. Mental health counseling can be licensed in 49 states and work in a number of clinical settings. Psychiatrists have medical degrees and can prescribe medication. Psychoanalysts are trained in psychoanalytic institutes and engage in personal analysis. Psychiatric social workers usually get a master's degree and often work in family or community agencies. School psychologists work with children and adolescents in school settings, assisting them with cognitive, social, and behavioral interventions.

II. **Defining abnormal behavior.** The Diagnostic and Statistical Manual of Mental Disorders (DSM-IV-TR) has the current definition of mental disorders. The standards include when are behaviors significant, what are present distresses, painful symptoms and ascertaining increased risk. The statistical criterion defines abnormality as those behaviors that are infrequent. One problem with this standard is that it provides no consistent means for deciding what is rare and what is undesirable. Psychologists view abnormal behavior as deviating from what is considered normal in terms of distress, deviance, dysfunction and dangerousness, the "4 D's." Distress involves both physical and psychological pain. Deviance refers to odd behaviors, such as *hallucinations* (false sensory impressions) and *delusions* (false beliefs). Dysfunction is exhibited when a person's performance falls well short of his or her potential. Dangerousness is defined by Tarasoff v. Regents of the University of California which indicates that psychologists have "a duty to protect."

III. **Contextual and cultural limitations in defining abnormal behavior.** Multicultural perspectives recognize that all behaviors originate from a cultural context. One approach is *cultural universality*, the traditional viewpoint on abnormality, which states that there are universal symptoms and disorders. The opposite, *cultural relativism*, says that deviance designations reflect cultural values. Both approaches have merit. A central theme is what behaviors are widely considered to be abnormal given the culture and how the culture influences the identification and treatment of abnormal behavior.

IV. **The frequency and burden of mental disorders.** The goals of psychiatric epidemiology are to determine how frequent disorders are in the population, how such factors as age and gender affect their prevalence (i.e., the percentage of people in a population who suffer from a disorder at a given time), lifetime prevalence (i.e., the total proportion of people in the population who have ever had a disorder in their lives), and incidence (i.e., the onset or occurrence of a given disorder over some period of time). Another goal of epidemiology is to determine whether and how trends are changing. Current research into the epidemiology of mental disorders. Overall, men and women are equally likely to suffer from disorders; however, men are more likely to have alcohol problems and women are more likely to become depressed or anxious. Older people are vulnerable to cognitive impairments. Mental illness ranks higher than malignant disease with respect to lost years of healthy life. Fewer than one-third of people with disorders receive mental health services.

V.   **Stereotypes about the mentally disturbed.** One myth is that mentally disturbed people can be readily spotted. This is not true because there are no sharp dividing lines between normality and abnormality and because some forms of deviance can be hidden. Another myth is that mental disorder is always inherited. Genetics can play a role in some disorders, but even in those disorders where genes are thought to play a role, environmental stress is a crucial influence. Other myths are that people with mental disorders cannot be cured, that their problems stem from a lack of willpower, that mental illness is always a deficit and those who suffer disorders contribute nothing to society, and that they are more dangerous than other people.

VI. **Historical perspectives on abnormal behavior.** How people view mental disorders is related to the beliefs of their culture ad time. During prehistoric times, people believed in *demonology* (demonic possession, sorcery, or the behest of an offended ancestral spirit). Treatments included *trephining* (chipping open the skull so the evil spirit could escape) and *exorcism* (prayers, noisemaking, even starvation to drive out spirits). Naturalistic explanations during the Greco-Roman era, relied heavily on observations and explanations attributing disorders to organic factors such as brain pathology. Reversion to supernatural explanations in the Middle Ages. during the Dark Ages, the Catholic Church dominated all thought and reverted to supernatural explanations for mental disorders. In the 13th century, whole populations were sometimes affected by such forms of mass madness as *tarantism* (a dance mania) and *lycanthropy* (in which people believed themselves to be wolves). Witchcraft became a common explanation for abnormal behavior in the 15th-17th centuries, when the Catholic Church was under attack. Some mentally ill people were considered witches and received brutal punishment, but most accused witches were probably sane. The *Malleus Maleficarum* (Witch's Hammer) is published. The rise of humanism (the Renaissance) took place in the $14^{th} - 16^{th}$ centuries, stressing human welfare and rejecting the supernatural aspects of witchcraft. Johann Weyer asserted that people who had been thought to be witches were actually mentally disturbed. The reform movement (18th and 19th centuries) led to the moral treatment movement; it began in France (Philippe Pinel) and England (William Tuke). In America (Benjamin Rush), mental patients were also treated more humanely. Dorothea Dix pushed for the improvement of care for individuals with mental disorders and for the building of mental hospitals. Clifford Beers exposed the cruel treatment he and other patients experienced in mental institutions. Generally, treatment for the mentally ill has improved in this century.

VII. **Causes: Early viewpoints.** From Hippocrates' day to our own, organic explanations of abnormality have existed. During the late 1800s, there was a strong increase in this biological viewpoint, which was supported by the discovery that general paresis had an organic cause. Emil Kraepelin observed that certain symptoms occur in clusters, called syndromes, with each syndrome having a unique cause. Kraepelin classified the mental illnesses on the basis of organic causes. The *psychological viewpoint* is an alternative view that suggests emotions can cause mental disorders. Anton Mesmer used trances (mesmerism) to treat people with hysteria, sometimes successfully. Although he was declared a fraud, these treatments underscored the power of suggestion for curing disorder. *Mesmerism and Hypnotism* was studied and used by several French physicians (Liebeault, Bernheim, and Charcot) to treat hysteria during the late 1800s, this was called the *Nancy School*. Breuer found that reliving past experiences through catharsis removed symptoms, too. Sigmund Freud built upon this foundation. A dichotomous approach, behaviorism, was firmly rooted in laboratory research and stressed the importance of directly observable behaviors and the conditions of stimuli that evoked, reinforced, and extinguished them.

VIII. **Contemporary trends in abnormal psychology.** Twentieth-century views of abnormality have been influenced by the introduction of psychiatric drugs in the drug revolution of the1950s, which led to a great reduction in patients residing in mental institutions *(deinstitutionalization)*. Psychologists have initiated legislative efforts to gain prescription privileges to treat individuals with mental disorders Medical providers (psychiatrists) are opposed to non-medical personnel having prescription privileges, and not all psychologists support psychologists' expansion into the psychopharmacological realm, fearing that psychologists will lose their own professional identity. *Managed health care,* which attempts to contain costs by increasing the oversight of treatment by outside reviewers and by requiring treatment professionals to justify their therapies, may alter the types of care provided. Appreciation for research: professionals in abnormal psychology value research on both the biological and psychological bases of behavior for understanding and treating mental disorders. Diversity and multicultural psychology: Changes in the racial and ethnic diversity of the United States have helped create a new field called *multicultural psychology*. Racial, cultural, age, and gender differences in apparent mental disorders may be explained in terms of social conditioning (e.g., stereotyping), cultural values that are taught, and sociopolitical influences such as prejudice, which prompt healthy coping mechanisms that may be seen as symptoms. Bias in diagnosis is another explanation for differences in minority mental health.

IX.   **Implications** Increasingly, professionals value a *multi-path approach*, which acknowledges that biological, psychological, and social factors combine to explain most disorders.

KEY TERMS REVIEW

1.   The therapeutic use of verbal expression to release pent-up unconscious conflicts is called the _____.

2.   The belief that mental disorders are caused by psychological or emotional factors is called the _____.

3.   The ancient. surgical technique in which part of the skull was chipped away to provide an escape for evil spirits is called _____.

4.   The industrialization of health care, whereby organizations in the private sector control the delivery of services is called _____.

5.   Begun by Philippe Pinel, this movement was a shift toward more humane treatment for mentally disturbed patients. It was called the _____.

6.   A cluster of symptoms that tend to occur together, believed to be indicative of a particular disorder, is called a(n) _____.

7.   A program of systematic intervention whose purpose is to modify a client's behavior, emotions, or thoughts is called _____.

8.   The scientific discipline that seeks to describe, explain, predict, and control behaviors that are considered unusual is called _____.

9.   The philosophical movement that emphasizes human welfare and the worth of the individual, and that challenged supernatural explanations of deviant behavior, is called _____.

10. The belief that mental disorders have a physical or physiological basis is called the _____.

11. The belief that the origin and manifestation of disorders are equally applicable across all cultures is called _____.

12. The belief that lifestyles, cultural values, and world views affect the expression and determination of deviant behavior is called _____.

13. An attempt to describe, assess, and systematically draw inferences about an individual's psychological disorder is called a(n) _____.

14. The contemporary approach that sees the cause of most disorders as a combination of biological, psychological, and social factors is called the _____.

15. _____ is a clinically significant behavioral or psychological syndrome or pattern that occurs in an individual and that is associated with present distress (e.g., a painful symptom) or disability (i.e., impairment in one or more important areas of functioning) or with a significantly increased risk of suffering death, pain, disability, or an important loss of freedom

16. The ritual in which prayer, noise, and extreme measures such as starvation were used to cast evil spirits out of an afflicted person's body is called _____.

17. Group hysteria in which large numbers of people exhibit similar symptoms that have no apparent physical cause is called _____.

18. The field of psychology that stresses the importance of race, ethnicity, gender, and culture in understanding abnormal behavior is called _____.

19. A dysfunction or disease of the brain is called a _____.

20. The percent of individuals in a population who suffer from a mental disorder at a given point in time is called the _____.

21.   The rate of occurrence of a disorder over a period of time is referred to as _____.

22.   The total proportion of people in the population who have ever had a disorder in their life is the

_____.

23.   It appears that, _____, or abnormal behavior, is not the result of any singular cause but an interaction of many factors.

24.   _____ is a psychological perspective that stresses the importance of learning and behavior in explanations of normal and abnormal development

FACTUAL MULTIPLE-CHOICE QUESTIONS

1.   Psychologists attempt to change or control abnormal behavior through the process of

    a.   psychodiagnosis.
    b.   therapy.
    c.   research.
    d.   clinical assessment.

2.   According to the practical criterion for defining abnormality, when a person complains of an extended period of anxiety, fatigue, and other physical or mental symptoms but is able to fulfill his or her expected social roles, this is evidence of

    a.   dysfunction.
    b.   discomfort.
    c.   deviance.
    d.   delusions.

3.   False sensory impressions are called _____ contradictory evidence are called

_____.

    a.   dysfunctions; delusions
    b.   hallucinations; delusions
    c.   sensorimotor deviation; dementia
    d.   delusions; hallucinations

4.   Based on the National Institute of Mental Health epidemiological study of mental disorders in three major cities,

    a.   the rate of mental disorders has steadily decreased over the past twenty years.
    b.   approximately 1 in 50 Americans suffers from an emotional disorder.
    c.   depression is among the least common disorders in the United, States.
    d.   alcohol problems are more common in men than in women.

5.   Tarantism and lycanthropy are examples of _____, which occurred during the

_____.

    a.   mesmerism; 1200s
    b.   mass madness; 1200s
    c.   exorcism; 1800s
    d.   mass madness; time of ancient Greece and Rome

6.   Clifford Beers, Dorothea Dix, and Benjamin Rush were all

    a.   Americans who supported Freud's psychoanalytic theory.
    b.   researchers on hypnosis and hysteria.
    c.   involved in improving the treatment offered in mental institutions.
    d.   supporters of the idea that mental disorder stems from organic causes.

7.   The technique of mesmerism was a forerunner of

    a.   hypnotism.
    b.   drug therapy.
    c.   exorcism.
    d.   trephining.

8.   Most psychologists believe that mental disorders are caused by

    a.   psychological factors only.
    b.   heredity and brain deficits.
    c.   cultural factors only.
    d.   a combination, of biological, psychological, and societal influences, the multi-path approach.

9.   A clinical psychologists education includes

    a.   required training in psychoanalysis.
    b.   four years of medical school.
    c.   getting a Ph.D. or Psy.D. degree.
    d.   no training in assessment or prevention of abnormal behavior.

10.   Among all the mental health professionals, only the _____ can currently prescribe medication.

    a.   psychiatrist
    b.   clinical psychologist
    c.   psychiatric social worker
    d.   counseling psychologist

11.   Behaviorism has been _____ in treating maladaptive behaviors.

    a.   somewhat dangerous
    b.   fairly ineffective
    c.   prohibited
    d.   quite successful

CONCEPTUAL MULTIPLE-CHOICE QUESTIONS

1.   One limitation in using the statistical criterion for defining abnormal behavior is the inability to

    a.   distinguish rare behaviors that are desirable from those that are undesirable.
    b.   consider how frequently a behavior occurs in the population.
    c.   show a relationship between prediction and control of behavior.
    d.   use objective, empirical information about deviant behavior.

2.   Dr. Chiu argues that in defining abnormal behavior, psychologists should use the ideal mental health criterion because this criterion

    a.   is based on whether the individual's behavior is bizarre and inefficient and causes personal discomfort.
    b.   is the most comprehensive and has the fewest drawbacks.
    c.   considers deviations from positive goals assumed to be important for the individual.
    d.   is based on the frequency of deviant actions.

3.   In contrast to traditional views of abnormality, cultural relativism

    a.   rejects the idea that behaviors defined as abnormal in western culture are abnormal everywhere else.
    b.   emphasizes the idea that abnormality is best defined in terms of deviation from some ideal of mental health.
    c.   argues that there is no such thing as mental illness.
    d.   supports the idea that abnormality is based primarily on biological differences.

4. Dysfunction suggests that mental disorder be seen as
    a. a biologically caused phenomenon that is unaffected by society.
    b. having three components: rarity, deviation from ideal, and cultural norms.
    c. a functional deficiency caused by biological factors that is seen as harmful by society.
    d. the result of poor parenting, inadequate social resources, and unavailable treatment.

5. Which of the following statements is *accurate* concerning heredity and mental disorder?
    a. Heredity plays a powerful causal influence and the occurrence of most every mental disorder and environmental factors play almost no role.
    b. Heredity has been found to play almost no role in even the most serious mental disorders.
    c. Because most mental disorders are inherited, they cannot be cured.
    d. Although heredity plays an important role in some disorders, the environment plays a major role in all of them.

6. Which of the following treatments for abnormal behavior is correctly paired with its period in history?
    a. Exorcism—Middle Ages
    b. Trephining—Renaissance
    c. Exorcism—moral treatment era
    d. Cathartic method—moral treatment era

7. Modern interpretations of witchcraft suggest that
    a. people who were seen as voluntary witches were treated with sympathy and kindness.
    b. witches were often not insane.
    c. the church actually tried to stop the hunting of witches.
    d. the church believed that witches were suffering from brain pathology.

8. A person who discusses mental disorders in terms of syndromes and believes that they are caused solely by brain disease, heredity, or metabolic disturbances supports the
    a. psychogenic viewpoint.
    b. idea of demonology.
    c. biological viewpoint.
    d. biopsychosocial orientation.

9. One explanation for differences in rates of mental disorder among ethnic and racial groups is
    a. cultural universality.
    b. social conditioning.
    c. the absence of bias in diagnosis.
    d. some groups are not susceptible to psychological distress

10. Which of the following statements about managed health care is *accurate*?
    a. Managed-care organizations are exerting increasing control over the type and number of treatment sessions psychologists can offer.
    b. Managed care has led to a great increase in the cost of health care.
    c. Managed care is favored by psychologists because it gives them greater control over the treatment they give their parents.
    d. Over the past thirty years managed care has decreased the number of clinical psychologists in the United States.

11. Which of the following terms is used by clinical psychologists as a synonym for abnormal behavior?
    a. Psychopathology
    b. Behaviorism
    c. Psychoanalysis
    d. Cultural relativism

APPLICATION MULTIPLE-CHOICE QUESTIONS

1. Dr. Eberhardt has already collected information on a client through observations and psychological tests, and is now formulating a psychodiagnosis. Dr. Eberhardt is involved in which objective of abnormal psychology?

    a. Prediction
    b. Control
    c. Research
    d. Description

2. Dr. Smith says, "Abnormality is simply based on how infrequent a particular behavior is." Dr. Wright says, "Abnormality is defined by the values of the society in which it takes place." Dr. Smith's ideas reflect the _____ criteria; Dr. Wright's ideas reflect the _____ criteria.

    a. practical; traditional
    b. ideal mental health; cultural relativist
    c. ideal mental health; traditional
    d. statistical; cultural relativist

3. Although no one is present, Martin hears voices, and he firmly believes that Martians are poisoning his oatmeal. Martin's behavior illustrates the _____ component of the practical criteria for defining abnormality.

    a. dysfunction
    b. deviance
    c. multicultural
    d. discomfort

4. Dr. Chaves says, "Abnormality occurs when there is a biological dysfunction that produces socially defined harm to the individual." With whom would Dr. Chaves be in agreement?

    a. A cultural relativist
    b. A cultural universalist
    c. someone who believes in the dysfunction model
    d. Szasz

5. Imagine that you work in the admissions office of a mental health center that specializes in treating alcohol dependence. Your clients would most likely be

    a. people over age 65
    b. males between 25 and 44.
    c. young children.
    d. females.

6. Karen says that people with mental illness can never contribute to society until they are cured. Karen's viewpoint

    a. reflects a myth about mentally disturbed people: artists and writers have produced some of their greatest work while seriously disturbed.
    b. reflects the cultural relativism perspective: society determines what is illness and what is a contribution to society.
    c. is supported by epidemiological research.
    d. is mistaken because most mentally disturbed people are rarely cured.

7. Strabismus lives in ancient Greece. He goes to see his physician, Hippocrates, about his problem with sadness and fatigue. What is Hippocrates likely to say to Strabismus?

    a. "You need to have a portion of your skull removed; let me get my trephining gear."
    b. "Satan has possessed you; you need to have an exorcism."
    c. "Your body is out of balance, and perhaps your brain is disturbed; you need rest and good food."
    d. "Emotionally charged events from your past are affecting you; you need the cathartic method."

8.   Johann Weyer and Philippe Pinel would have probably agreed that
   a.   witches need to be starved and burned in order to save their souls.
   b.   abnormal behavior is best treated with hypnosis.
   c.   most people with behavior disorders have a form of brain pathology.
   d.   witchcraft is not an acceptable explanation for mental disturbance.

9.   Suzanne undergoes a process whereby, in a trance, she relives forgotten, emotionally charged events. Suzanne's treatment is called
   a.   the cathartic method.
   b.   mesmerism.
   c.   exorcism.
   d.   moral treatment.

ANSWER KEY: KEY TERMS REVIEW

1.   cathartic method

2.   psychological view

3.   trephining

4.   managed health care

5.   moral treatment movement

6.   syndrome

7.   therapy

8.   abnormal psychology

9.   humanism

10. biological view

11. cultural universality

12. cultural relativism

13. psychodiagnosis

14. biopsychosocial model

15. abnormal behavior

16. exorcism (18)

17. mass madness (20)

18. multicultural psychology (29)

19. brain pathology (19)

20. prevalence (12)

21. incidence (13)

22. lifetime prevalence (12)

23. psychopathology

24. behaviorism

ANSWER KEY: FACTUAL MULTIPLE-CHOICE QUESTIONS

1. b.   Therapy is a means of controlling maladaptive behavior and helping people change.

    a.   Psychodiagnosis identifies and labels a person's abnormality.

    c.   Research increases knowledge but does not exercise control over people.

    d.   Clinical assessment is a collection of procedures used to determine whether or not a person's behavior is normal or abnormal.

2. b.   Discomfort includes such physical reactions as asthma, fatigue, and nausea.

    a.   Dysfunctional involves a failure to perform actions that are expected for one's age and social situation.

    c.   Deviance takes the form of delusions, hallucinations, or other rare behaviors.

    d.   Delusions are mistaken beliefs that are not influenced by factual information.

3. b.   Hallucinations are false perceptions involving the senses; delusions are beliefs held by people despite contradictory evidence.

    a.   Dysfunctions are impairments in performing expected role-related behaviors.

    c.   Sensorimotor is part of Piaget's theory of cognitive development; dementia is a cognitive disorder.

    d.   The terms are reversed here.

4. d.   Alcohol abuse and dependence occur in 24 percent of men but only 4 percent of women.

    a.   The rate of disorders has seemed to stay fairly constant over the past twenty years.

    b.   Between 29 and 38 percent of the people in the three samples reported a disorder.

    c.   In some studies, depressive symptoms are estimated to occur in 44 million Americans; it is a common emotional disorder.

5. b.   Tarantism and lycanthropy are examples of mass madness that occurred in the 1200s.

    a.   Mesmerism occurred in the late 1700s and was not a form of mass madness.

    c.   Tarantism and lycanthropy involved disorder on a mass scale; exorcism is a form of treatment for individuals.

    d.   Tarantism and lycanthropy were reported during the Middle Ages (the 1200s).

6. c.   Beers, Dix, and Rush worked to humanize the treatment of the mentally ill in the United States.

    a.   Beers, Dix, and Rush all lived before Freud's ideas were known in the United States.

    b.   Charcot, Liebeault, and Bernheim were researchers who looked at hypnosis and its relation to hysteria.

    d.   Dix and Beers took no distinct stand on whether mental disorder was biogenic or not.

7.   a.   Mesmerism involved a trance-like state, much like hypnotism, during which the subject was highly suggestible.

     b.   Mesmerism made no use of drugs.

     c.   Mesmerism was not a religiously oriented treatment, as exorcism is.

     d.   Mesmerism did not involve the kind of skull surgery seen in trephining.

8.   d.   Most contemporary psychologists endorse a multi-path perspective owing to evidence from psychopharmacology, as well as research on how family upbringing and social forces affect mental health.

     a.   Most contemporary psychologists do not hold a purely psychogenic viewpoint.

     b.   Most contemporary psychologists do not hold a purely biological (biogenic) viewpoint.

     c.   Most contemporary psychologists do not hold a purely sociocultural viewpoint.

9   c.   Clinical psychologists obtain one of two doctoral degrees, the Ph.D. or the Psy.D.

     a.   Psychoanalysts require training in psychoanalysis and can be psychologists or psychiatrists; such training is not required in clinical psychology.

     b.   Psychiatrists are trained in medical schools.

     d.   Clinical psychologists are trained in the assessment and treatment of disturbed people. They also do original research work, which is the reason they are awarded the Ph.D. degree.

10. a.   Psychiatrists are trained in medicine and, as M.D.s, may prescribe medication. No other type of mental health professional is always trained in medicine.

     b.   Clinical psychologists are not trained in medicine. It is against the law for them to prescribe medication, although there has recently been legislative activity to permit them to do so under certain conditions.

     c.   Psychiatric social workers are not trained in medicine. It is against the law for them to prescribe medication.

     d.   Counseling psychologists have the same type of training as clinical psychologists; they cannot prescribe medication.

11. d.   Behaviorism has proven to have a high degree of success in treating maladaptive behaviors.

     a.   Behaviorism has not been known to be dangerous in treating maladaptive behaviors.

     b.   Behaviorism has not been ineffective in treating maladaptive behaviors.

     c.   Behaviorism has not been prohibited in treating maladaptive behaviors.

ANSWER KEY: CONCEPTUAL MULTIPLE-CHOICE QUESTIONS

1.   a.   The statistical criteria do not decide whether a rare behavior is desirable or not; they equate rare with abnormal.

     b.   The statistical criterion emphasizes frequency.

     c.   The statistical criterion concept is relevant to defining abnormality, not predicting or controlling behavior.

     d.   Statistics are considered to be objective and empirical.

2. c.   The ideal mental health criteria require setting a positive goal (an ideal) and judging how far from that goal an individual is.

    a.   Discomfort, deviance, and dysfunction reflect the practical criterion for defining abnormal behavior.

    b.   There are several drawbacks to the ideal mental health criterion, such as disagreement over what are ideal characteristics and traits, and uncertainty over what the goals of treatment should be.

    d.   Frequency of deviant actions reflects the statistical criterion of abnormal behavior.

3. a.   Cultural relativism focuses on the diversity of symptoms as they relate to social values. Proponents of cultural relativism do not believe that symptoms are universal across cultures.

    b.   Cultural relativism does not use the ideal mental health criteria.

    c.   Cultural relativism does not reject the possibility of mental illness; Thomas Szasz has questioned this idea.

    d.   Cultural relativism emphasizes social values, not biological differences.

4. c.   Mental disorder as a "harmful dysfunction," where harm is defined by society and *dysfunction* is defined by the biological sciences.

    a.   This does not take a pure biogenic view and accepts the importance of cultural factors.

    b.   These are separate criteria for defining "abnormal" and are unrelated.

    d.   The dysfunction view stresses biological factors as the cause of mental disorders.

5. d.   In some cases heredity gives a person a predisposition toward a disorder but in all cases, the environment determines whether any predisposition is expressed in behavior.

    a.   Environmental factors are influential in all forms of disorder.

    b.   Heredity plays a critical role in schizophrenia, bipolar disorder, and alcoholism.

    c.   Most mental disorders are not inherited, and most people can be cured.

6. a.   During the Middle Ages, abnormality was explained in terms of demonic possession. The treatment for possession was exorcism.

    b.   Trephining was principally used during prehistoric times.

    c.   Eighteenth-century moral treatment included discussions with a physician, work, and rest; exorcism in the Middle Ages was done by a clergyman.

    d.   The cathartic method was developed around the turn of the twentieth century, 50 to 75 years after the moral treatment era.

7. b.   A comprehensive review of the period by Spanos shows that many witches were not insane.

    a.   Voluntary witches were treated with brutality.

    c.   The church led the fight to hunt down and kill witches.

    d.   The church explained abnormal behavior in terms of the supernatural, not the biological.

8. c. The biological, (organic or biogenic) viewpoint sees disorders in terms of clusters of symptoms (syndromes) and believes that the causes are biological.

    a. A psychogenic approach argues that disorders are caused by parenting, environmental factors, and other forces outside the body.

    b. Demonology involves a belief that individuals are possessed by agents of the devil.

    d. The biopsychosocial model accepts the importance of biology, but also argues that psychological and social forces outside the person influence the development and course of disorders.

9. b. Social conditioning in the form of learned, stereotyped behavior is one explanation for apparent differences in rates of mental disorders in different groups.

    a. Cultural universality gives no emphasis to cultural influences and assumes disorders are the same in different cultural groups.

    c. It is the presence of bias in diagnosis that helps explain gender and cultural differences.

    d. One of the, few principles researchers agree upon is that all groups are susceptible to psychological distress.

10. a. Managed health care represents an industrialization of the helping professions. These organizations have greater control over the services that professionals can provide, in order to cut health care costs.

    b. Managed health care aims to reduce the cost of care and has had some success in doing so.

    c. Many psychologists are fearful of managed care because it puts control of the type and duration of treatment in the hands of large organizations such as insurance companies.

    d. Over the past thirty years, the number of clinical psychologists in the United States has grown from 12,000 to more than 40,000.

11. a. Psychopathology is a term clinical psychologists use as a synonym for abnormal behavior.

    b. Behaviorism is a psychological perspective that stresses learning and behavior in explaining abnormal development.

    c. Psychoanalysis offers an intrapsychic explanation of abnormal behavior.

    d. Cultural relativism is the belief that lifestyles, cultural values, and worldviews affect the expression of deviant behavior.

ANSWER KEY: APPLICATION MULTIPLE-CHOICE QUESTIONS

1. d. Psychodiagnosis involves description and definition of just what a person is experiencing.

    a. Prediction involves anticipation of future events; psychodiagnosis refers to current description.

    b. Control implies treatment, not description.

    c. Research can be done on any of the objectives of abnormal psychology.

2.   d.   The statistical criteria are based on the rarity of behavior; cultural relativism assumes that social values determine what is abnormal.

      a.   Infrequent behavior is the main component of the statistical criteria, not of the practical criteria.

      b.   The ideal mental health criteria do not base judgments on the rarity of behavior.

      c.   The ideal mental health criteria do not base judgments on the rarity of behavior.

3.   b.   Martin is exhibiting auditory hallucinations and delusions (about Martians), which are forms of deviance.

      a.   There is no explicit information indicating that Martin cannot perform tasks he is expected to perform-the definition of dysfunction.

      c.   There is no information indicating that Martin's behavior is related to his gender, ethnic background, or race, some of the issues important in the multicultural perspective.

      d.   If Martin complained about physical or psychological pain, that would be an indication of discomfort.

4.   c.   The dysfunction model argues that abnormality has a biological component of dysfunction and a social component of harm to the individual defined by the culture.

      a.   Cultural relativism emphasizes social values not biological dysfunction.

      b.   Cultural universality would suggest that, regardless of culture, all disorders are the same in presentation, origin, and treatment.

      d.   Szasz's position is that mental illness is a myth and that "problems in living" are reflections of social problems only.

5.   b.   Alcohol problems are most common in men and in people between 25 and 44 years old.

      a.   Older people are more likely to suffer from cognitive impairments, not alcohol dependence.

      c.   It is very rare for children to develop alcohol dependence.

      d.   Men are more likely to have alcohol abuse and dependence disorders than women.

6.   a.   It is a myth that people with mental illness make no contributions. Picasso, Poe, and Hemingway all suffered from disorders when they created their artwork or books.

      b.   Cultural relativism makes no statement on the potential for mentally ill individuals to contribute to society.

      c.   Epidemiological research examines the number and distribution of disorders in a population, not the contributions of individuals who have them.

      d.   It is also a myth to suggest that mentally disturbed people cannot be successfully treated.

7.   c.   Hippocrates' theory of abnormality assumed that the body was out of balance and that there may be brain pathology.

      a.   Trephining was most common in prehistoric times, not in ancient Greece.

      b.   What made ancient Greece and Rome unique was that their physicians did not believe that demons caused disorder.

      d.   Ideas about catharsis and emotional memories were developed around the turn of the twentieth century.

8.   d.   Weyer was the first to challenge witchcraft; Pinel lived more than 100 years after witchcraft faded as a common explanation.

      a.   Neither Weyer nor Pinel believed that witchcraft existed.

      b.   Both Weyer and Pinel lived before hypnosis was first used.

      c.   Neither Weyer nor Pinel took a biogenic view of abnormal behavior.

9.   a.   The cathartic method, hypnosis, and other techniques seek to bring to consciousness painful, forgotten memories. Breuer, and later Freud, used the method to cure patients.

      b.   Mesmerism involved trances, but there was no goal of reviving memories.

      c.   Exorcism was a religious practice with the goal of driving out demons.

      d.   Moral treatment relied on work, rest, and prayer for cures.

OBJECTIVES DEFINED

1.   **What is abnormal psychology?**

- Abnormal psychology is the scientific study whose objectives are to describe, explain, predict, and control behaviors that are considered strange or unusual.

2.   **What criteria are used to determine normal or abnormal behaviors?**

- Nearly all definitions include statistical deviation from some normative standard. The *Diagnostic and Statistical Manual of Mental Disorders* (DSM-IV-TR) definition is used by most mental health practitioners. Thus, abnormality is determined by four criteria: distress, deviance, dysfunction, and dangerousness.

3.   **How do context and cultural differences affect definitions of abnormality?**

- Criteria used to define normality or abnormality must be considered in light of community standards and changes over time. What is considered acceptable behavior in urban environments, for example, may not be considered acceptable in rural communities. With the increasing diversity in our society, we have also become very sensitive to how culture and unique group characteristics affect the definition of psychopathology as well.

4.   **How common are mental disorders?**

- Over the course of a lifetime, approximately 30 percent of people suffer from mental health problems in the United States, and the human and economic costs are enormous. In addition, two-thirds of all people suffering from a diagnosable mental disorder are not receiving or seeking mental health services.

5.   **What are some common misconceptions of the mentally disturbed?**

- Unfortunately, many myths and stereotypes have emerged regarding people who suffer from a mental disorder. Beliefs that mental disorders are inherited, incurable, the result of weak-willed people, and that those who suffer from them will never contribute to society have caused undue worry and harm to many. The reality is that most people who have suffered from a mental disorder improve, are little different than ourselves, and go on to lead normal productive lives.

6.   **How have explanations of abnormal behavior changed over time?**

- Ancient peoples believed in demonology and attributed abnormal behaviors to evil spirits that inhabited the victim's body. Treatments consisted of trephining, exorcism, and bodily assaults.

- Rational and scientific explanations of abnormality emerged during the Greco-Roman era. Especially influential was the thinking of Hippocrates, who believed that abnormal behavior was due to organic, or biological, causes, such as a dysfunction or disease of the brain. Treatment became more humane.

- With the collapse of the Roman Empire and the increased influence of the church and its emphasis on divine will and the hereafter, rationalist thought was suppressed, and belief in the supernatural again flourished. During the Middle Ages, famine, pestilence, and dynastic wars caused enormous social upheaval. Forms of mass hysteria affected groups of people. In the fifteenth century, some of those killed in church-endorsed witch-hunts were people we would today call mentally ill.

- The Renaissance brought a return to rational and scientific inquiry along with a heightened interest in humanitarian methods of treating the mentally ill. The eighteenth and nineteenth centuries were a period characterized by reform movements.

7. **What were early viewpoints of the causes of mental disorders?**

- In the nineteenth and twentieth centuries, major medical breakthroughs fostered a belief in the biological roots of mental illness. An especially important discovery of this period was the microorganism that causes general paresis. Scientists believed that they would eventually find organic causes for all mental disorders.

- Mesmerism, and later hypnosis, supported another view, however. The uncovering of a relationship between hypnosis and hysteria corroborated the belief that psychological processes could produce emotional disturbances.

8. **What are some contemporary trends in abnormal psychology?**

- Five contemporary developments have had a major influence in the mental health professions: (1) the drug revolution in psychiatry, which not only allowed many of the more severely disturbed to be treated outside of a hospital setting but also lent credence to the biological viewpoint, (2) the push by psychologists for prescription privileges, (3) the development of managed health care, (4) an increased appreciation for research in abnormal psychology, and (5) the influence of multicultural psychology.

MARGIN DEFINITIONS

abnormal behavior "a clinically significant behavioral or psychological syndrome or pattern that occurs in an individual and that is associated with present distress (e.g., a painful symptom) or disability (i.e., impairment in one or more important areas of functioning) or with a significantly increased risk of suffering death, pain, disability, or an important loss of freedom"

abnormal psychology the scientific study whose objectives are to describe, explain, predict, and control behaviors that are considered strange or unusual

behaviorism psychological perspective that stresses the importance of learning and behavior in explanations of normal and abnormal development

biological view (organic view) the belief that mental disorders have a physical or physiological basis

biopsychosocial model a model in which mental disorders are the result of an interaction of biological, psychological, and social factors

brain pathology a dysfunction or disease of the brain

cathartic method a therapeutic use of verbal expression to release pent-up emotional conflicts

cultural relativism the belief that lifestyles, cultural values, and worldviews affect the expression and determination of deviant behavior

cultural universality the assumption that a fixed set of mental disorders exists whose obvious manifestations cut across cultures

exorcism treatment method used by the early Greeks, Chinese, Hebrews, and Egyptians in which prayers, noises, emetics, flogging, and starvation were used to cast evil spirits out of an afflicted person's body

humanism a philosophical movement that emphasizes human welfare and the worth and uniqueness of the individual

incidence the onset or occurrence of a given disorder over some period of time

lifetime prevalence the total proportion of people in the population who have ever had a disorder in their lives

managed health care the industrialization of health care, whereby large organizations in the private sector control the delivery of services

mass madness group hysteria in which a great many people exhibit similar symptoms that have no apparent physical cause

moral treatment movement movement instituted by Philippe Pinel that resulted in a shift to more humane treatment of the mentally disturbed

multicultural psychology an approach that stresses the importance of culture, race, ethnicity, gender, age, socioeconomic class, and other similar factors in its effort to understand and treat abnormal behavior

prevalence the percentage of people in a population who suffer from a disorder at a given point in time

psychodiagnosis an attempt to describe, assess, and systematically draw inferences about an individual's psychological disorder

psychological view the belief that mental disorders are caused by psychological and emotional factors rather than organic or biological ones

psychopathology a term clinical psychologists use as a synonym for abnormal behavior

syndromes certain symptoms that tend to occur regularly in clusters

therapy a program of systematic intervention whose purpose is to modify a client's behavioral, affective (emotional), and/or cognitive state

trephining a surgical method from the Stone Age in which part of the skull was chipped away to provide an opening through which an evil spirit could escape

CHAPTER 2

Models of Abnormal Behavior

TABLE OF CONTENTS

LEARNING OBJECTIVES

1.   Discuss what models of psychopathology have been used to explain abnormal behavior.

2.   Describe the multi-path model of mental disorders.

3.   Describe how much of mental disorders can be explained through our biological makeup.

4.   Discuss what psychological models are used to explain the etiology of mental disorders.

5.   Discuss the role social factors play in psychopathology.

6.   Discuss how sociocultural factors may play a role in the etiology of mental disorders.

CHAPTER OUTLINE

I.   **One-Dimensional models of mental disorders** Models are analogies that scientists use to describe things they cannot directly observe. Among the models that psychologists use is the medical model, which portrays psychological disorders as diseases or the psychosocial model. This chapter will introduce the multi-path model. The case of Steven V. is presented, which describes a college student suffering from depression and violent fantasies. The biological model suggests that abnormal behavior is caused by biological factors, especially involving genetic material and the brain. Psychological explanations such as Sigmund Freud's *psychodynamic model* emphasizes early childhood experiences. Behavioral explanations can be traced to inappropriate learning. Social explanations look at the social environment. Sociocultural explanations look at cultural factors to explain behavior.

II.   **A multi-path model of mental disorders**. What, then, is the "best" way to conceptualize the causes of mental disorders? An integrative and interacting *multi-path model* is a way of viewing disorders and their causes. The multi-path model is not a theory, but a way of looking at the variety and complexity of contributors to mental disorders. The etiology of mental disorders can be subsumed under four dimensions. Dimension One: Biological Factors This dimension includes genetics, brain anatomy, biochemical imbalances, central nervous system functioning, autonomic nervous system reactivity, etc. Dimension Two: Psychological Factors This dimension includes personality, cognition, emotions, learning, stress-coping, self-esteem, self-efficacy, values, developmental history, etc. Dimension Three: Social Factors This dimension includes family, relationships, social support, belonging, love, marital status, community, etc. Dimension Four:

Sociocultural Factors This dimension includes race, gender, sexual orientation, religion, socioeconomic status, ethnicity, culture, etc.

III. **Dimension one: biological factors**. Modern biological explanations of normal and abnormal behavior continue to share certain assumptions: (1) the things that make people who they are—their physical features, susceptibility to diseases, temperaments, and ways of dealing with stress—are embedded in the genetic material of their cells; (2) human thoughts, emotions, and behaviors are associated with nerve cell activities of the brain and spinal cord; (3) a change in thoughts, emotions, or behaviors will be associated with a change in activity or structure (or both) of the brain; (4) mental disorders are highly correlated with some form of brain or other organ dysfunction; and (5) mental disorders can be treated by drugs or somatic intervention The human brain is composed of billions of *neurons* (nerve cells) that receive and transmit information. The brain is divided into two hemispheres, each controlling the opposite side of the body. The brain structures most relevant to abnormal behavior include the thalamus, hypothalamus, reticular activating system, limbic system, and cerebrum. Other structures in the midbrain and hindbrain manufacture chemicals that are correlated with mental disorders. Biochemical theories suggest that chemical imbalances underlie mental disorders. Neurons are composed of *dendrites*, which receive signals from other neurons, and axons, which send the signals to other neurons. At the end of the *axon* is a gap called the *synapse*, into which chemicals called neurotransmitters are released. Imbalances in *neurotransmitters* are associated with many mental disorders. Certain medications can reduce symptoms of abnormal behavior by blocking or facilitating neurotransmitter activity. Biochemistry plays an important role in understanding abnormal behavior. Genetics also plays an important part in explaining the development of disorders. A person's *genotype* (genetic makeup) interacts with the environment to produce physical or behavioral characteristics (the person's *phenotype*). *The Human Genome Project* has mapped the location of all genes in the nucleus of a human cell and has completed its sequencing to provide a basic blueprint of the entire genetic material found in each cell of the human body. While single cells have been found to be responsible for a few diseases, most diseases are the result of many genes interacting with hormones, electrical signals and nutrient supplies internally, plus physical and social environments. Biology-based treatment techniques include: *Psychopharmacology* is the study of the effects of drugs on the mind and on behavior; it is also known as medication or drug therapy. Besides medication, *electroconvulsive therapy (ECT)* can be used to treat certain mental disorders. P*sychosurgery* is brain surgery performed for the purpose of correcting a severe mental disorder The treatment was used most often with patients suffering from schizophrenia and severe depression, although many who had personality and anxiety disorders also underwent psychosurgery. *Diathesis-stress theory* argues that people can inherit a vulnerability to developing an illness, but this tendency must be activated by environmental forces for the disorder to occur.

IV. **Dimension Two: psychological factors**. Especially important for the psychological dimension are conflicts in the mind, emotions, learned behavior, and cognitions in personality formation. Personality is a dynamic process resulting from three interacting components: the id, the ego, and the superego. The id operates on the pleasure principle, a need for immediate gratification. The ego is influenced by the reality principle. The superego is composed of the conscience and the ego ideal. Personality develops through five psychosexual stages (oral, anal, phallic, latency, and genital). Fixation at any of the stages affects emotional development. *Anxiety* is at the root of psychoanalytic thinking and takes three forms: realistic, moralistic, and neurotic. *Defense mechanisms* protect the individual from anxiety. These include, among others, repression, reaction formation, projection, rationalization, displacement, undoing and regression. Psychoanalytic therapy, or psychoanalysis, has three main goals: (1) uncovering repressed material, (2) having clients achieve insight into their inner motivations and desires, and (3) resolving childhood conflicts that affect current relationships. Psychoanalysts traditionally use four methods to achieve their therapeutic goals: free association, dream analysis, analysis of resistance and analysis of transference. Psychoanalysis has been criticized for basing its evidence on case studies, which are subject to distortion. Psychodynamic theory is biased against women and cannot be applied to a wide range of disturbed people. The *behavioral models* emphasize learning. The classical conditioning model involves the pairing of a neutral *(conditioned) stimulus* with an unconditioned stimulus that automatically produces certain responses called the *unconditioned response*. After repeated pairing, the conditioned stimulus alone can produce a weakened version of the response, call the *conditioned response*. Classical conditioning in psychopathology. These concepts can be said to explain the development of phobias and deviant sexual behavior. However, the passive nature of associative learning makes it a limited explanatory tool. Watson and the "little Albert" experiment are a good example. The *operant conditioning model* stresses the consequences of voluntary and controllable behaviors called *operant behaviors*. According to Thorndike's *law of effect*, these behaviors are more likely when they produce positive consequences and less likely when they produce negative consequences. Operant conditioning principles help explain such forms of psychopathology as self-injurious behavior. As in classical conditioning, operant concepts can be applied to treatment as well. The *observational learning model* suggests that an individual can acquire new behaviors simply by watching other people perform them through the process of vicarious conditioning or modeling. Observational learning in psychopathology assumes that exposure to disturbed models helps produce disturbed behavior. Behavioral models have made significant contributions to both the understanding and treatment of disorders. However, they are criticized for diminishing the importance of inner determinants of behavior. The cognitive models assume that thoughts modify our emotional states and behavior. People differ in their mediating processes, which determine our reactions, behaviors and self-evaluations. Our *schemas* (how we interpret events) influence our experiences. Cognitive theorists focus on irrational beliefs (Ellis) or dysfunctional "automatic thoughts" (Beck). Beck's work on depression helped him identify a hierarchy of cognitive content. Ellis describes an A-B-C theory of personality in which A is an event, B is a belief, and C is a consequent behavior or emotion. Beck describes six types of faulty or distorted thinking: arbitrary inference, selective abstraction, overgeneralization, magnification and exaggeration, personalization, and polarized thinking. Cognitive approaches to therapy have clients monitor their thoughts; recognize the connections between thoughts, emotions, and behaviors; examine the evidence for their assumptions; and substitute more reality-oriented interpretations. The *humanistic* and *existential approaches* emphasize the need to appreciate the world form the individual's vantage point. They also highlight freedom of choice and the wholeness of the individual. Psychologists Carl Rogers and Abraham Maslow suggested that people are motivated by the actualizing tendency to enhance the self (*self-actualization*). Development of abnormal behavior occurs when society imposes conditions of worth on people so that their *self-concept* and actualizing tendency become incongruent. This incongruence produces behavior disorders. In Rogers' person-centered therapy, people are free to grow toward their potential. The therapist uses reflection of feelings and acceptance rather than advice to help the client actively evaluate his or her experience. The existential perspective is not a systematized school of thought but a set of attitudes that is less optimistic than humanism. It views the individual within the human condition and focuses more on responsibility to others. Both approaches lack scientific grounding, are vague, and apply therapies that are ineffective with severely disturbed clients. Criticisms of the humanistic and existential approaches point to their "fuzzy," ambiguous, and nebulous nature and to the restricted population in which these approaches can be applied.

V.   **Dimension Three: social factors**. In contrast to traditional psychological models, social-relational models emphasize how other people, especially significant others, influence our behavior. This viewpoint holds that all people are enmeshed in a network of interdependent roles, statuses, values, and norms. One of these, the family systems model, assumes that the behavior of one family member directly affects the entire family system. Criticisms of the family systems model include difficulty defining it from different cultural viewpoints and its confusion of cause and effect over the issue of family abuse.

VI. **Dimension Four: sociocultural factors**. Gender factors, women are consistently subjected to greater stressors than their male counterparts. Lower socioeconomic class is related to lower sense of self-control, poorer physical health, and higher incidence of depression. Early attempts to explain differences between various minority groups and their white counterparts tended to adopt one of two models. The first, the inferiority model, contends that racial and ethnic minorities are inferior in some respect to the majority population. The second model—the deprivations or deficit model—explained differences as the result of "cultural deprivation." It implied that minority groups lacked the "right" culture. Both models have been severely criticized as inaccurate, biased, and unsupported in the scientific literature. The Multicultural Model is the new approach emphasizing that being culturally different does not equal deviancy, pathology, or inferiority. The model recognizes that each culture has strengths and limitations and that differences are inevitable. Criticisms of the Multicultural Model include that the multicultural model operates from a relativistic framework; that is, normal and abnormal behavior must be evaluated from a cultural perspective. The reasoning is that behavior considered disordered in one context—seeing a vision of a dead relative, for example—might not be considered disordered in another time or place.

VII. **Implications.** Each model—whether biological, psychodynamic, behavioral, cognitive, existential-humanistic, family systems, or multicultural—represents different views of pathology. In practice, most clinicians recognize that models of psychopathology do not completely contradict one another on every point. As the multi-path model suggests, elements of various perspectives can complement one another to produce a broad and detailed explanation of a person's condition

KEY TERMS REVIEW

1. The optimistic viewpoint that people are born with self-direction and the ability to fulfill their potential is called the _____.

2. In psychoanalytic theory, the ego-protection strategies that operate unconsciously to shelter the person from anxiety are called _____.

3. The therapy based on Freud's view that unconscious conflicts must be aired and understood by the patient is called _____.

4. The theory that a predisposition to mental illness is inherited and that this predisposition is activated by environmental factors is called the _____.

5. _____ is a treatment aimed at helping couples understand and clarify their communications, role relationships, unfulfilled needs, and unrealistic or unmet expectations.

6. The set of attitudes that agrees with humanism but that is less optimistic and that highlights alienation and responsibility to others is called the _____.

7. An analogy used by scientists to describe something that cannot be directly observed is called a(n) _____.

8. _____ is a term that means causes of disorders.

9. The view that adult disorders arise from the unconscious operation of repressed anxieties originally experienced in childhood is called the _____.

10. A person's genetic makeup is called his or her _____.

11. The observable result of the interaction of the genotype and the environment is called the _____.

12. The impulsive, pleasure-seeking aspect of our being, usually associated with the id, that seeks immediate gratification is called the _____.

13. Usually associated with the ego, the, awareness of environmental demands and adjustments made to meet these demands are called the _____.

14. An inherent tendency for people to strive toward the realization of their full potential is called _____.

15. _____ is a contemporary attempt to explain differences in minority groups that suggests that behaviors be evaluated from the perspective of a group's value system as well as by other standards used in determining normality and abnormality.

16. In psychoanalytic theory, human beings develop through a sequence of stages (oral, anal, phallic, latency, and genital), which collectively are called _____.

17. The space between a sending neuron and a receiving neuron is called the _____.

18. The rootlike structures of a neuron that receive information are called the _____.

19. The long extension of the neuron that transmits a signal to the end of that neuron is called the _____.

20. Nerve cells are also called _____.

21. Chemicals that are released into the synapse so that neural messages are facilitated or blocked are called _____.

22. A model that assumes conscious thoughts affect an individual's emotions and response to a stimulus is called the _____.

23. The theory that assumes individuals learn new behaviors by watching other people and imitating them is called _____.

24. The theory of learning in which involuntary responses to new stimuli are learned through association is called _____.

25. The model of psychopathology that emphasizes the influence of the family on individual behavior is called the _____.

26. A theory of learning, applying primarily to voluntary behaviors, that assumes these behaviors are controlled by the consequences that follow them is called _____.

27. Theories of psychopathology that are concerned with the role of learning are called _____.

28. In classical conditioning, the learned response made to a previously neutral stimulus is called the _____.

29. In classical conditioning, a previously neutral stimulus that, after conditioning, acquires the ability to produce a conditioned response is called a(n) _____.

30. _____ is a model of models that provides an organizational framework for understanding the numerous causes of mental disorders, the complexity of their interacting components, and the need to view disorders from a holistic framework.

31. The underlying assumptions held by a person that influence how he or she interprets events are called _____.

32. In classical conditioning, the unlearned response made to the unconditioned stimulus is called the _____.

33. In classical conditioning, the stimulus that elicits the unconditioned response is called the
_____.

34. A voluntary and controllable behavior that "operates" on an individual's environment is called a(n) _____.

35. The process of learning by observing models and imitating them is called _____.

36. _____ is an individual's assessment of his or her own value and worth.

37. The psychoanalytic therapeutic technique in which the patient says whatever comes to mind for the purpose of revealing his or her unconscious is called _____.

38. _____ is a form of therapy that involves the simultaneous treatment of two or more clients and may involve more than one therapist.

39. The process by which a patient reenacts early conflicts by carrying over and applying to the analyst feelings and attitudes that the patient had toward significant others in the past is called _____.

40. The _____ was an early attempt to explain differences in minority groups that contends that racial and ethnic minorities are inferior in some respect to the majority population.

41. The _____ was an early attempt to explain differences in minority groups that contends that differences are the result of "cultural deprivation."

42. During psychoanalysis, a process in which the patient unconsciously attempts to impede the analysis by preventing the exposure of repressed material _____.

FACTUAL MULTIPLE-CHOICE QUESTIONS

1. A psychologist who believes that genetics, brain chemistry, and damage to the nervous system are the major causes of mental disorder subscribes to the _____model.
    a. psychoanalytic
    b. existential
    c. biological
    d. multicultural

2. According to Freud, _____ is present at birth and impulsively seeks immediate gratification of pleasure needs.
    a. the id
    b. the ego
    c. the superego
    d. fixation

3. According to Freud, fixation in a psychosexual stage
    a. cannot be overcome.
    b. reduces the person's need for ego defense mechanisms.
    c. explains the development of conscience.
    d. arrests future emotional development.

4. Early theories that attempted to account for cultural differences in psychopathology
    a. relied on what Thorndike called "the law of effect."
    b. balanced European-American concepts of mental health with non-Western ones.
    c. looked at ethnic minorities as inferior to or deprived of white middle-class values.
    d. explained the differences in terms of bias in diagnosis.

5. Conditions of worth, conditional positive regard, and incongruence are all associated with the _____ approach to abnormal behavior.
   - a. humanistic
   - b. diathesis-stress
   - c. psychodynamic
   - d. object relations

6. Because they are voluntary behaviors, social skills are learned through
   - a. classical conditioning.
   - b. operant conditioning.
   - c. extinction.
   - d. the pairing of conditioned and unconditioned stimuli.

7. Research indicates that when children watch television violence, they often imitate the aggressive actions in their own lives. This illustrates
   - a. classical conditioning.
   - b. modeling.
   - c. operant conditioning.
   - d. the cognitive model of psychopathology.

8. According to Albert Ellis, negative emotions are the result of
   - a. irrational beliefs about events that occur in our lives.
   - b. modeling inappropriate behaviors.
   - c. pairing certain conditioned stimuli with negative unconditioned responses.
   - d. faulty communications in which verbal messages contradict nonverbal messages.

9. In _____ therapy, problems are seen in terms of power struggles, control, and the need to reestablish boundaries.
   - a. strategic family
   - b. conjoint family
   - c. rational-emotive
   - d. cognitive restructuring

10. Which psychopathology model claims that each culture has strengths and limitations and that those differences are inevitable?
    - a. Inferiority model
    - b. Deficit model
    - c. Multicultural model
    - d. Family systems model

CONCEPTUAL MULTIPLE-CHOICE QUESTIONS

1. The biological model of schizophrenia would be supported if researchers found that
   - a. schizophrenia occurred most frequently among those from the lower socioeconomic groups.
   - b. a specific neurotransmitter imbalance occurred only in people with the disorder.
   - c. people with the disorder had a forebrain that controlled higher mental functions.
   - d. people who suffered from the disorder came from families with great marital conflict.

2. Genotype is to _____ as phenotype is to _____.
   - a. genetic makeup; observable behavioral or physical characteristics
   - b. abnormal; normal
   - c. environmental forces; biological inheritance
   - d. observable behavioral or physical characteristics; genetic makeup

3. Psychodynamic theory has, been criticized because

    a. it has failed to have much impact on the field of psychology.
    b. it relies too heavily on evidence from scientific, laboratory investigations.
    c. it fails to examine the impact of the unconscious on psychopathology.
    d. its form of therapy cannot be applied to a range of disturbed people.

4. Which state-merit about the humanistic and existential theories is *accurate*?

    a. They believe that biological and instinctual forces determine each individual's behaviors.
    b. They argue that the individual's subjective view of events is more important than the events themselves.
    c. They emphasize the need to break down personality into its component parts.
    d. They reject the idea of an actualizing tendency.

5. In classical conditioning, the _____ is initially neutral, but can evoke a conditioned response if it is paired with the _____.

    a. unconditioned stimulus; conditioned response
    b. operant stimulus; classical stimulus
    c. unconditioned response; conditioned stimulus
    d. conditioned stimulus; unconditioned stimulus

6. Which of the following is probably best explained by classical conditioning?

    a. Learning how to use chopsticks in a Chinese restaurant
    b. Becoming silent when your friend continually interrupts anything you say
    c. Two people getting the same grade on a test, but only one of them feeling proud of it
    d. Developing a fear of cars after being in a traffic accident

7. In _____ behavior is controlled by preceding stimuli; in _____ learning, is based on the consequences of behavior.

    a. modeling; cognitive-behavioral theory
    b. classical conditioning; operant conditioning
    c. operant conditioning; modeling
    d. classical conditioning; cognitive-behavioral theory

8. Which statement is *accurate* concerning the family systems model?

    a. It suggests that all phenomena can be understood in terms of learning based on associations between stimuli.
    b. It suggests that abnormal behavior in an individual reflects unhealthy dynamics in the family.
    c. It suggests that family dynamics cannot be changed once they have been established.
    d. It assumes that genetics explains why some families have certain behavior problems generation after generation.

9. The terms *African American, American Indian, Asian American,* and *Hispanic American*

    a. are universally recognized as appropriate labels to define ethnic minorities in the U.S.
    b. are convenient labels recognized by the U.S. government, but they are not without controversy.
    c. are most preferred by ethnic minority groups regardless of age.
    d. are the most comprehensive and accurate description of all ethnic groups.

10. All of the following are traditional methods of therapy used by psychoanalysts *except*

    a. free association.
    b. transference.
    c. replication.
    d. resistance.

11. Which of the following is *not* a successful feature of a group therapy dynamic?

     a. The group experience allows each client to become involved in a social situation and to see how his or her behavior affects others

     b. Group members can develop new communication skills, social skills, and insights.

     c. Groups help members feel less isolated and less fearful about their problems.

     d. Group members are able to freely debate each other without regard for personal feelings.

12. The inferiority model and the deficit model have been _____

     a. praised for being fair and objective measures of racial and ethnic disparities.

     b. criticized for being unsubstantiated and biased.

     c. praised in Europe but criticized in the United States.

     d. slowly gaining legitimacy in the field of abnormal psychology.

APPLICATION MULTIPLE-CHOICE QUESTIONS

1. Dr. Chapman thinks of the brain as a kind of computer that takes in data, processes it, stores it, and retrieves it at a later date. Dr. Chapman is

     a. an eclectic thinker.

     b. taking a humanistic view of the brain.

     c. a supporter of the biological approach.

     d. using a model to think about the brain.

2. Dr. Mandler says, "We know that this patient has a high genetic vulnerability to the disorder. Given the current difficulties in his life, it is logical that he would develop a severe case of the disorder." Which perspective does Dr. Mandler's statement illustrate?

     a. Psychoanalytic

     b. Diathesis-stress

     c. Behavioral

     d. Humanistic

3. Kate is an outspoken feminist. With which perspective is she likely to have the most disagreements?

     a. Eclectic

     b. Biopsychosocial

     c. Humanistic

     d. Psychodynamic

4. Paula R. says, "I cannot decide on anything! I am drifting, and I have no direction." Dr. Pratt responds by reflecting Paula's feelings, but not by providing her with advice. What type of therapy does this illustrate best?

     a. psychoanalysis

     b. Rogers's person-centered therapy

     c. modeling therapy

     d. cognitive therapy

5. In the Case of Steven V,, Steven becomes sexually aroused when watching violent movies. From a classical conditioning viewpoint, a violent movie is a(n) _____ for Steven.

     a. conditioned response

     b. conditioned stimulus

     c. operant behavior

     d. schema

6. Dr. Lawrence says to a client, "Your phobia of spiders came about because your mother set an example by jumping on a chair and shrieking any time a spider was within twenty yards of her." Dr. Lawrence's explanation follows the_____ model.
   a. family systems
   b. cognitive
   c. operant conditioning
   d. observational learning

7. Dr. McNally says to a depressed client, "You are not depressed because of bad events; you are depressed because you have the irrational belief that any bad event is a catastrophe that is totally unfair and inhumane." Dr. McNally's statement illustrates
   a. Ellis's A-B-C theory of personality.
   b. what Beck refers to as the law of effect.
   c. the strategic approach to depression.
   d. the humanistic approach to psychopathology.

8. Mr. and Mrs. Juarez are very concerned about their daughter's performance in school. They see her as "sick," but their therapist thinks they are diverting attention from their own troubled marriage. What kind of therapist are the Juarezes probably seeing?
   a. A cognitive therapist
   b. A behavior therapist
   c. A family systems therapist
   d. A psychoanalytic therapist

9. A psychologist who agrees with the contemporary multicultural model would be most likely to make which of the following statements?
   a. "Minority groups experience more psychopathology than whites do because minority group children are deprived of a cultural background rich in good values."
   b. "The strongest reason for cultural differences in psychopathology is genetics."
   c. "The best way to understand human personality is to examine the individual at a micro level: his or her personal experiences, impulses, and thoughts."
   d. "Culture is central to all theories of pathology and must balance European concepts with non-European ones."

10. Juan thinks of himself as a relatively smart person, with a pleasant disposition, but not very good looking. Juan's beliefs about himself is known as
    a. self-reliance.
    b. self-concept.
    c. self-indulgence.
    d. self-gratification.

ANSWER KEY: KEY TERMS REVIEW

1. humanistic perspective

2. defense mechanisms

3. psychoanalysis

4. diathesis-stress theory

5. couples therapy

6. existential approach

7. model

8. etiology
9. psychodynamic model
10. genotype
11. phenotype
12. pleasure principle
13. reality principle
14. self-actualization
15. multicultural model
16. psychosexual stages
17. synapse
18. dendrites
19. axon
20. neurons
21. neurotransmitters
22. cognitive model
23. observational learning theory
24. classical conditioning
25. family systems model
26. operant conditioning
27. behavioral models
28. conditioned response
29. conditioned stimulus
30. multi-path model
31. schema
32. unconditioned response
33. unconditioned stimulus
34. operant behavior
35. modeling
36. self-concept
37. free association
38. group therapy
39. transference
40. inferiority model
41. deficit model
42. resistance

ANSWER KEY: FACTUAL MULTIPLE-CHOICE QUESTIONS

1. c. The biological model assumes that biological factors such as genetics, brain chemistry, hormones, and nervous system damage account for abnormal behavior.

    a. Psychoanalysts emphasize unconscious conflicts and childhood sources of anxiety.

    b. Existentialists take a psychogenic view that emphasizes personal freedom and responsibility.

    d. The multicultural model emphasizes social factors and is, therefore, a variant of the psychogenic view.

2. a. The id is the portion of personality that psychoanalysts describe as pleasure- seeking, impulsive, and unable to delay gratification. We can see this sort of behavior in newborns.

    b. The ego develops out of the id and is reality oriented.

    c. The superego develops at age 5 or 6 and is oriented toward morality.

    d. Fixation occurs when traumas arrest emotional development at any of the psychosexual stages.

3. d. Psychoanalytic theorists stress how fixation arrests emotional development and contributes to symptoms in adults.

    a. Healthy individuals can overcome or transcend fixation that occurs earlier. In part, this is why therapy provides hope.

    b. Fixation arrests emotional development and, if anything, increases the need for defenses against anxiety.

    c. Conscience is one aspect of the superego.

4. c. Two of the earlier ways of looking at cultural differences (inferiority and deprivation) placed white, middle-class values as the standard and looked at nonwhite cultures as inadequate.

    a. Thorndike's "law of effect" was an early behavioral explanation of how we learn through operant conditioning.

    b. Contemporary multicultural approaches balance European and non-European concepts; older approaches did not.

    d. Contemporary multicultural approaches consider diagnostic bias as an explanation for apparent cultural differences in psychopathology.

5. a. All three are important concepts in Rogers's theory. When there are conditions of worth, incongruence is likely—resulting in behavior disorders.

    b. Diathesis-stress theory combines genetic vulnerability and environmental factors to explain abnormal behavior.

    c. Freud's psychodynamic approach emphasizes unconscious impulses and sources of anxiety.

    d. Object relations theorists stress early mother-child relationships

6. b.   Operant conditioning involves the learning of voluntary behaviors.

    a.   Classical conditioning involves the learning of involuntary behaviors.

    c.   Extinction decreases the frequency of a behavior.

    d.   The pairing of stimuli is a part of classical conditioning.

7. b.   These children are imitating others, the essence of modeling.

    a.   Classical conditioning involves the pairing of stimuli and the learning of associations to make involuntary responses.

    c.   Operant conditioning occurs when behavior is changed by experiencing direct consequences

    d.   Cognitive models emphasize irrational or maladaptive thought processes.

8. a.   Ellis's rational-emotive therapy says that negative emotions are the result of irrational beliefs.

    b.   Modeling involves imitation of others.

    c.   The pairing of stimuli is the essence of classical conditioning.

    d.   Virginia Satir stresses faulty communications in families.

9. a.   Strategic family therapy attempts to change the power relationships and boundaries in distressed families.

    b.   Conjoint family therapy tries to change the communication patterns in distressed families.

    c.   Rational-emotive therapy focuses on the irrational thoughts of individuals.

    d.   Cognitive restructuring helps clients identify and change their thought processes.

10. c.   The multicultural model claims that each culture has strengths and limitations and that such differences are inevitable.

    a.   The inferiority model contends that racial and ethnic minorities are inferior in some respect to the majority population.

    b.   The deficit model contends that differences are the result of "cultural deprivation."

    d.   The family systems model assumes that the behavior of one family member directly affects the entire family system

ANSWER KEY: CONCEPTUAL MULTIPLE-CHOICE QUESTIONS

1. b.   The linking of specific neurotransmitter imbalances and mental disorders is a major theme of the biogenic model.

    a.   The biological model downplays the role of socioeconomic factors and emphasizes brain structure and chemistry.

    c.   The forebrain controls higher mental functions in all people so it would not be additional evidence for a biogenic model of schizophrenia.

    d.   Marital conflict is an environmental and psychological factor that is not included in a purely biogenic perspective.

2. a. The definition of genotype is one's genetic makeup; the phenotype is how genetic makeup and environmental factors interact to produce an observable set of physical and behavioral characteristics.

    b. Genotype can be abnormal or normal; phenotype can be abnormal or normal.

    c. Genotype is what we inherit; phenotype is what can be seen (the product of genes and environment).

    d. Genotype is defined as one's genetic makeup; phenotype is the observable pattern of physical and behavioral characteristics in a person.

3. d. Psychoanalysis, which relies on talking and abstraction, is not appropriate for people with poor verbal skills.

    a. Psychoanalytic thinking has had a tremendous impact on the field of psychology.

    b. Psychoanalytic theory has been criticized for relying on case studies and for putting no importance on laboratory investigations.

    c. Psychoanalytic theory puts heavy emphasis on the unconscious.

4. b. Central to both humanistic and existential theories is the importance placed on how the individual subjectively views the world.

    a. Humanistic and existential thinkers suggest that people are free to make life choices; they reject the ideas of biological destiny and instinctual forces.

    c. Humanistic and existential thinkers value the integrity of the human personality and argue against breaking it down into components or formulas.

    d. The actualizing tendency is a core idea in humanistic theory.

5. d. The conditioned stimulus is neutral with respect to a response until it has been paired with the unconditioned stimulus that can elicit the response in question.

    a. The unconditioned stimulus is not neutral; it automatically elicits the unconditioned response.

    b. Operant is a word used to describe behavior in the operant conditioning model.

    c. Stimuli are paired in classical conditioning, not responses and stimuli.

6. d. Classical conditioning involves an involuntary response (fear) that is paired with previously neutral stimuli (cars).

    a. Using chopsticks is voluntary behavior, and it is therefore more related to operant or modeling approaches.

    b. Talking is a voluntary behavior being affected by consequences.

    c. This illustrates how individuals interpret events—a component of the cognitive behavioral approach.

7. b. Behaviors learned through classical conditioning are controlled by stimuli preceding the response. In operant conditioning, behaviors are controlled by events that follow them.

    a. Modeling is part of observational learning; cognitive-behavioral theory stresses thinking processes.

    c. Operant conditioning is based on consequences; modeling is a part of observational learning.

    d. Stimuli that precede responses do control classical conditioning, but cognitive-behavioral theory stresses thinking processes.

8. b. Family systems theory suggests that symptoms in an individual reflect unhealthy family dynamics.

    a. Classical conditioning emphasizes the pairing of stimuli.

    c. Although family systems theory recognizes that change that threatens homeostasis is unwelcome, the whole thrust of therapy is to produce change toward healthy dynamics.

    d. The biological model stresses genetics; the family systems approach would emphasize parents' rules and behavior patterns.

9. b. Although overgeneralization and some inaccuracy may result from using the labels, the U.S. Census Bureau and Office of Management and Budget use these terms.

    a. While commonly used, these categories are practical choices, and do not reflect the more complex cases where individuals have mixed ancestry.

    c. Particular terms may be accepted by some generations but not others; for example, the term African American may be less accepted to blacks holding strong political views developed during the 1960s.

    d. These descriptions are generalizations and do not account for the nuances and differences that exist between ethnic groups; for example, there are about thirty distinct Asian American subgroups.

10. c. Replication is not a traditional therapy method used by psychoanalysts.

    a. Free association is a traditional therapy method used by psychoanalysts in which the patient says whatever comes to mind for the purpose of revealing his or her unconscious.

    b. Transference is a traditional therapy method used by psychoanalysts in which a patient reenacts early conflicts by carrying over and applying to the analyst feelings and attitudes that the patient had toward significant others in the past.

    d. Resistance is a traditional therapy method used by psychoanalysts in which the patient unconsciously attempts to impede the analysis by preventing the exposure of repressed material.

11. d. Debating without regard for other members' feelings is not a feature of successful group therapy.

    a. When the group experience allows each client to become involved in a social situation and to see how his or her behavior affects others is a feature of successful group therapy.

    b. When group members can develop new communication skills, social skills, and insights is a feature of successful group therapy.

    c. When groups help members feel less isolated and less fearful about their problems is a feature of successful group therapy.

12. b.   The deficit model and the inferiority model have been criticized for being biased and unsubstantiated.

     a.   The deficit model and the inferiority model have not been praised for helping to explain racial and ethnic disparities.

     c.   The deficit model and the inferiority model have not been praised in Europe.

     d.   The deficit model and the inferiority model have not been gaining legitimacy.

ANSWER KEY: APPLICATION MULTIPLE-CHOICE QUESTIONS

1.   d.   A model is an analogy; the analogy between computer and brain may help Dr. Chapman understand the brain better.

     a.   An eclectic approach uses ideas from different theories to find whatever works best to explain and treat a condition.

     b.   Humanistic thinkers do not consider the human mind to be like a machine.

     c.   Nothing indicates whether Dr. Chapman believes that biological factors cause disorders, so it is unclear whether the doctor supports the biogenic view.

2.   b.   Diathesis-stress theory emphasizes just these ideas: that inherited vulnerability combines with environmental stress to cause disorders.

     a.   Psychoanalytic theorists put little emphasis on genetics.

     c.   Behavioral theorists emphasize learning.

     d.   Humanistic theorists highlight freedom, individuality, and self-actualization.

3.   d.   Psychoanalytic theory has been criticized by feminists for taking a biased view of women, particularly seeing males as the standard against which normality is based.

     a.   Eclectic professionals borrow from a variety of theories, so it is unlikely that an outspoken feminist would be in disagreement with behavioral, cognitive, biological, and systems models.

     b.   The biopsychosocial perspective accepts the importance of sociocultural factors as well as biological and psychological ones.

     c.   The humanistic approach has not proposed any concepts inconsistent with a feminist approach.

4.   b.   Rogers's person-centered therapy gives the client unconditional positive regard by reflecting feelings and allowing the person to find his or her own direction.

     a.   Psychoanalysis makes unconscious impulses conscious through projective techniques and other methods.

     c.   Modeling therapy presents the client with behaviors to imitate and directs the person to do so.

     d.   Cognitive therapy challenges the irrational beliefs of the client.

5. b. The movies were probably initially neutral (with respect to sex), but were paired with situations for sexual arousal and came to be a conditioned stimulus for arousal.

    a. Sexual arousal would be an example of a conditioned response.

    c. Operant behaviors are voluntary actions that "operate" on the environment.

    d. A schema is a set of personal assumptions that influences how we see, value, and experience the world.

6. d. Observational learning involves learning through modeling; in this case, from the mother.

    a. Family systems would examine the relationships and communications in the family.

    b. A cognitive approach would look at the irrational beliefs the client has about spiders.

    c. Operant conditioning involves direct learning, not observation.

7. a. Ellis's A-B-C theory of personality holds that negative emotions stem not from events but from the irrational beliefs we have about them.

    b. Beck is a cognitive theorist, but the "law of effect" is an early operant conditioning idea.

    c. The strategic approach to family therapy emphasizes power relationships.

    d. The humanistic approach emphasizes incongruence, conditions of worth, and blocked self-actualization.

8. c. Family systems therapists see individual pathology stemming from faulty family dynamics.

    a. A cognitive therapist would help them to examine their thinking about their daughter's performance and to develop more realistic expectations.

    b. A behavior therapist would stress the environmental factors that reduce their daughter's school performance.

    d. Psychoanalytic therapists focus on the individual's unconscious conflicts.

9. d. The multicultural model notes that all behavior has a cultural influence and that non-European perspectives are as valid as European ones.

    a. This statement reflects, the deprivation approach of Reissman; it suggests that non-European cultures are lacking appropriate values; the multicultural approach values all cultures.

    b. Genetic inferiority is not a viable explanation in the multicultural model.

    c. The multicultural model proposes that development be seen at multiple levels including the family and culture.

10. b. Self-concept is an individual's assessment of his or her own value and worth.

    a. Self-reliance is not an individual's assessment of his or her own value and worth; self-concept is.

    c. Self-indulgence is not an individual's assessment of his or her own value and worth; self-concept is.

    d. Self-gratification is not an individual's assessment of his or her own value and worth; self-concept is.

OBJECTIVES DEFINED

1. **What models of psychopathology have been used to explain abnormal behavior?**

- One-dimensional models have been traditionally used to explain disorders. They have become increasingly inadequate because mental disorders are multidimensional.

2. **What is the multi-path model of mental disorders?**

- The multi-path model is proposed to explain the interaction of biological, psychological, social, and sociocultural contributors to mental disturbances. The model is not a theory but a way of looking at the variety and complexity of contributors to mental disorders. In some respects it is a meta-model, a model of models that provides an organizational framework for understanding the numerous causes of mental disorders, the complexity of their interacting components, and the need to view disorders from a holistic framework.

3. **How much of mental disorders can be explained through our biological makeup?**

- Biological models cite various organic causes of psychopathology, including genetics, brain anatomy, biochemical imbalances, central nervous system functioning, and autonomic nervous system reactivity. A good deal of biochemical research has focused on identifying the role of neurotransmitters in abnormal behavior. Researchers have also found correlations between genetic inheritance and certain psychopathologies. Mental health research reveals that a predisposition to a disorder, not the disorder itself, may be inherited. Gene-environment interactions are a two way process that are reciprocal in nature.

4. **What psychological models are used to explain the etiology of mental disorders?**

- Psychodynamic models emphasize childhood experiences and the role of the unconscious in determining adult behavior. The early development of psychodynamic theory is credited to Freud. Psychoanalytic therapy attempts to help the patient achieve insight into his or her unconscious.

- Behavioral models focus on the role of learning in abnormal behavior. The traditional behavioral models of psychopathology hold that abnormal behaviors are acquired through association (classical conditioning) reinforcement (operant conditioning) or modeling. Negative emotional responses such as anxiety can be learned through classical conditioning: a formerly neutral stimulus evokes a negative response after it has been presented along with a stimulus that already evokes that response. Negative voluntary behaviors may be learned through operant conditioning if those behaviors are reinforced (rewarded) when they occur. In observational learning, a person learns behaviors, which can be quite complex, by observing them in other people and then imitating, or modeling, those behaviors.

- Cognitive models are based on the assumption that conscious thought mediates, or modifies, an individual's emotional state and/or behavior in response to a stimulus. Cognitive therapeutic approaches are generally aimed at normalizing the client's perception of events.

- The humanistic perspective actually represents many perspectives and shares many basic assumptions with the existential perspective. Both view an individual's reality as a product of personal perception and experience. Both see people as capable of making free choices and fulfilling their potential. Both emphasize the whole person and the individual's ability to fulfill his or her capacities.

5.   **What role do social factors play in psychopathology?**

- Impaired or lack of social relationships have been found to be correlated with increased susceptibility to mental disorders. Good relationships seem to immunize people against stressors.

- From the perspective of family systems, abnormal behavior is viewed as the result of distortion or faulty communication or unbalanced structural relationships within the family. Children who receive faulty messages from parents or who are subjected to structurally abnormal family constellations may develop behavioral and emotional problems.

- Three social treatments described are family therapy, couples therapy, and group therapy.

6.   **What sociocultural factors may play a role in the etiology of mental disorders?**

- Proponents of the sociocultural approach believe that race, culture, ethnicity, gender, sexual orientation, religious preference, socioeconomic status, physical disabilities, and other variables are powerful influences in determining how specific cultural groups manifest disorders, how mental health professionals perceive disorders, and how disorders will be treated.

- Cultural differences have been perceived in three ways: (1) the inferiority model, in which differences are attributed to the interplay of undesirable elements in a person's biological makeup; (2) the deprivations or deficit model, in which differences in traits or behaviors are blamed on not having the "right culture"; and (3) the multicultural model, in which differences do not necessarily equate with deviance.

MARGIN DEFINITIONS

axon an extension on the cell body that sends signals to neurons, some a considerable distance away

behavioral models models of psychopathology concerned with the role of learning in abnormal behavior

classical conditioning a process in which responses to new stimuli are learned through association

cognitive models models based on the assumption that conscious thought mediates an individual's emotional state and/or behavior in response to a stimulus

conditioned response (CR) in classical conditioning, a learned response to a previously neutral stimulus that has acquired some of the properties of another stimulus with which it has been paired

conditioned stimulus (CS) in classical conditioning, a previously neutral stimulus that has acquired some of the properties of another stimulus with which it has been paired

couples therapy a treatment aimed at helping couples understand and clarify their communications, role relationships, unfulfilled needs, and unrealistic or unmet expectations

defense mechanisms in psychoanalytic theory, an ego-protection strategy that shelters the individual from anxiety, operates unconsciously, and distorts reality

deficit model early attempt to explain differences in minority groups that contends that differences are the result of "cultural deprivation"

dendrites numerous short rootlike structures on the cell body whose function is to receive signals from other neurons

diathesis-stress theory theory that holds that people do not inherit a particular abnormality but rather a *predisposition* to *develop illness* (diathesis) and that certain environmental forces, called *stressors,* may activate the predisposition, resulting in a disorder

etiology causes of disorders

existential approach a set of attitudes that has many commonalities with humanism but is less optimistic, focusing (1) on human alienation in an increasingly technological and impersonal world (2) on the individual in the context of the human condition, and (3) on responsibility to others as well as to oneself

family systems model, model that assumes that the behavior of one family member directly affects the entire family system

free association psychoanalytic therapeutic technique in which the patient says whatever comes to mind for the purpose of revealing his or her unconscious

genome all the genetic material in the chromosomes of a particular organism

genotype a person's genetic makeup

group therapy a form of therapy that involves the simultaneous treatment of two or more clients and may involve more than one therapist

humanistic perspective the optimistic viewpoint that people are born with the ability to fulfill their potential and that abnormal behavior results from disharmony between the person's potential and his or her self-concept

inferiority model early attempt to explain differences in minority groups that contends that racial and ethnic minorities are inferior in some respect to the majority population

model an analogy used by scientists, usually to describe or explain a phenomenon or process they cannot directly observe

modeling process of learning by observing models (and later imitating them)

multicultural model contemporary attempt to explain differences in minority groups that suggests that behaviors be evaluated from the perspective of a group's value system as well as by other standards used in determining normality and abnormality

multi-path model a model of models that provides an organizational framework for understanding the numerous causes of mental disorders, the complexity of their interacting components, and the need to view disorders from a holistic framework

neurons nerve cells that transmit messages throughout the body

neurotransmitters chemical substance released by the axon of the sending neuron and involved in the transmission of neural impulses to the dendrite of the receiving neuron

observational learning theory theory that suggests that an individual can acquire new behaviors by watching other people perform them

operant behavior a voluntary and controllable behavior, such as walking or thinking, that "operates" on an individual's environment

operant conditioning a theory of learning that holds that behaviors are controlled by the consequences that follow them

phenotype observable physical and behavioral characteristics caused by the interaction between the genotype and the environment

pleasure principle the impulsive, pleasure-seeking aspect of our being from which the id operates

psychoanalysis therapy whose goals are to uncover repressed material, have clients achieve insight into inner motivations and desires, and resolve childhood conflicts that affect current relationships

psychodynamic models models that view disorders as the result of childhood trauma or anxieties and that hold that many of these childhood-based anxieties operate unconsciously

psychosexual stages in psychodynamic theory, the sequence of stages—oral, anal, phallic, latency, and genital—through which human personality develops

reality principle an awareness of the demands of the environment and of the need to adjust behavior to meet these demands from which the ego operates

resistance during psychoanalysis, a process in which the patient unconsciously attempts to impede the analysis by preventing the exposure of repressed material

schema a set of underlying assumptions heavily influenced by a person's experiences, values, and perceived capabilities

self-actualization an inherent tendency to strive toward the realization of one's full potential

self-concept an individual's assessment of his or her own value and worth

synapse minute gap that exists between the axon of the sending neuron and the dendrites of the receiving neuron

transference process by which a patient reenacts early conflicts by carrying over and applying to the analyst feelings and attitudes that the patient had toward significant others in the past

unconditioned response (UCR) in classical conditioning, the unlearned response made to an unconditioned stimulus

unconditioned stimulus (UCS) in classical conditioning, the stimulus that elicits an unconditioned response

CHAPTER 3

Assessment and Classification of Abnormal Behavior

TABLE OF CONTENTS

LEARNING OBJECTIVES

1.   Determine the kinds of standards tests or evaluation procedures must meet when attempting to make an accurate evaluation or assessment of a person's mental health.

2.   Describe the kinds of tools clinicians employ in evaluating the mental health of people.

3.   Discuss how mental health problems are categorized or classified.

CHAPTER OUTLINE

I.   **Reliability and validity** Evaluation of information about an individual leads to a *psychodiagnosis,* which involves describing and drawing inferences about the person's psychological state. The psychodiagnosis clarifies the picture of that state, may lead to a treatment program, provides a way of communicating about disorders, and serves to standardize assessment procedures. To be useful, assessment tools must show *reliability*, the degree to which a procedure or test will give the same results repeatedly under the same circumstances. Three types of reliability are test-retest reliability, internal consistency and interrater reliability. Measures that are reliable can also demonstrate *validity*, the degree to which a procedure or test actually performs the function it was designed to perform. Predictive validity indicates how well a measure predicts future behavior. Three other aspects of validity are criterion-related, construct and content validity. Standardization in administration and the presence of standardization samples affect reliability and validity.

II. **The assessment of abnormal behavior** *Assessment* is the process of gathering information and drawing conclusions about a person's traits, skills, abilities, functioning and emotional problems to use in developing a diagnosis. It requires obtaining information from many sources: observations in either controlled or naturalistic settings are usually made in conjunction with an interview and can have diagnostic significance. A person who is aware of being observed may show *reactivity*, altering normal responses. Interviews stress different information depending on the interviewer's theoretical orientation. Standardized interviews, such as the Diagnostic Interview and the Structured Clinical Interview. Consistency and Interrater reliability, and the less structured mental status examination are widely used. Straightforward questions may not yield usable or accurate information. Psychological tests have a wide range of application. They provide a standard situation for responses and allow comparison of results with normative samples. *Projective personality tests* present ambiguous stimuli and ask for responses that "project" the person's motives. *The Rorschach technique* is a series of cards displaying inkblots.

What people see in the blots and why they see what they do are interpreted in terms of psychoanalytic symbolism. *The Thematic Apperception Test (TAT)* uses pictures of people and asks the person to tell a story about each picture. The style and themes of the stories are used to gain insight into conflicts and personality. The sentence-completion test and the draw-a-person test are other examples of projective tests. The difficult question of should the Rorschach technique be used for making assessments is discussed. Projective tests tend to have low reliability and validity. *Self-report inventories* supply the test taker with a list of alternative answers. *The Minnesota Multiphasic Personality Inventory (MMPI)* consists of 567 statements that are answered "true," "false," or "cannot say," and was revised to become the MMPI-2. MMPI-2 responses are scored on ten clinical and three validity scales. Profiles of scale results indicate personality styles. *The Beck Depression Inventory (BDI)* is an example of a test focused on a particular trait or problem. Inventories have been criticized for being restrictive, pathology oriented, and easily faked. Still, inventories are widely used, and some show both reliability and validity since the techniques used in making mental measurement—*psychometrics*—are becoming increasingly sophisticated. *Intelligence tests* are designed to measure cognitive functioning, called the *intelligence quotient (IQ),* and to detect organic brain disorders. *The Wechsler Adult Intelligence Scale* (now revised in its third edition as the WAIS-III) and two other forms for children (WISC-III) and preschoolers (WPPSI-III) are widely used. Also used is the *Stanford-Binet Scale*. Ethnic groups have attacked IQ tests for being culturally biased, and it is clear that reliance on IQ has led to discrimination. Social competency cannot be adequately assessed with IQ tests. The *Kaufman Assessment Battery for Children (K-ABC)* are tests that address this and other criticisms. Tests for cognitive impairment are tests to detect and assess brain damage to the central nervous system (*organicity*) including the *WAIS-III,* the *Bender-Gestalt Visual-Motor Test,* the *Halstead-Reitan Neuropsychological Test Battery*, and the *Luria-Nebraska Neuropsychological Battery*. Neurological tests are neurological medical procedures such as computerized axial tomography (CT scan), positron emission tomography (PET scan), the electroencephalograph (EEG), and magnetic resonance imaging (MRI) used to assess brain conditions. Functional MRIs provide high resolution, noninvasive views of neural activity detected by a blood oxygen level dependent signal. There is a strong anti testing movement in the United States. Criticisms include the undesirable social consequences of using test results and problems of using tests on people from non-Western cultures. Computer assessment has been viewed as a potential substitute for some testing. Studies of computer assessment have yielded encouraging results, but its validity must be established.

III. **The classification of abnormal behavior** The goal of a *classification system* is to provide distinct categories for different behavior problems. Classification systems should provide distinct categories that are used consistently but that still accommodate imperfect cases. Problems with early diagnostic classification systems Kraepelin's system and the original DSM were based on medical model principles and the hope that similar disorders would have a common *etiology* (cause). *The Diagnostic and Statistical Manual of Mental Disorders (DSM)* was first published in 1952 and is now revised for the sixth time (DSM-IV-TR). Interrater reliability of recent editions of the DSM has been good for broad categories, but less reliable for specific diagnoses. Older editions of the DSM were criticized for having poor reliability and validity, including an inability adequately to predict the future course of a disorder (*prognosis*). This newest version (2000) evaluates an individual on five dimensions or axes: Axis I, clinical syndromes; Axis II, personality or specific development disorders; Axis III, general medical conditions; Axis IV, psychosocial problems; and Axis V, global assessment of the highest level of adaptive functioning at the present time and over the past year. The five axes are intended to provide comprehensive and useful information. The broad categories of mental disorders discussed in the text are: disorders usually first diagnosed in infancy, childhood, or adolescence; delirium, dementia, amnestic, and other cognitive disorders; mental disorders due to a general medical condition; substance-related disorders; schizophrenia and other psychotic disorders; mood disorders; anxiety disorders; somatoform disorders; factitious disorders; dissociative disorders; sexual and gender identity disorders; eating disorders; sleep disorders; impulse control disorders not elsewhere classified; adjustment disorders; and personality disorders. The DSM-IV-TR addresses cross-cultural assessment more than previous DSM versions. Comorbidity refers to this co-occurrence of different disorders. It is too soon to provide an evaluation of DSM-IV-TR; however, critics of past DSMs argue it is biased toward the medical model, lacks a theoretical basis for classifying disorders, does not adequately address psychopathology in non-Western cultures, and classifies people into categories rather than seeing them as having more or less of certain characteristics. There is also controversy over some proposed conditions, such as premenstrual dysphoric disorder, as sexist diagnoses. The debates, however, have been valuable in suggesting new research issues. Objections to classification and labeling are viewed as a major problem .Classification can exaggerate the differences between normal and abnormal. It can also lead people to misinterpret normal behavior as pathological, affect the way people treat those who are labeled, change the behavior of people who are labeled (self-fulfilling prophecies), and fail to provide the information emphasized by managed-care organizations. Rosenhan's study with pseudopatients illustrates some of these problems.

IV.   **Implications.** We know that assessment has improved over time. Focus on reliability and validity, increased psychometric and statistical procedures, new technologies, and large numbers of research studies on assessment have all served to increase our ability to evaluate human beings.

KEY TERMS REVIEW

1.   The degree to which a procedure or test yields the same result repeatedly under the same circumstances is called _____.

2.   An assessment tool in which the test taker answers specific questions or responds to specific self-descriptive statements is called a(n) _____.

3.   A variety of standardized test instruments used to assess personality, maladaptive behavior, social skills, intellectual abilities, vocational interests, and cognitive impairment are called

     _____.

4.   The process of gathering information about an individual's traits, skills, abilities, emotional functioning, and psychological problems is called _____.

5.   A personality assessment technique in which the test taker is presented with ambiguous stimuli to which he or she is asked to respond is called a(n) _____.

6.   The degree to which a procedure or test actually performs the function that it was designed to perform is called _____.

7.   With regard to psychopathology, a system of distinct categories, indicators, and nomenclature for different patterns of behavior, thought processes, and emotional disturbances is called a(n)

     _____.

8.   An individual diagnosed with two or more mental disorders is said to show _____.

9.   The study and techniques of mental measurement are called _____.

10. The change in the way people usually respond, caused by their awareness that they are being observed is called _____.

11. A prediction of the future course of a particular disorder is called _____.

12. _____ is the use of identical procedures in the administration of tests; (in samples) it is the establishment of a norm or comparison group to which an individual's test performance can be compared.

FACTUAL MULTIPLE-CHOICE QUESTIONS

1. When different observers of the same individual agree on a diagnosis, this illustrates
    a. high predictive validity.
    b. low construct validity.
    c. high test-retest reliability.
    d. high interrater reliability.
2. Projective personality tests are most likely to be used by psychologists who agree with the
    a. psychodynamic perspective.
    b. medical model.
    c. behavioral perspective.
    d. family systems model.
3. Exner's system has become the standard way of scoring
    a. the Rorschach inkblot test.
    b. intelligence tests so that they are culturally unbiased.
    c. such projective tests as the draw-a-person and the sentence-completion test.
    d. the MMPI-2.
4. Which personality test has more than 550 items and reports, results on ten clinical scales and three validity scales?
    a. The TAT
    b. The Wechsler scales
    c. The MMPI-2
    d. The Bender-Gestalt
5. The Beck Depression Inventory is an example of a
    a. projective personality test.
    b. self-report inventory covering many traits.
    c. test for assessing organicity.
    d. self-report inventory aimed at detecting one specific problem.
6. Unlike the Stanford-Binet, the WAIS-III
    a. gives separate verbal IQ and performance IQ scores.
    b. is a structured interview as well.
    c. is used to assess children's intelligence.
    d. does not examine verbal IQ.
7. Which method of assessing brain function records brain wave patterns?
    a. Electroencephalograph (EEG)
    b. Bender-Gestalt Visual-Motor Test
    c. Computerized axial tomography (CAT) scan
    d. Magnetic resonance imaging (MRI)
8. Which statement about computer assessment is *accurate*?
    a. Computers tend to make more errors in scoring than humans.
    b. There is an abundance of research evidence assuring the scientific precision of computer assessment.
    c. Computer assessment tends to increase the cost of mental health care.
    d. Many clients enjoy being assessed by computer.

9. If a classification system provided useful information about the etiology and prognosis of disorders, it would be

    a. based on the behavioral model of abnormality.
    b. low in reliability but high in validity.
    c. considered a standardized instrument.
    d. telling about the cause and future course of disorders.

10. What information is revealed on Axis II of DSM-IV-TR?

    a. Level of functioning now and in the past year
    b. Any personality or specific developmental disorder
    c. Level of stress experienced in the past year
    d. The clinical syndrome, which is the focus of treatment

CONCEPTUAL MULTIPLE-CHOICE QUESTIONS

1. Which of the following statements about assessment is *accurate*?

    a. Assessment uses a wide range of information sources to get a clear picture of a client's problem.
    b. Assessment occurs when information is synthesized into a particular category.
    c. Assessment must use psychological tests in order to be valid.
    d. Assessment methods are not necessary for research.

2. Reactivity is a major problem for which of the following assessment methods?

    a. Observation
    b. Neurological procedures to detect brain damage
    c. Projective intelligence tests
    d. Structured interviews

3. The mental status examination and the Composite International Diagnostic Interview are likely to

    a. have low reliability because they employ naturalistic observation.
    b. produce very little reactivity because they employ naturalistic observation.
    c. have higher reliability because they are structured.
    d. be used for the same purposes as the CAT-scan and the electroencephalograph.

4. Which of the following statements about clinical interviews is *accurate*?

    a. Despite differences in theoretical orientations, psychologists tend to interview clients in the same way.
    b. Clinical interviews do not make use of observations.
    c. The quality of the relationship between interviewer and interviewee has a strong effect on the value of the interview.
    d. Interviews are most likely to be highly structured if performed by psychodynamic ally oriented psychologists.

5. Which of the following is characteristic of psychological tests?

    a. They predominantly measure intellectual functioning.
    b. They are given in standard situations, and norms exist for making assessments of individuals.
    c. They typically allow the examiner to use his or her own judgment about how to administer and score the test.
    d. They are typically used for research purposes only.

6. What did Kraepelin's system and the original DSM classification system have in common?

    a. High reliability
    b. An eclectic approach that described disorders rather than proposing specific causes for them
    c. Overreliance on the behavioral perspective
    d. Overreliance on the medical model

7. The poor reliability of the original DSM was mostly due to

    a. the poor training of the people who used it.
    b. its excessive use of specific behavior to define categories.
    c. inadequacies in the system itself.
    d. faking in the clients who were examined.

8. Anxiety disorders, mood disorders, and substance-related disorders are all categories of behavior that appear on which axis of the DSM-IV-TR?

    a. Axis I
    b. Axis III
    c. Axis V
    d. None; these categories have been omitted from the DSM-IV-TR

9. Diagnostic labels create all of the following problems *except* one. Which?

    a. They influence the behavior of the people who are labeled.
    b. They provide more information than is required by managed-care organizations.
    c. They influence others to treat the labeled person differently.
    d. They imply that the labeled person is qualitatively different from normal people.

10. What did the Rosenhan study with pseudopatients illustrate?

    a. The high reliability of the new DSM-IV-TR
    b. The ability of professionals to detect faking
    c. How self-fulfilling prophecies can make even normal people act "insane"
    d. How labels influence us to see abnormality even when people act normally

APPLICATION MULTIPLE-CHOICE QUESTIONS

1. A psychologist records the posture, facial expressions, and language patterns of adolescents in a local bowling alley. This represents assessment based on

    a. controlled observation.
    b. structured interviews.
    c. projective personality testing.
    d. naturalistic observation.

2. Gary thinks that projective tests are excellent because they reveal underlying conflicts and motives. Gary is probably in agreement with the _____ perspective on abnormal behavior.

    a. behavioral
    b. neuropsychological
    c. humanistic
    d. psychodynamic

3. A psychologist gives Larry two tests. In one test, Larry draws a picture of a person. In the other, he tells what he sees in ten symmetrical inkblots. The psychologist is assessing Larry by using

    a. objective personality tests.
    b. intelligence tests.
    c. projective personality techniques.
    d. one intelligence and one projective test.

4. Dr. Shaw says, "The more sophisticated we get at mental measurement, the higher the reliability and validity of our assessment instruments." Dr. Shaw is discussing

    a. the problem of classification and labeling.
    b. changes in the DSM that include cultural sensitivity.
    c. improving the cultural sensitivity of intelligence tests.
    d. psychometrics.

5. Alan is given the Luria-Nebraska Neuropsychological Battery and an MRI. We can assume that

    a. Alan is being assessed for brain damage.
    b. Alan is a young child.
    c. Alan's clinical psychologist is a behaviorist.
    d. Alan's clinical psychologist is a psychoanalyst.

6. Dr. Ireland asks, "Who will use the test results you ask for; for what purpose is this assessment requested?" These questions highlight _____ concerns about testing.

    a. standardization
    b. psychometric
    c. ethical
    d. biomedical

7. _____ will probably be less costly than traditional assessment methods because it does not require person-to-person contact. However, we are a long way from knowing whether it increases assessment validity.

    a. The Rorschach inkblot technique
    b. Computerized assessment
    c. Electroencephalograph (EEG)
    d. Brain imaging techniques

8. Ross has a phobia about going out in public. His wife recently and unexpectedly divorced him, and he has a heart condition. How would this information about Ross's life show up on the DSM-IV-TR?

    a. His phobia would be given on Axis II.
    b. His heart condition would be considered a form of organicity.
    c. His divorce would add to his stress rating on Axis IV.
    d. The phobia would not show up since it is not a disorder.

9. Oscar says, "The current diagnostic system is biased against minorities. No guidelines are given to help clinicians understand the cultural context of the client." Is Oscar correct?

    a. No, because the DSM-IV-TR has emphasized cross-cultural assessment.
    b. No, because previous editions of the DSM had specific guidelines for cultural contexts.
    c. Yes, Axis III and Axis IV of the DSM are biased against minorities.
    d. Yes, the diagnostic system relies solely on culturally biased IQ tests.

10. After Ellen is diagnosed as "schizophrenic," she begins to act so bizarrely that she seems more schizophrenic than before. This illustrates the problem of

    a. self-fulfilling prophecies.
    b. poor reliability in the DSM-IV-TR.
    c. diagnosis without the use of norms.
    d. reactivity in controlled observations.

ANSWER KEY: KEY TERMS REVIEW

1. reliability

2. self-report inventory

3. psychological tests and inventories

4.   assessment

5.   projective personality test

6.   validity

7.   classification system

8.   comorbidity

9.   psychometrics

10.   reactivity

11.   prognosis

12.   standardization

ANSWER KEY: FACTUAL MULTIPLE-CHOICE QUESTIONS

1.   d.   Interrater reliability is the degree of agreement in measurements or judgments made by two or more observers.

   a.   Predictive validity is shown-when a test accurately foretells future performance or behavior.

   b.   Low construct validity means that the measure fails to reliably detect a theoretically coherent pattern of behavior.

   c.   Test-retest reliability is consistency across time.

2.   a.   Because they reveal unconscious conflicts and symbolic behaviors, projective tests are favored by psychoanalysts.

   b.   The medical model would emphasize neurophysiological functioning.

   c.   The behavioral perspective would favor observations of behavior and its consequences.

   d.   The family systems model would examine actual communications in family settings.

3.   a.   Exner's scoring system, a more reliable method than previous systems, is now the standard way to score the Rorschach.

   b.   Intelligence tests themselves have been revised to be less culturally biased; Exner's system is used strictly with the Rorschach.

   c.   Exner's system is used strictly with the Rorschach.

   d.   The MMPI-2 is scored by computer.

4.   c.   The MMPI-2 consists of 567 statements and yields scores on ten scales to indicate abnormal behavior and three scales to see whether the test taker gave accurate answers.

   a.   The TAT is a projective test that uses pictures of people and asks the test taker to tell a story about them.

   b.   The Wechsler scales are intelligence tests.

   d.   The Bender-Gestalt asks test takers to copy designs.

5. d.   The Beck Depression Inventory asks for specific responses to items involving depression.

    a.   Because it asks the test taker specific questions, the Beck Depression Inventory cannot be a projective personality test.

    b.   Unlike the MMPI-2, the Beck Depression Inventory is focused an only one problem: depression.

    c.   The Beck Depression Inventory was not designed to assess brain damage.

6. a.   The Wechsler Adult Intelligence Scale, Revised (WAIS-R), like all Wechsler scales, yields both verbal and performance IQ scores.

    b.   The WAIS-R is an IQ test, not a diagnostic interview.

    c.   The Stanford-Binet can be given to children, but the WAIS-R is usually given to people over age 15.

    d.   The WAIS-R, like all Wechsler scales, has a verbal and a performance component.

7. a.   An electroencephalograph involves attaching electrodes to the scalp so that brain wave activity patterns can be recorded.

    b.   The Bender-Gestalt involves copying a number of designs.

    c.   CAT scans involve the use of multiple X-rays of the brain; they produce images of the brain not recordings of brain wave activity.

    d.   MRI produces a clear picture of the brain (or other structure) by surrounding the area with powerful magnetic fields.

8. d.   Research shows that many clients enjoy, even prefer, being assessed by computer.

    a.   Computers are likely to make fewer scoring errors than humans.

    b.   A chief criticism of computer assessment is the absence of definitive evidence that such assessments are precise.

    c.   Because machines can do the scoring tirelessly, costs are likely to be reduced.

9. d.   *Etiology* is the cause of a disorder; *prognosis* refers to the future course of the disorder.

    a.   The behavioral model is not uniquely interested in the causes and course of disorders.

    b.   One cannot have high validity without also having high reliability.

    c.   Standardization requires giving a test in the same manner each time-and using data from a large comparison group (a set of norms).

10. b.   Axis II indicates personality disorders or, in the case of children, developmental disorders.

    a.   Functioning level is indicated on Axis V.

    c.   Stress level is indicated on Axis IV.

    d.   The clinical syndrome—the main mental disorder—is listed on Axis I.

ANSWER KEY: CONCEPTUAL MULTIPLE-CHOICE QUESTIONS

1. a. Assessment involves collecting as much information as possible so that the clinician gains a better understanding of the client.

    b. When assessment information is synthesized, classification or psychodiagnosis is being done.

    c. Tests are a possible source of information, but they are not required.

    d. Assessment is critical for research.

2. a. Observation can lead to reactivity—the problem of people changing the way they act because they know someone is watching.

    b. Neurological procedures do not change the way people act, or at least they don't change the way people's *brains* act.

    c. Projective techniques are used in personality testing, not in intelligence testing.

    d. Structured interviews ask very specific questions, so although people may fake their answers, they do not change their actual behavior in response to the interviewer.

3. c. These interviews are fairly structured-predetermined questions are asked in a specific order, so reliability is likely to be higher than in unstructured interviews.

    a. Neither interview employs naturalistic observation.

    b. Interviews involve face-to-face contact, not naturalistic observation, so reactivity is always a possibility.

    d. CAT scans and electroencephalographs are used to detect brain damage; these interviews are to assess general mental status.

4. c. The relationship between interviewer and interviewee is one of three main reasons for interviewing errors.

    a. Different perspectives lead to different interview strategies: psychoanalysts use less structured formats than behaviorists.

    b. Interviews rely on the combination of observation and verbal information.

    d. Psychoanalysts are least likely to use structured interviews.

5. b. Tests commonly have these two characteristics: a standard situation in which they are given, and the use of norms for making comparisons.

    a. Psychological tests usually look for underlying traits, not intellectual functioning.

    c. Tests are usually standardized, so that they are given in a uniform manner.

    d. Tests are used for both research and clinical purposes.

6. d. Both the original DSM and Kraepelin's system were based on the biogenic idea that common symptoms have the same cause.

    a. The failing of both the original DSM and Kraepelin's system was poor reliability.

    b. Both systems relied on the medical model, not a broad range of ideas as occurs with an eclectic approach.

    c. Neither system relied on a behavioral approach; behaviorists are the prime movers of the alternative system.

7. c. 62.5 percent of the errors came from inadequacies in the system itself.

   a. Poor training was not a major reason for poor reliability.

   b. The DSM's poor reliability was traced to a lack of specific behavioral guidelines for diagnosis.

   d. Faking has not been found to be a major source of errors.

8. a. The principal mental disorders are listed on Axis I.

   b. Axis III lists physical illnesses or disorders that relate to the clinical syndrome (for example, a thyroid condition).

   c. Axis V rates the person's level of functioning currently and in the past year.

   d. The categories listed are included in DSM-IV-TR.

9. b. A criticism of labeling is that a single phrase fails to provide the detailed information on clients desired by managed-care organizations.

   a. Labels often influence the people who are given the labels to act differently, something called a self-fulfilling prophecy.

   c. One problem with labels is that labeled individuals are treated differently by others.

   d. Labeling has the problem of seeming to segregate people into qualitatively different groups.

10. d. Hospital staff started to see abnormal behavior in those labeled as schizophrenic.

    a. Rosenhan's study undercut the field's faith in the DSM's reliability because professionals could not detect faked symptoms.

    b. The results were the reverse of this. Patients and the ward could tell that the pseudopatients were faking, whereas professionals could not.

    c. The pseudopatients never acted insane; they continued to act normally while in the hospital.

ANSWER KEY: APPLICATION MULTIPLE-CHOICE QUESTIONS

1. d. A bowling alley is a "real world" place where natural behavior can be observed without interference.

   a. Although this illustrates observation, it is not being done in a controlled setting such as a laboratory or clinic.

   b. A structured interview would involve a predetermined list of questions and a limited set of responses.

   c. Projective tests such as the Rorschach or TAT present test takers with ambiguous stimuli.

2. d. Psychoanalysts have developed and used projective tests to get a general picture of functioning, underlying motives, and conflicts.

   a. Behaviorists do not stress underlying conflicts, and they are unlikely to use projective tests.

   b. Neuropsychologists focus on brain function, so they would be more likely to use the Luria-Nebraska or a medical test.

   c. Humanists are interested in the current, conscious, subjective world of clients more than in their underlying conflicts.

3.   c.   Larry is completing the draw-a-person test and the Rorschach test; both are projective because the stimuli presented to him are ambiguous.

      a.   Objective tests offer set responses, (e.g., "true" or "false") to predetermined, written items.

      b.   Intelligence tests also offer structured problems with a limited range of alternative responses.

      d.   Because both tests Larry is completing are projective, this cannot be the best answer.

4.   d.   Mental measurement, including the reliability and validity of assessment devices, is the subject called psychometrics.

      a.   Classification and labeling are activities that are separate from assessment and the instruments used in assessment.

      b.   The cultural sensitivity of the DSM is not directly related to issues of reliability and validity in assessment.

      c.   Improved cultural sensitivity of IQ testing is not directly related to issues of reliability and validity.

5.   a.   The Luria-Nebraska is a test battery used to assess brain damage; an MRI is also able to detect brain lesions, tumors, and other problems associated with brain damage.

      b.   Neither the Luria-Nebraska nor MRI is limited to being used with children.

      c.   A behaviorist would be interested in observable behaviors; Alan's clinical psychologist is probably a specialist in brain disorders with a biogenic orientation.

      d.   A psychoanalyst would be interested in unconscious conflicts; Alan's clinical psychologist is probably a specialist in brain disorders with a biogenic orientation.

6.   c.   These questions reflect the ethical concerns that many have about psychological tests.

      a.   When tests are standardized, the questions are asked and responses are scored in a consistent manner.

      b.   Psychometric concerns involve reliability and validity.

      d.   Biomedical concerns would highlight the impact of tests on the human body.

7.   b.   Computerized assessment can be done without personal contact, and studies say clients accept it.

      a.   The Rorschach involves person-to-person contact.

      c.   EEG requires one-on-one interaction.

      d.   Brain imaging techniques involve person-to-person contact.

8.   c.   The divorce is a strong stressor and would contribute to a high stress level rating on Axis IV.

      a.   Axis II lists personality and developmental disorders, not the clinical syndrome (in this case, phobia).

      b.   Organicity is restricted to brain damage, not damage to other organs.

      d.   Phobias are considered disorders and are shown on Axis 1.

9. a.   The DSM-IV-TR emphasizes cross-cultural assessment far more than previous versions of DSM.

    b.   Earlier editions of the DSM failed to include information on relevant cultural features of disorders.

    c.   These axes record information on health and stress, issues that are unrelated to culture.

    d.   IQ tests are not crucial to the diagnostic system except in matters of diagnosing mental retardation.

10. a.   Labels can change people's behavior in a process called self-fulfilling prophecy.

    b.   We would see poor reliability if one doctor diagnosed Ellen as schizophrenic and another considered her depressed.

    c.   Diagnosis without norms would occur if Ellen were considered schizophrenic without being compared with other schizophrenics.

    d.   Reactivity would occur if, knowing she was being observed, Ellen began to act differently.

OBJECTIVES DEFINED

1. **In attempting to make an accurate evaluation or assessment of a person's mental health, what kinds of standards must tests or evaluation procedures meet?**

- Assessment and classification of disorders are essential in the mental health field.

- In developing assessment tools and useful classification schemes, researchers and clinicians have been concerned with issues regarding reliability (stability or the degree to which a procedure or test yields the same results repeatedly, under the same circumstances) and validity (the extent to which a test or procedure actually performs the function it was designed to perform).

2. **What kinds of tools do clinicians employ in evaluating the mental health of people?**

- Clinicians primarily use four methods of assessment: observations, interviews, psychological tests and inventories, and neurological tests.

- Observations of external signs and expressive behaviors are often made during an interview and can have diagnostic significance.

- Interviews, the oldest form of psychological assessment, involve a face-to-face conversation, after which the interviewer differentially weighs and interprets verbal information obtained from the interviewee.

- Psychological tests and inventories provide a more formalized means of obtaining information. In personality testing, projective techniques, in which the stimuli are ambiguous, or self-report inventories, in which the stimuli are much more structured, may be used. Two of the most widely used projective techniques are the Rorschach inkblot technique and the Thematic Apperception Test (TAT). Unlike projective tests, self-report personality inventories, such as the MMPI-2, supply the test taker with a list of alternatives from which to select an answer. Intelligence tests can be used to obtain an estimate of a person's current level of cognitive functioning and to assess intellectual deterioration. Behavioral observations of how a person takes the test are additional sources of information about personality attributes. The WAIS, Stanford-Binet, and Bender-Gestalt tests can be used to assess brain damage. The Halstead-Reitan and Luria-Nebraska test batteries specifically assess brain dysfunction.

- Neurological medical procedures, including x-rays, CT and PET scans, EEG, and MRI, have added highly important and sophisticated means to detect brain damage.

3.   **How are mental health problems categorized or classified?**

- The first edition of DSM was based to a large extent on the biological model of mental illness and assumed that people who were classified in a psychodiagnostic category would show similar symptoms that stem from a common cause, that should be treated in a certain manner, that would respond similarly, and that would have similar prognoses. Critics questioned the reliability and validity of earlier versions of DSM.

- The current DSM-IV-TR contains detailed diagnostic criteria; research findings and expert judgments were used to help construct this latest version. As a result, its reliability appears to be higher than that of the previous manuals. Furthermore, data are collected on five axes so that much more information about the patient is systematically examined. DSM is now undergoing revisions for a forthcoming DSM-V edition.

- General objections to classification are based primarily on the problems involved in labeling and the loss of information about a person when that person is labeled or categorized.

- A number of ethical questions have been raised about classifying and assessing people through tests. These include questions about confidentiality, privacy, and cultural bias. Concerned with these issues, psychologists have sought to improve classification and assessment procedures and to define the appropriate conditions for testing and diagnosis.

MARGIN DEFINITIONS

assessment with regard to psychopathology, the process of gathering information and drawing conclusions about the traits, skills, abilities, emotional functioning, and psychological problems of an individual

classification system with regard to psychopathology, a system of distinct categories, indicators, and nomenclature for different patterns of behavior, thought processes, and emotional disturbances

comorbidity the co-occurrence of different disorders

prognosis a prediction of the future course of a particular disorder

projective personality test test in which the test taker is presented with ambiguous stimuli, such as inkblots, pictures, or incomplete sentences, and asked to respond to them in some way

psychological tests and inventories instruments used to assess personality, maladaptive behavior, development of social skills, intellectual abilities, vocational interests, and cognitive impairment.

psychometrics mental measurement, including its study and techniques

reactivity a change in the way a person usually responds, triggered by the person's knowledge that he or she is being observed or assessed

reliability the degree to which a procedure or test—such as an evaluation tool or classification scheme—will yield the same results repeatedly under the same circumstances

self-report inventories an assessment tool that requires test takers to answer specific written questions or to select specific responses from a list of alternatives

standardization in test administration, the use of identical procedures in the administration of tests; (in samples) the establishment of a norm or comparison group to which an individual's test performance can be compared

validity the extent to which a test or procedure actually performs the function it was designed to perform

CHAPTER 4

The Scientific Method in Abnormal Psychology

TABLE OF CONTENTS

LEARNING OBJECTIVES

1. Discuss the ways the scientific method is used to evaluate psychotherapy.

2. Discuss how the use of an experimental design differs from other ways of investigating phenomena.

3. Define correlations and how they are used to indicate the degree to which two variables are related.

4. Discuss analogue studies and when this type of investigation is used.

5. Describe field studies and how they are used.

6. Define the various types of single-participant studies and how they are used.

7. Discuss some of the advantages and shortcomings of the biological approach in understanding abnormal behavior.

8. Define epidemiological research and how it is used to determine the extent of mental disturbance in a targeted population.

9. Discuss some ethical concerns about how research is conducted and how researchers can best address these concerns.

CHAPTER OUTLINE

I. **The scientific method in clinical research.** The most general characteristic of science is its potential for self-correction. A *theory* is a group of principles and hypotheses that together explain some aspect of a particular area of inquiry. *Hypotheses* must be clearly stated and variables given definitions. Recent studies of child sexual abuse illustrate the range of definitions used. Measures must show reliability and validity. Appropriate comparison frequencies for a phenomenon *(base rates)* should be considered. For instance, if eating problems and child abuse are both commonly occurring events but one is unaware of this, one could mistakenly conclude that abuse causes eating problems. Finally, results should be evaluated in terms of both *statistical significance* (whether the results were due to a factor other than chance) and *clinical significance* (whether the results have clinical value). In large-sample studies, statistically significant differences are sometimes clinically meaningless.

II. **Experiments.** Experiments include *experimental* and *control groups*. Only the experimental group participants are exposed to the *independent variable* (the possible cause of behavior the experimenter manipulates). Measures of the *dependent variable* (the behavior believed to be controlled by the independent variable) are taken for participants in both groups. *Placebo groups* can be included to rule out the possibility that participants' expectations alter their behavior in the experimental group. Experimenter expectations can also be controlled by making the clinicians in a study blind (uninformed) as to the experimenter's hypothesis. To reduce the impact of both experimenter and participant expectations, there are *double-blind designs* where neither the individual working directly with the participant nor the participant is aware of who is in the experimental group. When changes in the dependent variable can unambiguously be attributed to the changes in the independent variable, a study is said to have *internal validity*. When results of a study can be generalized to other populations or situations, the study is said to have *external validity*.

III. **Correlations.** *Correlations* measure the degree to which changes in one variable are associated with changes in another variable. Statistically, these associations, correlation coefficients, are symbolized by *r*, which ranges from -1.00 to +1.00. Even if a correlational study shows a strong association, it is often difficult to determine whether Variable A caused changes in Variable B, Variable B caused changes in Variable A, or some third variable affected the other two.

IV. **Analogue studies.** (When the study of real-life situations is impractical or unethical, *analogue studies* are conducted in simulated, but controlled, circumstances. When analogue studies are too contrived, observations can be made in the real-life situation in what is called a *field study*. These are limited research strategies because they cannot determine the direction of causality and they introduce the potential for observers influencing behavior.

V. **Single-participant studies.** Although most research methods are aimed at making general statements about behavior and, therefore, use groups of people (the *nomothetic* orientation), in-depth studies are sometimes done on individuals (the *idiographic* orientation). The *case study* is used extensively by clinicians, and although it lacks control and objectivity, and thus cannot be used to show cause-and-effect relationships, it does examine and analyze conditions over a period of time. The *single-participant study* measures an individual's behavior over time. It observes changes that occur after some behavior modification has been applied. A second type of single-participant experiment obtains baselines on two or more behaviors and introduces the same intervention with each to see if the behaviors change with the intervention. A *multiple-baseline study* is a second type of single-participant experimental design in which baselines on two or more behaviors or the same behavior in two or more settings are obtained prior to intervention.

VI. **Biological research strategies.** *Genetic linkage studies* determine if a disorder follows a genetic pattern by identifying the family members of a person with a disorder (proband) who also suffer from it. *Endophenotypes* are measurable characteristics (neurochemical, endocrinological, neuroanatomical, cognitive, or neuropsychological) that can give clues regarding the specific genes involved in disorders. Researchers must be on guard for *iatrogenic* effects—those negative effects brought on by treatment. For example, traumatic events recalled during hypnosis may be a function of hypnotic suggestion more than accurate recollection. When a person carries a gene for a characteristic but fails to show the characteristic, there is incomplete *penetrance*. Symptoms that are distinctive for a disorder are considered *pathognomonic*. Finally, when clinical researchers use *biological challenge tests,* they observe for changes in behavior when chemicals (foods, allergens, or drugs) are introduced and for those behaviors to disappear when the chemical is absent.

VII. **Epidemiological and other forms of research.** A variety of research types, including survey research, longitudinal research, historical research, twin studies treatment outcome and treatment process studies, and program evaluation can use experimental, correlational, or single-subject methods. An important type of research is *epidemiological research*, which examines the rate and distribution of mental disorders. It can reveal the rate of new cases *(incidence)* or the total rate of cases *(prevalence)* as well as risk factors associated with the disorder.

VIII. **Ethical issues in research.** The scientific method can be abused and misused. The American Psychological Association has adopted the principle that the likely benefits of research must outweigh the risk or discomfort to its participants. Deception should be used only when alternatives are not possible. Only when alternatives are unavailable should animals be used as subjects, and then they should be treated in humane ways. Guidelines for research sensitive to minority ethnic and religious groups are also in place.

IX. **Implications.** Research has contributed greatly to our knowledge of mental disorders. However, the quality of the research design influences the degree of faith that we can have regarding the finding. It is difficult to call clinical psychology a science when so many theoretical orientations (over 400) offer differing etiologies for disorders.

KEY TERMS REVIEW

1. The degree to which variations in one variable are associated with increases or decreases in a second variable is called the _____.

2. The research technique in which behaviors are observed or recorded in non-laboratory conditions, in the natural environment is called a(n) _____.

3. The method of inquiry that involves systematic collection of data through controlled observation and provides for the testing of hypotheses based on those data is called the _____.

4. An investigation that attempts to simulate, as closely as possible, under controlled conditions a situation that occurs in real life is called _____.

5. The biological research method that attempts to determine whether a disorder follows a genetic pattern is, called a(n) _____.

6. A technique of scientific inquiry in which an independent variable is differentially manipulated for an experimental group and a control group, and the changes in a dependent variable are measured, is called a(n) _____.

7. Frequencies of phenomena that occur without treatment and that are used for comparing populations are called _____.

8. Research that studies the rate and distribution of mental disorders in a population is called _____.

9. In a psychological experiment, the variables (e.g., attitudes or behaviors) that are expected to change as a result of the manipulation of an independent variable are called _____.

10. The variable or condition that is manipulated by the experimenter and tested for its effects on the dependent variable is called the _____.

11. A description of variables under study in terms of the specific procedures used to measure them is called a(n) _____.

12. The intensive study of one individual that relies on observation, psychological tests, and historical data is called a(n) _____.

13. The unintended effects of treatment are considered _____ effects.

14. An experiment performed on a single individual in which the individual's own behavior is used as the control is called a(n) _____.

15. Measurable characteristics (neurochemical, endocrinological, neuroanatomical, cognitive, or neuropsychological) that can give clues regarding the specific genes involved in disorders are called _____.

16. A prediction concerning how an independent variable affects a dependent variable in an experiment is called a(n) _____.

17. A conjectural statement describing a relationship between two variables is called a(n) _____.

18. A group of principles that together explain some aspect of a specific area of study is called a(n) _____.

19. When a study is shown to be caused by changes in the independent variable, the study is said to have _____.

20. The degree to which findings of a particular study are generalizable to other populations or situations is known as _____.

21. A _____ is a second type of single-participant experimental design in which baselines on two or more behaviors or the same behavior in two or more settings are obtained prior to intervention.

FACTUAL MULTIPLE-CHOICE QUESTIONS

1. Epidemiological studies are concerned with
   a. independent and dependent variables.
   b. internal validity.
   c. incidence and prevalence.
   d. control groups and placebo groups.

2. Freud built his theories and developed his therapy with the use of a relatively small number of clients. His research was based on
   a. case studies
   b. field studies.
   c. longitudinal studies.
   d. historical studies.

3. In very large samples, you can have statistically significant results without having
   a. measured any variables.
   b. employed the nomothetic approach.
   c. clinically significant results.
   d. used numerical measurements

4. The _____ is the best research method for making cause-and-effect inferences.
   a. correlation
   b. historical research method
   c. case study
   d. experiment

5. In an experiment, which group is exposed to the independent variable?
   a. The control group
   b. The experimental group
   c. Both the control group and the experimental group
   d. The placebo group

6. Double-blind experimental designs are necessary
   a. when the control group's characteristics are unlike the experimental group's.
   b. to control for the effect of subjects' expectations.
   c. when no pretest has been done on the experimental group.
   d. to reduce the impact of both experimenter and participant expectations.

7. _____ are the research methods most often used in the study of rare conditions or when ethical standards only allow research in simulated, controlled situations.
   a. Longitudinal studies
   b. Correlations
   c. Case studies
   d. Analogue studies

8. When researchers go into a real-life situation and observe people's behavior they are using the research method called the
   a. analogue study.
   b. correlation.
   c. field study.
   d. historical study.

9. A single-subject study that measures changes in behaviors before and after a particular modification is applied is called the
   a. analogue experiment.
   b. case study.
   c. single-participant experiment.
   d. double-blind correlational study.

10. Prevalence and incidence rates are two concepts related to
    a. epidemiology.
    b. analogue studies.
    c. single-subject experiments.
    d. idiographic research.

CONCEPTUAL MULTIPLE-CHOICE QUESTIONS

1. Why is it premature to say that alcoholism is caused by the Al allele on a specific chromosome?
   a. The relationship between the gene and alcoholism is iatrogenic.
   b. The Al allele proved to be pathognomonic for alcoholism.
   c. The Al allele finding was replicated in other populations of alcoholics.
   d. Later studies showed no difference in the likelihood of the Al allele in control and alcoholic samples.

2. What are the main characteristics of the scientific method?
   a. Personal values and belief in rationality
   b. Personal belief and emotion
   c. Skepticism and self-correction
   d. Subjectivity and personal values

3. A researcher interested in thumb sucking and later adult personality would need to know how common thumb sucking is among children. The researcher would need to know
   a. if thumb sucking is genetic.
   b. the base rate for thumb sucking.
   c. whether there is a biological marker for thumb sucking.
   d. what is a placebo for thumb sucking.

4.   Unlike an experiment, in a correlational study,

   a.   only the control group is exposed to the independent variable.
   b.   there is no dependent variable.
   c.   statistics are not used to determine the strength of association between variables.
   d.   variables are not manipulated by the researcher.

5.   If the results of a correlation study showed that *r*= -0.73, what could be said?

   a.   There is a strong inverse relationship between the factors that were studied.
   b.   The association between the two factors is so weak that the study was a failure.
   c.   In 73 percent of the cases, one variable causes the other.
   d.   As the scores on one of the factors go up, scores on the other factor go up, too.

6.   Which statement about field studies is *accurate*?

   a.   The primary technique for data collection in field studies is observation.
   b.   The participants in field studies are most often individual cases.
   c.   Field studies occur in laboratories where variables and conditions can be controlled.
   d.   Researchers doing field studies need little special training.

7.   Correlations and experiments are to the _____ orientation as case studies and single-participant experiments are to the _____ orientation.

   a.   common-sense; scientific
   b.   scientific; nomothetic
   c.   idiographic; nomothetic
   d.   nomothetic; idiographic

8.   A study examining the level of certain neurotransmitters in people with a disorder and in a control group without the disorder is attempting to identify

   a.   endophenotypes.
   b.   iatrogenic effects.
   c.   double-blind effects.
   d.   penetrance.

9.   Which statement below accurately summarizes the American Psychological Association's guide lines for ethical research?

   a.   "Any research effort that might hurt a person or animal cannot be allowed."
   b.   "Most of human behavior is best left as a mystery."
   c.   "The value of any research effort must outweigh its potential risks."
   d.   "Animals may be treated in any manner as long as scientific truths are the result."

10.   Which type of study obtains baselines on two or more behaviors or the same behavior in two or more settings prior to intervention?

   a.   Field study
   b.   Multiple-baseline study
   c.   Case study
   d.   Analogue study

APPLICATION MULTIPLE-CHOICE QUESTIONS

1.   Jenny reads in the paper that scientists have found unusually high levels of a certain hormone in women who develop cancer. What information does Jenny need before she can believe the hormone increases her risk of cancer?

   a.   Evidence of statistical significance on huge samples.
   b.   Replication of the results by other scientists.
   c.   Evidence that the hormone has a very high base rate in the general population.
   d.   A correlation of about 0.00 between hormone concentrations and cancer.

2. In a research study, "alcoholism" is defined as a score of five or more on the Michigan Alcoholism Screening Test. This illustrates

    a. the use of an operational definition.
    b. a low-reliability measure.
    c. an iatrogenic effect.
    d. a base rate.

3. In an experiment to see whether diet influences depression, participants are randomly selected to eat either a high-protein-low-carbohydrate diet or their usual diet. At the end of six weeks on the diets, the experimental group is significantly less depressed. What is missing in this experiment?

    a. A control group
    b. A dependent variable
    c. An independent variable
    d. A placebo condition

4. In a study of the effects of a drug on anxiety, neither the participants nor the people dispensing the drug know who is getting a placebo and who is getting the drug being tested. This kind of study is considered

    a. correlational.
    b. a double-blind design.
    c. an analogue study.
    d. idiographic.

5. The longer Stephanie stays awake at night, the less efficient her study becomes. Which of the following best expresses the relationship between hours staying awake and study efficiency?

    a. $r = +1.00$
    b. A negative correlation
    c. A positive correlation
    d. $r = -1.00$

6. If a research study shows that life stress correlates positively with alcohol consumption, what can we conclude about the relationship between these two variables?

    a. That stress causes drinking
    b. That drinking causes stress
    c. That genetics cause both stress and drinking
    d. Nothing

7. Dr. Keys reports that one of her patients has sixteen distinct personalities. There are both male and female personalities. She reports that, through hypnosis, she has helped the personalities fuse into one competent individual. This report illustrates

    a. a correlation between sex-role typing and hypnosis.
    b. an analogue study, because the person did not receive hypnosis in the "real world."
    c. a case study.
    d. a single-participant experiment.

8. In order to study hyperactivity, a researcher asks Jimmy's teacher to keep track of how often he is out of his chair for five straight school days. Then, over the next twenty days, Jimmy is rewarded when he stays in his chair. His behavior improves. When the teacher stops the rewards, Jimmy gets worse, so rewards are returned, and his behavior improves again. This illustrates

    a. a positive correlation between reward and hyperactivity.
    b. an analogue study.
    c. a single-participant experiment.
    d. historical research.

9. Researchers interested in phobias identify 100 people who have a fear of animals. They assess the presence of a similar phobia in the parents and grandparents of all 100 people. This is an example of a(n) _____ study.
    a. longitudinal
    b. analogue
    c. biological challenge
    d. genetic linkage
10. Dr. Szezch is interested in the rate of new cases of childhood autism in Poland. Dr. Szezch is
    a. doing an analogue experiment.
    b. interested in the incidence of childhood autism.
    c. interested in the prevalence of childhood autism.
    d. doing unethical research.

ANSWER KEY: KEY TERMS REVIEW

1. correlation

2. field study

3. scientific method

4. analogue study

5. genetic linkage study

6. experiment

7. base rates

8. epidemiological research

9. dependent variables

10. independent variable

11. operational definition

12. case study

13. iatrogenic

14. single-participant experiment

15. endophenotypes

16. experimental hypothesis

17. hypothesis

18. theory

19. internal validity

20. external validity

21. multiple-baseline study

ANSWER KEY: FACTUAL MULTIPLE-CHOICE QUESTIONS

1. c. Epidemiological studies yield information on the incidence (the number of new cases) and prevalence (the percentage of cases in a population during a specified time period).

    a. These studies are not concerned with treatment of a disorder.

    b. These studies are concerned more so with external validity and representativeness.

    d. Control groups and placebo groups apply to experimental research.

2. a. Freud relied on case studies; while this method provides in-depth information about a single case, it lacks control and objectivity.

    b. Freud did his work in his office and used his clinical experiences as his laboratory.

    c. Freud's case studies involved relatively short periods of time.

    d. Freud was concerned with insight, not history.

3. c. In very large samples, statistically significant differences can have no clinical or real-world significance.

    a. There can be no statistical analyses unless there are variables that have been measured.

    b. The nomothetic approach uses groups of people as participants.

    d. Statistics can only be computed using numbers.

4. d. The greatest strength of the experiment is the manipulation of one factor by the experimenter and the consequent ability to make causal inferences.

    a. Correlational studies can only show an association between two variables, not what caused what.

    b. Historical research cannot create the experimental and control groups necessary to infer cause.

    c. Case studies examine individuals, provide no control groups, and make causal inferences impossible.

5. b. The definition of an experimental group is that it is exposed to the independent variable.

    a. The control group experiences the same factors as the experimental group *except* for the independent variable.

    c. If both groups were exposed to the independent variable, there would be no basis for comparing the two groups.

    d. The placebo group is led to believe it gets the independent variable, but it does not.

6. d. Double-blind studies make it impossible for either participants or those who interact with them to know whether the independent variable is being dispensed; this reduces the impact of expectations on both groups.

    a. Control group characteristics should be the same as the experimental group's except for the independent variable; double-blind strategies can only reduce expectation effects, not influence sample characteristics.

    b. Double-blind studies control for both experimenters' and participants' expectations.

    c. A lack of a pretest will make it impossible to tell whether a treatment made a difference; placebos cannot help with this problem.

7. d.   Analogue studies are used when it is impractical to study behavior in real-life situations, either because the behavior is rare or because control over the situation is impossible.

    a.   Longitudinal studies follow individuals across time; they do not involve simulated situations.

    b.   Correlations involve an examination of how two factors are associated.

    c.   Case studies involve an examination of one person or situation.

8. c.   Field studies involve "going into the field" to examine behavior in "the real world."

    a.   Analogue studies are done when researchers *cannot* go into a real-life situation.

    b.   Correlations involve an examination of how two factors are associated.

    d.   Historical research involves the collection of documents to shed light on behavior in a prior period.

9. c.   The single-participant experiment looks at one person's behavior at baseline (before the introduction of some intervention) and again afterward. The modification is often a form of treatment.

    a.   Analogue studies are simulations of naturally occurring situations and involve multiple subjects.

    b.   Case studies look at individuals in depth but do not systematically alter conditions.

    d.   Double-blind correlations do not exist since "blind" experiments involve the hiding of independent variables.

10. a.   Epidemiology is research that examines the distribution of cases, including new ones (incidence) and the total number (prevalence) within a given time period.

    b.   Analogue studies involve the simulation of real-life situations under more controlled circumstances.

    c.   Single-participant experiments look at one person's behavior, not that of many people.

    d.   The idiographic approach involves the in-depth study of individuals.

ANSWER KEY: CONCEPTUAL MULTIPLE-CHOICE QUESTIONS

1. d.   Lack of replication has led to reduced confidence that the Al allele is a marker for alcoholism.

    a.   An iatrogenic effect is one caused by treatment; there was no treatment and genes cannot be changed that way.

    b.   If the gene were pathognomonic (specific to the disorder) it would support the idea that it causes alcoholism.

    c.   If the finding were replicated in other alcoholic populations, the genetic cause of alcoholism would have been supported.

2. c.   The hallmarks of the scientific method are skepticism (cautiousness) and self-correction (replication and efforts directed at ruling out alternative explanations).

    a.   Scientists emphasize objective data rather than personal values.

    b.   Scientists seek ways to reduce the influence of personal belief and emotion in their search for answers.

    d.   Scientists try to be as free from subjectivity and personal values as possible.

3.   b.   Base rates are the frequencies of phenomena and are used to compare groups; if thumb sucking is very common, it may mean that there is little relationship between it and adult personality.

    a.   Genetics would have no relevance to this study.

    c.   Since the researcher is using thumb sucking as a predictor, it is unnecessary to find a biological marker for it.

    d.   Placebos are only necessary in experiments; this is not an experiment.

4.   d.   In correlations, the researcher does not manipulate a variable, but examines the association between scores on two or more variables that happen "naturally."

    a.   There are no control groups in correlational studies.

    b.   Dependent variables are measures of behavior; they are found in both experiments and correlational studies.

    c.   The statistic called the correlation coefficient (r) is used to assess the strength of associations in correlational studies.

5.   a.   When $r = -0.73$, there is a strong negative correlation, which indicates that as scores on one variable increase, scores on the other decrease—an inverse relationship.

    b.   A weak association would be indicated by an r around 0.00.

    c.   The correlation coefficient r is not a percentage, it is a measure of association.

    d.   This kind of positive correlation would yield a positive r, such as $r = +0.66$.

6.   a.   Field studies emphasize the observation of behavior in natural settings, so observation is a primary technique, although interviews and surveys are other possible means of recording data.

    b.   Field studies usually focus on groups of people in organizations or communities.

    c.   Field studies are done in naturalistic settings and never in laboratories.

    d.   Since observation is crucial to field studies, these researchers must be trained in making careful observations and in how not to influence the behaviors of others.

7.   d.   Correlations and experiments use groups of people (a nomothetic approach); case studies and single-participant experiments. focus on the individual (idiographic orientation).

    a.   Correlations and experiments are part of the scientific method; they do not necessarily rely on common sense.

    b.   Case studies and single-subject experiments use one person and are therefore the opposite of the nomothetic orientation, which looks for universal behavior from many subjects.

    c.   These are reversed.

8. a. Endophenotypes are measurable characteristics (neurochemical, endocrinological, neuroanatomical, cognitive, or neuropsychological) that can give clues regarding the specific genes involved in disorders.

    b. Iatrogenic effects are the side effects of treatment; there is no treatment in this study.

    c. *Double-blind* refers to a study design where neither the subjects nor the individuals who work directly with them know who is in the experimental or control groups.

    d. Penetrance refers to the degree to which people having a specific gene also have a specific characteristic.

9. c. APA guidelines try to strike a balance between the need to learn and the need to protect subjects; they suggest that any risk to the subject must be overshadowed by potential benefits.

    a. APA guidelines accept that some studies may induce embarrassment or pain in some subjects.

    b. APA guidelines encourage the pursuit of complete knowledge.

    d. APA guidelines have policies for the humane care of animal subjects.

10. b. A multiple-baseline study is when baselines on two or more behaviors or the same behavior in two or more settings are obtained prior to intervention.

    a. A field study is an investigative technique in which behaviors and events are observed and recorded in their natural environment

    c. A case study is an intensive study that relies on clinical data, such as observations, psychological tests, and historical and biographical information.

    d. An analogue study attempts to replicate or simulate, under controlled conditions, a situation that occurs in real life.

ANSWER KEY: APPLICATION MULTIPLE-CHOICE QUESTIONS

1. b. Only with replication of findings can we believe that there is stability in a scientific outcome; Jenny would be wise to be as skeptical as scientists are.

    a. Ironically, statistically significant results based on huge samples may mean that there is little clinical significance. Without clinical significance she has little reason to believe the factor increases her personal risk of cancer.

    c. If the base rate is high in the population, we will have a hard time seeing the hormone as causing a specific disorder since it will be present in m any without the disorder.

    d. Correlations near 0.00 indicate no association between variables.

2. a. Operational definitions define concepts in terms of how they are measured; in this case, alcoholism is defined in terms of a score on a questionnaire.

    b. Reliability refers to the consistency of a measure; the Michigan Alcoholism Screening Test has very strong reliability.

    c. An iatrogenic effect is caused by treatment; no treatment exists in this study.

    d. Base rates involve the frequency of a phenomenon; if the study looked at how often people score 5 on the Michigan Alcoholism Screening Test, that would entail base rates.

3.   d.   Without controlling for expectations about how diet will alter mood, we cannot tell whether it is the diet or expectations that cause changes in feelings. We need to disguise from participants the type of food they are eating—we need a placebo condition.

     a.   All experiments include control groups; in this case, it is the group that eats its normal diet.

     b.   All experiments include a measure of behavior (the dependent variable); in this case, it is depressive symptoms.

     c.   All experiments include an independent variable; in this case, it is the high-protein-low-carbohydrate diet.

4.   b.   *Double-blind* means that neither the participants nor those who come in contact with them know who is getting the independent variable.

     a.   Experimental groups receive the independent variable (the drug).

     c.   Analogue studies look at behavior in simulated situations.

     d.   Idiographic studies examine individuals in great detail; groups are being studied here.

5.   b.   As her time awake increases, study efficiency decreases; that is a negative correlation.

     a.   An *r* of +1.00 would be a perfect positive correlation; it would mean that every minute she was awake, her studying would get consistently *better* by a uniform amount.

     c.   A positive correlation would mean that as she stays awake longer, her efficiency increases.

     d.   A perfect negative correlation *(r = -1.00)* would mean that for every minute of staying awake, her efficiency would decrease by a set amount.

6.   d.   Correlations tell nothing about causality.

     a.   With correlational studies, no direction of causality can be determined.

     b.   With correlational studies, no direction of causality can be determined.

     c.   Correlational studies cannot determine whether a third variable causes the relationship in the other two.

7.   c.   Since only one person is being examined, it is a case study.

     a.   Since only one person is being examined, a correlation is impossible.

     b.   An analogue study would look at therapy in some simulated environment, not an actual therapy.

     d.   An experiment requires a control group or the use of a person's own behavior as a control (in the case of single-participant experiments).

8.   c.   Single-participants experiments examine behavior before and after a treatment is introduced.

     a.   Correlations use data from groups of people, not an individual person.

     b.   This work is taking place in an actual classroom, so it is not an analogue study, which would use a simulated setting.

     d.   Historical research would collect data from the past on a group of individuals.

9.   d.   Genetic linkage studies examine the frequency of a disorder in the family members of those who have the disorder.

      a.   A longitudinal study would repeatedly observe the same 100 people over time.

      b.   An analogue study would put individuals in a simulated situation so that an independent variable could be introduced.

      c.   A biological challenge test would introduce some chemical into the bodies of individuals to see if behavior changed.

10.   b.   Incidence is the number of new cases of a disorder in a population over a period of time.

      a.   An analogue study puts subjects in simulated situations.

      c.   Prevalence is the total number of cases of a disorder (old and new) in a population over a period of time.

      d.   There is nothing unethical about doing epidemiological research.

OBJECTIVES DEFINED

1.   **In what ways is the scientific method used to evaluate psychotherapy?**

- The scientific method is a method of inquiry that provides for the systematic collection of data, controlled observation, and the testing of hypotheses.

- Characteristics such as the potential for self-correction, the development of hypotheses, the use of operational definitions, a consideration of reliability and validity, an acknowledgment of base rates, and the requirement that research findings be evaluated in terms of their statistical significance enable us to have greater faith in our findings.

2.   **How does the use of an experimental design differ from other ways of investigating phenomena?**

- The experiment is the most powerful research tool we have for determining and testing cause-and-effect relationships. In its simplest form, an experiment involves an experimental hypothesis, an independent variable, and a dependent variable.

- The investigator manipulates the independent variable and measures the effect on the dependent variable. The experimental group is the group subjected to the independent variable. A control group is employed that is similar in every way to the experimental group except for the manipulation of the independent variable.

- Additional concerns include expectancy effects on the part of the participants and the investigator and the extent to which an experiment has internal and external validity.

3.   **What are correlations and how are they used to indicate the degree to which two variables are related?**

- A correlation is a measure of the degree to which two variables are related, not what causes the relationship. It is expressed as a correlation coefficient, a numerical value between -1 and $+1$, symbolized by r. Correlational techniques provide less precision, control, and generality than experiments, and they cannot be taken to imply cause-and-effect relationships.

4.   **What are analogue studies and when is this type of investigation used?**

- In the study of abnormal behavior, an analogue study is used to create a situation as close to real life as possible. It permits the study of phenomena under controlled conditions when such study might otherwise be ethically, morally, legally, or practically impossible. The generalizability of the findings to clinical populations has to be evaluated and cannot be automatically assumed.

5.   **What are field studies and how are they used?**

- The field study relies primarily on naturalistic observations in real-life situations. As opposed to analogue studies, events are observed as they naturally occur. However, a field study cannot determine causality, and it may be difficult to sort out all the variables involved.

6.   **What are the various types of single-participant studies and how are they used?**

- A case study is an intensive study of one individual that relies on clinical data, such as observations, psychological tests, and historical and biographical information. The case study is especially appropriate when a phenomenon is so rare that it is impractical to try to study more than a few instances.

- Single-participant experiments differ from case studies in that cause-and-effect relationships can be determined. They rely on experimental procedures; some aspect of the person's own behavior is taken as a control or baseline for comparison with future behaviors.

- A multiple-baseline study is a second type of single-participant experimental design in which baselines on two or more behaviors or the same behavior in two or more settings are obtained prior to intervention.

7.   **What are some of the advantages and shortcomings of the biological approach in understanding abnormal behavior?**

- Biological research strategies allow us to search for genetic factors involved in psychological disorders or to identify biological markers or indicators of a disorder. As with any approach, consideration of other factors may be minimized because the stress is on the biological model.

8.   **What is epidemiological research and how is it used to determine the extent of mental disturbance in a targeted population?**

- Epidemiological research examines the rate and distribution of mental disorders in a population. It can also provide insight into what groups are at risk for mental disturbance and what factors may influence disturbance.

- There is often confusion between prevalence and incidence rates. Prevalence rates are statements of new and existing cases during a specified time period. Incidence rates are statements of new cases only.

9.   **What are some ethical concerns about how research is conducted and how can researchers best address these concerns?**

- Like other tools, the scientific method is subject to misuse and misunderstanding, both of which can give rise to moral and ethical concerns. Such concerns have led the American Psychological Association (APA) to develop guidelines for ethical conduct and to establish ways for dealing with violations within the mental health professions. The APA has also published guidelines for those working with culturally diverse populations.

MARGIN DEFINITIONS

analogue study an investigation that attempts to replicate or simulate, under controlled conditions, a situation that occurs in real life

base rate the rate of natural occurrence of a phenomenon in the population studied

case study an intensive study of one individual that relies on clinical data, such as observations, psychological tests, and historical and biographical information

correlation the extent to which variations in one variable are accompanied by increases or decreases in a second variable

dependent variable a variable that is expected to change when an independent variable is manipulated in a psychological experiment

endophenotypes measurable characteristics (neurochemical, endocrinological, neuroanatomical, cognitive, or neuropsychological) that can give clues regarding the specific genes involved in disorders

epidemiological research the study of the rate and distribution of mental disorders in a population

experiment a technique of scientific inquiry in which a prediction—an experimental hypothesis—is made about two variables; the independent variable is then manipulated in a controlled situation, and changes in the dependent variable are measured

experimental hypothesis a prediction concerning how an independent variable will affect a dependent variable in an experiment

external validity the degree to which findings of a particular study can be generalized to other groups or conditions

field study an investigative technique in which behaviors and events are observed and recorded in their natural environment

genetic linkage studies studies that attempt to determine whether a disorder follows a genetic pattern

hypothesis a conjectural statement that usually describes a relationship between two variables

iatrogenic unintended effects of therapy—such as an unintended change in behavior resulting from a medication prescribed or a psychological technique employed by a therapist

independent variable a variable or condition that an experimenter manipulates to determine its effect on a dependent variable

internal validity the degree to which changes in the dependent variable are due solely to the effect of changes in the independent variable

multiple-baseline study a single-participant experimental design in which baselines on two or more behaviors or the same behavior in two or more settings are obtained prior to intervention

operational definitions concrete definitions of the variables that are being studied

scientific method a method of inquiry that provides for the systematic collection of data, controlled observation, and the testing of hypotheses

single-participant experiment an experiment performed on a single individual in which some aspect of the person's own behavior is used as a control or baseline for comparison with future behaviors

theory a group of principles and hypotheses that together explain some aspect of a particular area of inquiry

CHAPTER 5

Anxiety Disorders

TABLE OF CONTENTS

LEARNING OBJECTIVES

1. Discuss how biological, psychological, social, and sociocultural factors are involved in the development of anxiety disorders.

2. Discuss phobias, their causes, and how they are treated.

3. Describe panic disorder and agoraphobia, their causes, and how they are treated.

4. Describe generalized anxiety disorder, its causes, and how it is treated.

5. Define obsessive-compulsive disorder, its causes, and how it is treated.

CHAPTER OUTLINE

I. **Understanding anxiety disorders from a multi-path perspective.** Anxiety is a fundamental human emotion that has an adaptive function. *Anxiety disorders* meet one of the following criteria: the anxiety is a major disturbance, the anxiety is manifested only in a particular situation, or anxiety results from attempts to master other symptoms. In the current diagnostic system, anxiety disorders consist of *panic disorder, generalized anxiety disorder (GAD), phobias, obsessive-compulsive disorder..* In each of these disorders, a person can experience panic attacks—intense fear with symptoms such as a pounding heart and fear of losing control. There are three types of attacks: (1) situationally bound (occurring in response to a stimulus); (2) situationally predisposed (usually occurring in response to a stimulus); and (3) unexpected attacks. Most attacks are of the first two types. In the biological dimension there are two main biological factors affecting anxiety disorders: *brain structure* and *genetic influences*. In brain structure the *amygdala* (a part of the brain involved in the formation and memory of emotional events) plays a central role in anxiety disorders. It alerts other brain structures, such as the *hippocampus* and *prefrontal cortex*, when a threat is present, triggering a fear or anxiety response. In genetic influences there appears to be a modest contribution of genes to anxiety disorders. In the psychological, and social interactions dimensions many etiological theories of mental disorders are psychological in nature and tend to deemphasize either biological or social influences.

II. **Phobias.** A *phobia is* an intense, persistent, and unwarranted fear of an object or situation. Attempts to avoid the fear-inducing situation interfere with the person's life. Phobias are the most common mental disorder in the United States. *Social phobia is* an intense fear of being watched and humiliated. There are three types of social phobias: performance (involving such activities as public speaking), limited interactional (involving such interactions as going out on a date), and generalized (where extreme anxiety occurs in most social situations). The last category has been criticized for being too similar to avoidant personality disorder. Except for public speaking, social phobias are somewhat rare. Despite knowing that their fears are irrational, people with social phobias curtail many activities. Social phobias appear to be common in families who use shame as a method of control and who stress the importance of other people's opinions. *Specific phobias* are fears of specific objects and include a long list of disorders. In DSM-IV-TR there are five types: animal, natural environmental (for example, thunder); blood/injections or injury; situational (for example, heights); and other (a range of situations that may lead to choking or illness). Common phobias involve fear of public speaking, speaking to strangers, animals, and heights. They are twice as prevalent in women as in men and are rarely incapacitating. Etiology of phobias include genetic evidence that indicates phobias may stem from a predisposition to excessive autonomic reaction to stress, but genetic vulnerability has only a modest relationship to specific phobias. Psychoanalysts see phobias as symbolic of unconscious sexual or aggressive conflicts. The case of little Hans is used to explain a youth's fear of horses. Classical conditioning explains the development of some phobias. Observational learning and operant conditioning principles may explain some phobias. Retrospective reports indicate that conditioning experiences play a major causative role. However, research suggests other cause factors as well. Catastrophic thoughts and distorted cognitions may cause strong fears to develop and phobic individuals are more likely than other people to overestimate the odds of unpleasant events occurring, supporting a cognitive-behavioral perspective. Biochemical treatment of the phobias usually involves antidepressants, although SSRIs have also been used to treat social phobias. Behavioral treatment includes *exposure therapy* (the gradual presentation of the feared situation), which has been helpful in reducing fears and panic attacks in agoraphobic individuals and those with specific phobias; cognitive strategies aimed at changing unrealistic thoughts; systematic desensitization; modeling. A combined approach that includes cognitive, behavioral, and biological components is increasingly being used.

III.   **Panic disorder and agoraphobia** Free-floating anxiety characterizes both panic disorder and generalized anxiety disorder. Panic disorder is diagnosed when a person has recurrent panic attacks that alternate with periods of low anxiety. Such attacks are terrifying and may lead to agoraphobia. While attacks are fairly common, the disorder is not; the lifetime prevalence is about 3.5 percent. *Agoraphobia is* a fear of being in public places without the availability of help. It is twice as common for females as for males. The disorder often has a precipitating event, and thoughts play a key role. People with agoraphobia tend to react more intensely to anxiety symptoms than people with other anxiety problems. The biological perspective focuses on neural structures and neurochemical responses to stressful stimuli and notes that such factors as oxygen-monitoring receptors and response to sodium lactate influence panic attacks. Dysfunction in the locus ceruleus, a part of the central anxiety system in the brain, may account for panic disorders. Genetics also seem to play a role, particularly in panic disorder. Psychoanalysts suggest that internal (sexual and aggressive) conflicts are expressed in outward anxiety. The effectiveness of defenses used determines whether the person develops panic disorder or generalized anxiety disorder. The cognitive-behavioral thinkers argue that catastrophic thoughts and overattention to internal signals maintain and inflate anxiety symptoms. Research in which subjects had marked increases in cardiovascular activity after focusing on negative thoughts supports this argument.. In the social and sociocultural dimensions many patients with panic disorder report a disturbed childhood environment that involved separation anxiety, family conflicts, school problems, leaving home, or the loss of a loved one.) Medications, particularly the antidepressants, have proven useful in treating panic disorder, although relapse rates after ceasing the drugs is high. Benzodiazepines (Valium and Librium) have been used successfully to treat generalized anxiety disorder, but psychological treatment is also necessary. Behavior therapies, including relaxation training and cognitive restructuring, show promise. Treatment for panic disorder can include educating the client about the disorder, training in relaxation techniques, altering unrealistic thoughts, facing the, symptoms, and developing coping strategies. Cognitive-behavioral therapy seems particularly effective for generalized anxiety disorder.

IV. **Generalized anxiety disorder**. Generalized anxiety disorder is characterized by persistent anxiety, heart palpitations, tension, and restlessness, together lasting over six months. People with GAD worry over major and minor events and have more persistent but less severe physical symptoms than people with panic disorder. Estimated lifetime prevalence of GAD in the United States is 5 percent of the adult population, with females being twice as likely as males to receive this diagnosis. In the biological dimension there appears to be less support for the role of genetic factors in GAD than in panic disorder. In the psychological dimension psychoanalytic and cognitive behavioral theories have been developed regarding the etiology of GAD, and recent research has focused on the relationship between types of worry and GAD. In the social and sociocultural dimensions stressful conditions such as poverty, poor housing, prejudice, and discrimination can also contribute to GAD. Treatments include Benzodiazepines which have been successful in treating GAD, but because it is a chronic condition, medication dependence issues are a concern, particularly if there is a history of substance abuse.

V. **Obsessive-compulsive disorder** Obsessive-compulsive disorder is an anxiety disorder characterized by intrusive thoughts *(obsessions)* and the need to perform ritualistic actions *(compulsions)*. Once thought to be rare, obsessive-compulsive disorder has an estimated lifetime prevalence of approximately 1 percent. Common *obsessions* among adults involve bodily wastes, dirt or germs, and environmental contamination. Many "normal" individuals have obsessions, but those with obsessive-compulsive disorder report thoughts that last longer, produce more discomfort, and cannot be easily controlled. Compulsions are behaviors that are designed to reduce anxiety but that cause distress if not performed correctly. To the compulsive, these actions have the magical ability to ward off danger. The causes of obsessive-compulsive disorder are unclear. Biological models emphasize differences in brain function, genetic vulnerability, and effects of medication on individuals with obsessive-compulsive disorder. One theory, favored by psychoanalysts, suggests that obsessions substitute for unconscious conflicts and that compulsions are based in defense mechanisms such as undoing and reaction formation. The behavioral perspective emphasizes the anxiety-reducing functions of compulsions. In the social and sociocultural dimensions OCD is more common among the young and among individuals who are divorced, separated, or unemployed. Treatments include antidepressant medication, but only 60 to 80 percent of obsessive-compulsives respond to these drugs, relief is only partial, and relapse is a problem. The most effective behavioral treatment has been a combination of exposure therapy and response prevention.

VI. **Implications**. It is becoming clear that single model approaches are unable to explain why anxiety disorders develop in some individuals and not others.

KEY TERMS REVIEW

1. A strong subjective need to perform an act in order to reduce anxiety is called a(n)
    _____.

2. A strong, persistent, and unwarranted fear of a specific object or situation is called a(n)
    _____.

3. The therapeutic technique that involves continued actual or imagined exposure to a feared situation is called _____.

4. An excessive fear of being scrutinized in social situations is called a(n) _____.

5. Feelings of fear and apprehension are also called _____.

6. The disorder characterized by persistent high levels of anxiety and excessive worry over many life circumstances is called _____.

7. The therapy technique of gradually exposing the client to a feared situation is called _____.

8. An extreme fear of a specific object that is not classified as agoraphobia or a social phobia is called a(n) _____.

9. Disorders such as phobias and panic disorder that are characterized by irrational feelings of fear and apprehension are called _____.

10. The anxiety disorder that involves intrusive and uncontrollable thoughts, the need to perform specific acts repeatedly, or both is called _____.

11. The anxiety disorder characterized by severe episodes of apprehension and feelings of impending doom is called _____.

12. An intrusive, uncontrollable, and persistent thought or image is called a(n) _____.

13. The disorder involving an intense fear of open spaces or of being alone where help may not be available is called _____.

14. The therapeutic approach to phobias in which the phobic client observes a fearless individual coping with the fear-producing situation is called _____.

15. The behavior therapy technique in which relaxation is used to eliminate the anxiety associated with phobias and other fear-evoking situations is called _____.

16. A _____ is an intense fear accompanied by symptoms such as a pounding heart, trembling, shortness of breath, or fear of losing control or dying.

17. _____ is a cognitive strategy that attempts to alter unrealistic thoughts believed to be responsible for phobias.

FACTUAL MULTIPLE-CHOICE QUESTIONS

1. When anxiety produces changes in breathing, perspiration, and muscle tension, these changes reflect _____ manifestations of anxiety.
    a. behavioral
    b. somatic
    c. cognitive
    d. neurological

2. Which statement below concerning panic attacks is *accurate*?
    a. They always occur in specific situations and are preceded by warning signs of their occurrence.
    b. They are fairly common.
    c. They are extremely rare and occur only in people who suffer from panic disorder.
    d. They involve behavioral aspects of anxiety but not cognitive or somatic ones.

3. The chemical _____ seems to induce panic attacks in clients with panic disorder.
    a. imipramine
    b. serotonin
    c. alcohol
    d. sodium lactate

4. Which statement about the biological treatment of generalized anxiety disorder is *accurate*?

    a. The first effective treatment was a form of brain surgery called leucotomy.
    b. Medication helps reduce anxiety, but psychological treatment is also necessary for successful treatment.
    c. Antidepressants are more helpful than benzodiazepines.
    d. The most effective medication is sodium lactate.

5. Agoraphobia is

    a. much more common in men than in women.
    b. characterized by persistent unwanted thoughts and rituals.
    c. an intense fear of being in public places without available help.
    d. so similar to panic attack that the two have been merged in the DSM-IV-TR.

6. Which of the following is not a type of social phobia?

    a. performance
    b. limited interactional
    c. generalized
    d. agoraphobia

7. The behavior therapy that teaches clients to relax while imagining a feared stimulus is called

    a. systematic desensitization.
    b. cognitive restructuring.
    c. flooding.
    d. modeling therapy.

8. An effective combination of approaches for treating agoraphobia might include

    a. sodium lactate and exposure therapy.
    b. antidepressants and exposure to public places.
    c. social isolation and eye movement desensitization and reprocessing.
    d. flooding and preparedness learning.

9. The preferred behavioral treatment for obsessive-compulsive disorder is

    a. relaxation training and biofeedback.
    b. biofeedback and response prevention.
    c. cognitive restructuring and positive reinforcement.
    d. flooding and response prevention.

10. Which of the following behavioral therapies gradually introduces the patient to increasingly difficult encounters with a feared situation?

    a. Exposure therapy
    b. Systematic desensitization
    c. Cognitive restructuring
    d. Modeling therapy

CONCEPTUAL MULTIPLE-CHOICE QUESTIONS

1. Recurrent unexpected panic attacks and at least one month of worry over having another are the criterion for diagnosing

    a. agoraphobia.
    b. panic disorder.
    c. generalized anxiety disorder.
    d. posttraumatic stress disorder.

2. Constant worry over major and minor life events, poor concentration, and physiological symptoms that are less extreme than a panic attack but last more than six months are the chief characteristics of
    a. acute stress disorder.
    b. social phobia.
    c. obsessive-compulsive disorder.
    d. generalized anxiety disorder.

3. Cognitive behavioral theorists suggest that generalized anxiety disorder develops when
    a. people discover they can avoid the negative consequences of panic attacks by avoiding situations in which they occur.
    b. the consequence of a fear response is punished or extinguished.
    c. a feedback loop between catastrophic thoughts and somatic symptoms increases anxiety.
    d. people mistakenly believe they have control over situations and their internal arousal level.

4. A psychodynamic explanation for specific phobias stresses
    a. prepared learning.
    b. irrational beliefs that mistakenly predict negative events.
    c. how symptoms are a compromise between the ego and the id's need to gratify sexual impulses.
    d. how parents provide modeling for the fears that develop in early childhood.

5. Research on the genetic cause of agoraphobia
    a. suggests that both heredity and modeling may account for it being prevalent in first-degree relatives of agoraphobics.
    b. has shown no higher vulnerability in parents or siblings of agoraphobic patients than in control groups.
    c. indicates that what is inherited is an underactive autonomic nervous system.
    d. suggests that the neurotransmitter imipramine is deficient in these clients.

6. If preparedness were not an issue in the development of phobias,
    a. it would be unlikely that we would find any phobias for cars or airplanes.
    b. we would find that any object was as likely as any other to be a source of terror.
    c. genetics would be the sole reason for phobias.
    d. classical conditioning could no longer be considered a reason for phobias.

7. A persistent and unwanted fear of being contaminated by dirt and germs illustrates _____ and is often associated with the _____ of hand washing.
    a. a phobia; obsession
    b. an obsession; compulsion
    c. a compulsion; phobia
    d. preparedness; compulsion

8. Which of the following statements about the psychoanalytic theory of obsessive-compulsive disorder is *accurate*?
    a. It is based on observational learning.
    b. It adequately explains the majority of cases of obsessive-compulsive disorder.
    c. It is essentially the same thing as preparedness theory.
    d. It assumes that symptoms originate out of defenses against unconscious conflicts.

9. Which theory and concept pair concerning the cause of obsessive-compulsive disorder is *accurate*?
    a. Biological: orbital frontal cortex activity
    b. Biological: sodium lactate sensitivity
    c. Behavioral: reaction formation and undoing
    d. Behavioral: catastrophic thinking

APPLICATION MULTIPLE-CHOICE QUESTIONS

1. Dr. Thomas says, "They can occur in response to a specific feared stimulus or come an unexpectedly. When you have one, you think you might be dying of a heart attack. They are fairly common: Between one-quarter and one-third of college students report having had one in the past year." What is Dr. Thomas referring to?

    a. Obsessions
    b. Compulsions
    c. Posttraumatic stress reactions
    d. Panic attacks

2. Gene is diagnosed as suffering from generalized anxiety disorder, whereas Paul is diagnosed with panic disorder. What is the main difference between the two diagnoses?

    a. In panic disorder, the person shows relatively low anxiety levels between panic episodes.
    b. In panic disorder, the person is constantly worried about a wide range of life situations.
    c. In generalized anxiety disorder, the person primarily experiences the somatic aspects of anxiety.
    d. In generalized anxiety disorder, the person performs rituals as a way of reducing anxiety.

3. Ben is being treated for panic disorder. His therapist tells him, "You need to change from thinking 'I'll pass out if I walk into that store' to 'I can control my anxiety.'" What perspective on anxiety disorders does this illustrate?

    a. Classical conditioning
    b. Psychoanalytic
    c. Cognitive-behavioral
    d. Biological

4. Dr. Harlan is a researcher investigating the relationship between the locus ceruleus and a specific anxiety symptom. Which symptom is she most likely interested in?

    a. Obsessions
    b. Fear of being in public
    c. Compulsions
    d. Panic attack

5. Charlene is receiving biological treatment for her panic disorder. It is most likely that she is getting

    a. electroshock treatments.
    b. antidepressants.
    c. biofeedback.
    d. sodium lactate.

6. Laurie is terribly afraid of being seen in restaurants or movie theaters because she fears she will make a complete fool of herself in some way. She recognizes that her fear is irrational, but the fear completely controls her. Laurie's problem best illustrates

    a. a social phobia.
    b. agoraphobia.
    c. phobophobia.
    d. generalized anxiety disorder.

7. A psychologist says, "The case of little Hans (and his 'widdler') illustrates that classical conditioning might cause phobias. Unfortunately, other attempts to replicate that study have failed." What part of the psychologist's statement is *inaccurate*?

    a. It is inaccurate to say that the case of little Hans illustrates classical conditioning.
    b. It is inaccurate to say that the case of little Hans involved phobias.
    c. It is inaccurate to say that the case of little Hans examined the cause of a disorder.
    d. It is inaccurate to say that the results of the case were not replicated.

8. Suppose we found that, of 100 people with phobias, 80 percent had a fear of animals, 10 percent had a fear of germs and dirt, and the remainder feared enclosed places. None of the people had phobias about machinery. This finding would support the _____ approach to phobias.

    a. cognitive-behavioral
    b. psychoanalytic
    c. exposure
    d. preparedness

9. A psychiatrist says, "Even in normal populations, there are people who are fearful of contamination and of being out of control. They check everything to lessen their worries." What kind of problem is the psychiatrist describing?

    a. Posttraumatic stress disorder
    b. Obsessions
    c. Panic disorder
    d. Reaction formation

10. After being unsuccessfully treated with antidepressants for obsessive-compulsive disorder, Wayne is looking for a treatment technique that is both effective and takes little time. A psychologist might suggest _____ to Wayne.

    a. biofeedback
    b. psychoanalytic psychotherapy
    c. exposure therapy and response prevention
    d. systematic desensitization

ANSWER KEY: KEY TERMS REVIEW

1. compulsion

2. phobia

3. flooding

4. social phobia

5. anxiety

6. generalized anxiety disorder

7. exposure therapy

8. specific phobia

9. anxiety disorders

10. obsessive-compulsive disorder

11. panic disorder

12. obsession

13. agoraphobia

14. modeling therapy

15. systematic desensitization

16. panic attack

17. cognitive restructuring

ANSWER KEY: FACTUAL MULTIPLE-CHOICE QUESTIONS

1. b.   Sweating, muscular tension, heart palpitations, cold hands and feet, perspiration, and diarrhea are all somatic manifestations of anxiety.

    a.   Behavioral aspects of anxiety involve avoidance of places where anxiety has occurred in the past.

    c.   Cognitive manifestations of anxiety include worrying, indecisiveness, and confusion.

    d.   There are no neurological manifestations of anxiety, but if there were, they would involve changes in nervous system structures.

2. b.   Although panic disorder is uncommon, many people report having had at least one panic attack; nearly 45 percent of college women report an attack in the past year.

    a.   Panic attacks can occur in specific situations, but can also come on without warning.

    c.   Panic disorder is defined by recurrent panic attacks, but many "normal" people have one or two such attacks over a lifetime.

    d.   Panic attacks are so distressing because they affect behavior, thought, and physical functioning.

3. d.   Sensitivity to sodium lactate appears to be a biological difference between those who are vulnerable to panic disorder and those who are not.

    a.   Imipramine is an antidepressant drug that reduces symptoms of anxiety.

    b.   Serotonin is a neurotransmitter that appears to regulate emotional experience.

    c.   Alcohol does not increase anxiety; it tends to reduce it.

4. b.   Medication, such as benzodiazepines, helps reduce symptoms, but anxiety management training seems necessary to alter avoidance responses.

    a.   Leucotomy was originally used as a surgical treatment for obsessive-compulsive disorder.

    c.   Benzodiazepines have proven to be more effective than antidepressants when treating generalized anxiety disorder.

    d.   Sodium lactate increases the likelihood of panic attack, rather than reducing it.

5. c.   Agoraphobia is an intense fear of being in public without support or assistance, and leads to avoidance of such situations.

    a.   Agoraphobia is two or three times more likely in women.

    b.   Persistent thoughts and rituals are symptoms of obsessive-compulsive disorder.

    d.   Agoraphobia may develop after panic attacks, but the two are separate disorders.

6. d.   Agoraphobia is not considered a type of social phobia; rather, as an intense fear of being in public places where escape or help may not be readily available, it is classified separately.

    a.   Performance refers to excessive anxiety over activities such as playing a musical instrument, public speaking, eating in a restaurant, or using public restrooms.

    b.   Limited interactional refers to excessive fear only in specific social situations, such as going out on a date or interacting with an authority figure.

    c.   Generalized refers to extreme anxiety displayed in most social situations.

7.   a.   Systematic desensitization involves teaching relaxation skills and then pairing relaxation with imagined or real anxiety-producing situations on a gradual basis.

     b.   Cognitive restructuring focuses on how we think about situations and our behavior in them.

     c.   Flooding represents "cold turkey" extinction and high levels of anxiety; it is the opposite of systematic desensitization.

     d.   Modeling therapy involves imitation of effective individuals and does not rely on relaxation training or classical conditioning.

8.   b.   Successful treatment of agoraphobia has included antidepressants, which appear to reduce anxiety, and behavior therapy, which gets individuals to face fearful situations.

     a.   Sodium lactate induces panic attacks; it is unrelated to treating agoraphobia.

     c.   Social isolation would intensify agoraphobia; eye movement desensitization and reprocessing treatment is used for PTSD.

     d.   Flooding is used for obsessive-compulsive disorder, and preparedness is an explanation for the cause of phobias, not a treatment method.

9.   d.   It is necessary to extinguish both anxiety (through flooding) and ritualistic actions (through response prevention).

     a.   Relaxation training may be helpful, but biofeedback will have little effect on reducing ritualistic actions.

     b.   Biofeedback will have little effect on reducing ritualistic actions.

     c.   Positive reinforcement will not reduce the likelihood of ritualistic actions.

10. a.   Exposure therapy involves gradually introducing the patient to increasingly difficult encounters with a feared situation.

     b.   Systematic desensitization uses muscle relaxation to reduce the anxiety associated with specific and social phobias.

     c.   Cognitive restructuring attempts to alter unrealistic thoughts thought to be responsible for phobias.

     d.   Modeling therapy demonstrates another person's successful interactions with the feared object or situation.

ANSWER KEY: CONCEPTUAL MULTIPLE-CHOICE QUESTIONS

1.   b.   Panic disorder is diagnosed when there are recurrent panic attacks and at least one month of worry about another occurring or about the consequences of a previous one.

     a.   Agoraphobia involves intense fear of going out in public without assistance.

     c.   Generalized anxiety disorder is characterized by constant worry. and anxiety symptoms that are less intense than those in panic disorder.

     d.   Posttraumatic stress disorder is diagnosed when symptoms occur after an event outside the normal range of life stressors (for example, experiencing a tornado).

2. d.   Generalized anxiety disorder is characterized by constant worry over both minor and major events, indecisiveness and poor concentration, and physiological manifestations of anxiety such as sweating and muscle tension.

   a.   Psychogenic amnesia is a dissociative disorder characterized by memory loss.

   b.   Panic disorder is characterized by intermittent yet terrifying episodes, but relatively low anxiety levels otherwise.

   c.   Obsessive-compulsive disorder is diagnosed when a person has worrisome thoughts that lead to ritualistic actions such as hand washing or repetitive checking.

3. c.   Cognitive behaviorists say that when individuals think catastrophic thoughts or pay extra attention to bodily changes, they trigger somatic symptoms, which foster more negative thoughts and greater anxiety.

   a.   Generalized anxiety disorder is not associated with panic attacks; the anxiety in the disorder is constant and at a low level.

   b.   Consequences are the focus of operant conditioning principles, and if a response is extinguished it should disappear rather than strengthen.

   d.   Thoughts before and during panic attacks involve being out of control.

4. c.   Psychodynamic explanations stress unconscious conflicts between id and ego.

   a.   Preparedness is a biological concept.

   b.   Irrational beliefs are cognitive concepts.

   d.   Modeling is a social learning concept.

5. a.   Just because a disorder runs in families. does not mean that inheritance is the cause; imitation of parents is just as likely an explanation.

   b.   First-degree relatives do show higher percentages of cases.

   c.   If anything is inherited, it is an overactive autonomic nervous system.

   d.   Imipramine is an antidepressant medication, not a neurotransmitter.

6. b.   If preparedness did not enter into the equation, every object would have an equal chance of being a source of phobia if it were paired with anxiety.

   a.   Preparedness suggests that post-technical age objects (such as cars) do not easily become conditioned stimuli.

   c.   Preparedness only suggests that certain categories of objects are easily associated with anxiety; no prediction is made as to the importance of genetics as the cause.

   d.   Classical conditioning could still be the explanation; all that changes is the object that induces terror.

7. b.   An obsession is an unwanted and unstoppable thought; a compulsion is a ritualistic behavior to ward off the worry.

   a.   A phobia is an intense, irrational fear of an object, not an unwanted thought.

   c.   A phobia is an intense, irrational fear, not a ritualistic action.

   d.   Preparedness deals with the likelihood of certain stimuli becoming the target of a phobia, not with persistent thoughts.

8.   d.   As a psychodynamic explanation, substitution says that symptoms at the surface substitute for conflicts below the surface.

      a.   Substitution, not observation, is a psychoanalytic explanation.

      b.   Although psychoanalytic explanations have clinical appeal, they do not explain the majority of cases.

      c.   Preparedness is a concept used to explain the cause of specific phobias.

9.   a.   Research shows that higher glucose metabolism is found in the orbital frontal cortex of people with obsessive-compulsive disorder than in controls.

      b.   Sodium lactate is a biogenic explanation for panic disorder.

      c.   Psychoanalysts, not behaviorists, would emphasize these defense mechanisms.

      d.   Cognitive theorists, not behaviorists, would emphasize catastrophic thinking.

ANSWER KEY: APPLICATION MULTIPLE-CHOICE QUESTIONS

1.   d.   Panic attacks involve heart palpitations and can occur in response to a specific situation or be unexpected; college students report they are fairly common.

      a.   Obsessions are unwanted, persistent anxiety-arousing thoughts. They do not come on without warning.

      b.   Compulsions are stereotyped, ritualistic actions that reduce anxiety.

      c.   Posttraumatic stress disorder occurs in response to a specific, highly stressful event.

2.   a.   In between panic attacks, those with panic disorder are relatively low in anxiety; those with generalized anxiety disorder are never low in anxiety.

      b.   It is in generalized anxiety disorder that worry is constant.

      c.   In both disorders, anxiety produces somatic complaints; in panic disorder, the anxiety is so great the patient may think he or she will die.

      d.   Rituals are associated with obsessive-compulsive disorder.

3.   c.   Cognitive-behavioral theorists stress how thinking influences the experience of anxiety.

      a.   Classical conditioning focuses on the external stimuli that are associated with fear responses.

      b.   Psychoanalytic explanations look for the unconscious conflicts that surface in symbolic symptoms.

      d.   Biological explanations stress the genetics of patients and their sensitivity to such chemicals as sodium lactate.

4.   d.   People with panic disorder have been found to have unusually high sensitivity in the locus ceruleus, a portion of the central anxiety system of the brain.

      a.   Obsessions are associated with heightened frontal cortex activity.

      b.   Social phobias have no clear relationship to brain abnormalities.

      c.   Compulsions are associated with heightened frontal cortex activity.

5. b. Antidepressants such as imipramine have been helpful in reducing the frequency and intensity of panic attacks.

    a. Electroshock treatments may be helpful in depression, but not in panic disorder.

    c. Biofeedback is not actually a biological treatment; it is based on operant conditioning.

    d. Sodium lactate seems to increase panic attacks in patients, but not in controls.

6. a. Social phobias are characterized by irrational fears of performing actions in public that will be evaluated.

    b. Agoraphobia is an intense fear of being in public (in general) without available help.

    c. Phobophobia is a fear of having a phobia.

    d. Generalized anxiety disorder involves worry about almost everything, not a specific target as in phobias.

7. a. The case of little Hans underscored psychodynamic explanations and was unrelated to classical conditioning.

    b. The case of little Hans was used by Freud to explain how the surface symptoms of a phobia stemmed from unconscious (oedipal) conflicts.

    c. The case of little Hans was about the causes of phobia.

    d. As a case, the results have not been replicated; evidence does not sustain Freud's analysis of phobia.

8. d. Preparedness is the concept that pretechnical objects related to evolution are more likely to be objects of phobic fear than technical ones such as cars and machinery.

    a. Cognitive-behavioral explanations focus on thoughts.

    b. Psychoanalytic explanations focus on unconscious conflicts.

    c. Exposure is the treatment technique of extinguishing anxiety through habituation.

9. b. Contamination worries and checking behaviors are seen in the obsessional activities of many people.

    a. Posttraumatic stress disorder involves events, not thoughts.

    c. Panic disorder involves fears of attacks, not worries over contamination.

    d. Reaction formation is a defense mechanism, not a disorder.

10. c. Exposure (continued exposure to the feared stimulus) and response prevention (stopping avoidance of the stimulus).

    a. Biofeedback has not been helpful in treating obsessive-compulsive disorder.

    b. Psychoanalytic therapy takes a long time.

    d. Systematic desensitization may be helpful, but it is more time-consuming than flooding.

OBJECTIVES DEFINED

1. **How are biological, psychological, social, and sociocultural factors involved in the development of anxiety disorders?**

- All of these factors are involved in anxiety disorders but the contribution of each varies from individual to individual and circumstance to circumstance.

- Biological contributors include an inherited overactive fear circuitry in the brain and neurotransmitters abnormalities. However, anxiety disorders may also not develop in vulnerable individuals in a supportive family or social environment. The impact of stressors can also be mitigated by personality variables such as a sense of control and mastery. Sociocultural factors such as power and status, discrimination, and poverty may be responsible for the greater representation of women with anxiety disorders.

2. **What are phobias, what are their causes, and how are they treated?**

- Phobias are strong fears that exceed the demands of the situation. Social phobias are irrational fears about situations in which the person can be observed by others. Specific phobias include all the irrational fears that are not classed as social phobias or agoraphobia. Commonly feared objects include small animals, heights, and the dark.

- Biological explanations are based on studies of the influence of genetic, biochemical, and neurological factors or on the idea that humans are prepared to develop certain fears. In the psychodynamic view, phobias represent unconscious conflicts that are displaced onto an external object. Behavioral explanations include the classical conditioning view, in which phobias are based on an association between an aversive event and a conditioned stimulus; conditioning through observational learning; the role of thoughts that are distorted and frightening; and reinforcement for fear behaviors.

- The most effective treatments for phobias seem to be biochemical (antidepressants) and behavioral (exposure and flooding, systematic desensitization, modeling, and graduated exposure).

3. **What is panic disorder and agoraphobia, what are their causes, and how are they treated?**

- Panic disorder is marked by episodes of extreme anxiety and feelings of impending doom. It is characterized by attacks that seem to occur "out of the blue." Agoraphobia is an intense fear of being in public places where escape or help may not be possible; it can keep people from leaving home because attempts to do so may produce panic attacks.

- The causes of panic disorder and agoraphobia include biological factors (genetic contribution, neural structures, and neurotransmitters), psychological factors (the psychodynamic view stresses the importance of internal sexual and aggressive impulses, the cognitive-behavioral view emphasizes the importance of catastrophic thoughts regarding bodily sensations), and social and sociocultural factors (such as a disturbed childhood environment and gender-related issues).

- Treatments for panic disorder and agoraphobia include biochemical treatments (benzodiazepines and antidepressants) and behavioral treatments (identification of catastrophic thoughts, correcting them, and substituting more realistic ones).

4. **What is generalized anxiety disorder, what are its causes, and how is it treated?**

- Generalized anxiety disorder involves chronically high levels of anxiety and excessive worry that is present for six months or more.

- There appears to be less support for the role of genetics in GAD than other anxiety disorders, although there are some reports of abnormalities with the GABA receptors or overactivity of the anxiety circuitry in the brain. Psychoanalysts believe the disorders are unfocused because they stem from internal conflicts in the unconscious. Cognitive behavioral theorists emphasize erroneous beliefs regarding the purpose of worry or the existence of dysfunctional schemas. Social and sociocultural factors such as poverty and discrimination can also contribute to GAD.

- Drug therapy (antidepressant medications), behavioral therapies, and psychodynamic therapies have been used to treat these disorders.

5. **What is obsessive-compulsive disorder, what are its causes, and how is it treated?**

- Obsessive-compulsive disorder involves thoughts or actions that are involuntary, intrusive, repetitive, and uncontrollable. Most persons with obsessive-compulsive disorder are aware that their distressing behaviors are irrational.

- Neuroimaging shows increased metabolic activity in the orbital frontal cortex in those with OCD. Freud believed the disorder represented the replacement of thoughts of a threatening conflict with a less threatening behavior or thought. According to the anxiety-reduction hypothesis, obsessions and compulsions develop because they reduce anxiety. Cognitive-behavioral therapists have focused on factors such as confirmatory bias, probability bias, and morality bias. Social and sociocultural dimensions are also important in the etiology of OCD. It is more common among individuals who are divorced, separated, or unemployed and occurs less frequently among African Americans and Hispanic Americans.

- Some antidepressants have been effective in treating OCD. However, antianxiety medications are less effective with this disorder than other anxiety disorders. The treatment of choice is a combination of flooding and response prevention, sometimes combined with cognitive therapy.

MARGIN DEFINITIONS

agoraphobia an intense fear of being in public places where escape or help may not be readily available

anxiety a fundamental human emotion that produces bodily reactions that prepare us for "fight or flight"; anxiety is anticipatory; the dreaded event or situation has not yet occurred

anxiety disorder fear or anxiety symptoms that interfere with an individual's day-to-day functioning

cognitive restructuring cognitive strategy that attempt to alter unrealistic thoughts thought to be responsible for phobias

compulsions the need to perform acts or to dwell on thoughts to reduce anxiety

exposure therapy therapy that involves gradually introducing to the patient to increasingly difficult encounters with a feared situation

flooding a technique that involves continued actual or imagined exposure to a fear-arousing situations at high-anxiety level

generalized anxiety disorder (GAD) disorder characterized by persistent, high levels of anxiety and excessive worry over many life circumstances that last more days than not for over six months

modeling therapy procedures that include filmed modeling, live modeling, and participant modeling effective in treating certain phobias

obsessions intrusive, repetitive thoughts or images that produce anxiety

obsessive-compulsive disorder (OCD) a disorder characterized by obsessions or compulsions

panic attacks intense fear accompanied by symptoms such as a pounding heart, trembling, shortness of breath, or fear of losing control or dying

panic disorder recurrent unexpected panic attacks and at least one month of apprehension over having another attack or worrying about the consequences of an attack

phobia a strong, persistent, and unwarranted fear of some specific object or situation

social phobia an intense, excessive fear of being scrutinized in one or more social or performance situations

specific phobia an extreme fear of a specific object (such as snakes) or situation (such as being in an enclosed place)

systematic desensitization cognitive strategy that uses muscle relaxation to reduce the anxiety associated with specific and social phobias

CHAPTER 6

Dissociative Disorders and Somatoform Disorders

TABLE OF CONTENTS

LEARNING OBJECTIVES

1. Describe dissociations. Discuss what forms they can take, how they are caused, and how they are treated.

2. Define when physical complaints become a psychological disorder. Name the causes and treatments of these conditions.

CHAPTER OUTLINE

I. **Dissociative and somatoform disorders** The *dissociative disorders* show altered or disrupted identity, memory, or consciousness; the *somatoform disorders* involve physical symptoms that have no physiological basis. Both disorders occur because of some psychological need and both rely on self-reports, and so are subject to faking.

II. **Dissociative disorders.** There are four dissociative disorders: dissociative amnesia, dissociative fugue, dissociative identity disorder (formerly called multiple-personality disorder), and depersonalization disorder. Except for depersonalization, dissociative disorders are rare, although there has been a dramatic increase in reports of dissociative identity disorder. *Dissociative amnesia* is the partial or total loss of important personal information, often occurring in response to a stressful event. There are five types. *Localized amnesia* is characterized by total memory loss for a particular, short time period, and is the most common form. In *selective amnesia*, the memory loss is for details about an incident. Total loss of memory for one's past life is the criterion for *generalized amnesia*; *systematized amnesia* involves the loss of memory for only selected types of information; total loss of memory from one point in time to another occurs in *continuous amnesia*. Repression of a traumatic event seems to be the main reason for *psychogenic amnesia*. In *dissociative fugue*, memory loss is accompanied by flight to another area and establishment of a new identity. Recovery from this and from psychogenic amnesia is usually abrupt and complete. *Depersonalization disorder is* characterized by feelings of unreality or distorted perceptions of the body or environment. It is more common than the other dissociative disorders, tends to be chronic, is often accompanied by mood or anxiety disorders, and can be precipitated by stress. In dissociative identity disorder (multiple-personality disorder) two or more (often many more) distinct personalities exist in one individual. Not all personalities are aware of one another. However, even objective testing with physiological measurements produces conflicting findings about the existence of distinct personalities. Although this condition was once thought to be rare, there has been a dramatic increase in reported cases, perhaps because of the influence of therapists while clients are under hypnosis. People with dissociative identity disorder often report a history of childhood abuse. Diagnosis in childhood is possible, but misdiagnosis is common, both by seeing the disorder in people who have other problems and by failing to see multiple personality in people diagnosed with other disorders. Diagnosis is much more common in the United States and Canada than in other parts of the world. The causes of dissociative disorders are subject to a good deal of conjecture because faking is always a possibility. In the biological dimension a number of studies using PET scans and MRIs on individuals diagnosed with DID have found variations in brain activity when comparing different personalities .The psychological perspective sees repression of, unpleasant emotions as the cause of dissociative disorders. Splits in consciousness protect the individual from anxiety and pain. The Social and sociocultural dimensions, conceptualizes DID as a syndrome with rule-governed and goal-directed experiences, and displays of multiple role enactments created, legitimized, and maintained by social reinforcement. The disorder may also be the unintended effect of treatment, an *iatrogenic* condition. The expectations of therapists and their use of hypnosis, which increases suggestibility, may create memories of abuse and personalities. Recovery from dissociative amnesia, dissociative fugue, and depersonalization disorder often occurs spontaneously; therefore, treatment often aims at reducing the depression or anxiety these conditions produce. Dissociative identity disorder is usually treated with psychotherapy and hypnosis, but not with notable success.

III.   **Somatoform disorders.** The principal symptoms of *somatoform disorders* are complaints of physical symptoms that have no apparent physiological cause. Faking is possible, but when symptoms such as fever are consciously induced, they are considered *factitious disorders* rather than *malingering,* which involves voluntary faking for monetary or other rewards. In *somatization disorder,* individuals have physical complaints in four or more different sites in the body, symptoms for which there are no physiological explanations. Complaints include gastrointestinal, sexual and pseudoneurological symptoms. If the individual does not fully meet the criteria but has at least one physical complaint for six months, the diagnosis would be undifferentiated somatoform disorder. Patients shop around for doctors and often have unneeded surgery. Somatization disorder, formerly called hysteria, is rarely diagnosed in men although over one third of males referred for unexplained somatic complaints meet the criteria for the disorder. In *conversion disorder,* there is a significant physical impairment, such as paralysis in a limb or sensory problems, without physical basis. When neurological or other processes prove the symptoms impossible (such as in glove anesthesia), diagnosis is readily made; otherwise, it is quite hard to differentiate conversion disorder from actual illnesses or faking. Pain that is excessive, lingers too long, or is unrelated to a physiological cause is characteristic of *pain disorder.* As with ordinary pain, there is a complex interaction among perception, thinking, and behavior. In *hypochondriasis,* there is a consistent preoccupation with illness in the face of doctors' repeated assurances of health. Those with hypochondriasis often have a history of illness and parents who focused on illness. Fear, anxiety, and depression are common complaints. *Body dysmorphic disorder* involves an excessive concern with an imagined or slight physical defect such as facial features, excessive hair, or the shape of genitals. Individuals with this disorder frequently check their appearance in the mirror and fear that others are looking at the defect. They make frequent requests for plastic surgery regardless of the treatment's outcome. Because the disorder involves obsessive thinking and delusions, its placement in the diagnostic category of somatoform disorders has been questioned. It is also not clear where normal concerns about appearance end and the disorder begins. Etiology and treatment of somatoform disorders include the following. The biological dimensions in general, using twin or family studies found there is little evidence for heredity in somatoform disorders. Psychoanalysts believe that repression accounts for the process of converting unconscious conflicts into physical symptoms. There is *primary gain* in the reduction of anxiety and *secondary gain* in the sympathy the individual receives. Behavioral theorists contend that a "sick role" is reinforced by others and helps the person escape from responsibilities. The social and sociocultural dimension stresses that, historically, social norms did not provide women with appropriate channels for the expression of aggressive or sexual needs. As a result, women developed hysterical symptoms.. Biological treatment includes antidepressant medications; the SSRIs have shown promise with somatoforms disorders, primarily somatization and somatoform pain disorders. The most promising interventions for somatoform disorders involve the cognitive-behavioral approach. A fundamental focus is an understanding of the clients' views regarding their problem

IV.   **Implications.** The two primary models for dissociative disorders include the psychoanalytically based posttraumatic model (PTM) and the sociocognitive model (SCM). Both models account for only certain etiological aspects of dissociative disorders.

KEY TERMS REVIEW

1.   The somatoform disorder characterized by a persistent preoccupation with one's health is called _____.

2.   The dissociative disorder in which psychogenic amnesia is accompanied by flight from familiar surroundings and adoption of a new identity is called _____.

3.   The dissociative disorder in which an individual reports feelings of unreality or distortions of self and the environment is called _____.

4.   The disorder that involves chronic complaints about a number of physical symptoms for which there is no physical basis is called _____.

5.   The somatoform disorder in which there appears to be a significant impairment of physical function without an underlying organic cause is called _____.

6.   Mental disorders characterized by disruption or alteration of one's identity, memory, or consciousness are called _____.

7.   Mental disorders involving complaints of physical symptoms that mimic authentic medical conditions but have no physical basis are called _____.

8.   The somatoform disorder characterized by severe physical discomfort that has a psychological rather than a physical basis is called _____.

9.   The dissociative disorder characterized by an inability to recall information of personal significance, usually after a traumatic event, is called _____.

10.   The dissociative disorder in which two or more relatively distinct personalities exist in one individual is called _____.

11.   The somatoform disorder that involves preoccupation with an imagined physical defect is called _____.

12.   The inability to recall events from a period in the past to present is called _____.

13.   The inability to recall the entire past, due to some psychosocial crisis, is called _____.

14.   The inability to recall all events during a specific period is the most common type of amnesia and is called _____.

15.   When some psychosocial stress results in the inability to recall only some aspects of a situation, the condition is called _____.

16.   A problem that is the result of the therapist's treatment is considered _____.

17.   Deliberately self-induced or simulated physical or mental conditions without apparent incentive are called _____.

18.   Faking an illness to obtain a goal is called _____.

19. If an individual has at least one physical complaint for six months, but does not meet the criteria for somatoform disorder, the diagnosis would be _____.

FACTUAL MULTIPLE-CHOICE QUESTIONS

1. Amnesia, fugue, and depersonalization disorder are all examples of

   a. somatoform disorders
   b. anxiety disorders.
   c. dissociative disorders.
   d. iatrogenic disorders.

2. In localized amnesia, the memory loss is

   a. total; nothing can be remembered about one's past life.
   b. almost always due to a biological cause.
   c. only for specific details of a specific event.
   d. complete for a specific period in one's life.

3. When people develop amnesia and then travel to a new area where they establish a new identity, the problem is called

   a. dissociative fugue.
   b. generalized amnesia.
   c. dissociative identity disorder.
   d. dissociative phobia.

4. The most common dissociative disorder involves feelings of unreality about one's body or the environment. These intense experiences may lead sufferers to wonder whether they are losing their minds. The disorder being described is called

   a. dissociative identity disorder.
   b. dissociative fugue.
   c. somatoform disorder.
   d. depersonalization disorder.

5. The majority of people with dissociative identity disorder report a history of

   a. vague physical complaints.
   b. excessively permissive upbringing
   c. physical and sexual abuse.
   d. having one traumatic incident in adulthood.

6. In recent years, the number of _____ cases reported by mental health professionals has increased.

   a. conversion disorder
   b. depersonalization disorder
   c. hypochondrias
   d. dissociative identity disorder

7. Somatization disorder was previously called

   a. hysteria.
   b. iatrogenic.
   c. dementia praecox.
   d. manic-depression.

8. Because it involves symptoms that mimic physical disorders, it is difficult to differentiate
   _____ from faking and from organic problems.

   a. depersonalization disorder
   b. body dysmorphic disorder
   c. conversion disorder
   d. dissociative amnesia

9. A history of physical illness, a low pain threshold, and parents who focused on the symptoms of
   illness are all believed to be factors related to

   a. body dysmorphic disorder.
   b. hypochondriasis.
   c. dissociative identity disorder.
   d. factitious disorder.

10. Family therapists would see somatoform complaints as a way of

    a. avoiding family responsibilities.
    b. crying for help.
    c. responding to childhood abuse and neglect.
    d. repressing unpleasant emotions related to an earlier trauma.

CONCEPTUAL MULTIPLE-CHOICE QUESTIONS

1. Why is it difficult to tell whether the personalities in dissociative identity disorder truly exist?

   a. The personalities usually exhibit dissociative amnesia.
   b. Not even physiological measures produce consistent results.
   c. The personalities almost always appear at the same time.
   d. One personality typically does not have memory of what another personality has
      experienced.

2. In dissociative identity disorder, it is rare to find

   a. more than three distinct personalities.
   b. that the personalities are distinct from one another.
   c. that every personality is aware of every other one.
   d. evidence that there is dissociation.

3. Among the dissociative disorders, the development of _____ is thought to be
   partially iatrogenic (induced by certain treatment methods).

   a. dissociative identity disorder
   b. depersonalization disorder
   c. dissociative amnesia
   d. body dysmorphic disorder

4. Avoidance of stress is the main factor in the _____ theorist's explanation of
   dissociative disorders.

   a. iatrogenic
   b. biological
   c. behavioral
   d. psychodynamic

5. Long-term psychotherapy is usually not necessary for _____ because it usually
   stops spontaneously.

   a. dissociative amnesia
   b. dissociative identity disorder
   c. hypochondriasis
   d. factitious disorders

6. In somatoform disorders, the fundamental symptom is

   a. the involuntary separation of consciousness in response to traumatic events.
   b. irrational fears of specific objects.
   c. physical symptoms, such as ulcers and diabetes, that develop in response to stress.
   d. involuntarily produced physical symptoms that occur in the absence of organic causes.

7. Unlike somatoform disorders, factitious disorders

   a. are complicated by depression and anxiety.
   b. are under voluntary control.
   c. involve a separation of consciousness.
   d. stem from repression of psychological conflicts.

8. Which statement about somatization disorder is *accurate?*

   a. The disorder is defined in terms of numerous physical complaints.
   b. The disorder is main symptom is exaggerated or lingering pain.
   c. The disorder is related to physical and sexual abuse during childhood.
   d. The disorder is more common in men than in women.

9. Primary gain and secondary gain are concepts that _____ theorists use to explain the adaptive qualities of somatoform disorders.

   a. psychodynamic
   b. biological
   c. learning
   d. sociocultural

APPLICATION MULTIPLE-CHOICE QUESTIONS

1. Nora has no recollection of the events just before her house burned down, although she recalls running to a neighbor's house to call for the fire department. Nora's amnesia illustrates

   a. dissociative fugue.
   b. continuous amnesia.
   c. selective amnesia.
   d. depersonalization disorder.

2. Paula is diagnosed as having dissociative identity disorder. One personality, Mark, protects her from trouble, while another personality, Kim, is sexually promiscuous. All three personalities are aware of one another. What is unusual about Paula's case of multiple personality?

   a. There are rarely three separate personalities.
   b. Rarely are all personalities aware of one another.
   c. A male personality is rarely found in a female patient.
   d. Sexually promiscuous personalities are rare.

3. "Dissociative identity disorder is an adaptive response to unbearable psychological torture: the repression is so complete that distinct personalities are protected from any memory of the trauma." What kind of psychologist could say this?

   a. A behavior therapist
   b. A biologically oriented psychologist
   c. A therapist who believes the disorder is iatrogenic
   d. A psychoanalyst

4. Dr. Greise says to a patient's husband, "Whenever she says she is feeling as though she or the world is getting distorted and unreal, you should ignore her. Make sure you show attention, though, when she is in control." The disorder being treated is _____ and Dr. Greise is a _____ theorist.

   a. depersonalization disorder; behavioral
   b. dissociative identity disorder; psychoanalytic
   c. pain disorder; behavioral
   d. depersonalization disorder; biological

5. Dr. O'Neil says, "These disorders involving physical symptoms are diagnosed by what they aren't: they aren't under voluntary control, they aren't faked, and they aren't due to physiological causes." What is Dr. O'Neil talking about?

   a. Dissociative disorders
   b. Anxiety disorders
   c. Factitious disorders
   d. Somatoform disorders

6. Sharon has complained about more than fifteen physical problems over the past year and has had surgery four times even though there is no evidence of physiological causes. She constantly "shops around" for doctors. Sharon suffers from

   a. conversion disorder.
   b. dissociative amnesia.
   c. somatization disorder.
   d. hypochondriasis.

7. Milton began complaining of leg paralysis after he lost his job. There is no evidence of a physical cause. He does not stand to benefit from having these symptoms. Milton suffers from

   a. conversion disorder.
   b. malingering.
   c. somatization disorder.
   d. hypochondriasis.

8. Dr. Wimsey says, "There is no doubt that this patient is preoccupied with health concerns and possible death, and that there are no physiological reasons behind the complaints. However, the insistence on one complaint (chest pains) means that the diagnosis should be _____ rather than _____.

   a. hysteria; malingering
   b. conversion disorder; somatization disorder
   c. hypochondriasis; somatization disorder
   d. malingering; hypochondriasis

9. Dr. Blue notes that women have more somatoform disorders than men, perhaps because they experience few situations in which they are in control of their lives. It is likely that Dr. Blue is a _____.

   a. sociocultural
   b. behavioral
   c. biological
   d. psychodynamic

10. "Physicians, nurses, and eventually, spouses are trained to respond to complaints of pain. Unless attention to (and reinforcement for) such complaints is ended, you cannot expect the somatoform pain patient to improve." Who might say this?
    a. A psychoanalyst
    b. A psychiatrist who treats disorders with medication
    c. A behavior therapist
    d. A humanistic psychotherapist

ANSWER KEY: KEY TERMS REVIEW

1. hypochondriasis
2. dissociative fugue (or fugue state)
3. depersonalization disorder
4. somatization disorder
5. conversion disorder
6. dissociative disorders
7. somatoform disorders
8. pain disorder
9. dissociative amnesia
10. dissociative identity disorder
11. body dysmorphic disorder
12. continuous amnesia
13. generalized amnesia
14. localized amnesia
15. selective amnesia
16. iatrogenic
17. factitious disorders
18. malingering
19. undifferentiated somatoform disorder

ANSWER KEY: FACTUAL MULTIPLE-CHOICE QUESTIONS

1. c. Dissociative disorders involve a division of consciousness, usually producing memory problems, as is seen in amnesia and dissociative identity.

   a. Somatoform disorders involve physical complaints; they include such problems as hypochondriasis and conversion disorder.

   b. Anxiety disorders do not produce memory problems; they include phobias and panic disorder.

   d. Although some believe dissociative identity disorder can be iatrogenic (therapist-caused), the other disorders are seen as originating in the individual's inadequate response to stress.

2. d. Localized amnesia is complete memory loss for a specific time; for example, one may not remember being robbed and threatened.

   a. Complete loss of previous experience occurs in generalized dissociative amnesia.

   b. Localized amnesia can be caused by psychosocial stressors. Dissociative disorders, by definition, are psychogenic.

   c. Selective amnesia involves loss of memory of specific aspects of a traumatic incident, such as amnesia for some events related to a devastating tornado.

3. a. The central characteristic of fugue is dissociative amnesia together with travel to a new region to establish a new identity.

   b. Generalized amnesia involves complete loss of memory of previous experience.

   c. Dissociative identity disorder is characterized by distinct personalities, not by travel to another area.

   d. *Dissociative phobia* is a made-up term; *dissociative is* usually associated with amnesia or fugue, and *phobia* is a disorder on its own.

4. d. Depersonalization disorder is characterized by feeling unreal, seeing distortions in the environment or ones body parts, and fear of going crazy; such reactions in times of stress are common.

   a. Dissociative identity disorder is characterized by distinct personalities, not a sense of unreality; it is also considered rather rare.

   b. Dissociative fugue is characterized by travel to a new region and establishment of a new identity.

   c. Somatoform disorders involve physical complaints such as anesthesia, paralysis, or dizziness.

5. c. Most cases of dissociative identity disorder seem to develop out of childhood abuse, as in the case of Sybil.

   a. Vague physical complaints are more likely to be related to hypochondriasis or somatization disorder than to dissociative identity disorder.

   b. Dissociative identity disorder is not associated with permissive upbringing.

   d. Single traumatic events are more likely to be associated with dissociative amnesia; dissociative identity disorder usually involves a childhood full of trauma.

6. d. There has been an enormous upsurge in reported cases of dissociative identity disorder recently; one clinician alone reported 130 cases.

   a. There is no evidence that conversion disorder has increased recently.

   b. There is no evidence that depersonalization disorder has increased recently.

   c. There is no evidence that hypochondriasis has increased recently.

7. a. An older name for somatization disorder was *hysteria;* until the DSM-III it was lumped together with conversion disorder.

   b. *Iatrogenic is* a term for disorders that are the unintended effect of treatment.

   c. *Dementia praecox is* the older term for schizophrenia.

   d. *Manic-depression* is the older term for the mood disorder called bipolar disorder.

8. c. Conversion disorder involves somatic complaints that might be due to organic causes or sheer fakery.

    a. Depersonalization is a dissociative disorder, not a somatoform disorder, which would involve physical complaints.

    b. Body dysmorphic disorder involves exaggerated concern about a body part, such as too much hair or too long a nose.

    d. Dissociative amnesia is a memory problem, not one connected with somatic complaints.

9. b. Hypochondriasis is a preoccupation with illness and death that stems from actual illness and parental modeling.

    a. Too little is known about body dysmorphic disorder to speculate on preexisting factors.

    c. The major preexisting factors in dissociative identity disorder seem to be child abuse, an ability to dissociate, and a lack of environmental support.

    d. Too little is known about factitious disorders to speculate on preexisting factors.

10. a. The impact of these complaints is to disrupt family functioning by taking the patient "off the hook" for his or her responsibilities.

    b. Family therapists do not see these physical complaints as cries for help.

    c. Family therapists tend to focus on current relationships, not childhood issues; also, abuse is more related to dissociative disorder.

    d. Psychoanalysts, not family therapists, would stress the repression of emotions.

ANSWER KEY: CONCEPTUAL MULTIPLE-CHOICE QUESTIONS

1. b. Current attempts to identify the disorder through EEGs, cerebral blood flow, and other physiological measures have been inconclusive and contradictory (Miller & Triggiano, 1992).

    a. Dissociative amnesia is another DSM-IV disorder; this fact is unrelated to the case in detecting the existence of separate personalities.

    c. Personalities typically appear one at a time.

    d. The asymmetry in awareness is not complete; this fact is unrelated to the ease in detecting the existence of separate personalities.

2. c. Usually one personality has limited or no awareness of the others; this is the basic dissociation of consciousness.

    a. Many more than three personalities have been reported: Chris Sizemore (the real "Eve") had more than twenty, and one clinician says the average is thirteen to fourteen!

    b. The diagnosis of dissociative identity disorder rests on the notion that the personalities are distinct.

    d. Dissociative identity disorder is a form of dissociative disorder because one part of the person (along with memories for that part) dissociates itself from the rest.

3. a. Research indicates that the suggestion of a therapist can influence the reporting of multiple-personality-like symptoms.

    b. Depersonalization disorder does not seem to be induced by therapy.

    c. Dissociative amnesia is triggered by traumatic events, not by therapy.

    d   Body dysmorphic disorder does not seem to be induced by therapy.

4. c. Behavioral theory looks at dissociative symptoms in terms of rewards and punishments, the rewards being attention and avoidance of stressful situations.

    a. Iatrogenic refers to a problem that is the result of the therapist's treatment.

    b. Biological theory does not emphasize avoidance; it emphasizes genetics and body processes.

    d. Psychodynamic theory emphasizes repression of traumatic events.

5. a. Dissociative amnesia often ends as abruptly as it begins.

    b. Dissociative identity disorder is often a lifelong problem; it is difficult to treat even with extensive psychotherapy.

    c. Hypochondriasis is usually a lifelong problem; it is as much a lifestyle as a psychological disorder.

    d. Factitious disorders are poorly understood but are believed to be linked to deep-seated and enduring problems.

6. d. When physical symptoms are not caused by organic factors and do not seem to be voluntarily induced (as they are in factitious disorders), the diagnosis is somatoform disorder.

    a. The separation of consciousness is a fundamental symptom of the dissociative disorders.

    b. Irrational fears of objects are associated with phobias.

    c. Actual physical damage associated with stress is called stress-related illness or psychophysiological illness.

7. b. In factitious disorders the person may either inject himself/herself with agents that produce fever or consciously mimic physical disorders.

    a. It is not believed that factitious disorders are complicated by depression and anxiety.

    c. Dissociative disorders involve the division of consciousness.

    d. Factitious disorders are poorly understood, but repression is more involved in somatoform disorders.

8. a. In the DSM-IV-TR, the criteria for somatization disorder are pain complaints in four different sites, two gastrointestinal symptoms, one sexual symptom, and one pseudoneurological symptom. The range of complaints is a prime way of differentiating this disorder from hypochondriasis.

    b. Lingering and exaggerated pain are symptoms of pain disorder.

    c. Childhood abuse is more related to dissociative identity disorder than to somatization disorder.

    d. Somatization disorder is more common in women than in men.

9. a. Psychoanalysts consider the primary gain in somatoform disorders to be relief from unconscious conflicts and the secondary gain to be attention from others, which meets dependency needs.

    b. Biological theory stresses the pain and sensory thresholds of people with somatoform disorders

    c. Learning theory highlights the positive consequences of making physical complaints.

    d. Sociocultural theorists argue that women develop somatoform disorders because they have typically had social restrictions placed upon them.

ANSWER KEY: APPLICATION MULTIPLE-CHOICE QUESTIONS

1. c. Selective amnesia involves partial memory loss for a specific traumatic event.

    a. Dissociative fugue is characterized by amnesia, travel to a new place, and the establishment of a new identity.

    b. Continuous amnesia is a rare form of dissociative disorder in which there is complete memory loss for the past until a specific point in time.

    d. Depersonalization disorder is characterized by feelings of body distortion and unreality.

2. b. Typically, one or more of the separate personalities are unaware of the existence of the others.

    a. Three or more separate personalities are commonly found in multiple personality.

    c. In many cases, male personalities are found in females (as in the case of Sybil) and female personalities are found in males (as in the case of Billy Milligan).

    d. Often, one of the personalities is sexually promiscuous or aggressive (taking on id qualities).

3. d. Psychoanalysts emphasize the function of repression in all dissociative disorders.

    a. Behavior therapists stress how dissociation is a coping strategy for daily stress.

    b. Biological theorists have rarely commented on multiple personality, but would emphasize brain function or genetics if they did.

    c. Those who believe dissociative identity disorder is iatrogenic would discount the importance of trauma and repression.

4. a. Depersonalization disorder involves complaints of feeling unreal; behaviorists would treat the problem through extinction of the complaints and rewards for "healthy talk."

    b. Dissociative identity disorder does not involve feelings of unreality; psychoanalysts would try to unlock unconscious factors.

    c. Pain disorder is about pain, not body distortions or feelings of unreality.

    d. The biological viewpoint would use medication for treatment.

5. d. Part of the problem of diagnosing somatoform disorders (particularly conversion) is that the factors Dr. O'Neil mentions are other possible explanations for the complaints.

    a. Dissociative disorders involve a split in consciousness, usually involving memory loss, not physical symptoms.

    b. Anxiety disorders are not thought to be faked and involve only physical complaints that are secondary to the anxiety.

    c. Factitious disorders *are* under voluntary control.

6. c. Somatization disorder involves multiple physical complaints that often lead to unnecessary surgery.

    a. Conversion disorder usually involves paralysis or sensory problems (blurred vision, for instance), and there is rarely much "doctor shopping."

    b. Dissociative amnesia is characterized by memory loss, not physical complaints.

    d. Hypochondriasis involves a preoccupation with health problems and often centers on one vague complaint.

7. a. Conversion disorder often involves paralysis in an extremity and begins shortly after a major stressor.

    b. Malingering is when a person consciously fakes his or her symptoms.

    c. Somatization disorder involves multiple complaints.

    d. Hypochondriasis is characterized by a preoccupation with illness; rarely is the complaint about a specific dysfunction like leg paralysis.

8. c. Chest pains and fear of death are the kinds of complaints associated with hypochondriasis; in somatization disorder, many more diverse and vague complaints would be made.

    a. Hysteria is an older name for both conversion and somatization disorder.

    b. Conversion disorder usually involves one complaint (extremity paralysis or sensory loss), not the multiple complaints seen in somatization disorder.

    d. Malingering is unlikely to involve a fear of death.

9. a. Sociocultural theorists note that hysteria was more common when women had fewer social roles in which they could express aggression or sexuality.

    b. Behavioral theorists highlight the reinforcements for sick behavior.

    c. Biological theorists stress the lower pain tolerance and heightened internal awareness of somatoform patients.

    d. Psychoanalysts relate the physical complaints to repressed unpleasant memories and conflicts.

10. c. Behavior therapists want to extinguish pain complaints by reducing the attention patients receive for them.

    a. Psychoanalysts would stress the repression behind such complaints and the need for unconscious feelings to become conscious.

    b. Psychiatrists (medical doctors) are likely to be attentive to pain complaints rather than to suggest that they be ignored.

    d. Humanistic therapists would accept as valid the subjective experience of the patient and would not encourage this kind of selective attention.

OBJECTIVES DEFINED

1. **What are dissociations? What forms can they take? How are they caused, and how are they treated?**

-   Dissociation involves a disruption in consciousness, memory, identity, or perception and may be transient or chronic.

-   Dissociative amnesia and dissociative fugue involve a selective form of forgetting in which the person loses memory of information that is of personal significance. Depersonalization disorder is characterized by feelings of unreality—distorted perceptions of oneself and one's environment. Dissociative identity disorder involves the alternation of two or more relatively independent personalities in one individual.

-   Biological explanations for DID have focused on studies finding variations in brain activity when comparing different personalities. Some researchers believe that childhood trauma and chronic stress can result in permanent structural changes in the brain. Psychoanalytic perspectives attribute these disorders to the repression of impulses that are seeking expression and ways of coping with childhood abuse. Sociocultural explanations for dissociation include exposure to media portrayals of dissociation and role enactment. Social explanations include childhood abuse, subtle reinforcement, responding to the expectations of a therapist, or mislabeling dissociative experiences.

-   Dissociative amnesia and dissociative fugue tend to be short-lived and to remit spontaneously; behavioral therapy has also been used successfully. Dissociative identity disorder has most often been treated with psychotherapy and hypnosis, as well as with behavioral and family therapies. In most cases, the therapist attempts to fuse the several personalities.

2. **When do physical complaints become a type of disorder? What are the causes and treatments of these conditions?**

-   Somatoform disorders involve complaints about physical symptoms that mimic actual medical conditions but that have no apparent organic basis. Instead, psychological factors are directly involved in the initiation and exacerbation of the problem. Somatization disorder is characterized by chronic multiple complaints and early onset. Conversion disorder involves a physical impairment that has no organic cause. Pain disorder is a condition in which reported severe pain has a psychological rather than a physical basis. Hypochondriasis involves a persistent preoccupation with bodily functioning and disease. Body dysmorphic disorder involves preoccupation with an imagined bodily defect.

-   Biological explanations have suggested that there is increased vulnerability to somatoform disorder when individuals have high sensitivity to body sensations, a lower pain threshold and/or a history of illness or injury. The psychoanalytic view holds that somatoform disorders are caused by the repression of sexual conflicts and their conversion into physical symptoms. Other psychological factors include social isolation, high anxiety or stress, and catastrophic thoughts regarding bodily sensations. Social explanations suggest that the role of "being sick" is reinforcing. Parental models for injury or illness can also be influential. From a sociocultural perspective, somatoform disorders result from societal restrictions placed on women, who are affected to a much greater degree than men by these disorders. Additionally, social class, limited knowledge about medical concepts, and cultural acceptance of physical symptoms can play a role.

MARGIN DEFINITIONS

body dysmorphic disorder (BDD) preoccupation with an imagined defect in appearance in a normal-appearing person or an excessive concern over a slight physical defect

continuous amnesia an inability to recall any events that have occurred between a specific time in the past and the present time

conversion disorder physical problems or impairments in sensory or motor functioning controlled by the voluntary nervous system suggesting a neurological disorder but with no underlying organic cause

depersonalization disorder disorder characterized by feelings of unreality concerning the self and the environment

dissociative disorders a group including the disorders of dissociative amnesia, dissociative fugue, dissociative identity disorder, and depersonalization disorder all of which involve some sort of dissociation, or separation, of a part of the person's consciousness, memory, or identity

dissociative fugue confusion over personal identity (often involving the partial or complete assumption of a new identity), accompanied by unexpected travel away from home

dissociative identity disorder (DID) a condition in which two or more relatively independent personalities appear to exist in one person; also known as multiple-personality disorder

factitious disorder a mental disorder in which the symptoms of physical or mental illnesses are deliberately induced or simulated with no apparent incentive

generalized amnesia a complete loss of memory of the individual's entire life

hypochondriasis a persistent preoccupation with one's health and physical condition, even in the face of physical evaluations that reveal no organic problems

localized amnesia a failure to recall all the events that happened in a specific short period, often centered on some highly painful or disturbing event

malingering faking a disorder to achieve a specific goal

pain disorder a disorder characterized by reports of severe pain that appear to have no physiological or neurological basis, are in excess of what would be expected from an existing physical condition, or that linger long after a physical injury has healed

selective amnesia an inability to remember certain details of an incident

somatization disorder a disorder involving chronic complaints of specific bodily symptoms that have no physical basis

somatoform disorder a disorder involving physical symptoms or complaints that have no physiological basis, believed to occur due to an underlying psychological conflict or need **dissociative amnesia** the partial or total loss of important personal information, sometimes occurring suddenly after a stressful or traumatic event, due to psychological, not physical, factors

systematized amnesia the loss of memory for only selected types of information

undifferentiated somatoform disorder the diagnosis given an individual who does not fully meet the criteria for somatization disorder but who has at least one physical complaint of six months' duration

CHAPTER 7

Stress Disorders

TABLE OF CONTENTS

LEARNING OBJECTIVES

1. Describe acute and posttraumatic stress disorder and how they are diagnosed.

2. Describe what causes acute and posttraumatic stress disorders.

3. Discuss the different treatments for acute and posttraumatic stress disorders.

4. Discuss the role that stressors play on physical health, and define the associated psychophysiological disorders.

5. Define the causes psychophysiological disorders.

6. Define the methods that have been developed to treat psychophysiological disorders.

CHAPTER OUTLINE

I. **Acute and posttraumatic stress disorders.** *Acute stress disorder (ASD)* produces dissociation, a reliving of a traumatic experience, and avoidance of reminders of the experience. It lasts for more than two days and less than twenty-nine and occurs within four weeks of the stressful event. In the National Comorbidity Survey, the lifetime prevalence of PTSD for American adults is 6.8 percent, with about twice as many women as men receiving the diagnosis. *Posttraumatic stress disorder (PTSD)* is an anxiety disorder, lasting thirty or more days, characterized by delayed reactions to extraordinarily distressing events. Symptoms include re-experiencing the event, intrusive memories and dreams, emotional numbing, and heightened autonomic arousal.

II. **Etiology of acute and posttraumatic stress disorders**. Recent research suggests that some extreme stressors may produce PTSD in almost everyone. There appears to be a strong correlation between the level of danger perceived from a trauma and the likelihood of developing PTSD. Although men are more likely to be exposed to stressors, women seem to be twice as likely to suffer from PTSD. Preexisting anxiety disorder or a family history of anxiety occurs in many with PTSD. As compared with trauma-exposed individuals who do not have PTSD, those who develop the disorder show a sensitized autonomic system. The psychological dimension asks what are preexisting or psychological contributions to developing a stress disorder? Specific psychological vulnerabilities have been identified, although the precise role they play varies from individual to individual. The Social Dimension investigates the effects of poor or inadequate support during childhood which has also been identified as possibly contributing to the development of the stress disorders. The sociocultural dimension investigates recent immigrants and refugees from countries in which there have been civil disturbances or conflict which may have elevated rates of the stress disorders.

III. **Treatments of acute and posttraumatic stress disorders.** A range of treatments for PTSD exists. Biological interventions generally consist of antidepressants and SSRIs, although the associated side effects often result in discontinuation of their use. Exposure and cognitive therapies may also be effective.

IV. **Physical stress disorders: psychophysiological disorders**. Anxiety and stress have some role in sudden death syndrome, unexpected death that often seems to have no physical basis. Sudden death among Hmong immigrants in the United States may be due to severe culture shock. Psychophysiological disorders involve actual tissue damage (such as coronary heart disease), a disease process (immune impairment), or physiological dysfunction (as in asthma or migraine headaches). Coronary heart disease (CHD) involves the narrowing of cardiac arteries, resulting in the restriction or partial blockage of the flow of blood and oxygen to the heart. Symptoms of CHD may include chest pain (angina pectoris), heart attack, or, in severe cases, cardiac arrest. Approximately 452,300 Americans die of coronary heart disease each year, although the rate has been declining. Migraine, tension, and cluster headaches are among the most common psychophysiological complaints. About 90 percent of males and 95 percent of females have at least one headache during a given year. Over 45 million Americans suffer from chronic, recurring headaches. Asthma is a chronic inflammatory disease of the airways in the lungs. Bronchiospasms, excessive mucus secretion, and edema, constrict the airways, making it difficult to completely empty the lungs and therefore reducing the amount of air that can be inhaled. Stress on the immune system caused by viral conditions, such as herpes infection, Acquired Immune Deficiency Syndrome (AIDS), and even the common cold may be influenced by cognitive and emotional factors. There are a variety of biological, behavioral, cognitive, and social pathways that affect the immune system. Part of the stress response involves the release of neurohormones, such as corticosteroids and endorphins, which compromise immune functioning. Stress reactions release chemicals that suppress immune system components such as lymphocytes (B-, T- and natural killer cells) and phagocytes.

V. **Etiology of psychophysiological disorders.** The biological dimension indicates that stressors can directly produce physiological changes through the release of neurohormones (epinephrine, norepinephrinecatecholamines, and cortisol). Psychological and personality characteristics can also mediate the effects of exposure to stressors. *Somatic weakness theory* proposes that certain organs are weakened by earlier experience and are vulnerable to disease under stress. The *autonomic response specificity hypothesis* argues that each person has a unique way of responding to stressors. The *general adaptation syndrome* may be combined with the previous two theories to understand illness as a disease of adaptation. Psychological dimension explored a longitudinal study of remaining employees after nearly half of the workforce was removed during downsizing showed that while two-thirds developed health problems, one-third appeared to thrive. The individuals who did well had three characteristics: (1) commitment—they were involved in ongoing changes rather than giving up and feeling isolated; (2) control—they made attempts to influence decisions and refused to feel powerless, and (3) challenge—changes were viewed as opportunities. Sociocultural Dimension looks at conflicts with societal stressors, discrimination, and cultural expectations can have a significant impact on health.

VI. **Treatment of psychophysiological disorders**. Treatment programs for psychophysiological disorders generally consist of both medical treatment for the physical symptoms and psychological therapy to eliminate stress and anxiety. Behavioral medicine comprises a range of disciplines that study the social and psychological issues in health and apply that knowledge to stress management approaches. In relaxation training, individuals are taught to alternately tense and relax muscle groups in the body. In biofeedback training, clients are informed about small internal changes (such as in blood pressure and heart rate). They learn to control these internal processes and eventually do not need the monitoring devices. Essentially an operant technique, biofeedback has been used to treat a range of psychophysiological disorders, from headache to asthma. Stress management programs often include such cognitive-behavioral interventions as self-instructional techniques and cognitive restructuring.

VII. **Implications.** Psychologists are becoming increasingly aware that single-cause models of psychophysiological illness are inadequate. Not everyone exposed to the same set of stressors develops a psychophysiological disorder

KEY TERMS REVIEW

1. Severe headaches that result from the dilation of cerebral blood vessels after an initial contraction of cranial arteries are called _____.

2. The chronic inflammatory disease characterized by attacks in which breathing becomes extremely difficult as a result of constriction of lung airways is called _____.

3. The therapeutic technique in which the individual acquires the ability to relax the muscles of the body is called _____.

4. The cardiovascular disease in which the flow of blood and oxygen to the heart is restricted because of narrowed arteries in or near the heart is called _____.

5. _____ is a disorder characterized by anxiety and dissociative symptoms that occur within one month after exposure to a traumatic stressor.

6. A physical or psychological demand placed on an individual by some external situation is called a(n) _____.

7. The therapeutic technique in which the individual receives information about internal physiological functions and learns to control them is called _____.

8. A headache that may be produced by prolonged contraction of scalp and neck muscles is called a(n) _____.

9. High blood pressure with no known organic cause is called _____.

10. A model that assumes that the body's physical and psychological reaction to biological stressors involves three stages of response (alarm, resistance, exhaustion) is called the _____.

11. A physical disorder that has a strong psychological basis or component is called a(n) _____.

12. An individual's internal reaction to the physical or psychological demands placed on him or her by the environment is called _____.

13. An excruciating headache that tends to occur near the eye or cheek and produces tears or a blocked nose is called a(n) _____.

14. _____ is a disorder characterized by anxiety, dissociative, and other symptoms that last for more than one month and that occur as a result of exposure to extreme trauma.

FACTUAL MULTIPLE-CHOICE QUESTIONS

1. Because any physical disorder can have a psychological component, the term now being used by psychologists to describe stress-related illnesses is

    a. psychosomatic.
    b. adaptive.
    c. somatopsychic.
    d. psychophysiological.

2. Alarm, resistance, and exhaustion are terms associated with the _____ model of stress-related illness.

    a. general adaptation
    b. life change
    c. decompensation
    d. transaction

3. When levels of T-cells, B-cells, and phagocytes are high, this is an indication that the individual has

    a. HIV.
    b. a strong immune system.
    c. a weak immune system.
    d. few neurohormones.

4. As a result of marital separation or bereavement, people often experience

    a. an increase in NK cells.
    b. impairments in the immune system.
    c. an increase in phagocytes and lymphocytes.
    d. a lowering of their life change units.

5. When a person has high blood pressure without physiological reason, the disorder is called

    a. coronary heart disease.
    b. essential hypertension.
    c. angina pectoris.
    d. psychosomatic blood pressure.

6. An African American who is excessively angry and deficient in psychosocial resources is believed to be at particularly high risk for developing

    a. tension headaches.
    b. asthma.
    c. high blood pressure.
    d. defective NK cells.

7. Headaches that are preceded by neurological symptoms such as blurred vision and that are caused by uncontrolled blood flow to the brain are called

    a. tension headaches.
    b. classic migraine headaches.
    c. cluster headaches.
    d. common migraine headaches.

CONCEPTUAL MULTIPLE-CHOICE QUESTIONS

1. Research on nursing home residents indicates that those who live the longest

    a. have the highest catecholamine levels.
    b. relinquish most of their decision-making power to the nursing home staff.
    c. tend to suppress their anger.
    d. are allowed to make certain decisions that increase their sense of control.

2. The majority of psychologists and physicians believe that psychological moods
   a. have no effect on the progression of cancer.
   b. determine whether or not a person develops cancer.
   c. are an important factor in the development of cancer only for women.
   d. may have an impact on cancer, but research is too inconclusive to be sure.

3. Recent research examining depression before a diagnosis of cancer found that
   a. the cancer death rate was two times greater for people with high depression scores than for those with low depression scores.
   b. cancer was unrelated to depression scores.
   c. the cancer death rate was two times lower for people with high depression scores than for those with low depression scores.
   d. high depression scores predicted cancer death, but only when people were also anger suppressors.

4. The relationship between stress and the development of various psychophysiological disorders is best understood by understanding the effect of stress on
   a. HPA dysregulation.
   b. passive coping.
   c. the immune system.
   d. somatization disorders.

5. The autonomic response specificity hypothesis suggests that
   a. if a stressor goes on long enough, any person's body will become exhausted.
   b. each individual has a unique way of reacting to stressors.
   c. each type of psychophysiological disorder has a specific conflict associated with it.
   d. certain body parts respond to certain levels of life change.

6. The concept of _____ explains how bronchial irritation can become associated with stressors and other stimuli so that conflicts produce asthma attacks.
   a. operant conditioning
   b. the hardy personality
   c. general adaptation
   d. classical conditioning

7. The voluntary control of a physiological response such as heart rate can be demonstrated by using
   a. biofeedback.
   b. progressive relaxation.
   c. classical conditioning.
   d. modeling.

8. Psychophysiological disorders differ from somatoform disorders in that
   a. somatoform disorders involve actual bodily disease, whereas psychophysiological disorders are psychogenic.
   b. psychophysiological disorders involve actual bodily disease, whereas somatoform disorders are psychogenic.
   c. somatoform disorders are caused by immune system dysregulation, whereas psychophysiological disorders are psychogenic.
   d. somatoform disorders are treated successfully with behavioral therapy, whereas psychophysiological disorders are not successfully treated.

9. Which of the following is NOT a true statement regarding acute stress disorder and posttraumatic stress disorder?

   a. They both develop in response to an extreme trauma.
   b. The prevalence of acute stress disorder may be underestimated.
   c. A person suffering from acute stress disorder is likely to receive a diagnosis of posttraumatic stress if the symptoms last more than four weeks.
   d. Individuals suffering from posttraumatic stress often have flashbacks and nightmares, but those suffering from acute stress do not.

APPLICATION MULTIPLE-CHOICE QUESTIONS

1. Dr. Morgan is trying to decide if a medical condition is affected by a psychological factor. She thinks that as long as there is a temporal relationship between psychological factors and the onset of or the delay in recovery from a medical condition, the diagnosis that it is an affected condition can be made. Is she correct?

   a. No, the psychological factor must interfere with treatment.
   b. No, the psychological factor must add to the health risk of the individual.
   c. No, the psychological factor must interfere with treatment and add to health risk.
   d. Yes, she is correct.

2. Gina's reactions to a snarling dog are a rapid heartbeat and the secretion of hormones by her adrenal glands that temporarily reduce the efficiency of her immune system. These reactions are

   a. an illustration of the somatic weakness hypothesis.
   b. the exhaustion stage of the general adaptation syndrome.
   c. an illustration of the hardy personality.
   d. the alarm stage of the general adaptation syndrome.

3. In the past three months, Vera has changed jobs twice, has learned that her parents plan to divorce, and has gone on a vacation. The life change model of stress suggests that

   a. only the job changes are stressors.
   b. the way she interprets these events will determine whether or not she becomes ill.
   c. All these changes increase her chances of becoming ill.
   d. she is now in the alarm stage of adapting to stressors.

4. Barbara has never outwardly expressed anger in her life. On the MMPI, she shows a very high depression score. What physical illness is she at higher risk for developing?

   a. General paresis
   b. Coronary heart disease
   c. Cancer
   d. Asthma

5. John, age 36, is a poor black man with a Type A personality. He is almost always angry and upset. John is at highest risk for developing which disorders?

   a. Asthma and migraine headaches
   b. Essential hypertension and coronary heart disease
   c. Cancer and migraine headaches
   d. Sudden death syndrome and asthma

6. Don says, "When I was small, I was exposed to severe air pollution that damaged my lungs. Now whenever I am under stress, I develop a bad cough and wheezing." Don's explanation reflects the
   _____ hypothesis on psychophysiological illnesses.

   a. operant conditioning
   b. psychodynamic
   c. neurotransmitter
   d. autonomic weakness

7. To treat his hypertension, Carl is hooked up to a machine that shows small changes in his blood pressure. The information that he is lowering his blood pressure acts as reinforcement. Carl's treatment is
    a. progressive relaxation.
    b. cognitive restructuring.
    c. biofeedback.
    d. implosive therapy.

ANSWER KEY: KEY TERMS REVIEW

1. migraine headaches
2. asthma
3. relaxation training
4. coronary heart disease
5. acute stress disorder
6. stressor
7. biofeedback training
8. tension headache
9. essential hypertension
10. general adaptation syndrome
11. psychophysiological disorder
12. stress
13. cluster headache
14. posttraumatic stress disorder

ANSWER KEY: FACTUAL MULTIPLE-CHOICE QUESTIONS

1. d. To convey the idea that any physical condition can be related to psychological states, the new term used is psychophysiological.

    a. Psychosomatic is the old term that implied that only some disorders were related to psychological states.

    b. Adaptive may be related to the general adaptation syndrome view of psychophysiological illnesses, but this represents only one viewpoint.

    c. Somatopsychic is a term that describes a non-Western view that illness produces emotional disorder.

2. a. There are three stages in the general adaptation syndrome: alarm, resistance, and exhaustion.

    b. The life change model stresses the role of small and large life events; it predicts that higher life change scores lead to greater illness.

    c. Decompensation is a model of psychological response to stress, developed by De La Fuente, that has three stages, too: impact, attempted resolution, and decompensated adjustment.

    d. The transaction model emphasizes actual situations and the appraisal of events.

3. b.   The white blood cells in the immune system (lymphocytes, B-cells and T-cells, and phagocytes) help maintain health by recognizing and destroying pathogens such as bacteria, viruses, fungi, and tumors.

    a.   One indicator of HIV/AIDS is low levels of the white blood cells (lymphocytes, B-cells and T-cells, and phagocytes).

    c.   This would be just the opposite. A weak immune system would be characterized by low levels of these white blood cells.

    d.   Neurohormones, such as corticosteroids and endorphins, have a negative impact on the immune system: corticosteroids have an immunosuppressive action, while endorphins decrease natural killer cells' tumor-fighting ability.

4. b.   A variety of impairments in the immune system, including decreased NK cell responsiveness, are found during stress.

    a.   When people are under stress, their NK cells are less responsive.

    c.   Phagocytes and lymphocytes are immune system components weakened by stress.

    d.   Separation and bereavement are life events associated with high numbers of life change units.

5. b.   Essential hypertension exists when blood pressure is high but cannot be traced to a direct cause.

    a.   Coronary heart disease is a more general term for conditions that reduce the efficiency and longevity of the heart.

    c.   Angina pectoris is a term for pains in the chest caused by heart disease.

    d.   Psychosomatic blood pressure is a made-up term.

6. c.   Poor blacks (who have fewer psychosocial resources) and those who express or suppress either anger excessively are most likely to have essential hypertension.

    a.   Episodic tension headaches are not overrepresented by African-Americans.

    b.   Asthma is primarily a problem in youths and is not related to any particular personality pattern or ethnicity.

    d.   There is no evidence that defective NK cells are related to ethnicity or personality.

7. b.   Classic migraines have such neurological signs as blurred vision and tingling sensations prior to appearance of the headache itself.

    a.   Tension headaches are characterized by a feeling of pressure and by lower intensity than migraine headaches, and they do not have neurological symptoms.

    c.   Cluster headaches are not believed to be related to blood flow; they involve excruciating pain around the eye.

    d.   Common migraine headaches do not have the neurological symptoms of classic migraines.

ANSWER KEY: CONCEPTUAL MULTIPLE-CHOICE QUESTIONS

1. d.   Research by Rodin and Langer indicates that personal control in nursing-home residents is associated with longer life.

    a.   High catecholamine levels are a sign of stress and may lead to early death rather than long life.

    b.   Reduced personal control is associated with shortened life span in nursing homes.

    c.   Suppression of anger is, if anything, related to an increased likelihood of essential hypertension.

2. d.   There are too many methodological problems in the current research to permit definite conclusions about the role of moods in cancer.

    a.   There is too much evidence linking personality and cancer to dismiss the entire topic.

    b.   Cancer is related to diet, pollution, genetics, and many other nonpersonality dimensions.

    c.   There is no evidence that women alone develop cancer because of emotions.

3. a.   Research shows that high depression scores on the MMPI predict future mortality due to cancer.

    b.   Cancer is related to high scores on the depression scale of the MMPI.

    c.   The reverse of this is true: As depression scores increase, so does the risk of later cancer (at least in one study).

    d.   The research reports no interaction between depression and anger suppression.

4. c.   Research indicates that prolonged stress negatively affects the immune system.

    a.   Stress may activate the hypothalamic-pituitary-adrenocortical (HPA) axis, which mobilizes energy, but this effect may be positive or negative.

    b.   Passive coping occurs when the individual cannot attempt to minimize exposure to the stressor and must tolerate it.

    d.   Somatization disorder occurs when a person has a long-standing history of physical complaints for which medical tests indicate the person is normal.

5. b.   Autonomic response specificity argues that each person has a unique way of reacting to stressors.

    a.   The general adaptation model predicts that exhaustion occurs after a stressor has gone on too long.

    c.   Psychoanalytic theory (Alexander) suggests that each disorder is associated with a particular unconscious conflict.

    d.   There is no theory that suggests that body parts react differently to different levels of stress.

6. d.   Classical conditioning focuses on the pairing of stimuli and would explain the generalization of attacks to a variety of stimuli.

    a.   Operant conditioning stresses the consequences of responses; it would examine the rewards for having an attack.

    b.   Hardiness is associated with reduced risk of illness in the face of stressors.

    c.   General adaptation is a model that proposes a generic response to stressors.

7. a. Biofeedback is an operant procedure that gives one control over autonomic responses such as heart rate and skin temperature.

   b. Progressive relaxation (Jacobson) involves tensing and relaxing muscle groups throughout the body.

   c. Classical conditioning is a passive process, unlike the operant conditioning that occurs in biofeedback.

   d. Modeling entails the imitation of others; none of this occurs in biofeedback.

8. b. Psychophysiological disorders involve tissue damage, whereas somatoform disorders are psychogenic in nature.

   a. The reverse is true; psychophysiological disorders involve tissue damage, whereas somatoform disorders are psychogenic in nature.

   c. Psychophysiological disorders are not psychogenic; they involve tissue damage.

   d. Psychophysiological disorders may be treated with cognitive-behavioral techniques, relaxation, biofeedback, and medications.

9. d. People suffering from ACD often do in fact have flashbacks and nightmares.

   a. This is true. They do both develop in response to extreme trauma.

   b. This is true. ACD is potentially underestimated.

   c. This is true. ACD symptoms extending beyond four weeks would typically change diagnosis to PTSD.

ANSWER KEY: APPLICATION MULTIPLE-CHOICE QUESTIONS

1. d. Because she sees a temporal relationship, the diagnostic criterion has been met.

   a. The DSM-IV-TR says that any one of three relationships between psychological factors and the medical condition must exist: a temporal relationship or interference with treatment or additional health risk.

   b. The DSM-IV-TR says that any one of three relationships between psychological factors and the medical condition must exist: a temporal relationship or interference with treatment or additional health risk.

   c. The DSM-IV-TR says that any one of three relationships between psychological factors and the medical condition must exist: a temporal relationship or interference with treatment or additional health risk.

2. d. The first stage of the general adaptation syndrome (alarm) involves a general mobilization of body functions that reduces immune system strength.

   a. The somatic weakness hypothesis would be illustrated by Gina having heart trouble after this episode.

   b. The exhaustion stage is illustrated by the breakdown of tissues that have experienced prolonged resistance.

   c. The hardy personality is one that shows openness to change, commitment, and a sense of personal control.

3.   c.   The life change model suggests that all events-negative and positive, large and small increase the likelihood of illness.

      a.   The life change model would consider all the events as examples of stressors.

      b.   The interpretation of events is a key component of the transaction model.

      d.   The general adaptation syndrome suggests that alarm occurs soon after a stressor.

4.   c.   Cancer has been found to be more common both in people who are extreme anger suppressors and in those with high depression scores on the MMPI.

      a.   There is no evidence that general paresis (deterioration of the brain due to syphilis) is related to a particular personality pattern.

      b.   Coronary heart disease is related to hostility, but not to suppressed anger.

      d.   Asthma is primarily a biological disorder, although fear of separation from others is related to some attacks.

5.   b.   Essential hypertension is related to race and anger expression; coronary heart disease is related to Type A personality.

      a.   Ethnicity and personality are unrelated to asthma and migraines.

      c.   Cancer may be related to depression and anger suppression, but migraines are not related to any of the factors listed in John's case.

      d.   Sudden death syndrome is found among Hmong males; ethnicity and personality are not strongly related to asthma.

6.   d.   Autonomic weakness theory suggests that each person has a unique physiological reaction to all types of stressful situations.

      a.   Operant conditioning would focus on the consequences of a wheezing attack, such as increased attention.

      b.   Psychodynamic thinking would examine the unconscious conflicts underlying a wheezing attack.

      c.   Neurotransmitters play no role in the development of a cough.

7.   c.   Biofeedback is an operant procedure that uses machinery to give information that leads to the voluntary altering of internal processes.

      a.   Progressive relaxation involves the tensing and relaxing of muscle groups.

      b.   Cognitive restructuring features changing the way people think about stressors and about their ability to cope.

      d.   Implosive therapy is used to extinguish fears by having people experience high levels of anxiety.

OBJECTIVES DEFINED

1.   **What are acute and posttraumatic stress disorder and how are they diagnosed?**

- Acute and posttraumatic stress disorders involve exposure to a traumatic event, resulting in intrusive memories of the occurrence, attempts to forget or repress the memories, emotional withdrawal, and increased arousal.

- Acute stress disorder (ASD) is characterized by anxiety and dissociative symptoms that occur within one month after exposure to a traumatic stressor. Posttraumatic stress disorder (PTSD) is characterized by anxiety, dissociative, and other symptoms that last for more than one month and that occur as a result of exposure to extreme trauma.

2. **What causes acute and posttraumatic stress disorders?**

- Various biological, psychological, sociocultural, and social factors have been implicated in the stress disorders. Possible biological factors involve a sensitized autonomic system, involvement of stress hormones, and brain cell damage. Psychological factors include level of cognitive functioning, trait anxiety and depression, and classic conditioning. Poor or inadequate support during childhood has also been identified as possibly contributing to the development of the stress disorders, as have various sociocultural factors such as immigration status and gender.

3. **What are the different treatments for acute and posttraumatic stress disorders?**

- Antidepressant medication has been successful in the treatment of ASD and PTSD, as has exposure to cues associated with the trauma. Cognitive-based therapies such as psychoeducation have also proven effective in some cases.

4. **What role do stressors play on physical health and what are the psychophysiological disorders?**

- Any external events or situations that places a physical or psychological demand on a person can serve as a stressor and can affect physical health. Stressors can range from chronic irritation and frustration to acute and traumatic events.

- A psychophysiological disorder is any physical disorder that has a strong psychological basis or component. Psychophysiological disorders involve actual tissue damage (such as coronary heart disease), a disease process (immune impairment), or physiological dysfunction (as in asthma or migraine headaches). Examples of psychophysiological disorders include coronary heart disease (CHD), essential hypertension, migraine, tension, and cluster headaches, and asthma.

- Not everyone develops an illness when exposed to the same stressor or traumatic event because stress is an internal psychological or physiological response to a stressor. Individuals reacting to the same stressor may do so in very different ways.

5. **What causes psychophysiological disorders?**

- Various biological, psychological, sociocultural, and social factors have been implicated in the psychophysiological disorders.

- Biological explanations include (1) chronic activation of the sympathetic nervous system and continual release of neurohormones, (2) genetic contributions, and (3) somatic weakness, autonomic response specificity, and general adaptation syndrome.

- Psychological contributors include characteristics such as helplessness versus control, optimism, hostility, self-efficacy and the role of classical and operant conditioning in acquiring or maintaining these disorders.

- Social contributors include having an inadequate social network, abrasive interpersonal interactions, a stressful environment, and being unmarried for men.

- Sociocultural factors such as the gender, racial or ethnic background are risk factors in certain physiological disorders. Stressful environments associated with poverty, prejudice or racism as well as cultural conflicts have been related to illnesses.

6.   **What methods have been developed to treat the psychophysiological disorders?**

- These disorders are treated through stress management or anxiety management programs, combined with medical treatment for physical symptoms or conditions.

- Relaxation training and biofeedback training, which help the client learn to control muscular or organic functioning, are usually a part of such programs.

- Cognitive-behavioral interventions, which involve changing anxiety-arousing thoughts, have also been useful.

MARGIN DEFINTIONS

acute stress disorder (ASD) disorder characterized by anxiety and dissociative symptoms that occur within one month after exposure to a traumatic stressor

asthma chronic inflammatory disease of the airways in the lungs

biofeedback training a therapeutic approach, combining physiological and behavioral approaches, in which a patient receives information regarding particular autonomic functions and is rewarded for influencing those functions in a desired direction

cluster headaches excruciating stabbing or burning sensations located in the eye or cheek

coronary heart disease (CHD) the narrowing of cardiac arteries, resulting in the restriction or partial blockage of the flow of blood and oxygen to the heart

essential hypertension a chronic condition characterized by blood pressure of 140 (systolic) over 90 (diastolic) or higher

general adaptation syndrome (GAS) a three-stage model for understanding the body's physical and psychological reactions to biological stressors

migraine headaches moderate to severe pain resulting from constriction of the cranial arteries followed by dilation of the cerebral blood vessels

posttraumatic stress disorder (PTSD) disorder characterized by anxiety, dissociative, and other symptoms that last for more than one month and that occur as a result of exposure to extreme trauma

psychophysiological disorder any physical disorder that has a strong psychological basis or component

relaxation training therapeutic technique in which a person acquires the ability to relax the muscles of the body in almost any circumstance

stress an internal psychological or physiological response to a stressor

stressors external events or situations that place a physical or psychological demand on a person

tension headaches produced by prolonged contraction of the scalp and neck muscles, resulting in vascular constriction and steady pain

CHAPTER 8

Personality Disorders

TABLE OF CONTENTS

LEARNING OBJECTIVES

1. Discuss personality disorders and how they are viewed.

2. Describe which personality disorders are considered odd or eccentric.

3. Describe which personality disorders are considered dramatic, emotional, or erratic.

4. Describe which personality disorders are considered anxious and fearful.

5. Discuss how the multi-path model explains antisocial personality disorder.

6. List what types of therapy are used in treating antisocial personality disorder.

CHAPTER OUTLINE

I. **Diagnosing personality disorders** *Personality disorders* involve longstanding, inflexible, and maladaptive behavior patterns that produce personal and social difficulties, personal distress, or problems in functioning in society. They account for about 5 to 15 percent of admissions to hospitals and outpatient clinics; lifetime prevalence for all of them is 9 to 13 percent. Men are more likely than women to be diagnosed with some of the personality disorders, whereas women are more likely to be diagnosed with others. There are reasons to suggest that the gender distribution may be due to bias in diagnosing. Diagnosis is made on Axis II of the DSM, but diagnosis is difficult because symptoms represent extremes of normal personality traits, are rarely stable across situations, and may overlap with other disorders. Further, clinicians often render diagnoses inconsistent with DSM criteria. To be considered disorders personality patterns must cause significant impairment in functioning or subjective distress, a constellation of characteristics must be found, the personality pattern must characterize the person's current and long-term functioning, and the pattern must not be limited to episodes of illness. Further, there may be questions about the universality of these disorders and the cultural validity of DSM-IV-TR personality disorders.

II. **Disorders characterized by odd or eccentric behaviors** *Paranoid personality disorder* is characterized by suspiciousness, hypersensitivity, and reluctance to trust others. DSM-IV-TR estimates the prevalence of paranoid personality disorder as between 0.5 and 4.4 percent. Psychodynamic explanations emphasize the role of projection in the disorder, *Schizoid personality disorder* is marked by aloofness and voluntary social isolation. To avoid conflicts and emotional involvements, these people withdraw from others or comply superficially with requests from others. The relationship between this disorder and schizophrenia is not clear. *Schizotypal personality disorder* involves odd thoughts and actions, such as speech oddities or beliefs in personal magical powers, and poor interpersonal relationships. It occurs in approximately 3 percent of the population. Odd though their behaviors are, individuals with this disorder are not as impaired as people with schizophrenia.

III. **Disorders characterized by dramatic, emotional, or erratic behaviors.** Prevalence is about 1 percent. *Antisocial personality disorder* involves exploitation of others, irresponsibility, and guiltlessness, and is far more common in men than women. In the United States, the incidence of antisocial personality disorder is estimated to be about 2.0–3.6 percent overall; rates differ by gender with more men than women diagnosed with the disorder. *Borderline personality disorder* is characterized by extreme fluctuations in mood: friendly one day, hostile the next. People with this disorder also lack identity, feel lost and empty they engage in self-destructive behaviors. The core aspects seem to be difficulty in regulating emotions, and intense, unstable relationships. Females are three times more likely to receive the diagnosis than men. The disorder has been conceptualized from a psychodynamic perspective (object splitting—either people are completely good or completely bad), a social learning viewpoint (conflict between attachment to others and avoidance of such engagement), and a cognitive approach (distorted attributions and assumptions). *Histrionic personality disorder* is marked by self-dramatization, exaggerated emotional expression, and attention-seeking behaviors. It affects 1 to 3 percent of the population. Biological factors, such as autonomic or emotional excitability, and environmental factors, such as parental reinforcement of attention-seeking behaviors, may influence the development of histrionic personality disorder. *Narcissistic personality disorder* involves an exaggerated sense of self-importance, exploitative attitude, and lack of empathy.

IV. **Disorders characterized by anxious or fearful behaviors** Individuals with *avoidant personality disorder* desire interpersonal contact but fear social rejection; they avoid situations that might lead to criticism. Their primary defense mechanism is fantasy, and their social skills are weak. Prevalence is about 1 percent of the population, with no gender differences and there seems to be disagreement about whether it is a separate diagnosis from social phobia or an extension of that disorder. People with *dependent personality disorder* are characterized by an extreme lack of self-confidence, reliance on others for decisions, and an ingrained assumption that they are inadequate and must be cared for by others. Prevalence of the disorder is about 2.5 percent. *Obsessive-compulsive personality disorder* is marked by excessive perfectionism, devotion to details, rigidity, and indecisiveness. Unlike obsessive-compulsive disorder, there are no recurrent unwanted thoughts or ritualistic actions. Prevalence is about 1 percent, but a recent study place it at 7.9 percent with twice as many males as females having the disorder.

V. **Multi-path analysis of one personality disorder: Antisocial personality disorder**. There has been an extraordinary amount of research in the biological dimension devoted to trying to uncover the biological basis of APD. Indeed, early researchers concentrated primarily on using genetics, central nervous system abnormalities, and autonomic nervous system abnormalities to explain the disorder. Under genetic influences many people have speculated that some individuals are born to "raise hell." It is not uncommon for casual observers to remark that antisocials, criminals, and sociopaths appear to have an inborn temperament toward aggressiveness, sensation seeking, impulsivity, and a disregard for others. Central nervous system abnormality suggest that adults with antisocial personalities tend to have abnormal brain wave activity similar to that of young children. Other interesting research points to the involvement of the autonomic nervous system (ANS) in the prominent features of APD. Genetic predisposition to fearlessness or lack of anxiety also have been investigated. Psychological dimension explanations of personality disorders and specifically APD tend to fall into three camps: psychodynamic, cognitive, and social learning. According to psychodynamic approaches, the psychopath's absence of guilt and frequent violation of moral and ethical standards are the result of faulty superego development. Cognitive explanations of APD stress the relationship of core beliefs that influence behavior. These core beliefs operate on a nonconscious level, occur automatically, and influence emotions and behaviors. Learning theories stress a number of different forces in explaining APD: (1) inherent neurobiological characteristics that delay or impede learning, (2) lack of positive roles models in developing prosocial behaviors, or (3) presence of poor role models. In all cases, whether we are speaking about classical conditioning, operant conditioning, or social modeling, it is proposed that biology or social/developmental factors combine in unique ways to influence the development of APD. In the social dimension many factors that have been implicated in the development of personality disorders, but relationships within the family—the primary agent of socialization—are paramount in the development of antisocial patterns. The study of culture and personality has always been of fascination to early anthropologists who believed that culture shapes its development or that it represents an expanded extension of personality. *Impulse control disorders* are unrelated to personality disorders and are included in this chapter for the sake of convenience. These disorders involve an inability to resist the temptation to perform some act, a feeling of tension before the act, and a sense of excitement, release, and sometimes guilt afterward. *Intermittent explosive disorder* is marked by brief episodes of losing control, leading to destruction of property or assaults on other people. *Kleptomania* involves stealing, even when the article is not needed. It appears to be more common in women than men. *Pathological gambling* involves an inability to resist impulses to gamble and afflicts 1 to 3 percent of American adults. Cognitive-behavioral approaches focus on the erroneous beliefs gamblers have about their ability to influence outcomes that are governed by chance. *Pyromaniacs* repeatedly and deliberately set fires without the motive of revenge. Children who are fire-setters are more often boys than girls and have problems with impulsivity and hostility. *Trichotillomania* is the inability to refrain from pulling out one's hair. It is probably more common in women than men; about 1 percent of college students have a past or current history of the disorder.

VI. **Treatment of antisocial personality disorder** Owing to their lack of anxiety, antisocial personalities are poorly motivated to change. Behavior modification and cognitive therapies have been somewhat helpful, but effective treatments for antisocial personality are rare. The focus might be placed on youths, who are more amenable to treatment.

VII. **Implications.** Although personality disorders have generated rich clinical examples and speculation, not much empirical research has been conducted to provide definitive insights into the causes of the disorders. Many researchers use the five-factor model of personality, which describes personality patterns in terms of *neuroticism* (emotional adjustment and stability), *extraversion* (preference for interpersonal interactions, being fun-loving and active), *openness to experience* (curiosity, willingness to entertain new ideas and values, and emotional responsiveness), *agreeableness* (being good-natured, helpful, forgiving, and responsive), and *conscientiousness* (being organized, persistent, punctual, and self-directed).

KEY TERMS REVIEW

1. The personality disorder characterized by intense fluctuations in mood, self-image, and interpersonal relationships is called _____.

2. The personality disorder characterized by failure to conform to social rules, lack of guilt feelings for wrongdoing, and superficial relationships is called _____.

3. The impulse control disorder in which there is a recurrent failure to resist impulses to steal objects is called _____.

4. The personality disorder characterized by self-dramatization, exaggerated emotions, and attention-seeking behavior is called _____.

5. The group of maladaptive behavior patterns that are longstanding and interfere with productive living and that stem from distorted personality structure are called _____.

6. The personality disorder characterized by unwarranted suspiciousness, hypersensitivity, and a reluctance to trust others is called _____.

7. The disorders characterized by a failure to resist the temptation to perform an act that is harmful to oneself or others are called _____.

8. The personality disorder characterized by such oddities of thinking and behavior as frequent digressions in speech or a belief in personal magical powers is called _____.

9. The impulse control disorder that is marked mainly by deliberate fire setting is called _____.

10. The impulse control disorder characterized by an inability to resist pulling out one's hair is called _____.

11. The personality disorder characterized by a fear of rejection and humiliation and, as a result, reluctance to enter into social relationships, is called _____.

12. The personality disorder characterized by extreme reliance on others and an unwillingness to assume responsibility is called _____.

13. The impulse control disorder characterized by an inability to refrain from gambling is called _____.

14. The personality disorder characterized by social isolation and emotional coldness is called _____.

15. The personality disorder characterized by perfectionism, indecision, devotion to details, and rigidity in behavior is called _____.

16. The personality disorder characterized by egocentrism and an exaggerated sense of self-importance is called _____.

17. The impulse control disorder marked by loss of control overaggressive impulses is called _____.

18. _____ is a new impulse control disorder in the 2012 edition of DSM-V characterized by persons using the Internet so frequently that they isolate themselves from family and friends.

FACTUAL MULTIPLE-CHOICE QUESTIONS

1. Which statement below is accurate concerning the personality disorders?
   a. They are recorded on Axis I of the DSM-IV-TR.
   b. They have symptoms that can overlap with those of other disorders.
   c. Symptoms first appear in young adulthood.
   d. They are characterized by an inability to resist temptation.
2. Neuroticism, extraversion, and agreeableness are
   a. characteristics of the antisocial personality disorder.
   b. components of the five-factor model of personality.
   c. personality characteristics that are not influenced by cultural norms.
   d. characteristics found in all personality disorders.
3. Which of the following statements about histrionic personality disorder is *accurate*?
   a. It involves attention-seeking behavior and exaggerated emotional expression.
   b. It is characterized by withdrawal from other people.
   c. It is related to abnormally low levels of arousal.
   d. It is considered a disorder involving odd or eccentric behaviors.

4. How do narcissistic personalities relate to other people?

    a. Narcissistic personalities do not trust others.
    b. Narcissistic personalities rely on others' opinions.
    c. Narcissistic personalities feel superior to others.
    d. Narcissistic personalities avoid other people.

5. Extreme fluctuations in mood, an unstable identity, a sense of being empty, and intense but erratic interpersonal relationships are characteristics of _____ personality disorder.

    a. borderline
    b. antisocial
    c. histrionic
    d. dependent

6. Which description of antisocial personality is *accurate*?

    a. It is three times more common in women than in men.
    b. It is characterized by marked irresponsibility and lack of empathy.
    c. Attention to details and lack of expressed warmth are common symptoms.
    d. Development of symptoms usually occurs after the age of 18.

7. What is the incidence of antisocial personality in males in the United States?

    a. .5 percent
    b. 3 percent
    c. 20 percent
    d. 45 percent

8. _____ psychologists would explain the cause of antisocial personality in terms of inadequate superego development.

    a. Behavioral
    b. Physiological
    c. Humanistic
    d. Psychoanalytic

9. Both Lykken assume that antisocial personalities

    a. are fearless.
    b. are able to learn from punishment.
    c. have an excessively active autonomic nervous system.
    d. have an underlying fear of being humiliated by others.

10. According to psychodynamic theory, the irresistible actions and the feelings of excitement and guilt related to them in the impulse control disorders are evidence of

    a. traumatic experiences in early childhood.
    b. the sexual symbolism in these disorders.
    c. excessive superego development.
    d. anal fixation.

CONCEPTUAL MULTIPLE-CHOICE QUESTIONS

1. The principal feature of paranoid personality disorder is

    a. excessive attention to details and general perfectionism.
    b. wide fluctuations in mood and self-image.
    c. unwarranted suspiciousness.
    d. a desire to be alone.

2. Schizoid personality, disorder differs from schizotypal personality disorder in that in schizoid personality disorder there

     a.   is a withdrawal from other people.
     b.   is a possible genetic relationship to schizophrenia.
     c.   is unwarranted suspiciousness of other people.
     d.   are odd thoughts that border on delusions.

3. In this personality disorder, people believe they are innately inadequate and must rely on others for protection and information. They rarely express their own opinions. What is being described?

     a.   Borderline personality disorder
     b.   Dependent personality disorder
     c.   Narcissistic personality disorder
     d.   Obsessive-compulsive personality disorder

4. Perfectionism is to _____ personality disorder as fear of humiliation is to _____ personality disorder.

     a.   borderline; obsessive-compulsive
     b.   obsessive-compulsive; avoidant
     c.   narcissistic; histrionic
     d.   obsessive-compulsive; histrionic

5. Cleckley's indicators include lack of anxiety and superficial charm; the DSM-IV-TR criteria include breaking social norms and acting impulsively. What is being described?

     a.   Narcissistic personality disorder
     b.   Histrionic personality disorder
     c.   Antisocial personality disorder
     d.   Impulse control disorders

6. Which of the following is a problem when criminal psychopaths are used in research an antisocial personality disorder?

     a.   Very few antisocial personalities engage in criminal behavior.
     b.   Criminals, unlike antisocial personalities, tend to request treatment for psychological problems.
     c.   Criminals may not be representative of nonprison psychopaths.
     d.   Criminals tend to be male, whereas noncriminal psychopaths tend to be female.

7. Twin and adoption studies of antisocial personalities tend to

     a.   support the idea that the disorder is inherited.
     b.   reject the idea that the disorder is inherited.
     c.   explain why females are especially likely to develop the disorder.
     d.   highlight the role of the superego in the disorder.

8. Research on antisocial personalities shows that they make fewer errors in avoiding punishment when

     a.   they are given tranquilizers.
     b.   punishment means losing money.
     c.   punishment is highly uncertain.
     d.   their arousal level is low.

9. In general, there are few effective treatments for antisocial personality disorder because

     a.   there are so few people with the disorder.
     b.   antisocial personalities suffer from extreme anxiety.
     c.   the neurotransmitter imbalance of antisocial personalities cannot be offset by medication.
     d.   antisocial personalities are unmotivated for treatment.

10. What do pyromania, kleptomania, and trichotillomania have in common?

   a. They all affect women more than men.
   b. They are all personality disorders.
   c. They all involve lower than normal levels of arousal.
   d. They are all impulse control disorders.

APPLICATION MULTIPLE-CHOICE QUESTIONS

1. Irma, age 29, spends her days alone in her room playing records and looking at magazines. She has no desire to talk with others, and has had no intimate relationships in her life. Irma illustrates which personality disorder?

   a. Avoidant
   b. Obsessive-compulsive
   c. Schizoid
   d. Antisocial

2. Dr. Clopper says, "Georgette is an unusual case of histrionic personality. She constantly seeks attention, dramatically 'performs' emotions, and demands perfection of herself and others." What is unusual about the case?

   a. Most histrionics are shy and withdrawn.
   b. Most histrionics are not perfectionistic.
   c. Most histrionics are unable to express emotions.
   d. Most histrionics are men.

3. "The incompetence of my subordinates upsets me. If I didn't have ignorant people holding me down, I'd get the promotions I deserve." People with which personality disorder are most likely to make such statements?

   a. Narcissistic
   b. Dependent
   c. Obsessive-compulsive
   d. Avoidant

4. A psychologist says, "Because of early childhood experiences, these people see others as either all good or all bad. That accounts for their tremendous swings in mood and self-image." The psychologist is giving a _____ explanation for _____ personality disorder.

   a. behavioral; antisocial
   b. psychodynamic; borderline
   c. psychodynamic; avoidant
   d. behavioral; borderline

5. Shandra is an accountant with a passion for details. She is so perfectionistic, she drives everyone else crazy. These behaviors best illustrate the _____ personality disorder.

   a. schizotypal
   b. avoidant
   c. narcissistic
   d. obsessive-compulsive

6. Juan is diagnosed as a primary psychopath. He exploits other people and feels guilt about it. He has been imprisoned repeatedly for small crimes because he acts impulsively and fails to learn from his mistakes. What is unusual about this case?

   a. Most antisocial personalities are women.
   b. Most antisocial personalities learn from mistakes.
   c. Most antisocial personalities experience no guilt.
   d. Most antisocial personalities plan their crimes carefully.

7.   While interviewing a client whom he suspects should be diagnosed with _____,
     Dr. Hill asks many questions about whether the client's father was an impulsive criminal, a hostile
     and rejecting parent, or physically abusive.

     a.   borderline personality disorder
     b.   kleptomania
     c.   antisocial personality disorder
     d.   pathological gambling

8.   Tom is diagnosed as an antisocial personality. He takes several psychological tests and is
     measured for physiological arousal when under stress. What ought to be the results of the tests and
     physiological measures?

     a.   He is highly fearful, but has a low arousal level.
     b.   He is a "Big T" and has a low arousal level.
     c.   He is a "little t" and has a high arousal level.
     d.   He is fearless and has a high arousal level.

9.   A psychologist says, "Unlike pyromania and kleptomania, this impulse control disorder does not
     involve an action that is harmful to others. Indeed, the irresistible response in this disorder is
     physically painful to the person with the disorder." What disorder is being discussed?

     a.   Trichotillomania
     b.   Intermittent explosive disorder
     c.   Antisocial personality disorder
     d.   Pathological gambling

10. A student goes to the library to study about impulse control disorders. The student is likely to find
     that

     a.   there is little research on their cause.
     b.   they are very similar to anxiety disorders.
     c.   behavioral and cognitive behavioral therapies are totally ineffective.
     d.   the cause of these disorders is neurological.

ANSWER KEY: KEY TERMS REVIEW

1.   borderline personality disorder

2.   antisocial personality disorder

3.   kleptomania

4.   histrionic personality disorder

5.   personality disorders

6.   paranoid personality disorder

7.   impulse control disorders

8.   schizotypal personality disorder

9.   pyromania

10. trichotillomania

11. avoidant personality disorder

12. dependent personality disorder

13. pathological gambling

14. schizoid personality disorder

15. obsessive-compulsive personality disorder

16. narcissistic personality disorder

17. intermittent explosive disorder

18. Internet addiction

ANSWER KEY: FACTUAL MULTIPLE-CHOICE QUESTIONS

1. b.   One problem with diagnosing personality disorders is that symptoms, such as suspiciousness, overlap with those of other disorders, such as paranoia or paranoid schizophrenia.

   a.   The major clinical syndrome is recorded on Axis I; personality disorders are listed an Axis I.

   c.   Personality disorders usually become evident during adolescence or earlier.

   d.   An inability to resist temptation is associated with the impulse control disorders.

2. b.   The five-factor model (FFM) of personality includes neuroticism, extraversion, openness to experience, agreeableness, and conscientiousness.

   a.   The antisocial personality disorder is characterized by impulsivity, thrill seeking, and law breaking; it is not associated with neuroticism or agreeableness.

   c.   People from different cultures exhibit different personality characteristics; it is unlikely that these three are immune from cultural forces.

   d.   Some of the components of the five-factor model may be present in some of the personality disorders; what all personality disorders have in common are inflexible, maladaptive patterns of behavior that cause distress or functional impairment.

3. a.   Histrionic personality disorder is characterized by attention-seeking behavior, exaggerated emotional displays, and egocentric self-dramatization.

   b.   Histrionics need the attention of others; they seek out people rather than withdrawing from them.

   c.   There is no evidence that low arousal is related to histrionic personality disorder.

   d.   Histrionic personality disorder is categorized with those disorders involving "emotional or erratic behaviors."

4. c.   Narcissistic personalities feature inflated self-importance, which is propped up by devaluing others.

   a.   Paranoid personalities do not trust other people.

   b.   Dependent personalities rely on others' opinions.

   d.   Schizoid personalities tend to avoid other people.

5. a.   Extreme fluctuations in mood and self-image, impulsivity, and underlying feelings of purposelessness are key symptoms of borderline personality disorder.

   b.   Antisocial personalities use other people and do little self-evaluation, so there is rarely a time of low self-image.

   c.   Histrionic personalities can have mood swings, but this is coupled with attention-seeking behavior, seductiveness, and shallowness.

   d.   Dependent personalities rely on others for advice and information.

6. b.   Irresponsibility, impulsivity, lack of empathy, and lack of remorse are key features of antisocial personality.

    a.   The reverse is true: antisocial personality is three times more likely in men than in women.

    c.   Attention to details is a sign of obsessive-compulsive personality disorder.

    d.   All personality disorders show symptoms in adolescence or earlier.

7. b.   Although it is estimated that prevalence for antisocial personality disorder is 2 percent of the adult population in the United States, the prevalence for males is 3 percent.

    a.   1 percent or less is the incidence for females in the United States.

    c.   20 percent is roughly seven times the U.S. male incidence rate.

    d.   45 percent is roughly fifteen times the U.S. male incidence rate.

8. d.   Psychoanalysts see morality and self-control as stemming from the superego; lack of parental identification produces a faulty superego.

    a.   Behaviorists would stress modeling and inconsistent reinforcement.

    b.   Physiological psychologists would stress nervous system abnormalities.

    c.   Humanistic psychologists are not typically concerned with antisocial personalities but might stress social conditions.

9. a.   Lykken and Farley report that psychopaths enjoy taking risks and showing their fearlessness.

    b.   Eysenck's research shows that they learn slowly.

    c.   Fearlessness and lack of anxiety stem from underarousal in the autonomic nervous system.

    d.   Fear of humiliation is a problem for people with avoidant personality disorder.

10. b.   Psychoanalysts see each forbidden behavior as linked to sex; for instance, gambling and masturbation or stealing and sexual gratification.

    a.   Early traumatic experiences are not necessarily associated with these disorders.

    c.   Excessive superego concern is expressed in perfectionism and a need to obey all rules.

    d.   Anal fixation is associated with stinginess and stubbornness.

ANSWER KEY: CONCEPTUAL MULTIPLE-CHOICE QUESTIONS

1. c.   Paranoid personality disorder is characterized by suspiciousness without cause and by emotional distance from others.

    a.   Excessive attention to details is a feature of obsessive-compulsive personality disorder.

    b.   Wide fluctuations in mood and self-image are related to borderline personality disorder.

    d.   A desire to be alone can be associated with the schizoid personality disorder and with complete normality.

2. a. Although both personality disorders have some symptoms in common with schizophrenia, schizoid personality disorder is marked by the social withdrawal that is seen in schizophrenia.

    b. The genetic links to schizophrenia are not as clear for schizoid personality disorder as they are for schizotypal.

    c. Unwarranted suspiciousness is most important in paranoid personality disorder.

    d. Odd thoughts are the key symptom of schizotypal personality disorder; social withdrawal is seen as secondary to cognitive difficulties.

3. b. Dependent personalities rely on others for their ideas because they have low self-confidence.

    a. Borderline personalities have mood swings; they have no trouble expressing opinions.

    c. Narcissistic personalities devalue others to inflate their own self-concept and feel superior to others.

    d. Obsessive-compulsives take on many responsibilities and attempt to execute them perfectly.

4. b. Perfectionism is a core feature of people with obsessive-compulsive personality disorder, and avoidant personalities fear criticism from and embarrassment in front of others.

    a. Perfectionism is a characteristic of obsessive-compulsive personalities, not borderlines.

    c. Narcissistic personalities do not strive for perfectionism; if they are sloppy, they blame others.

    d   Histrionic personalities seek attention from others; they do not fear being humiliated.

5. c. Antisocial personality disorder has these two sets of symptoms, which overlap somewhat.

    a   Narcissistic personality involves an inflated self-concept; there is no alternative diagnostic criteria.

    b. Histrionics are attention seekers who have exaggerated emotional displays.

    d. Impulse control disorders only involve recurrent failure to resist an urge.

6. c. Imprisoned psychopaths have been studied because they are clearly a captive audience, but it is unclear whether they are representative; they might be more impulsive than others, since they got caught.

    a. Research with nonprison populations shows that antisocials engage in a great deal of criminal behavior.

    b. Antisocials, both inside and outside of prison do not feel there is anything wrong with them.

    d. There is no evidence that nonprison psychopaths are any more likely to be female, but even if there were this bias, c is a more general answer.

7. a. Both kinds of studies find that the greater the genetic similarity of one person to an antisocial personality, the greater the likelihood that that person is antisocial, too.

    b. Twin and adoption studies support genetic theory.

    c. Females are less likely to develop the disorder.

    d. The superego is related to psychoanalysis.

8.   b.   When punishment was defined as losing money (rather than electric shock), antisocial personalities learned the avoidance task better.

      a.   Tranquilizers would further reduce the already low arousal level of antisocial personalities.

      c.   Antisocial personalities learn less well when there is high uncertainty about when punishment will occur.

      d.   A reason that they learn poorly is that their arousal level is too low.

9.   d.   Because of underarousal, antisocial personalities are not motivated for treatment; they usually consider therapy a joke.

      a.   With an incidence of 3 percent among males in the United States, antisocial personality disorder is fairly common.

      b.   Antisocial personalities experience abnormally low levels of anxiety.

      c.   There is no clear neurotransmitter imbalance.

10.   d.   Since all these disorders involve both an inability to resist some behavior and excitement or guilt when engaged in that behavior, they are impulse control disorders.

      a.   There is no evidence for a sex difference in these disorders.

      b.   None of them is a personality disorder.

      c.   Antisocial personality involves abnormally low levels of arousal; there is no evidence for such a deficit in these disorders.

ANSWER KEY: APPLICATION MULTIPLE-CHOICE QUESTIONS

1.   c.   Social isolation is the key symptom of schizoid personality disorder.

      a.   Although avoidant personalities may spend time alone, they crave attention and uncritical acceptance.

      b.   Obsessive-compulsive personality disorder is marked by attention to detail and perfectionism.

      d.   Antisocial personalities seek others out so that they can exploit them.

2.   b.   Histrionics are impressionistic and vague; they are not perfectionists.

      a.   Histrionics seek attention, so they are rarely withdrawn.

      c.   Histrionics are constantly expressing emotions that appear, after a while, to be superficial.

      d.   More women are diagnosed with histrionic personality disorder than men, perhaps because it is a caricature of traditional femininity.

3.   a.   The central feature of narcissistic personality disorder is inflated self-importance, which is demonstrated by devaluing others.

      b.   Dependent personalities would not make a statement like this; they have very low self-confidence.

      c.   Obsessive-compulsive personality disorder is marked by perfectionism and a lack of warmth.

      d.   Avoidant personality disorder involves hypersensitivity to criticism by others.

4.   b.   Psychoanalysts believe that the borderline person has split the world into "good objects" and "bad objects," which accounts for the extreme mood swings seen in the disorder.

    a.   Behaviorists would stress the reinforcements for exploiting others (antisocial personality).

    c.   Avoidant personality disorder does not involve such wide fluctuations of mood.

    d.   Behaviorists would stress the reinforcements for being changeable.

5.   d.   Individuals diagnosed with obsessive-compulsive personality disorder are devoted to details and insist that everything be done perfectly.

    a.   Schizotypal personalities have odd thoughts and ways of speaking.

    b.   Avoidant personality disorder involves hypersensitivity to criticism and fantasies of being loved.

    c.   Inflated self-importance is the hallmark of narcissistic personality disorder.

6.   c.   Primary psychopaths feel no guilt over their antisocial actions.

    a.   Most antisocial personalities are men.

    b.   Most antisocial personalities fail to learn from mistakes.

    d.   Impulsivity is a central feature of antisocial personality disorder; antisocial personalities rarely plan their crimes carefully.

7.   c.   Family and socialization theory suggests that antisocial personality develops in families where fathers model antisocial behavior and parents are hostile and rejecting.

    a.   Borderline personality disorder may be related to splitting the world into "all good" and "all bad."

    b.   There is no evidence that kleptomania stems from parental rejection or the modeling of impulsivity.

    d.   Pathological gambling is too little understood to suggest this pattern of development.

8.   b.   Farley has coined the term "Big T" for thrill seekers such as psychopaths; Lykken's and other research show psychopaths to be low in autonomic arousal.

    a.   Research shows that antisocial personality is associated with fearlessness.

    c.   "Little t's" avoid reckless activity, making them the opposite of antisocial personalities.

    d.   High arousal during stress is true of nonpsychopaths; psychopaths keep their cool when everyone else would be emotional.

9.   a.   Trichotillomania—uncontrolled hair pulling—harms only oneself, not others.

    b.   The physical and verbal aggression of intermittent explosive disorder certainly hurts others.

    c.   Antisocial personality disorder involves the exploitation of others and invariably produces harmful consequences for others.

    d.   Pathological gambling may be harmful to oneself, but cannot be seen as physically damaging.

10. a. There is very little research on the cause of impulse control disorders.

    b. Impulse control disorders have more similarities with substance abuse disorders and sexual deviations.

    c. Booth's (1988) review shows that behavioral and cognitive behavioral methods can be helpful.

    d. There is no evidence that impulse control disorders are caused by neurological factors.

OBJECTIVES DEFINED

1. **What are personality disorders and how are they viewed?**

- Personality disorders are enduring, inflexible, long-standing maladaptive personality traits that cause significant functional impairment, subjective distress or a combination of both. DSM-IV-TR lists ten specific personality disorders; each causes notable impairment of social or occupational functioning or subjective distress for the person. They are usually manifested in adolescence, continue into adulthood, and involve disturbances in personality characteristics.

- There are differences in thought as to whether personality disorders should be viewed categorically or in a dimensional manner (extremes on a continuum of normal personality traits). The personality disorders include a diversity of behavioral patterns in people who are typically perceived as being odd or eccentric; dramatic, emotional, and erratic; or anxious and fearful.

2. **What personality disorders are considered odd or eccentric?**

- The three personality disorders in this cluster are paranoid personality disorder (suspiciousness, hypersensitivity, and mistrust); schizoid personality disorder (social isolation and indifference to others); and schizotypal personality disorder (peculiar thoughts and behaviors).

3. **What personality disorders are considered dramatic and emotional?**

- The four personality disorders in this cluster are antisocial personality disorder (failure to conform to social or legal codes of conduct); borderline personality disorder (intense mood and self image fluctuations); histrionic personality disorder (self-dramatization and attention seeking behaviors); and narcissistic personality disorder (sense of self importance and lack of empathy).

4. **What personality disorders are considered anxious and fearful?**

- The three personality disorders in this cluster are avoidant personality disorder (fear of rejection and humiliation); dependent personality disorder (reliance on others and inability to assume responsibility); and obsessive-compulsive personality disorder (perfectionism and interpersonally controlling).

5. **How does the multi-path model explain antisocial personality disorder?**

- Because personality is at the core of the disorder, etiological explanations focus on factors that influence personality. Genetics and neurobiological factors (underarousal of ANS and low anxiety), psychodynamic, cognitive and learning formulations, social or parental and family environments, and sociocultural factors (gender, race, and culture) all seem to contribute in a highly complex fashion.

6. **What types of therapy are used in treating antisocial personality disorder?**

- Traditional treatment approaches are not particularly effective with antisocial personalities. It may be that successful treatment can occur only in a setting in which behavior can be controlled. That is, treatment programs may need to provide enough control so that those with antisocial personalities cannot avoid confronting their inability to form close and intimate relationships and the effect of their behaviors on others.

MARGIN DEFINITIONS

antisocial personality disorder a personality disorder characterized by a failure to conform to social and legal codes, by a lack of anxiety and guilt, and by irresponsible behaviors

avoidant personality disorder a personality disorder characterized by a fear of rejection and humiliation and a reluctance to enter into social relationships

borderline personality disorder a personality disorder characterized by intense fluctuations in mood, self-image, and interpersonal relationships

dependent personality disorder a personality disorder characterized by reliance on others and an unwillingness to assume responsibility

histrionic personality disorder a personality disorder characterized by self-dramatization, exaggerated expression of emotions, and attention-seeking behaviors

impulse control disorder a disorder in which the person fails to resist an impulse or temptation to perform some act that is harmful to the person or to others; the person feels tension before the act and release after it

intermittent explosive disorder impulse control disorder characterized by separate and discrete episodes of loss of control over aggressive impulses, resulting in serious assaults on others or destruction of property

Internet addiction a new impulse control disorder in the 2012 edition of DSM-V characterized by persons using the Internet so frequently that they isolate themselves from family and friends

kleptomania an impulse control disorder characterized by a recurrent failure to resist impulses to steal objects

narcissistic personality disorder a personality disorder characterized by an exaggerated sense of self-importance, an exploitative attitude, and a lack of empathy

obsessive-compulsive personality disorder a personality disorder characterized by perfectionism, a tendency to be interpersonally controlling, devotion to details, and rigidity

paranoid personality disorder a personality disorder characterized by unwarranted suspiciousness, hypersensitivity, and a reluctance to trust others

pathological gambling an impulse control disorder in which the essential feature is a chronic and progressive failure to resist impulses to gamble

personality disorder a disorder characterized by inflexible, long-standing, and maladaptive personality traits that cause significant functional impairment, subjective distress, or a combination of both for the individual

pyromania an impulse control disorder having as its main feature deliberate and purposeful fire setting on more than one occasion

schizoid personality disorder a personality disorder characterized by social isolation, emotional coldness, and indifference to others

schizotypal personality disorder a personality disorder characterized by peculiar thoughts and behaviors and by poor interpersonal relationships

trichotillomania an impulse control disorder characterized by an inability to resist impulses to pull out one's own hair

CHAPTER 9

Substance-Related Disorders

TABLE OF CONTENTS

LEARNING OBJECTIVES

1. Define the substance-use disorders.

2. Explain why people develop substance-use disorders.

3. Describe what kinds of interventions and treatments are available for substance-use disorders and what treatments work?

CHAPTER OUTLINE

I.   **Substance-use disorders.** *Substance-related disorders* involve drug use that alters one's psychological state and causes significant physical, social, or occupational problems and sometimes results in abuse or dependence. *Substance-use* disorders involve abuse or dependence; substance-induced disorders involve withdrawal or delirium. DSM-IV-TR defines *substance abuse as* recurrent use over twelve months that leads to impairment or distress, and continues despite problems. *Substance dependence* adds the concepts of tolerance (needing increased dosages) and *withdrawal* (physical or emotional symptoms after reduced intake). Further, *intoxication* refers to central nervous system effects, following ingestion of a drug that involves maladaptive behaviors or thinking. Dependence is the more serious condition. Depressants or sedatives cause generalized depression of the central nervous system and a slowing of responses. They induce feelings of calm, but may also make people more social and open because of lowered inhibitions. Alcohol-use disorder involves alcohol abuse and alcohol dependence; people with these disorders are referred to as alcoholics, and their disorder is alcoholism. Problem drinking often begins as a way to reduce anxiety and expands to heavier drinking. Some drink daily, others binge. About 35 percent of Americans abstain from alcohol, but 10 percent of the drinkers consume 50 percent of all alcohol consumed in this country. Men drink two to five times as much a women; and heavy drinking is most common between ages 18 and 25. Its short-term psychological effects include poor judgment, feelings of happiness, and reduced concentration, but the precise effects are influenced by the situational context. Long-term effects are serious: some drinkers become preoccupied with thoughts of alcohol, experience blackouts, lose control over their consumption; deteriorating Physiological effects can include liver damage, heart disease, and cancers of the mouth and throat. Moderate use is associated with lowered risk of heart disease. Narcotics, which include opium and its derivatives morphine, heroin, and codeine, act as sedatives and are addictive. Tolerance builds rapidly and withdrawal is severe. Twenty-five percent of AIDS cases involve persons who abuse intravenous drugs. Prevalence of addiction decreases with age. Synthetic barbiturates are legal medications and are used mostly by middle-aged and older people to induce sleep and relaxation; however, next to narcotics, they represent the largest category of illegal drugs. By themselves, barbiturates can be addictive and can be accidentally overdosed; combined with alcohol, barbiturates can lead to fatal overdoses. Polysubstance use, using more than one chemical substance at the same time, may (among other things) result in synergistic effects that depress the central nervous system and cause death. One of the most widely prescribed benzodiazepines in the country is Valium, a central nervous system depressant used to reduce anxiety and muscle tension. Three times as many females as males, and whites as compared with blacks, use benzodiazepines. A *stimulant* energizes the central nervous system. One example is an *amphetamine,* which increases alertness and inhibits both appetite and sleep. Tolerance builds quickly, and chronic high doses can lead to aggressive behavior. Lifetime prevalence of amphetamine abuse or dependence is about 2 percent. Caffeine and nicotine are both legal and widely used stimulants. Caffeine has mild effects; nicotine is the single most preventable cause of death in the United States. Although 72 percent of the adult population in the United States reported never having smoked cigarettes, about 30 percent of the U.S. population currently smokes. Nicotine dependence symptoms are unsuccessful attempts to stop, withdrawal symptoms after stopping, and continued use despite such illnesses as emphysema. *Cocaine* induces feelings of self confidence in users. It is a fashionable drug, and there are from one to three million cocaine abusers in need of treatment in the United States. Cocaine is typically snorted. Crack, a rock like, purified form of cocaine, is smoked, resulting in rapid euphoria followed by depression. Cocaine and amphetamines alter moods by increasing brain dopamine levels. Crack is a major social concern because it is inexpensive, easy to acquire, produces an intense high, leads to rapid addiction, and is associated with crime. *Hallucinogens* are not believed to be physically addicting, although psychological dependence may occur. They produce hallucinations, vivid sensory awareness, and perceptions of increased insight. Over 40 percent of the U.S. population has used *marijuana,* although it is illegal. Technically, the DSM-IV-TR does not consider marijuana a hallucinogen. Marijuana is a mild hallucinogen that produces euphoria, passivity, and memory impairment. There is considerable controversy concerning its short- and long-term physical and psychological effects. *Lysergic acid diethylamide (LSD)* is a psychotornimetic drug that alters visual and auditory perceptions and can produce flashbacks. It does not produce physical dependence. *Phencyclidine (PCP)* is an extremely dangerous hallucinogen because it often leads to assaultive and suicidal behavior

II. **Etiology of substance-use disorders**. The biological dimension studies the genetic transmission of alcoholism is supported by evidence with children of alcoholics adopted by nonalcoholics and by twin research. Although the incidence of alcoholism is four times higher among male biological offspring of alcoholic fathers compared with the offspring of non-alcoholic father, no specific genes have been found to explain the causes of alcoholism. Biological markers for alcoholism have been suggested in the form of neurotransmitter differences and insensitivity to alcohol but firm causal links are yet to be found. There is less research on the hereditary basis for other substances. The psychological dimension uses behavioral explanations that originally focused on the tension-reducing properties of alcohol. However, in which alcoholics and social drinkers were led to believe they were drinking alcohol when they actually got tonic, showed that expectation has a strong influence on use. In the Cognitive area a number of researchers have focused less on tension reduction and more on the expectancies that are learned in substance use. Individuals who use drugs may come to expect feeling relaxed, confident, high, less anxious, and so on In the social dimension almost all explanations of substance use, social or interpersonal factors are considered important. For example, one may try drinking and maintain drinking because of pressures from peers, modeling after parents who drink, pressures from peers to drink and expecting to feel less anxious in social situations. In the sociocultural dimension drinking varies according to sociocultural factors such as gender, age, socioeconomic status, ethnicity, religion, and country. As mentioned previously, males and young adults consume more alcohol than females and older adults, respectively. Interestingly, consumption tends to increase with socioeconomic status, although alcoholism is more frequent in the middle socioeconomic classes

III. **Intervention and treatment of substance-use disorders**. A first step in most treatment programs is detoxification, the elimination of the chemical from the body. The second step tries to prevent the person from returning to the substance. Self-help groups, such as Alcoholics Anonymous, which stress support, spiritual awareness, and public self-revelations, are often helpful, but less so than members assert. The pharmacological approach uses chemicals such as Antabuse for alcohol and methadone for heroin treatment which can be useful but have the problem of individuals ceasing to take the medication. Naltrexone has been helpful for reducing alcohol and heroin cravings. Reasons for resuming smoking include physiological and psychological factors. Cognitive and behavioral therapies include aversion therapy, covert sensitization, rapid smoking, nicotine fading, spacing of cigarettes, relaxation training and coping-skills training; reinforcing abstinence has been effective for opiod-dependent person. There is considerable controversy about treatment for controlled drinking for alcoholics. In addition to the problem of retraining patients to drink socially, the researchers themselves have been attacked. Most treatment uses a multimodal effort, including inpatient individual and group therapy followed by outpatient treatment and support groups. Self-help programs often seek to educate the public about the negative consequences of substance use. In view of the many factors that maintain drug-use disorders, some treatment programs make systematic use of combinations of approaches, especially with approaches that have been shown to be effective. For example, alcoholics may be detoxified through Antabuse treatment and simultaneously receive behavioral training (via aversion therapy, biofeedback, or stress management) as well as other forms of therapy Prevention programs have been initiated to discourage drug and alcohol use before it begins or to reduce consumption among users. Campaigns to educate the public about the detrimental consequences of substance use, to reestablish norms against drug use, and to give coping skills to others who are tempted by drug use are waged in the media. Effectiveness of treatment research evidence indicates that treatment programs are effective in reducing substance abuse and dependence, although outcomes have been small to moderate and estimates vary from study to study.

IV. **Implications.** All human beings consume substances that alter moods, affect performance and skills, and change body and brain processes. In substance-use disorders, individuals cannot refrain from using drugs or they use them despite harmful effects. We now know that drugs alter brain processes and functioning in long-lasting ways.

KEY TERMS REVIEW

1. The treatment aimed at removing all alcohol (or other substance) from a user's body is called _____.

2. Excessive use of a substance leading to lack of control over use and impaired functioning is called _____.

3. Substance abuse or dependence in which the substance being used is alcohol is called _____.

4. The physical or emotional symptoms, such as shaking and irritability that appear when intake of a regularly used substance is halted are called _____.

5. A substance that causes general depression of the central nervous system and a slowing of responses is called a sedative or a(n) _____.

6. The pathological pattern of excessive use of a substance that results in impaired social and occupational functioning but not tolerance or withdrawal is called _____.

7. _____ are variables related to, or etiologically significant in, the development of a disorder.

8. A behavioral strategy designed to promote the abstinence of drugs is called
    _____.

9. People who abuse and depend on alcohol are called _____.

10. Substances known as "uppers" that speed up central nervous system activity and produce increased alertness and euphoria and, in chronic users, paranoia are called
    _____.

11. Substances known as "downers" that powerfully depress the central nervous system and can induce physical dependency and lethal overdose are called _____.

12. A drug that induces feelings of euphoria and self-confidence in users and is usually inhaled is called _____.

13. An aversive conditioning technique in which the individual imagines a noxious stimulus in t he presence of a behavior is called _____.

14. The conditioning procedure in which the response to a stimulus is decreased by pairing it with an aversive stimulus is called _____.

15. A substance that produces hallucinations, vivid sensory awareness, or feelings of increased insight is called a(n) _____.

16. The mildest and most commonly used hallucinogen is called _____.

17. An addictive substance that depresses the central nervous system, provides relief from pain and anxiety, and is derived from opium is called a(n) _____.

18. A psychoactive substance that energizes the central nervous system and causes elation, hyperactivity, and appetite suppression is called a(n) _____.

19. A maladaptive pattern of use extending over a twelve-month period and characterized by inability to control use and by tolerance or withdrawal symptoms is called _____.

20. The condition in which increasing doses of a substance are necessary to achieve a desired effect is called _____.

21. Substance dependence based not on any single substance but on the repeated use of at least three groups of substances for a period of twelve months is called _____.

22. Behavioral techniques used in drug treatment programs that are designed to improve one's communication, problem solving, and peer pressure refusal abilities are called
    _____.

FACTUAL MULTIPLE-CHOICE QUESTIONS

1. When increasing doses of a substance are necessary to achieve a desired effect, this
    a. is considered a substance-induced disorder.
    b. indicates tolerance for the drug.
    c. shows that the user will experience withdrawal.
    d. indicates the key symptom of substance abuse.
2. In the United States, substance-related disorders would most likely be expected in which population?
    a. Females under age 30
    b. African Americans and Hispanic Americans
    c. Males under age 30
    d. White males over age 45

3.   Which statement about alcohol consumption is accurate?

    a.   Roughly 50 percent of the alcohol consumed in the United States is consumed by 10 percent of the drinkers.

    b.   Women drink more frequently than men.

    c.   About 50 million Americans have been problem drinkers at some time in their lives.

    d.   Less than 10 percent of American adults abstain from drinking.

4.   Which of the following is a physiological effect of chronic alcohol use?

    a.   Intoxication

    b.   Flashbacks

    c.   Liver cirrhosis

    d.   Lung disease

5.   _____ are a category of drug that is widely prescribed for reduction of anxiety and muscle tension.

    a.   Hallucinogens

    b.   Opiates

    c.   Amphetamines

    d.   Benzodiazepines

6.   Which statement about marijuana is *accurate*?

    a.   It is the least commonly used hallucinogen.

    b.   When intoxicated, users are excited and time seems to pass quickly.

    c.   Prior experience and the setting in which it is used influence its effects.

    d.   It produces serious physiological withdrawal effects.

7.   The hallucinogen that is most related to uncontrolled aggression and delusional states is called

    a.   PCP.

    b.   marijuana.

    c.   LSD.

    d.   crack cocaine.

8.   Results from the study in which alcoholics and social drinkers drank either tonic or alcohol indicate that

    a.   alcoholism is a disease in which one loses control over drinking.

    b.   a subject's expectations have little effect on how much he or she drinks.

    c.   expectations are important only for social drinkers.

    d.   the disease concept of loss of control is inaccurate.

9.   According to Schachter, most smokers have difficulty quitting because of

    a.   expectation, since nicotine cannot be physically addicting.

    b.   the drug's ability to produce hallucinations.

    c.   physical addiction to nicotine.

    d.   the social pressures that smokers feel to fit in with their peers.

10.   Multimodal treatment for substance-related disorders entails

    a.   working with people who are addicted to several different chemicals.

    b.   extinguishing behaviors to many different cues and situations.

    c.   detoxifying people before they become involved with Alcoholics or Narcotics Anonymous.

    d.   inpatient treatment group therapy, individual psychotherapy, self-help groups, and behavior therapy.

CONCEPTUAL MULTIPLE-CHOICE QUESTIONS

1. The major difference between substance abuse and substance dependence is that in substance dependence,

    a. the problem has lasted one month or more.
    b. social functioning has been affected.
    c. there are signs of tolerance or withdrawal symptoms.
    d. the person shows other signs of mental disorder.

2. Heroin, barbiturates, and benzodiazepines have what in common?

    a. They are all depressants or sedatives.
    b. They are all illegal.
    c. None of them produces tolerance.
    d. None of them can be lethal.

3. Which drugs have their stimulant effect by increasing dopamine levels?

    a. Amphetamine and cocaine
    b. Alcohol and narcotics
    c. Marijuana and LSD
    d. Barbiturates and cocaine

4. There are two general explanations for substance-related disorders: _____ and _____.

    a. personality; environment
    b. biology; psychological/ cultural factors
    c. social class; education
    d. learning; psychoanalytic factors

5. Results of twin and adoption studies tend to

    a. support the idea that alcoholism is due to preexisting personality characteristics.
    b. reject the idea that alcoholism is hereditary.
    c. support the idea that alcoholism is a sociocultural phenomenon.
    d. support the idea that alcoholism is hereditary.

6. Which of the following is a biological marker related to alcoholism?

    a. Central nervous system functioning differences between alcoholics and nonalcoholics
    b. High concordance among identical twins
    c. The fact that children of alcoholics have a higher rate of alcoholism themselves
    d. Physiological response to Antabuse

7. Research by Shedler and Block compared the psychological adjustment of adolescents who abstained from drugs, experimented with drugs, or used drugs heavily. The results showed that

    a. heavy drug use caused maladjustment.
    b. abstainers were the least likely to have adjustment problems.
    c. those who experimented with drugs were best adjusted.
    d. all the "experimenters" became maladjusted, heavy users.

8. Which of the following statements strengthens the belief that cultural values play an important role in drinking patterns?

    a. Alcohol is a central nervous system depressant in all races.
    b. Although France and Italy have high rates of alcohol consumption, the rate of alcoholism is high in the U.S. and Russia.
    c. Recent research demonstrates that pregnant women who drink heavily have higher risk of giving birth to children with FAS.
    d. Antisocial behavior and depression are frequently associated with alcoholism.

9.   Early behavioral explanations for alcoholism emphasized findings that

a.   cats placed in approach-avoidance conflicts learn to prefer milk mixed with alcohol over regular milk.

b.   rats will refuse to drink alcohol-spiked water when they are under stress.

c.   in conditioning experiments, rats' responses indicate that alcohol is a more aversive stimulus than electric shocks.

d.   responses to alcohol in stress-producing situations are more a function of our expectations than of the chemical's effect.

10. The problem with methadone treatment is that

a.   it is part of an aversive behavior therapy that, clients drop out of before completing treatment.

b.   it substitutes one addiction for another.

c.   it relies heavily on the Alcoholics Anonymous requirement of spiritual awareness.

d.   it intensifies the experience of narcotic withdrawal.

APPLICATION MULTIPLE-CHOICE QUESTIONS

1.   Karen has been using marijuana for several months. Using the drug has led to several minor traffic accidents and a marked drop in her school grades. Her friends find her uninvolved and unhappy. She can go for several days without using pot and feels no craving. What diagnosis is appropriate for Karen?

a.   Substance use without abuse

b.   Substance abuse

c.   Substance dependence

d.   Addiction to stimulants

2.   You hear that an acquaintance smokes a drug that comes in the form of small pieces he calls "rocks." When he has smoked the drug he becomes euphoric, but when it is out of his system he feels depressed. What drug is he using?

a.   Cocaine

b.   LSD

c.   Crack

d.   Marijuana

3.   Fran looks back on her days of drug use and says, "The good trips were filled with startling hallucinations and feelings of ecstasy. But weeks later, I'd have 'flashbacks' at truly inopportune times, like when I was driving on the freeway." What drug did Fran use?

a.   Heroin

b.   Marijuana

c.   LSD

d.   Crack cocaine

4.   Dr. Enberg says, "Alcoholism is caused by frustration of oral dependency needs in infancy. Alcohol allows the expression of repressed feelings and gratification of oral needs." These remarks reflect the perspective.

a.   behavioral

b.   family systems

c.   biological-physical

d.   psychodynamic

5.   Dr. Gomez says, "There are two personality factors that are associated with drinking problems: low intelligence and a tendency to become depressed." Is anything wrong with the doctor's statement?

    a.   Yes, the personality factors associated with alcoholism are repression and antisocial behavior.

    b.   No, the doctor's statement is accurate.

    c.   Yes, no personality factors are associated with drinking problems.

    d.   Yes, the personality factors associated with alcoholism are antisocial behavior and depression.

6.   Jane quit smoking cigarettes in July and promised not to smoke another one. Now, in August, having had one cigarette, she feels guilty. Losing all sense of personal control, she smokes two packs of cigarettes the same day. According to behavioral explanations, what happened?

    a.   Nicotine sets up a physiological chain reaction that no one can stop.

    b.   She fell victim to the abstinence violation effect.

    c.   She experienced what is called covert sensitization.

    d.   She had stopped taking her Antabuse tablets.

7.   Sima says that when she first used narcotics, they produced a euphoric high, and that after the drug was out of her system there were only mild problems "coming down." Now, however, she only uses narcotics because they control the intense withdrawal effects of not using them. Her story best matches _____ model of drug use.

    a.   the cognitive-behavioral learned expectancy

    b.   Tiffany's automatic processes

    c.   the biogenic detoxification

    d.   Solomon's opponent-process

8.   Alvin says, "My treatment was successful because I became a part of a fellowship that provides support and increases spiritual awareness. That group saved my life!" What kind of treatment is Alvin describing?

    a.   Methadone maintenance

    b.   Systematic desensitization

    c.   Alcoholics Anonymous

    d.   Group behavior therapy

9.   Stanley is being treated for a substance-related disorder with a patch of medication he wears on his arm. The patch slowly helps him overcome the withdrawal effects of the substance he is trying to stop using. What is Stanley's problem?

    a.   LSD

    b.   Marijuana

    c.   Nicotine

    d.   Caffeine

10.   The mayor of a town says, "Drug prevention programs have never been shown to work. We must put our efforts into treatment of drug problems. Even so, treatment is only modestly effective, since only one-third of treated alcoholics remain abstinent, and most treated narcotics addicts are readdicted within a year of treatment." What portion of the mayor's statement is *inaccurate?*

    a.   It is inaccurate to say that. prevention has never been shown to work.

    b.   It is inaccurate to say that drug treatment has been modestly effective.

    c.   It is inaccurate to say that one-third of treated alcoholics are using again within a year of treatment.

    d.   It is inaccurate to say that most treated narcotic addicts are using again within a year of treatment.

ANSWER KEY: KEY TERMS REVIEW

1. detoxification
2. substance-related disorder
3. alcoholism
4. withdrawal
5. depressant
6. substance abuse
7. risk factors
8. reinforcing abstinence
9. alcoholics
10. amphetamines
11. barbiturates
12. cocaine
13. covert sensitization
14. aversion therapy
15. hallucinogen
16. marijuana
17. narcotic
18. stimulant
19. substance dependence
20. tolerance
21. polysubstance dependence
22. skills training

ANSWER KEY: FACTUAL MULTIPLE-CHOICE QUESTIONS

1. b.   Tolerance is defined as the need for increased doses of a drug to achieve. a particular effect.

   a.   Substance-induced disorders are those that cause delirium and other cognitive disorders.

   c.   Withdrawal occurs when there is distress when drug use stops

   d.   Substance abuse involves impairment due to drug use but does not require signs of tolerance; substance dependence involves tolerance.

2. c.   Substance-related disorders are most prevalent in youths and young adults and far more so in men than women.

   a.   Females are much less likely to have substance-related disorders than men.

   b.   White Americans have higher lifetime prevalence for drug abuse and dependence than African Americans or Hispanic Americans.

   d.   Although white males are more prone to substance-related disorders than nonwhites and women, the chief age groups for disorders are youths and young adults

3.   a.   Statistics show that a small number of drinkers (10 percent) account for half of all alcohol consumed.

     b.   Men drink two to five times as much as women.

     c.   The estimate is closer to 10 to 15 million; about 14 percent of the adults in the United States have drinking problems.

     d.   Roughly one-third of Americans do not drink at all.

4.   c.   Liver cirrhosis is one of the many serious physiological effects of chronic alcohol use; heart failure and cancers of the mouth and throat are others.

     a.   Intoxication is the physical and psychological effect of acute doses of a substance.

     b.   Flashbacks are symptoms of LSD use only.

     d.   Lung disease is an outcome of smoking, not drinking.

5.   d.   Benzodiazepines, such as Valium, are prescribed frequently for anxiety and tension reduction.

     a.   Hallucinogens are all illegal drugs, so they are not prescribed.

     b.   Opiates are narcotics; they are not prescribed for anxiety reduction.

     c.   Amphetamines are stimulants; they increase muscle tension.

6.   c.   The exact effects that marijuana has on the user are influenced by the persons past experience with the drug and by the setting in which it is taken.

     a.   Marijuana is the most commonly used hallucinogen.

     b.   The main effects of marijuana are calm, euphoria, passivity, and a feeling that time has slowed down.

     d.   There is no evidence of physiological withdrawal effects when people stop using marijuana.

7.   a.   Phencyclidine (PCP or "angel dust") is a hallucinogen that can produce homicidal aggression and delusions of such invincibility that people jump out of windows expecting to fly.

     b.   Marijuana is a mild hallucinogen that causes passivity, not aggressiveness.

     c.   Heroin is not a hallucinogen; it usually promotes relaxation rather than aggression.

     d.   Crack is a stimulant, not a hallucinogen.

8.   d.   That alcoholics primed with alcohol did not drink more alcohol when they thought it was tonic undercuts the disease notion of loss of control.

     a.   If alcoholism were a disease involving loss of control, the only thing that would have influenced drinking would have been drinking alcohol, not expectation.

     b.   The subjects' expectations had a great impact on the amount they drank.

     c.   Expectations were important for both groups.

9.   c.   Schachter's work suggests that the body craves nicotine, and that continued smoking is an attempt to avoid withdrawal.

     a.   Schachter's work suggests that nicotine is strongly addicting.

     b.   Nicotine is not a hallucinogen.

     d.   Schachter's work stresses the physiological needs of smokers, not their psychological needs.

10. d.   Multimodal treatment uses a wide range of individual, group, and self-help measures to stop substance abuse and find alternative behaviors.

     a.   The term for people who are addicted to several substances is *polysubstance abusers*.

     b.   Extinction connotes only behavior therapy; multimodal treatment may use behavior therapy and several others.

     c.   Detoxification is not a form of treatment per se; Alcoholics Anonymous is only one method of treatment.

ANSWER KEY: CONCEPTUAL MULTIPLE-CHOICE QUESTIONS

1.   c.   The key feature of substance dependence is tolerance or withdrawal symptoms.

     a.   Both substance abuse and substance dependence are associated with use over a period of at least twelve months.

     b.   Substance abuse and substance dependence both impair social functioning.

     d.   Mental disorders may or may not be associated with abuse or dependence.

2.   a.   All three are depressants or sedatives—they slow down the working of the brain.

     b.   Barbiturates are prescribed drugs but are often obtained illegally; benzodiazepines (such as Valium) are widely available from doctors.

     c.   All three produce tolerance.

     d.   All three can be lethal, particularly barbiturates.

3.   a.   Amphetamines and cocaine are central nervous stimulants that prevent the reuptake of dopamine and therefore increase its concentration in certain brain synapses.

     b.   Alcohol and narcotics are depressants.

     c.   Marijuana and LSD are hallucinogens, not stimulants.

     d.   Barbiturates are depressants.

4.   b.   Causes are usually seen as internal and biogenic (especially genetics) or psychological/cultural (personality and social factors); however, an integration of the two schools of thought is quite common.

     a.   Both personality and environment are part of the psychological/cultural viewpoint.

     c.   Social class and education are both cultural factors.

     d   Learning and psychodynamic perspectives are both psychological; biogenic factors are important in understanding substance-related disorders.

5. d.   Concordance ratios of MZ twins are higher than those of DZ twins, and children of alcoholics who are adopted by nonalcoholics have higher rates of drinking problems—both support the role of heredity.

    a.   Support for personality factors comes from longitudinal studies, which find that impulsive and antisocial youths are more likely than others to develop drinking problems.

    b.   Evidence from this work tends to support the genetic position.

    c.   Support for the sociocultural position comes from evidence that different cultures have different rates of consumption and alcoholism.

6. a.   Research shows that the central nervous system functioning of sons of alcoholics differs from that of sons of nonalcoholics, which suggests a biological marker for alcoholism.

    b.   Concordance shows that the disorder may be inherited or may be the product of similar expectations; it does not indicate a biological marker.

    c.   Children of alcoholics may learn to be alcoholics; this does not indicate a biological marker.

    d.   As far as we know, all individuals have a negative physiological reaction to Antabuse when they drink.

7. c.   Much to the surprise of many, those who experimented with drugs but did not use heavily had the best social adjustment.

    a.   Shedler and Block found that maladjustment preceded heavy drug use in adolescents.

    b.   Abstainers had more adjustment problems than experimenters; they tended to be inflexible and had poorer social skills.

    d.   Experimenters did not become heavy users.

8. b.   If cultures differ in their rates of alcoholism, it *may* be because the cultures teach different values concerning what is deviant drinking.

    a.   If alcohol has the same physiological effect on all people, culture is irrelevant.

    c.   Fetal alcohol syndrome is a physiological effect that appears to be unrelated to cultural values.

    d.   That antisocial behavior and depression are related to drinking is support for a personality explanation.

9. a.   Early behaviorists stressed the role of alcohol as an anxiety-reducing chemical, which was supported by the research with cats.

    b.   If rats did this (and they don't), it would undercut the early behaviorist position, which stressed anxiety reduction.

    c.   Such a finding would undercut the behaviorist position.

    d.   The importance of expectation is a recent behavioral explanation for why alcohol sometimes has anxiety-reducing properties and sometimes doesn't.

10. b. Because methadone produces a euphoria and is addictive, it substitutes one substance-related problem for another.

    a. Methadone treatment is unrelated to behavior therapy and is far from aversive since it produces a euphoria.

    c. Methadone treatment is unrelated to Alcoholics Anonymous.

    d. The goal of methadone is to do the opposite—to reduce the impact of heroin withdrawal.

ANSWER KEY: APPLICATION MULTIPLE-CHOICE QUESTIONS

1. b. Karen's use is clearly pathological and the symptoms have occurred during the same twelve-month period, so she shows signs of substance abuse; since there are signs of neither tolerance or withdrawal, we need to rule out substance dependence.

    a. Karen's drug use has led to social and occupational (school) impairments; this cannot be considered nonabusive use.

    c. Without signs of tolerance or withdrawal, one cannot diagnose this as substance dependence.

    d. Marijuana is not a stimulant; it is a mild hallucinogen.

2. c. Crack is a purified form of cocaine that is sold as small "rock" that are smoked; its effects are sudden euphoria followed by depression once the drug is out of the system.

    a. Cocaine is usually snorted (inhaled into the nose) rather than smoked; it occurs in a powder form, not small, solid pieces.

    b. LSD is not smoked and it produced hallucinations rather than euphoria and depression.

    d. Although marijuana is smoked, it is not in solid pieces, nor does it produce depression when it is out of the person's system.

3. c. One of LSD's unique properties is that hallucinations can occur weeks after use has stopped; these are called flashbacks.

    a. Heroin does not produce hallucinations, and there is no evidence of it producing flashbacks.

    b. Marijuana produces only the mildest of hallucinations and no flashbacks.

    d. Crack cocaine produces a strong and rapid high, but there is no evidence of hallucinations or flashbacks.

4. d. The psychodynamic perspective emphasizes early childhood influences and the symbolic nature of adult drinking.

    a. The behavioral perspective stresses modeling, anxiety reduction, and expectations.

    b. The family systems perspective stresses the adaptive role of drunkenness in the family.

    c. The biological-physical perspective emphasizes the role of genetic vulnerability.

5. d. Peter Nathan (1988) has shown that antisocial behavior and depression are the two factors most related to drinking problems.

    a. This is inaccurate because, although psychoanalysts focus on repression, no empirical relationship between it and alcoholism has been documented.

    b. The is inaccurate because intelligence has no relationship to alcoholism.

    c. This is inaccurate; two personality factors *have* been related to alcoholism.

6. b. The abstinence violation effect is the feeling of having "blown it" when one gives in to temptation once; according to Marlatt, it is a principal reason for relapses.

    a. Behaviorists do not believe that physiological loss of control occurs when people relapse.

    c. Covert sensitization is a treatment method using imagery.

    d. Antabuse is used in the treatment of alcohol.

7. d. Opponent process theory says that initial drug use has positive effects, but that chronic use involves a lessened high and a dramatically intensified withdrawal effect; chronic use is therefore motivated by avoidance of the withdrawal effects.)

    a. A cognitive-behavioral learned expectancy approach would emphasize the beliefs she had about narcotics—their social benefits.

    b. Tiffany's autonomic processes model highlights the lack of thinking marks chronic drug use.

    c. Detoxification is a first stage in treatment and is not an explanation for chronic drug use.

8. c. Alcoholic Anonymous is a group treatment that uses self-revelation, support, and spiritual involvement.

    a. Methadone maintenance is not done in groups; it is administered individually on a daily basis to offset the craving for heroin.

    b. Systematic desensitization is an individual treatment that uses classical conditioning principles.

    d. Behavior therapy, if done in groups, would not focus on the spiritual, but would teaching coping skills.

9. c. Transdermal nicotine patches have proven to be useful in wearing cigarette smokers from their addiction to nicotine.

    a. LSD does not produce withdrawal effects.

    b. Marijuana does not produce withdrawal effects.

    d. Caffeine does not produce serious withdrawal effects and is not treated with transdermal patches.

10. a. Prevention programs can be successful; the text describes on that reduced smoking in junior high students

    b. Treatment of drug problems has been modestly effective since a minority of those treated remain drug-free for a period of time after treatment.

    c. One-third of alcoholic getting treatment remain abstinent one year after treatment.

    d. Most treated narcotics addicts are readdicted within a year of treatment.

OBJECTIVES DEFINED

1. **What are substance-use disorders?**

*   People often use chemical substances that alter moods, levels of consciousness, or behaviors. The use of such substances is considered a disorder when abuse or dependence occurs. *Substance abuse* is defined as a maladaptive pattern of recurrent use over a twelve-month period, during which the person is unable to reduce or cease intake of a harmful substance, despite knowledge that its use causes social, occupational, psychological, medical, or safety problems. *Substance*

dependence is a more serious disorder, involving not only excessive use but also tolerance and withdrawal in many cases.

- Substances are largely classified on the basis of their effects. Three major categories have been created: Depressants, stimulants, and hallucinogens.

- Alcohol, which is widely used, is considered a depressant. Other depressants include narcotics, barbiturates, and benzodiazepines and can also cause psychological, physiological, or legal problems.

- Stimulants energize the central nervous system, often inducing elation, grandiosity, hyperactivity, agitation, and appetite suppression. Amphetamines and cocaine/crack cocaine, as well as widely used substances such as caffeine and nicotine, are considered stimulants.

- Hallucinogens, another category of psychoactive substances, often produce hallucinations, altered states of consciousness, perceptual distortions, and sometimes violence. Included in this category are marijuana, LSD, and PCP.

2.   **Why do people develop substance-use disorders?**

- There appears to be no single factor that can account for drug abuse or for dependence on other substances such as depressants, stimulants, and hallucinogens. Biological/genetic, psychological, social, and sociocultural factors are all important.

- In terms of biological factors, research has demonstrated that heredity is important in abuse and dependency of some substances such as alcohol. Chronic drug use seems to alter brain chemistry, crowds out other pleasures, reduces good decisions, and becomes a consuming, compulsive desire for the drug.

- Psychological approaches to substance-use disorders have emphasized learning of drug use patterns, the tension- and anxiety-reducing properties of drugs, and expectancies over the effects of drug use.

- Social or interpersonal factors are important in the consumption of substances. Teenagers and adults have been found to use drugs because of parental models, social pressures from peers, and increased feelings of comfort and confidence in social relationships.

- Sociocultural factors such as gender, ethnicity, and culture are related to alcohol and drug use. Cultural norms, attitudes, and practices affect the availability, access, and tolerance of substance use.

3.   **What kinds of interventions and treatments are available for substance-use disorders, and does treatment work?**

- A variety of treatment approaches have been used, including detoxification, drug therapies, psychotherapy, and behavior modification. The treatment prescribed for drug users depends on the type of drug and on the user. Heroin addicts usually undergo detoxification followed by methadone maintenance and forms of treatment such as residential treatment programs, psychotherapy, cognitive or behavior therapy, and group therapy. Many alcoholics are helped by treatment, and some achieve abstinence by themselves. For addiction to cigarette smoking, aversive procedures such as "rapid smoking," nicotine fading (the use of brands containing less and less nicotine), and transdermal nicotine patches have had some success. Prevention programs have also been extensively used in an attempt to discourage substance use.

- Treatment for substance-use disorders has had mixed success. Multimodal approaches (the use of several treatment techniques) are probably the most effective. Evidence indicates that relapse is particularly likely during the first three months after treatment. The risk of relapse decreases as a function of time.

MARGIN DEFINITIONS

alcoholic person who abuses alcohol and is dependent on it

alcoholism substance-related disorder characterized by abuse of, or dependency on, alcohol, which is a depressant

amphetamine a drug that speeds up central nervous system activity and produces increased alertness, energy, and, sometimes, feelings of euphoria and confidence; also called "uppers"

aversion therapy conditioning procedure in which the response to a stimulus is decreased by pairing the stimulus with an adverse stimulus

barbiturate substance that is a powerful depressant of the central nervous system; commonly used to induce relaxation and sleep; and capable of inducing psychological and physical dependency; also called "downers"

cocaine substance extracted from the coca plant; induces feelings of euphoria and self-confidence in users

covert sensitization aversive conditioning technique in which the individual imagines a noxious stimulus occurring in the presence of a behavior

depressant (sedative) substance that causes generalized depression of the central nervous system and a slowing down of responses

detoxification alcohol or drug treatment phase characterized by removal of the abusive substance; after that removal, the user is immediately or eventually prevented from consuming the substance

hallucinogen substance that produces hallucinations, vivid sensory awareness, heightened alertness, or perceptions of increased insight; use does not typically lead to physical dependence , although psychological dependency may occur

marijuana the mildest and most commonly used hallucinogen; also known as "pot" or "grass"

narcotic drug such as opium and its derivatives—morphine, heroine, and codeine—that depresses the central nervous system; acts as a sedative to provide relief from pain, anxiety, and tension; is addictive

polysubstance dependence substance dependence in which dependency is not based on the use of any single substance but on the repeated use of at least three substances (not including caffeine and nicotine) for a period of twelve months

reinforcing abstinence (contingency management) treatment technique in which the individual is given behavioral reinforcements for abstinence from substance use

risk factors variables related to, or etiologically significant in, the development of a disorder

skills training teaching skills for resisting peer pressures or temptations, resolving emotional conflicts or problems, or for more effective communication

stimulant substance that is a central nervous system energizer, including elation, grandiosity, hyperactivity, agitation, and appetite suppression

substance abuse maladaptive pattern of recurrent use that extends over a period of twelve months; leads to notable impairment or distress; and continues despite social, occupational, psychological, physical, or safety problems

substance dependence maladaptive pattern of use extending over a twelve-month period and characterized by unsuccessful efforts to control use despite knowledge of harmful effects; taking more of substance than intended; tolerance; and/or withdrawal

substance-related disorder   ailment arising from the use of psychoactive substances that affect the central nervous system, causing significant social, occupational, psychological, or physical problems, and that sometimes result in abuse or dependence

tolerance   condition in which increasing doses of a substance are necessary to achieve the desired effect

withdrawal   condition characterized by distress or impairment in social, occupational, or other areas of functioning, or physical or emotional symptoms such as shaking, irritability, and inability to concentrate after reducing or ceasing intake of a substance

CHAPTER 10

Sexual and Gender Identity Disorders

TABLE OF CONTENTS

LEARNING OBJECTIVES

1. Define normal and abnormal sexual behaviors.

2. Discuss what the normal sexual response cycle tells us about sexual dysfunctions.

3. Discuss what causes sexual dysfunctions.

4. Define the types of treatments that are available for sexual dysfunctions.

5. Explain why homosexuality is not considered a mental disorder.

6. Describe how aging affects the sexual activity of the elderly.

7. Define the causes of gender identity disorder and how it is treated.

8. Describe the paraphilias, what causes them, and how they are treated.

9. Discuss if rape is an act of sex or aggression.

CHAPTER OUTLINE

I. **What is "normal" sexual behavior?** This chapter discusses sexual dysfunctions, gender identity disorders, and paraphilias, as well as sexual coercion. The sexual and gender identity disorders are the hardest to distinguish from "normal" sexual behavior because of cultural differences as well as moral and legal judgments. Normal sexual behavior is poorly understood and differs depending upon the historical period and one's culture. The question of compulsive sexual behavior (CSB) became particularly salient with President Clinton's affair with Monica Lewinsky. Although it is not classified by DSM-IV-TR, sexual scientists use such terms as hypersexuality, erotomania, nymphomania, and satyriasis to refer to this phenomenon. The first reliable information concerning human sexuality came from the survey research work of Alfred Kinsey. Masters and Johnson used laboratory research to study physiological sexual responses. More recently, the Janus Report described sexual practices in the United States. The sexual response cycle has an *appetitive (desire) phase,* when fantasies about sex increase. The *excitement phase occurs* when direct sexual stimulation (not necessarily physical) increases blood flow to the genitals. The *orgasm phase* produces involuntary contractions and the release of sexual tension. Men ejaculate then have a refractory period where additional stimulation does not produce orgasm; women are capable of multiple orgasms. The body then returns to relaxation during the *resolution phase.* Decreased functioning in any of these phases can be criteria for a sexual dysfunction.

II.   **Dysfunction disorders** involve any persistent disruption in the normal sexual response cycle. DSM-IV-TR requires that factors such as frequency, chronicity, distress, and impact on functioning be considered in the diagnosis. *Sexual desire disorders* involve a lack of interest in or aversion to sex. These are more common in women than in men, and there are many questions about what "normal" sexual interest is (about 20 percent of the adult population is believed to suffer from this disorder). *Sexual arousal disorders* are problems occurring during the excitement phase of the sexual response cycle. *Erectile disorder is* the man's inability to maintain an erection sufficient for intercourse. Physical conditions may account for a large minority of cases. Distinguishing biogenic erectile dysfunction from psychogenic cases is difficult. Primary dysfunction is when a man has never been successful in intercourse; secondary dysfunction means the problem is situational. *Female sexual arousal disorder* involves lack of vaginal lubrication or erection of the nipples. This disorder, too, can be primary or secondary. *Orgasmic disorders* involve the inability to achieve orgasm after receiving adequate stimulation in the excitement phase. *Female orgasmic disorder* means a woman is unable to achieve orgasm. Many questions arise about whether the lack of an orgasm is a normal variant of sexual behavior or a disorder. *Male orgasmic disorder,* the inability to ejaculate intravaginally, is relatively rare and little is known about it. *Premature ejaculation* is a common disorder involving an inability to delay ejaculation during intercourse, but definitions of "premature" vary. *Sexual pain disorders* include *dyspareunia* (persistent pain in the genitals before, during, or after intercourse) and *vaginismus* (involuntary muscular contraction of the outer vagina). DSM-IV-TR also notes sexual dysfunction owing to a general medical condition and substance-induced sexual dysfunction.

III.   **Etiology of sexual dysfunctions** Many dysfunctions are due to a combination of biological and psychological factors. The biological dimension indicates lower levels of testosterone or higher levels of estrogens such as prolactin (or both) have been associated with lower sexual interest in both men and women and with erectile difficulties in men   The psychological dimension understand that sexual dysfunctions may be due to psychological factors alone or to a combination of psychological and biological factors The social dimension examines social upbringing and current relationships as important in sexual functioning. It seems plausible that the attitudes parents display toward sex and affection and toward each other can influence their children's attitudes The sociocultural dimensions makes it clear that sexual behavior and functioning are influenced by gender, age, cultural scripts, educational level, and country of origin. While the human sexual response cycle is similar for women and men, gender differences are clearly present: women (1) are capable of multiple orgasms, (2) entertain different sexual fantasies than men, (3) have a broader arousal pattern to sexual stimuli, (4) are more attuned to relationships in the sexual encounter, and (5) take longer than men to become aroused.

IV.   **Treatment of Sexual Dysfunction.** Biological dimension uses treatments including exercise, oral medication (Viagra), surgery, and injections into the penis of substances that induce erection. Psychological treatments includes predisposing causes, such as early experiences and upbringing, and current concerns, such as poor marital relations and performance anxiety. Research shows that anxiety and self-focus impair performance. Treatment often includes education, anxiety reduction, structured behavioral exercises, and improved communication. Specific treatments for dysfunctions include masturbation as treatment for female orgasmic disorder, the "squeeze technique" for premature ejaculation, and relaxation and insertion of dilators for vaginismus.

V.   **Homosexuality.** The American Psychological Association no longer consider homosexuality to be a mental disorder, however some individuals still harbor this belief. Homosexuality is not a mental disorder. There are no physiological differences in sexual arousal, no differences in psychological disturbance, no gender identity distortions that differentiate homosexuals and heterosexuals.

VI.   **Aging, sexual activity, and sexual dysfunction.** Sexuality continues into old age, although physiological changes can lead to changes in sexual activity. Patterns of sexuality during middle age are maintained. The Janus survey suggests that sexual activity and enjoyment remain high among those 65 and older.

VII. **Gender identity disorders.** *Gender identity disorders,* often called transsexualism, involve a conflict between anatomical sex and gender self-identification. A second disorder is called gender identity disorder not otherwise specified. Transsexuals, have a lifelong conviction that they are in the body of the wrong sex. Sex role conflicts start at an early age; they are more common in boys than in girls. Prevalence estimates range from 1 in 100,000 to 1 in 30,000 among males and about one-quarter that rate among females. The etiology of GID is unclear. Because the disorder is quite rare, investigators have focused more attention on other sexual disorders. In all likelihood, a number of variables interact to produce GID. Again, a multi-path analysis would reveal multiple influences, but biological factors seem to be strongly implicated. In the area of biological influences the research in this area suggests that neurohormonal factors, genetics, and possible brain differences may be involved in the etiology of GID. Psychological and social explanations of GID must also be viewed with caution. In psychodynamic theory, all sexual deviations symbolically represent unconscious conflicts that began in early childhood Most treatment programs with children having gender identity disorder assign boys to male therapists, to facilitate identification with a male, and teach behavior modification skills to the parents. Sex conversion treatment involving hormones and surgery can alter the apparent sex of transsexuals; woman-to-man changes seem to have more positive outcomes. It is particularly positive for those who are highly motivated and carefully screened, who have stable work records and good social support, although many transsexuals remain depressed and suicidal after surgery. Controversy exists whether sex-conversion surgery or psychotherapy should be advanced in treating individuals with gender identity disorders.

VIII. **Paraphilias.** *Paraphilias* are sexual disorders lasting at least six months in which repeated intense sexual urges exist for nonhuman objects, real or simulated suffering, or nonconsenting others. Either the urge is acted upon or causes severe distress. Sex offenders often have multiple paraphilias. They are overwhelmingly male problems. *Fetishism* is a strong sexual attraction to inanimate objects, such as shoes or underwear. As a group, fetishists are not dangerous. In *transvestic fetishism,* the person obtains sexual arousal by dressing in the clothes of the opposite sex. Most transvestites are heterosexual males who use cross-dressing to facilitate sexual intercourse, but many transvestites feel they have both male and female personalities. Paraphilias involving nonconsenting persons include. **E**xhibitionism involves urges, acts, or fantasies about exposing one's genitals to strangers. Women commonly report being victims. Most exhibitionists are young married men who want no further contact with the women to whom they expose themselves. *Voyeurism* is sexual gratification obtained primarily from observing others' genitals or others engaged in sex. Acts are repetitive and premeditated. *Frotteurism* involves intense sexual urges to touch and rub against nonconsenting individuals. *Pedophilia* is characterized by adults obtaining erotic gratification from sexual fantasies about or involving sexual contact with children. Paraphilias involving pain or humiliation include *Sadism* and *masochism* which involve associations between pain or humiliation and sex. Sadists inflict pain; masochists receive it. Often people engage in both roles. Some cases develop from early experiences with pain, but causal explanations are currently weak. Some research findings suggest biological causes for paraphilias but replication is needed. Psychodynamic theory links paraphilias to unresolved oedipal conflicts, particularly castration anxiety. Treatment involves making these unconscious conflicts conscious. Behavioral theory stresses early conditioning experiences, masturbation fantasies, and a lack of social skills. Treatment seeks to extinguish inappropriate behaviors and reinforce appropriate ones. Results of behavioral treatments are positive but largely based on single-subject reports.

IX.   **Rape.** *Rape* is defined in the text as forced intercourse accomplished through force or threat of force; statutory rape is sexual intercourse with someone under a certain age (depending on the particular state). Rape can be seen as either a sexual act, a violent act, or both. Victims may experience prolonged distress and sexual dysfunction. Consistent with posttraumatic stress disorder, survivors may experience rape trauma syndrome. Rapists are most often motivated by power and anger, not by sex; 5 percent are rapists who enjoy inflicting pain on their victims. In the sociocultural perspective a variety of views of the causes of rape have been proposed. Some researchers theorized that rape was committed by mentally disturbed men, and studies were initiated to find personality characteristics that might be associated with rap. Another explanation of rape and sexual aggression is posited by sociobiological models. Sexual aggression, according to this view, has an evolutionary basis. Sex differences have evolved as a means of maximizing the reproduction of the human species: men have much more to gain in reproductive terms by being able to pass on their genes rapidly to a large number of women, which increases their chances of having offspring. Many believe that sex offenders are not good candidates for treatment. High recidivism rates are often associated with sexual aggression, and the most frequent action is punishment (incarceration). Both conventional and more controversial treatments have been used or proposed.

X.   **Implications.** Sexuality and the expression of sex are considered not only normal and pleasurable aspects of human existence but an intimate expression of life itself. Because human sexuality plays such an important role in our lives, sexual problems can cause great consternation. As a result, much public and scholarly interest and attention have been directed toward problematic sexual behaviors.

KEY TERMS REVIEW

1.   The disorder characterized by an extremely strong sexual attraction to a particular nongenital part of the anatomy or an inanimate object is called _____.

2.   The disorder in which an adult obtains erotic gratification through fantasies about or sexual contact with children is called _____.

3.   The paraphilia characterized by the sexual desire to rub against or the act of rubbing against the body of a nonconsenting individual is called _____.

4.   The disorder characterized by conflict between an individual's anatomical sex and his or her sexual identity is called _____.

5.   The condition in which there is recurrent or persistent pain in the genitals before, during, or after sexual intercourse is called _____.

6.   The sexual disorder in which erotic or sexual gratification is obtained by receiving pain or punishment is called _____.

7.   An act of intercourse accomplished through force or the threat of force is called

    _____.

8.   Sexual relations between close relatives are called _____.

9.   The sexual dysfunctions characterized by a lack of interest in or aversion to sexual arousal are called _____.

10. The disorder in which sexual gratification is obtained by inflicting pain or punishment on others is called _____.

11. The sexual dysfunction in which a woman has a persistent delay or inability to achieve orgasm despite adequate stimulation is called

12. Sexual disorders in which unusual or bizarre acts or objects are required for sexual arousal or in which such urges are distressing are called _____.

13. The sexual dysfunction in which men experience persistent delay or inability to achieve orgasm despite adequate stimulation is called _____.

14. The inability of a male to attain or maintain an erection that is sufficient for sexual intercourse is called _____.

15. The dysfunction characterized by ejaculation before penile entry into the vagina or so soon after entry that sexual relations are unsatisfactory is called _____.

16. The disorder in which sexual gratification is obtained by secretly observing strangers disrobe or engage in sex is called _____.

17. The paraphilia in which a person derives sexual gratification from cross-dressing is called _____.

18. The disorder characterized by urges, acts, or fantasies about exposing one's genitals to strangers is called _____.

19. Sexual dysfunctions that occur during the excitement phase and relate to difficulties in feeling sexual pleasure are called _____.

20. _____ is a term used by many sex therapists to describe individuals who seem to crave constant sex at the expense of relationships, work productivity, and daily activities).

21. The sexual pain disorder in which there are involuntary spasms of the outer third of the vagina wall is called _____.

22. Emotional symptoms such as distress, phobic reactions, and sexual dysfunction following unwanted coerced sexual contact defines the _____.

23. A disruption of any part of the normal sexual response cycle is known as a _____.

24. A woman who experiences persistent delays or inability to achieve an orgasm even though there is adequate stimulation is said to have _____.

FACTUAL MULTIPLE-CHOICE QUESTIONS

1. Who of the following is *not* an important contributor to the study of sex research and therapy?
    a.   Kinsey
    b.   Masters & Johnson
    c.   Kaplan
    d.   Beck

2. Research with nonclinical samples of homosexuals suggests that
    a.   they are more inclined to develop psychoses than are heterosexuals.
    b.   lesbians are far more disturbed than male homosexuals.
    c.   distress over being homosexual rarely, if ever, occurs.
    d.   there is no more psychopathology in homosexuals than in heterosexuals.

3. Which of the following is *not* a DSM-IV-TR disorder?
    a.   Premature ejaculation
    b.   Sexual addiction
    c.   Hypoactive sexual desire disorder
    d.   Dyspareunia

4. A woman who has experienced orgasm in the past but currently cannot be brought to orgasm should be diagnosed as having

    a. a sexual desire disorder.
    b. primary vaginismus.
    c. secondary female orgasmic disorder.
    d. a secondary paraphilia.

5. Which of the following are related to sexual pain disorders?

    a. Lack of sexual desire and lack of orgasm
    b. Vaginismus and dyspareunia
    c. Premature ejaculation and erectile dysfunction
    d. Hypoactive sexual desire and erectile dysfunction

6. The inability to obtain sexual arousal unless one is wearing the clothes of the opposite sex indicates

    a. transvestic fetishism.
    b. gender identity disorder.
    c. exhibitionism.
    d. fetishism.

7. Contrary to popular belief, most _____ tend to be people who are relatives or friends of their victims.

    a. exhibitionists
    b. pedophiles
    c. masochists
    d. transvestites

8. Which of the following is a paraphilia that involves intentional pain or humiliation?

    a. Transvestic fetishism
    b. Premature ejaculation
    c. Voyeurism
    d. Sadomasochism

9. The behavioral treatment called aversive behavior rehearsal involves shame and is most appropriate for treating

    a. gender identity disorder.
    b. exhibitionism.
    c. premature ejaculation.
    d. homosexuality.

10. Anger and power are two of the more common motivations for

    a. sadomasochists.
    b. rapists.
    c. transvestic fetishists.
    d. exhibitionists.

CONCEPTUAL MULTIPLE-CHOICE QUESTIONS

1. Sexual deviation disorders

    a. are unaffected by legal or moral judgments.
    b. can be reliably diagnosed because they all entail personal distress.
    c. are difficult to define because they involve legal and moral judgments.
    d. involve an inability to perform at some stage in the normal sexual response cycle.

2.   Which sexual dysfunction, believed to affect 20 percent of the adult population, is difficult to diagnose because we know little about the "normal" frequency of sexual fantasies and activities?

   a.   Paraphilia
   b.   Premature ejaculation
   c.   Sexual desire disorder
   d.   Primary erectile dysfunction

3.   Which of the following is a current psychological factor that increases the likelihood of erectile dysfunction?

   a.   Excessive levels of testosterone
   b.   A strict moral upbringing
   c.   Unresolved castration anxiety
   d.   Pressure to perform sexually

4.   Transsexuals tend to

   a.   show sex role conflicts at an early age.
   b.   be women.
   c.   outgrow their gender identity disorder.
   d.   engage in gender-inappropriate behavior, but have no desire to change their physical characteristics.

5.   Absence of a male role model, lack of male playmates, and parental encouragement of cross-dressing are psychological factors in the development of

   a.   pedophilia.
   b.   premature ejaculation.
   c.   sexual desire disorders.
   d.   gender identity disorders.

6.   Rubbing against a nonconsenting person is to _____ as observing others in sexual activity is to _____.

   a.   transvestic fetishism; exhibitionism
   b.   frotteurism; voyeurism
   c.   transvestic fetishism; voyeurism
   d.   frotteurism; exhibitionism

7.   According to psychoanalytic theory, sadomasochism and other sexual deviations are caused by

   a.   the pairing of certain stimuli with sexual arousal in early childhood.
   b.   cultural requirements of males and females.
   c.   unconscious conflicts related to castration anxiety.
   d.   a lack of superego controls.

8.   Behavioral approaches to treating pedophilia would focus on

   a.   strengthening the association between sexual arousal and children.
   b.   bringing to consciousness unconscious fears and conflicts.
   c.   the need to imprison convicted offenders.
   d.   extinguishing sexual responses to fantasies about children.

9.   "Cultural spillover" theory suggests that a culture where violence is encouraged or condoned *will* have

   a.   very few incidents of sexually deviant behavior.
   b.   a high rate of sexually dysfunctional men.
   c.   a high rate of exhibitionism, voyeurism, and other paraphilias.
   d.   more rapes than in other cultures.

10. Which statement about the treatment of sex offenders is *true*?

    a. Imprisonment is the main form of "treatment."
    b. Controlled research shows that psychotherapy is more effective than biological treatments.
    c. Treatment for rapists is far more successful than for any other type of offender.
    d. Surgical castration has been found to have no effect on sexual fantasies or recidivism rates.

APPLICATION MULTIPLE-CHOICE QUESTIONS

1. Kara has inhibited sexual desire, whereas Fred occasionally has problems maintaining an erection. Kara's problem is an example of a disorder in the _____ stage of the sexual response cycle; Fred's problem is in the _____ stage.

    a. excitement; orgasm
    b. appetitive; excitement
    c. appetitive; resolution
    d. excitement; appetitive

2. Dr. Knowlton says, "By masturbating, women can completely eliminate this common problem. However, there is good reason to believe that, without manual stimulation, the problem will continue during normal intercourse." What problem is Dr. Knowlton discussing?

    a. Functional vaginismus
    b. Transvestic fetishism
    c. Primary inhibited sexual orgasm
    d. Gender identity disorder in women

3. John received a penile implant as treatment for a sexual problem. It is likely that the problem was

    a. premature ejaculation.
    b. low sexual desire.
    c. pedophilia.
    d. erectile dysfunction.

4. Mrs. Johnson is instructed by a therapist to stimulate her husband's penis while it is outside the vagina until he senses an ejaculation about to occur. She is then to stop stimulation and continue only after a short time has gone by. What sexual dysfunction is probably being treated?

    a. Mrs. Johnson's sexual pain disorder
    b. Mr. Johnson's, premature ejaculation
    c. Mr. Johnson's erectile dysfunction
    d. Mrs. Johnson's sexual desire disorder

5. At an early age, Albert avoided all traditionally male activities and felt that he was a girl trapped in the body of a boy. As an adult, he had a sex change operation and is now called Alberta. This case illustrates

    a. gender identity disorder.
    b. sexual desire disorder.
    c. pedophilia.
    d. transvestic fetishism.

6. Doris derives sexual gratification from fondling men's underwear. She is a shy, married woman who also must dress in men's clothes to have satisfactory intercourse with her husband. What is unusual about Doris's case?

    a. Men are more likely to have paraphilias than women.
    b. People rarely have more than one paraphilia.
    c. Transvestites are almost always homosexuals.
    d. People with paraphilias are rarely shy or married.

7. Todd, age 26, responds to attractive women in public by fantasizing about exposing his genitals, then returning to the same place and actually exposing himself. Todd would probably be diagnosed with

   a. gender identity disorder.
   b. sexual dysfunction of the arousal stage.
   c. voyeurism.
   d. exhibitionism.

8. Donald, who likes to look at attractive women, wonders whether he is really a voyeur. Which incident below would indicate that he is?

   a. He drove fifty miles to see bottomless dancers.
   b. He bought ten copies of nudist magazines.
   c. He prefers "peeping" to having sex with his wife.
   d. He spends the summer at a swimming pool so that he can watch women in swimsuits.

9. Harold is in behavior therapy for exhibitionism. His therapist is helping him learn appropriate ways of deriving sexual gratification and is modeling improved social skills. What component of Harold's therapy, common in a learning approach, is missing?

   a. Harold is not examining unconscious castration anxieties.
   b. Harold is not receiving medical treatment to reduce his sex drive.
   c. Harold is not receiving the "squeeze technique."
   d. Harold's inappropriate behaviors are not receiving aversive conditioning.

10. Gina has become intensely fearful of the dark. Since a particular incident occurred, she has little desire for sex, and when she has sex, there are flashbacks of that incident. It's a good bet that Gina

    a. has survived a rape.
    b. has a husband with erectile dysfunction.
    c. was a victim of an exhibitionist.
    d. has a paraphilia.

ANSWER KEY: KEY TERMS REVIEW

1. fetishism

2. pedophilia

3. frotteurism

4. gender identity disorder

5. dyspareunia

6. masochism

7. rape

8. incest

9. sexual desire disorders

10. sadism

11. female orgasmic disorder

12. paraphilias

13. male orgasmic disorder

14. male erectile disorder

15. premature ejaculation

16. voyeurism

17. transvestic fetishism

18. exhibitionism

19. sexual arousal disorders

20. compulsive sexual behavior

21. vaginismus

22. rape trauma syndrome

23. sexual dysfunction

24. female sexual arousal disorder

ANSWER KEY: FACTUAL MULTIPLE-CHOICE QUESTIONS

1.   d.   Beck is associated with the cognitive therapy for depression.

     a.   Kinsey published a study of male sexuality (1948) and female sexuality (1953).

     b.   Masters & Johnson published several studies in the 1960s and 1970s.

     c.   Kaplan's research deals with the treatment of sexual dysfunctions.

2.   d.   Nonclinical homosexual samples are no more disturbed than nonclinical heterosexual samples.

     a.   Comparisons of nonclinical samples of homosexuals and heterosexuals show no significant difference in psychological adjustment.

     b.   If anything, lesbians show better psychological adjustment than male homosexuals.

     c.   Most psychologists agree that ego dystonicity (distress) over ones homosexual orientation affects every homosexual at some point.

3.   b.   DSM-IV-TR does not recognize sexual addiction as a disorder.

     a.   Premature ejaculation is considered a male orgasm disorder.

     c.   About 20 percent of the population are thought to suffer from hypoactive sexual desire disorder.

     d.   Dyspareunia is painful intercourse.

4.   c.   A secondary disorder is one that is currently a problem but was not at some previous time.

     a.   Sexual desire disorders involve a lack of interest in sexual behavior.

     b.   Vaginismus involves uncontrolled spasms.

     d.   A paraphilia is arousal associated with a bizarre object or situation; inhibited orgasm is not a paraphilia but a dysfunction.

5.   b.   Vaginismus (spasms in the vagina) and dyspareunia (pain during intercourse) are forms of sexual pain disorders.

     a.   Lack of sexual desire is a problem in the appetitive stage, not during excitement and orgasm, as is true with vaginismus.

     c.   Premature ejaculation and erectile dysfunction are male dysfunctions unrelated to pain.

     d.   Erectile dysfunction is unrelated to pain.

6. a.   Transvestic fetishism involves sexual arousal when cross-dressing, but not as a function of gender identity disorder.

    b.   Cross-dressing related to gender identity disorder is not done for sexual arousal; the person feels he or she is trapped in the body of the wrong sex.

    c.   Exhibitionism is revealing one's genitals in order to shock someone else.

    d.   Fetishism involves extremely strong attraction to an inanimate object (bras, shoes, and so on).

7. b.   Pedophiles tend to be fathers, stepfathers, or friends of the children they abuse.

    a.   Exhibitionists almost always expose themselves to strangers.

    c.   Masochists receive pain and humiliation; they do not victimize others.

    d.   Transvestites do not victimize others; they merely cross-dress to obtain sexual gratification.

8. d.   Sadomasochism may be scripted and mutual, but pain, humiliation, and helplessness are its goals.

    a.   Transvestites do not victimize others.

    b.   Premature ejaculation, a sexual dysfunction, causes anguish to the premature ejaculator.

    c.   Voyeurs tend to be harmless; they want only to "peep," not to have sex.

9. b.   ABR helps exhibitionists see the impact they have on victims, and it controls compulsive exposing.

    a.   ABR involves getting the patient to see his effect on a victim; those with gender identity disorder have no victims.

    c.   Premature ejaculation is shaming enough without additional "treatment."

    d.   Homosexuality is a life lived in an atmosphere of unacceptance; there are no intended victims in this lifestyle.

10. b.   Three common motives for rapists are power, anger, and sadism.

    a.   The motivation behind most sadomasochism is helplessness.

    c.   Transvestic fetishism is motivated by sexual arousal, not power.

    d.   Exhibitionists may want to impress and shock women, but anger is not a common motive.

ANSWER KEY: CONCEPTUAL MULTIPLE-CHOICE QUESTIONS

1. c.   Because there are many conflicting legal and moral perspectives on acceptable sex, definitions of deviance are difficult.

    a.   Religious and legal authorities have made many pronouncements about which sexual acts are moral or illegal, and these color definitions of sexual deviation.

    b.   Not all sexual deviations involve personal distress; for example, fetishists can be quite content with their behavior.

    d.   Only the sexual dysfunctions involve an inability to perform; gender identity disorders and paraphilias involve no such problem.

2. c. Perhaps the most common of the sexual dysfunctions, sexual desire disorders are more common in women, but without knowing what is "normal," the diagnosis is difficult.

    a. Paraphilias are relatively rare, occur in men more than in women, and are not sexual dysfunctions.

    b. Premature ejaculation is a dysfunction that occurs exclusively in men.

    d. Females do not achieve erections.

3. d. Pressure and anxiety over performance are current factors that are particularly important causes of erectile dysfunction.

    a. Excessive levels of testosterone would increase masculine behavior.

    b. Childhood upbringing is an example of a predisposing factor.

    c. Unresolved castration anxiety is an example of a predisposing factor.

4. a. Transsexuals show gender identity abnormalities at a young age.

    b. Most transsexuals are men.

    c. Transsexuals maintain their gender identity disorder throughout adulthood.

    d. Transsexuals feel trapped in the wrong body and desire a change in physical characteristics.

5. d. Lack of male role models and cross-dressing are early experiences in many cases of gender identity disorder.

    a. Pedophilia, sexual involvement with children, is unrelated to cross-dressing.

    b. Premature ejaculation is a sexual dysfunction unrelated to male role models or cross-dressing.

    c. Sexual desire disorders are unrelated to cross-dressing.

6. b. Rubbing against a nonconsenting person is the core symptom of frotteurism; voyeurism involves watching others engage in sexual activity or observing unsuspecting undressed people.

    a. Rubbing against a nonconsenting person is the core symptom of frotteurism.

    c. Transvestic fetishism is deriving sexual arousal from cross-dressing.

    d. Exhibitionism involves exposing one's genitals to unsuspecting individuals for shock value.

7. c. Psychoanalytic theory asserts that all sexual deviations stem from unconscious fears of castration that go back to the oedipal stage of development.

    a. Classical conditioning proposes that certain stimuli are paired.

    b. Sociocultural theory would stress the roles of men and women.

    d. Masochism would not involve too few superego controls, but excessively harsh controls.

8. d. Behavioral treatment would extinguish sexual responses to fantasies about children and later introduce social skills and sexual responses to more appropriate adult stimuli.

    a. Learning approaches would want to weaken and eliminate any association between children and sexual arousal.

    b. Only in psychoanalytic therapy would raising unconscious issues be important.

    c. Imprisonment is not a form of behavioral treatment since it teaches nothing.

9. d. Research indicates that where violence is condoned, there is a "spillover effect" and rape is more common.

    a. Cultural spillover theory is associated with increased rates of one sexually deviant behavior: rape.

    b. Cultural spillover theory is unrelated to sexual dysfunction.

    c. Cultural spillover theory is unrelated to the paraphilias.

10. b. There has been no controlled research comparing psychotherapy and biological treatment.

    a. Imprisonment is the "treatment" most sex offenders get; it does not usually change their behavior.

    c. Rapists have not been found to be effectively treated; child molesters and exhibitionists seem to be treated more effectively.

    d. In one study, surgical castration led to reduced sexual activity and fantasy; results from Europe indicate low recidivism rates after castration.

ANSWER KEY: APPLICATION MULTIPLE-CHOICE QUESTIONS

1. b. Sexual desire is part of the appetitive stage, and erections are part of the excitement stage in the normal sexual response cycle.

    a. Erectile dysfunctions are associated with the excitement stage.

    c. Erectile dysfunctions are associated with the excitement stage.

    d. Sexual desire is part of the appetitive stage, not the excitement stage.

2. c. Female orgasmic disorder is often seen as a problem of insufficient stimulation; Wakefield (1988) claims it exists in less than 1 percent of women.

    a. Functional vaginismus usually stems from partners suffering from impotence, strict upbringing, sexual trauma, or dyspareunia.

    b. Transvestic fetishism is a male problem.

    d. Gender identity disorders in women would stem from very early childhood upbringing or biological differences, not from masturbatory practices.

3. d. Penile implants are frequently a successful treatment for erectile dysfunction when hormone replacement therapies and psychological treatments have failed.

    a. Premature ejaculation is treated with the squeeze technique.

    b. Low sexual desire is a problem caused by relationship stress or medication, not physical equipment.

    c. Pedophilia. is not a sexual dysfunction.

4. b. Premature ejaculation is treated by increasing the time during which stimulation occurs prior to ejaculation.

    a. A sexual pain disorder (vaginismus) would be treated by relaxation and insertion of successively larger dilators.

    c. Treatment of erectile dysfunction would increase stimulation, not stop it.

    d. Sexual desire disorder is treated with education, relaxation, and couples therapy.

5. a.   Gender identity disorder involves the feeling of being trapped in the body of the wrong sex.

    b.   The term *sexual desire disorder* is reserved for adults who have no interest in sexual activity or who avoid it.

    c.   Pedophiles do not feel trapped; they sexually abuse children.

    d.   Transvestites cross-dress, but they do so for sexual arousal, not because they identify with the opposite sex.

6. a.   Paraphilias are quite rare in females.

    b.   In most cases, people have more than one paraphilia; for example, child molesters often commit rape or expose themselves.

    c.   Most transvestites are married heterosexual males.

    d.   Most people with paraphilias are socially unskilled.

7. d.   The key symptom of exhibitionism is fantasizing about and actually exposing one's genitals in the manner Todd illustrates.

    a.   Gender identity disorders involve a conflict between genetic sex and preferred sex-appropriate dress and behavior.

    b.   Exposing ones genitals constitutes a paraphilia, not a sexual dysfunction.

    c.   Voyeurism involves observing sexual behavior in unsuspecting individuals or looking at disrobed people who do not consent to being observed.

8. c.   When observing is preferred over sex, the disorder can be diagnosed.

    a.   This does not illustrate the risk taking and exclusive preference shown in the disorder.

    b.   This does not illustrate the risk taking and exclusive preference shown in the disorder.

    d.   This does not illustrate the risk taking and exclusive preference shown in the disorder.

9. d.   Behavior therapists would first ensure that the problem behavior had been extinguished before moving on to more appropriate alternatives.

    a.   Psychoanalytic, not behavior, therapy would emphasize unconscious castration anxieties.

    b.   Behavior therapists do not rely on medicine to alter this behavior.

    c.   The squeeze technique is used to treat premature ejaculation.

10. a.   Rape trauma syndrome is a cluster of negative consequences following rape, such as sexual dysfunction, fear reactions, and psychological distress, including flashbacks, during sex, of the rape.

    b.   Erectile dysfunction may be upsetting, but fears and flashbacks in women are unheard of.

    c.   Victims of exhibitionism may be distressed, but there are no reports of either effects on the desire for sex or the production of flashbacks.

    d.   Few women have paraphilias.

OBJECTIVES DEFINED

1. **What are normal and abnormal sexual behaviors?**

- One of the difficulties in diagnosing abnormal sexual behavior is measuring it against a standard of normal sexual behavior. No attempt to establish such criteria has been completely successful, but these attempts have produced a better understanding of the normal human sexual response cycle.

2. **What does the normal sexual response cycle tell us about sexual dysfunctions?**

- The human sexual response cycle has four stages: the appetitive, arousal, orgasm, and resolution phases. Each may be characterized by problems, which may be diagnosed as disorders if they are recurrent and persistent.

- Sexual dysfunctions are disruptions of the normal sexual response cycle. They are fairly common in the general population and may affect a person's ability to become sexually aroused or to engage in intercourse. Many result from fear or anxiety regarding sexual activities; the various treatment programs are generally successful.

3. **What causes sexual dysfunctions?**

- The multi-path model illustrates how biological (hormonal variations and medical conditions), psychological (performance anxieties), social (parental upbringing and attitudes), and sociocultural (cultural scripts) dimensions contribute to sexual dysfunctions.

4. **What types of treatments are available for sexual dysfunctions?**

- Depending on the specific dysfunction, treatments vary from biological interventions such as hormone replacement in the treatment of low sexual desire, penile implants or drugs like Viagra for ED, to education and communications training to combat negative attitudes or misinformation about sex, and to structured sexual exercises for learning new behaviors and warding off performance anxieties.

5. **Is homosexuality a mental disorder?**

- Many myths and misunderstandings continue to surround homosexuality. The belief that homosexuality is deviant seems to relate more to homophobia than to scientific findings. DSM-IV-TR no longer considers homosexuality to be a psychological disorder.

6. **How does aging affect the sexual activity of the elderly?**

- Despite myths to the contrary, sexuality extends into old age. However, sexual dysfunction becomes increasingly prevalent with aging, and the frequency of sexual activity typically declines.

7. **What causes gender identity disorder and how is it treated?**

- Specified GID involves strong and persistent cross-gender identification. Transsexuals feel a severe psychological conflict between their sexual self-concepts and their genders. Children with this problem identify with members of the opposite gender, deny their own physical attributes, and often cross-dress.

- Some transsexuals seek sex-conversion surgery, although behavioral therapies are increasingly being used. For children, treatment generally includes the parents and is behavioral in nature.

8. **What are the paraphilias, what causes them, and how are they treated?**

- The paraphilias are of three types, characterized by (1) a preference for nonhuman objects for sexual arousal, (2) repetitive sexual activity with nonconsenting partners, or (3) the association of real or simulated suffering with sexual activity.

- Biological factors such as hormonal or brain processes have been studied as the cause of paraphilias, but the results have not been consistent enough to permit strong conclusions about the role of biological factors in the paraphilias. Psychological factors also play a role.

- Treatments are usually behavioral and are aimed at eliminating the deviant behavior while teaching more appropriate behaviors.

9. **Is rape an act of sex or aggression?**

- Rape is not listed in DSM-IV-TR, but it is a serious problem. There appears to be no single cause for rape and rapists seem to have different motivations and personalities.

- Some researchers feel that sociocultural factors can encourage rape and violence against women; others believe that biological factors coupled with sociocultural factors are important in explaining rape.

MARGIN DEFINITIONS

compulsive sexual behavior   a term used by many sex therapists to describe individuals who seem to crave constant sex at the expense of relationships, work productivity, and daily activities

dyspareunia   recurrent or persistent pain in the genitals before, during, or after sexual intercourse

exhibitionism   disorder characterized by urges, acts, or fantasies about the exposure of one's genitals to strangers

female orgasmic disorder   a sexual dysfunction in which the woman experiences persistent delay or inability to achieve an orgasm with stimulation that is adequate in focus, intensity, and duration after entering the excitement phase; also known as *inhibited female orgasm*

female sexual arousal disorder   the inability to attain or maintain physiological response and/or psychological arousal during sexual activity

fetishism   sexual attraction and fantasies involving inanimate objects such as female undergarments

frotteurism   disorder characterized by recurrent and intense sexual urges, acts, or fantasies or touching or rubbing against a nonconsenting person

gender identity disorder (transexualism)   disorder characterized by conflict between a person's anatomical sex and his or her gender identity, or self-identification as male or female

incest   a form of pedophilia; can also be sexual relations between people too closely related to marry legally

male erectile disorder   an inability to attain or maintain an erection sufficient for sexual intercourse and/or psychological arousal during sexual activity

male orgasmic disorder   persistent delay or inability to achieve an orgasm after the excitement phase has been reached and sexual activity has been adequate in focus, intensity, and duration; usually restricted to an inability to ejaculate within the vagina; also known as *inhibited male orgasm*

masochism   a paraphilia in which sexual urges, fantasies, or acts are associated with being humiliated, bound, or made to suffer

paraphilia   sexual disorder of at least six months' duration in which the person has either acted on or is severely distressed by recurrent urges or fantasies involving non-human objects, nonconsenting persons, or suffering or humiliation

pedophilia   disorder in which an adult obtains erotic gratification through urges, acts, or fantasies involving sexual contact with a prepubescent child

premature ejaculation ejaculation with minimal sexual stimulation before, during, or shortly after penetration

rape trauma syndrome a two-phase syndrome that rape victims may experience, including such emotional reactions as psychological distress, phobic reactions, and sexual dysfunction

rape a form of sexual aggression that refers to sexual activity (oral-genital sex, anal intercourse, and vaginal intercourse) performed against a person's will through the use of force, argument, pressure, alcohol or drugs, or authority

sadism form of paraphilia in which sexually arousing urges, fantasies, or acts are associated with inflicting physical or psychological suffering on others

sexual addiction a popular term referring to a person's desire and need to engage in constant and frequent sexual behavior (frequently labeled *compulsive sexual behavior*)

sexual arousal disorder disorder characterized by problems occurring during the excitement phase of the sexual response cycle and relating to difficulties with feelings of sexual pleasure or with the physiological changes associated with sexual excitement

sexual desire disorder sexual dysfunction that is related to the appetitive phase of the sexual response cycle and is characterized by a lack of sexual desire

sexual dysfunction a disruption of any part of the normal sexual response cycle that affects sexual desire, arousal, and response

transvestic fetishism intense sexual arousal obtained through cross-dressing (wearing clothes appropriate to the opposite gender); not to be confused with transsexualism

vaginismus involuntary spasm of the outer third of the vaginal wall, preventing or interfering with sexual intercourse

voyeurism urges, acts, or fantasies involving observation of an unsuspecting person disrobing or engaging in sexual activity

CHAPTER 11

Mood Disorders

TABLE OF CONTENTS

LEARNING OBJECTIVES

1. Discuss the symptoms of unipolar depression.

2. Describe what causes unipolar depression.

3. Discuss what kinds of treatment are available for people with unipolar depression and how effective they are.

4. Describe the symptoms of bipolar or manic depressive disorder.

5. Discuss the causes of bipolar disorder.

6. Discuss the primary means of treating bipolar disorder.

CHAPTER OUTLINE

I. **Unipolar depression.** Mood disorders, which rank among the top ten causes of worldwide disability, are disturbances in emotions that cause discomfort or hinder functioning. *Depression* is by far the most common mood disorder and is characterized by sadness, feelings of worthlessness, and social withdrawal. *Mania* is characterized by elevated mood, expansiveness, and irritability. Depression and mania are different from normal mood changes because they are more intense, last longer, and may occur for no apparent reason. Lifetime prevalence for depression ranges from 8 to 19 percent. . The affective (emotional) symptoms of depression are sadness, dejection, crying spells, and feelings of worthlessness. Cognitive symptoms include profound pessimism, loss of interest, and suicidal thoughts. The cognitive triad (negativism, about self, others and the future) is found in depressives. Behavioral symptoms include poor personal hygiene, slowed speech and movement (psychomotor retardation), and social withdrawal. Physiological symptoms of depression include disturbances of eating, constipation, sleeping, sexual activity, and menstruation. Depressive disorders are considered unipolar, whereas disorders with manic and depressive episodes are *bipolar disorders*. Depressive disorders include major depressive disorder, dysthymic disorder, and depressive disorders not otherwise specified. Symptoms must be present for at least two weeks and must represent a change from typical functioning to be considered signs of a mood disorder. About half of those who have a depressive episode have another. *Dysthymic disorder* is a chronic condition (at least two years) involving depressed mood, low self-esteem, fatigue, and apathy. DSM-IV-TR also lists *symptom* features—characteristics that accompany mood disorders but are not criteria for diagnosis. These include *melancholia* (loss of pleasure, depression worse in the morning) and *catatonia* (immobility and negativism). *Course specifiers* in DSM-IV-TR indicate whether the mood disorder is cyclic (how quickly moods shift from manic to depressive), *seasonal, postpartum* (after giving birth), or *longitudinal* (length between relapses). Unipolar and bipolar disorders are distinguished from one another because in bipolar, inheritance plays a bigger role, the age of onset is earlier, depressive episodes involve greater motor retardation, and lithium provides effective relief. Lifetime prevalence of bipolar disorder is roughly 1 percent. Finally, there is no sex difference for bipolar disorder, but major depression is far more common in women.

II. **Etiology of unipolar depression.** Biological approaches to the causes of mood disorders generally focus on genetic predisposition, physiological dysfunction, or combinations of the two. There is now overwhelming evidence that mood disorders carry significant genetic components whose ultimate phenotypic expression is highly dependent on environmental factors. But how is heredity involved in major mood disorders? Research shows that dysfunctions in neurotransmission in the brain, perhaps influenced by heredity, is associated with depression. Because the prefrontal region, amygdala, and hippocampus of the brain are involved in emotional regulation, investigators have been searching for possible leads. Considerable interest has also focused on possible abnormalities in neuroendocrine regulation in depression. People experiencing depression tend to have high levels of cortisol, a hormone secreted by the adrenal cortex In the psychological dimensions, psychoanalysts suggest that separation and anger are potent causal factors. Separation can be real or symbolic, but is different from normal mourning. Guilt can account for some depressive symptoms, and anger (at the lost person) turned against the self accounts for others. Behaviorists suggest that reduced reinforcements lead to reduced reinforceable activity, thus producing a downward spiral. A lack of self-reinforcement, social skills, and a tendency to create more stressors are also associated with depression. Lewinsohn and his colleagues have developed a comprehensive view of depression: Stress disrupts established behavior patterns, positive reinforcement declines, self-critical and low-confidence thoughts produce depressed affect, which makes functioning more difficult. Cognitive theorists suggest that depressives' *schemas* for interpreting events produce low self-esteem. According to Beck, depressives operate from a primary triad involving negative expectations about self, others, and the future. Four errors in logic typify this schema: arbitrary inference, selected abstraction, overgeneralization and magnification and minimization. Cognitive-learning approaches include *learned helplessness* and *attributional style*. Learned helplessness argues that depression occurs when, after experiencing uncontrollable stressors, a person comes to believe that he or she has no effect on the environment. Coupled with a certain attributional style, learned helplessness leads to the passivity that characterizes depression. The pessimistic attributional style sees the causes of bad events as internal, global (true for many situations), and stable (a permanent condition). Attributional style may be related to achievements, health, and depression although the causal relationships are not established. Lewinsohn, et al., tested the diathesis-stress processes involved in both Beck's and Seligman's theories, found more support for Beck's than Seligman's and high levels of negative cognitions coupled with stress tended to predict depression; counterintuitively, that only at low levels of stress did negative attributional styles predict depression; and that these models did not predict nondepressive disorders. The social dimension explanations stress differences in prevalence rates and symptom pictures across cultures. Stress theory argues that individuals have a vulnerability to depression (diathesis), exposure to stressors, and limited resources such as social supports; cross-cultural factors have been noticed in this regard. The sociocultural dimension studies gender differences in depression and concludes they may not be real because women are more likely to be seen in treatment and may report their symptoms more readily than men. Diagnostic bias and misdiagnosis of male depression are other explanations. Real differences may be due to biology, gender roles, or social restrictions on women. Nolen-Hoeksema concluded that women are more likely than men to ruminate in response to depressed mood.

III. **Treatment for unipolar depression**. Biomedical treatments are interventions that alter the physical or biochemical state of the patient. The principal medications used to treat depression are *tricyclic antidepressants, heterocyclic antidepressants, monoamine oxidase (MAO) inhibitors,* and *SSRIs* such as fluoxetine *(Prozac).* Tricyclics block the reuptake of norepinephrine but cause side effects such as drowsiness, insomnia, and agitation. MAO inhibitors have a serious interaction with tyramine, found in many cheeses and other fermented products. Prozac, a widely used SSRI, blocks the reuptake of serotonin. *Electroconvulsive therapy (ECT),* usually reserved for severe depressives who do not respond to medications, works rapidly but can cause memory loss, so is controversial. Interpersonal psychotherapy is a short-term, psychodynamic-eclectic treatment that focuses on current conflicts in relationships and links these to earlier life experiences and traumas. Cognitive behavioral therapy teaches the patient to identify, examine, and replace distorted negative thoughts with more realistic ones. Patients increase their activity level and improve their social skills. Both forms of treatment are effective and equal to medication. Cognitive behavioral training reduces the risk of relapses and can be helpful in preventing depression.

IV. **Bipolar disorders.** The symptoms of mania have the following characteristics: the affective symptoms of mania are elation or irritability and grandiosity; cognitive symptoms include accelerated and disjointed speech; behaviorally, at the level of hypomania, people are overactive but not delusional. Mania involves increased levels of activity, incoherence, and sleeplessness. In severe forms, hallucinations and delusions appear and the person is uncontrollable. Cognitive symptoms of mania include grandiosity, flightiness, pressured (or intrusive) thoughts, lack of focus and attention, and poor judgment. In terms of behavioral symptoms, individuals with mania are often uninhibited, engaging impulsively in sexual activity or abusive discourse. The most prominent physiological or somatic symptom is a decreased need for sleep, accompanied by high levels of arousal. The energy and excitement these patients show may cause them to lose weight or to go without sleep for long periods. The essential feature of bipolar disorders is the occurrence of one or more manic or hypomanic episodes; the term *bipolar* is used because the disorders are usually accompanied by one or more depressive episodes. Criteria for diagnosing bipolar disorder in DSM specify that manic episodes last at least one week in the case of mania and four days in the case of hypomania. Bipolar disorders include subcategories that describe the nature of the disorder. Bipolar I disorders include *single manic episode, most recent episode hypomanic, most recent episode manic, most recent episode mixed, most recent episode depressed,* and *most recent episode unspecified.* Bipolar II disorder includes *recurrent major depressive episodes with hypomania.* Persons in whom manic but not depressive episodes have occurred are extremely rare; in such cases, a depressive episode will presumably appear at some time. As in the case of dysthymia, *cyclothymic disorder* is a chronic and relatively continual mood disorder in which the person is never symptom free for more than two months. With lifetime prevalence between 0.4 and 1 percent, cyclothymia is less common than dysthymia. The risk that a person with cyclothymia will subsequently develop a bipolar disorder is 15 to 50 percent.

V. **Etiology of bipolar disorders.** Biological explanations of the causes of mood disorders emphasize evidence that genetic factors play a role, particularly in bipolar disorder. Concordance rates for bipolar disorder average 72 percent for identical twins and 14 percent for fraternals; the percentages are 40 and 11 for unipolar mood disorders. Genetic factors may predispose people to a deficit of activity in certain neurotransmitters.

VI. **Treatment for bipolar disorders**. Drugs such as lithium are often used in the treatment of bipolar disorder, although there are side effects. Patient compliance with lithium treatment is another impediment.

VII. **Implications.** We know that depression is relatively widespread and seriously affects people throughout the world. No single theory can adequately account for depression or bipolar disorder. Increasingly, researchers have proposed multi-path explanatory models. They try to link genetic findings, brain-body functioning, and psychological, social, and sociocultural factors in mood disorders.

KEY TERMS REVIEW

1. A pattern of thinking or a cognitive set that determines an individual's reactions and responses is called a(n) _____ .

2. The DSM-IV-TR category including major depressive disorder, dysthymic disorder, and depressive disorders not otherwise specified and generally known as the unipolar disorders is also called _____ .

3. The emotional state characterized by great elation, seemingly boundless energy, and irritability is called _____ .

4. Severe disturbances of emotions or affect involving depression, mania, or both are called _____ .

5. The disorders in which both depression and mania are exhibited and those in which only mania has been exhibited are called _____ .

6. A disorder whose symptoms include depressed mood, loss of interest, sleep disturbances, and an inability to concentrate, lasting at least two weeks, is called _____ .

7. _____ is a mood disorder in which only depression occurs and is characterized by intense sadness, feelings of futility and worthlessness, and withdrawal from others.

8. A mild, chronic mood disorder characterized by nonpsychotic mood swings is called _____ .

9. A, mild, chronic mood disorder characterized by nonpsychotic depression is called _____ .

10. Acquiring the belief that one is impotent and cannot control the outcomes in one's life is called _____ .

FACTUAL MULTIPLE-CHOICE QUESTIONS

1. The prevalence of mania is _____ that of major depression.
   a. about one-half
   b. about the same as
   c. more than two times
   d. about one-tenth

2. When a mild depression continues for most days over a two-year period and includes symptoms of social withdrawal, pessimism, and loss of interest, the appropriate diagnosis is
   a. dysthymic disorder.
   b. exogenous depression.
   c. cyclothymic disorder.
   d. major depression.

3. Mood disorders that occur during certain seasons of the year or after a woman gives birth are considered disorders
   a. that are endogenous.
   b. with certain symptom features.
   c. that are bipolar.
   d. with course specifiers.

4. Symbolic loss, grief work, and anger turned inward are central concepts in the
    _____ theory of depression.

    a. psychodynamic
    b. cognitive
    c. learned helplessness
    d. operant conditioning

5. When things are going poorly, depressives make attributions that are

    a. external, unstable, and global.
    b. internal, global, and stable.
    c. internal, unstable, and specific.
    d. external, stable, and global.

6. Low levels of _____ are most commonly found in people suffering from major
    depression.

    a. REM sleep
    b. norepinephrine
    c. dexamethasone
    d. Prozac and lithium carbonate

7. One type of drug used to treat unipolar depression has a number of serious side effects related to
    diet. These drugs are known as

    a. MAO inhibitors.
    b. catecholamines.
    c. tricyclics.
    d. Prozac.

8. Electroconvulsive therapy (ECT) is usually used for treating _____ but it causes
    side effects, such as _____.

    a. bipolar disorder; gastrointestinal difficulties
    b. severely depressed patients; confusion and memory loss
    c. dysthymic individuals; increased REM sleep and decreased norepinephrine
    d. mildly depressed individuals; dependency on the therapist and increasing apathy

9. Lithium carbonate is usually used in the treatment of

    a. dysthymic disorder.
    b. bipolar disorder.
    c. unipolar depression.
    d. melancholia.

10. All of the following are typical symptoms of unipolar depression *except*

    a. loss of sex drive.
    b. crying spells.
    c. occasional manic spells.
    d. social withdrawal.

CONCEPTUAL MULTIPLE-CHOICE QUESTIONS

1. When a person's mood disturbance involves hyperactivity, irritability, and expansiveness, the
    problem is considered

    a. depression.
    b. dysthymia.
    c. mania.
    d. schizophrenia.

2.   Difficulty in concentration, suicidal thoughts, and loss of motivation are

    a.   physiological signs of depression.
    b.   cognitive signs of depression.
    c.   elements of the cognitive triad.
    d.   affective signs of hypomania.

3.   Which of the following symptoms is characteristic of hypomania?

    a.   Slowed movements and speech
    b.   Extreme irritability, sleeplessness, and hallucinations
    c.   "High" mood, poor judgment, and grandiosity
    d.   Weight loss, feelings of worthlessness, and apathy

4.   When family and friends are sympathetic toward a depressed person, according to behavioral psychologists,

    a.   the person develops a negative cognitive schema.
    b.   the family shows a negative attributional style.
    c.   the depression will deepen.
    d.   this will challenge the depressive's irrational beliefs.

5.   According to _____, the cure for depression requires increased activity levels and improved social skills; according to _____ the cure for depression is changed schemas and improved self-esteem.

    a.   Beck; Seligman
    b.   Seligman; Lewinsohn
    c.   Freud; Beck
    d.   Lewinsohn; Beck

6.   If we see depression as a mistaken belief that outcomes are independent of our actions and that the disorder is a motivational problem, we are seeing it as a problem involving

    a.   unconscious conflicts.
    b.   sociocultural norms.
    c.   learned helplessness.
    d.   illogical attributional thoughts.

7.   The gender difference in _____ may be either "real" and due to hormonal differences or caused by _____.

    a.   bipolar disorder; diagnosticians' expectations about women
    b.   major depression; women's greater likelihood to ask for help
    c.   major depression; men's tendency to ruminate about their symptoms
    d.   bipolar disorder; women's greater likelihood to ask for help

8.   Studies to determine the biological factors that cause mood disorders have shown that

    a.   concordance rates for MZ and DZ twins are about the same for bipolar disorder.
    b.   the incidence of major depression is higher in individuals' adoptive families than in biological families.
    c.   concordance rates for bipolar disorder are higher for MZ twins than for DZ twins.
    d.   biological factors are more potent predictors of major depression than of bipolar disorder.

9.   The client monitors his or her thoughts and emotions, then increases pleasurable activities and social skills. These processes are components of

    a.   psychoanalytic therapy for depression.
    b.   psychoanalytic therapy for bipolar disorder.
    c.   cognitive-behavioral therapy for bipolar disorder.
    d.   cognitive-behavioral therapy for depression.

10. Which statement about cognitive therapy for depression is *accurate*?

    a. Cognitive therapy is less effective than medication but more effective than interpersonal psychotherapy.
    b. With cognitive therapy the risk of relapse is less than with medication.
    c. Cognitive therapy relates the person's current conflicts with traumas from the past.
    d. Cognitive therapy accepts the client's attributional style but changes their activity level.

APPLICATION MULTIPLE-CHOICE QUESTIONS

1. Jon is so depressed that if he thinks about himself or the future, all he can imagine is failure. He does not believe that anyone else can help him, either. Jon's symptoms illustrate

    a. the physiological symptoms of depression.
    b. the affective symptoms of depression.
    c. what Beck calls the cognitive triad of depression.
    d. what Freud calls learned helplessness.

2. Frank is diagnosed with bipolar disorder. His symptoms are elevated mood, disjointed talk, excessive sleep, and irritability at others. Which aspect of Frank's case is unusual?

    a. Most people with bipolar disorder are female.
    b. Most people with bipolar disorder remain awake for long periods.
    c. Most people with bipolar disorder are calm rather than irritable.
    d. Disjointed talk never occurs in bipolar disorder.

3. Sarah has had many mild swings of mood over the past two years. She has never been hypomanic so the correct diagnosis is

    a. dysthymic disorder.
    b. cyclothymic disorder.
    c. Bipolar I.
    d. Bipolar I.

4. Richard is depressed, and his therapist says, "The best way to feel better is to do more. Doing more increases your chances of being rewarded and finding pleasure in your activities." Richard's therapist illustrates

    a. the psychodynamic approach to treatment.
    b. Lewinsohn's learning approach to treatment.
    c. Beck's cognitive approach to treatment.
    d. the humanistic-existential approach to treatment.

5. Cathy throws a party one evening, but it rains so hard that the party must be canceled. Cathy concludes that she is worthless. According to Beck's cognitive theory, this error in logic is called

    a. magnification and minimization.
    b. undergeneralization.
    c. the cognitive triad.
    d. arbitrary inference.

6. Seligman suggests that depressives make a certain type of attribution for failure. Which statement below best illustrates that attributional style?

    a. "I didn't work hard enough, but tomorrow I will work harder."
    b. "The job was too hard for anyone to do; I can't blame myself."
    c. "I am stupid and I always will be stupid; it shows in everything I do."
    d. "Just because I fail in one area of life doesn't mean I'll fail in others."

7. Dr. Nemmah says, "Depressed women respond to some stressors by creating more crises for themselves. Their lack of effective coping makes the depression continue and get worse." This statement suggests that

    a. the gender difference for depression is more imagined than real.

    b. depressed women consciously try to further their depression.

    c. women who are depressed seek treatment at an earlier time than men.

    d. stress triggers depression and depression triggers stress.

8. Verne suffers from major depression. What can we predict about his sleep habits?

    a. He may have trouble getting to sleep or awaken earlier than he wants.

    b. He may have slower onset and less frequent REM sleep than others.

    c. He can fall asleep only when he uses cortisol.

    d. He will feel fatigued at night but rested during the day.

9. Kim is being treated for depression by a therapist who focuses on her current relationships and makes links to earlier life experiences and traumas. The treatment is briefer than traditional psychoanalytic therapy but uses some of the same concepts. What kind of therapy is Kim receiving?

    a. Beck's cognitive therapy

    b. Electroconvulsive therapy

    c. Seligman's attributional therapy

    d. Interpersonal psychotherapy

10. Martha has major depressive disorder. She was treated with tricyclics, and MAO inhibitors without success. Her therapist tells her, "The only effective treatment left is ECT." What is incorrect about this advice?

    a. ECT is only effective with people suffering from bipolar disorder.

    b. ECT is ineffective if tricyclic medication has been ineffective.

    c. Cognitive therapy is as successful as drug therapy.

    d. Lithium is the most successful treatment for major depressive disorder.

ANSWER KEY: KEY TERMS REVIEW

1. schema

2. depressive disorders

3. mania

4. mood disorders

5. bipolar disorders

6. major depression

7. unipolar depression

8. cyclothymic disorder

9. dysthymic disorder

10. learned helplessness

ANSWER KEY: FACTUAL MULTIPLE-CHOICE QUESTIONS

1. d. The prevalence of depression is more than 10 times that of mania.

    a. The prevalence of depression is more than 10 times that of mania.

    b. Mania is much less common than depression.

    c. Mania is much less common than depression.

2. a.   Dysthymic disorder is a mild depression that goes on for at least two years, so long that it seems congruent with the person's personality.

      b.   An exogenous depression is triggered by outside events and usually ends when the stressor does.

      c.   Cyclothymic disorder involves mild, but chronic, mood swings.

      d.   Major depression has more severe symptoms than those described here and must elicit behaviors foreign to the person's personality.

3. d.   Course specifiers describe the circumstances under which the disorders occur-seasonal, postpartum, cycling, and longitudinal patterns are examples.

      a.   Endogenous mood disorders are ones that are unrelated to environmental changes.

      b.   Symptom features include catatonia (lack of movement) and melancholia (lack of motivation) and focus on the behaviors of the individual, not the circumstances under which the disorders occur.

      c.   Bipolar disorders involve mood swings.

4. a.   Psychoanalysts believe that early childhood losses, incomplete grieving, and angry feelings turned toward oneself are important in depression.

      b.   The cognitive perspective emphasizes illogical thinking, negative schemas, and inappropriate attributions.

      c.   Learned helplessness argues that depression occurs when individuals mistakenly generalize, from a circumstance in which inescapable negative consequences occurred, the belief they have no control over the events in their lives.

      d.   The operant conditioning approach to depression highlights poor social skills, lack of reinforcement for actions, and reinforcement for inaction.

5. b.   Depressives are depressed because they blame themselves (internal) for everything (global) and assume that their inability is unchanging (stable).

      a.   Depressives tend to blame themselves (make internal attributions) when things go poorly.

      c.   If people say that they are at fault (internal) but that the fault is specific to one situation and may change, they are less apt to become depressed.

      d.   Depressives tend to blame themselves, not outside factors.

6. b.   Supporting the catecholamine hypothesis, low levels of norepinephrine activity are found in major depression and are changed by antidepressant drugs.

      a.   In major depression, REM sleep appears to be excessive.

      c.   Dexamethasone usually suppresses cortisol levels, but only in certain kinds of depression.

      d.   Prozac is an antidepressant medication; lithium carbonate is a treatment for bipolar disorder.

7. a.   MAO inhibitors are antidepressants that interact with tyramine (an amino acid found in many foods) and cause side effects that can be lethal.

    b.   Catecholamines are neurotransmitters that are associated with mood disorders; they are not drugs.

    c.   Tricyclics are antidepressants, but they have no known side effects resulting from food interactions.

    d.   Prozac is an antidepressant that does not, as far as we know, have any interaction with chemicals in the diet.

8. b.   ECT is used when drugs have not helped seriously depressed people. Common side effects include memory loss, and in about 1 in every 1000 cases there are serious medical complications.

    a.   Electroconvulsive therapy is reserved almost exclusively for treating severe unipolar depression.

    c.   Dysthymic disorder is too mild a depression for ECT to be used.

    d.   ECT's major side effect is memory loss, not dependency.

9. b.   Lithium carbonate is used almost exclusively to treat bipolar disorder; it brings down the highs and lifts the lows.

    a.   Dysthymic disorder is a mild, chronic depression; medical treatment would probably involve antidepressants.

    c.   Unipolar depression is most often treated with antidepressants.

    d.   Melancholia is a symptom feature of depressive disorders.

10. c.   Manic spells are not typically associated with unipolar depression.

    a.   Loss of sex drive is a typical symptom of unipolar depression.

    b.   Crying spells are a typical symptom of unipolar depression.

    d.   Social withdrawal is a typical symptom of unipolar depression.

ANSWER KEY: CONCEPTUAL MULTIPLE-CHOICE QUESTIONS

1. c.   Mania involves uncontrollably "high" moods that include excessive activity, sleeplessness, and irritability because others cannot keep up.

    a.   Depression is characterized by sadness, feelings of worthlessness, and reduced activity.

    b.   Dysthymia is a mild depression that goes on for long periods.

    d.   Schizophrenia is a thought disorder rather than a mood disorder.

2. b.   Cognitive (thought) symptoms of depression include poor concentration, thoughts of suicide and worthlessness, and negative self-statements.

    a.   Physiological (bodily) symptoms of depression include gastrointestinal problems, weight loss, and sleep problems.

    c.   The cognitive triad involves illogical ways of viewing oneself

    d.   The affective signs of hypomania are hyperactivity and grandiosity.

3.   c.   Hypomania, a milder form of mania, is marked by hyperactivity and poor judgment, but no hallucinations or delusions.

      a.   Hypomania is a form of bipolar disorder involving excessive and rapid activity.

      b.   Mania is the more severe form of bipolar disorder during which people are delusional, stay up for long hours, and speak wildly.

      d.   Feelings of worthlessness and apathy are key symptoms of depression.

4.   c.   According to operant theorists, when depressive behavior is rewarded through sympathetic attention, the depressed person will probably withdraw further and get worse.

      a.   Negative cognitive schemas are persistent thoughts that cause depression; kindness will not help one develop.

      b.   The depressive has a negative attributional style (gives internal and stable, global trait, reasons for any failure), not the family or friends.

      d.   Sympathy does not challenge irrational beliefs; in fact, it may strengthen them.

5.   d.   Lewinsohn is an operant theorist and emphasizes what people do; Beck is a cognitive theorist concerned with what they think.

      a.   Increases in social skills are more the concern of an operant therapist than of a cognitive therapist like Beck.

      b.   Lewinsohn is a believer in operant conditioning and puts less emphasis on cognitive issues like schemas and self-esteem.

      c.   Freud stressed the symbolic, not the social skills or activity levels of patients.

6.   c.   The concept of learned helplessness involves believing (mistakenly) that our actions have no impact on outcomes and that there is nothing to motivate us.

      a.   Unconscious conflicts suggest a psychodynamic approach: seeing depression as a function of separation and anger turned inward.

      b.   Sociocultural norms would highlight the ways depression is to be expressed and the situations in which members of the society are "permitted" to be depressed.

      d.   No attributional thoughts are illogical; depressives tend to see their failures as due to their own actions—the opposite of thinking that their actions have no consequences.

7.   b.   There is a considerable sex difference in reported rates of major depression, but this may only be an illusory difference because women are more likely to request help.

      a.   There is no sex difference in rates of bipolar disorder.

      c.   The sex difference in major depression is that women have a higher reported rate than men; women tend to ruminate about their symptoms more than men.

      d.   There is no sex difference in rates of bipolar disorder.

8.   c.   Higher concordance rates for MZ (70+ percent) than for DZ twins (10+ percent) indicate a strong genetic contribution.

      a.   Higher concordance rates for MZ (70+ percent) than for DZ twins (10+ percent) indicate a strong genetic contribution.

      b.   Rates are higher in biological families than in adoptive ones.

      d.   Biological factors appear to be better predictors of bipolar disorder than of major depression.

9.   d.   Cognitive-behavioral therapy stresses irrational thoughts and the need to change both those thoughts and the behaviors that typically reduce opportunities for pleasure.

      a.   Psychoanalysts would be interested in dreams and the symbolic meaning of depression, not in activities and social skills.

      b.   Psychoanalysts would be interested in dreams and the symbolic meaning of bipolar disorder, not in activities and social skills.

      c.   Bipolar disorder is usually treated with drugs, particularly lithium carbonate, since bipolar disorder appears to be an endogenous mood disorder.

10.   b.   Cognitive-behavioral therapy tends to yield lower relapse rates than medication treatment alone.

      a.   In general, interpersonal therapy, cognitive-behavioral therapy, and imipramine treatment were equally effective in treating depressive disorder.

      c.   Psychodynamic treatment addresses past events and their effect on current mood.

      d.   Cognitive-behavior therapy focuses on changing one's maladaptive thinking processes.

ANSWER KEY: APPLICATION MULTIPLE-CHOICE QUESTIONS

1.   c.   Beck stresses the cognitive aspects of depression; the cognitive triad consists of negative views of others, of oneself, and of the future.

      a.   Physiological symptoms include weight loss, sleeplessness, and gastrointestinal problems.

      b.   Affective symptoms include sadness and crying, slumped posture, and a sense of defeat.

      d.   Seligman, not Freud, is associated with learned helplessness.

2.   b.   When in the midst of a manic episode, bipolar patients can stay awake for days on end.

      a.   There is no sex difference in rates of bipolar disorder.

      c.   When people experience mania, they speed up activity and become irritable with others who cannot keep up.

      d.   As mania becomes more severe, the speed of speech increases and its coherence decreases.

3.   b.   Cyclothymic disorder is a mild form of bipolar disorder, with repeated mood swings, but without ever reaching the criteria for hypomania or depression.

      a.   Dysthymic disorder is a mild form of depression that can last for years but does not involve mood swings.

      c.   Bipolar I disorders involve a manic episode.

      d.   Bipolar II disorder is characterized by a hypomanic episode and periods of major depression.

4.   b.   The therapist's remarks mirror Lewinsohn's behavioral approach, which sees depression as a lack of reinforced activity.

      a.   The therapist's comments stress activity rather than separation, anger, or other symbolic issues that psychoanalysts would emphasize.

      c.   Beck's cognitive approach would examine and seek to change Richard's illogical thinking.

      d.   A humanistic-existential approach would not highlight the reinforcing aspects of activity.

5. d. Arbitrary inference occurs when a depressive draws a conclusion without evidence (for example, a rainy day does not indicate that one is worthless).

    a. Magnification is an exaggeration of limitations, and minimization is a diminution of achievements.

    b. The logical error is overgeneralization.

    c. The cognitive triad is a negative schema for self, others, and the future.

6. c. The depressive attributional style involves making internal and stable attributions for failure.

    a. How hard one works is an internal attribution, and suggesting the possibility for change makes the attribution unstable.

    b. Blaming an external factor (task difficulty) for failure contradicts the depressive's attributional tendency.

    d. Specific attributions are unlike the global attributions of the depressive attributional style.

7. d. Hammen's longitudinal research shows that depressive women respond to stress in ways that foster depression, but also that their depressive actions bring on more stress.

    a. Differences in diagnostic criteria and help-seeking are reasons the gender difference may be more imagined than real; this describes a real difference in behavior.

    b. The statement does not suggest that there is a conscious attempt to bring more pain into their lives.

    c. If anything, this statement suggests that depressives would get help later, after they have used inadequate coping methods.

8. a. Insomnia and early waking are classic symptoms of depression.

    b. Depressives demonstrate more rapid onset and greater frequency of REM sleep.

    c. Cortisol is a naturally occurring hormone and levels are higher in depressives.

    d. Fatigue during the day is a classic symptom of depression; depressives rarely feel well rested.

9. d. Interpersonal psychotherapy is a short-term, psychodynamic-eclectic treatment that looks at current relationships and their links to earlier life experiences.

    a. Beck's cognitive therapy focuses on examining and changing illogical schemas.

    b. Electroconvulsive therapy is a biological treatment rather than a talk therapy.

    c. Seligman's attributional therapy focuses on the mistaken causal explanations a depressive uses.

10. c. Research shows that cognitive therapy is as effective as medication; the two together are no more effective than either separately.

    a. ECT is used with severely depressed people and is much less effective with bipolar disorder.

    b. ECT is often successfully used when antidepressant medication is ineffective.

    d. Lithium is only effective in treating bipolar disorder.

OBJECTIVES DEFINED

1. **What are the symptoms of unipolar depression?**

- Depression involves affective, cognitive, behavioral, and physiological symptoms, such as sadness, pessimism, low energy, and sleep disturbances.

- Unipolar depression, the broad name for depressive disorders, involves the occurrence of depression without any history of mania. In DSM, two types of depressive disorders can be diagnosed: major depression, in which the depression is severe, and dysthymic disorder, in which the depression is less severe but long term.

2. **What causes unipolar depression?**

- Evidence shows that biological factors, including heredity, are important in predisposing one to depression. The functioning of neurotransmitters, brain structure activities, and cortisol levels in the body are associated with depression.

- Psychological theories of depression have been proposed by adherents of the psychodynamic, behavioral, cognitive, cognitive-learning, and sociocultural viewpoints. Psychodynamic explanations focus on separation and anger. Behavioral explanations focus on reduced reinforcement following losses. Cognitive explanations see low self-esteem as an important factor. According to the learned helplessness theory of depression, susceptibility to depression depends on the person's experience with controlling the environment. The person's attributional style—speculations about why he or she is helpless—is also important.

- Social explanations focus on relationships and interpersonal stressors and social supports that make one vulnerable to, or resilient against, depression.

- Sociocultural explanations have focused on cultural, demographic, and socioeconomic factors that influence the rates and symptoms of mood disorders. For example, women have a higher prevalence for depression than men and various biological and social psychological factors have been proposed for this gender discrepancy.

3. **What kinds of treatment are available for people with unipolar depression, and how effective are they?**

- Different forms of psychological and behavioral treatments have been found to be effective with depressive disorders. These include cognitive-behavioral treatment, which seeks to replace negative thoughts with more realistic (or positive) cognitions, and interpersonal therapy, which is a short-term treatment focused on interpersonal issues. Biomedical approaches to treating depression focus on increasing the amounts of neurotransmitters available at brain synapses or affecting the sensitivity of postsynaptic receptors through either medication or electroconvulsive therapy. Anti-depressant medication is effective but, unlike some psychological treatments, its effects last only as long as one continues with medication.

4. **What are the symptoms of bipolar or manic depressive disorder?**

- Bipolar disorder is characterized by the occurrence of mania, in which a person shows elation, lack of focus, impulsive actions, and almost boundless energy.

- In bipolar mood disorders, manic episodes occur or alternate with depressive episodes. DSM-IV-TR recognizes two levels of manic intensity. Hypomania and mania. Hypomania is the milder form in which affected people seem to be "high" in mood and overactive in behavior. People suffering from mania display more disruptive behaviors, including pronounced overactivity, grandiosity, and irritability. Their behaviors may be so extreme as to require restraint and medication.

5.   **What causes bipolar disorder?**

- In finding the causes of bipolar disorders, researchers have also focused on biological, psychological, social, and sociocultural factors. However, much more research has been devoted to unipolar depression. Research has shown that bipolar disorders seem to have stronger genetic basis and to have a reduced gender difference than those found in unipolar depression. Nevertheless, consistent with a multi-path model, bipolar disorder is affected by a number of different factors.

6.   **What are the primary means of treating bipolar disorder?**

- The most effective treatment for bipolar and manic disorders is lithium, a drug that lowers the level of neurotransmitters at synapses by increasing the reuptake of norepinephrine, although other drugs are being tested for use in these disorders. Research has increasingly shown that psychotherapy is also effective in treating bipolar disorders.

MARGIN DEFINITIONS

bipolar disorder a mood disorder in which depression is accompanied by mania, which is characterized by elevated mood, expansiveness, or irritability, often resulting in hyperactivity

cyclothymic disorder a chronic and relatively continual mood disorder in which the person is never symptom free for more than two months

depressive disorders disorders that include major depressive disorder and dysthymic disorder with no history of a manic episode; also called unipolar depression

dysthymic disorder (dysthymia) depressed mood which is chronic and relatively continual and does not meet the criteria for major depression

learned helplessness an acquired belief that one is helpless and unable to affect the outcomes in one's life

major depressive disorder a major depressive episode whose symptoms include a depressed mood or a loss of interest or pleasure, weight loss or gain, sleep difficulties, fatigue, feelings of worthlessness, inability to concentrate, and recurrent thoughts of death

mania characteristic of bipolar disorder, consisting of elevated mood, expansiveness, or irritability, often resulting in hyperactivity

mood disorders disturbances in emotions that cause subjective discomfort, hinder a person's ability to function, or both

schemas cognitive frameworks that help organize and interpret information

unipolar depression a mood disorder in which only depression occurs and that is characterized by intense sadness, feelings of futility and worthlessness, and withdrawal from others

CHAPTER 12

Suicide

TABLE OF CONTENTS

LEARNING OBJECTIVES

1.   Discuss what we know about suicide.

2.   Define the major explanations of suicide.

3.   Discuss who the victims of suicide are.

4.   Discuss how we can intervene or prevent suicides.

5.   Discuss if there are times and situations in which suicide should be an option.

CHAPTER OUTLINE

I.   **Correlates of suicide**. People may commit suicide if they feel depressed, like a failure, as though the quality of their life is poor, unwanted, as though their death is for a greater good and for many other reasons. Suicide is not a disorder in DSM-IV-TR, but is important in abnormal psychology, and the suicidal person has clear psychiatric symptoms. Suicide and suicidal ideation (thinking about it) may be separate from depression. As a topic, suicide has been hidden, but as the eleventh leading cause of death in the United States, it is now emerging as a focus of research and social discussion. Those who complete suicide attempts cannot be asked their reasons. Patterned after *medical autopsies*, a *psychological autopsy* attempts to make psychological sense of suicide by examining the person's case history, interviewing family and friends, and analyzing suicide notes. However, these sources of information are often unavailable or unreliable. Every sixteen minutes or so, someone in the United States takes his or her own life. Approximately 31,000 persons kill themselves each year. Suicide is among the top eleven causes of death in the industrialized parts of the world; it is the eighth leading cause of death among American males and the third leading cause of death among young people ages fifteen to twenty-four. Some evidence shows that the number of actual suicides is probably 25 to 30 percent higher than that recorded. Many deaths that are officially recorded as accidental—such as single-auto crashes, drownings, or falls from great heights—are actually suicides. Suicides among the young have increased dramatically in the past decade. Reasons for suicide include hopelessness, loneliness, helplessness, relationship problems, unspecified depression, money problems, and problems with their parents. Men complete suicide three times as often as women, but women attempt suicide three times as often. Suicides in the 15 to 24 year-old age group increased more than 40 percent during the past decade, and it is now the second leading cause of death for that age group. Media reports of suicides, especially of celebrities, seem to spark an increase in suicide. The completed suicide rate for men is about four times that for women, although recent findings suggest that the gap is closing as many more women are now incurring a higher risk. Further, women are more likely to make attempts, but it appears that men are more successful because they use more lethal means. Being widowed as compared to divorced appears to be associated with higher risk of suicide for white men and women and African American men. At older ages, however, divorce rather than widowhood increases the risk. Interestingly, the pattern reversal occurs much earlier among white women than for men. Physicians, lawyers, law enforcement personnel, and dentists have higher than average rates of suicide. Among medical professionals, psychiatrists have the highest rate and pediatricians the lowest. Suicide is represented proportionately among all socioeconomic levels. Level of wealth does not seem to affect the suicide rate as much as do changes in that level. Over 50 percent of suicides are committed by firearms, and 70 percent of attempts are accounted for by drug overdose. Men most frequently choose firearms as the means of suicide; poisoning and asphyxiation via barbiturates are the preferred means for women. Religious affiliation is correlated with suicide rates. Although the U.S. rate is 12.2 per 100,000, in countries in which Catholic Church influences are strong—Latin America, Ireland, Spain, and Italy—the suicide rate is relatively low. Suicide rates vary among ethnic minority groups in the United States. American Indian groups have the highest rate, followed by white Americans, Mexican Americans, African Americans, Japanese Americans, and Chinese Americans. American Indian youngsters have frighteningly high rates (26 per 100,000) as compared with white youths (14 per 100,000). As might be expected, suicide is the most frequent cause of death in U.S. jails. A suicide number that ranges from 90 to 230 per 100,000 means that the suicide rate in prisons is 16 times higher than in the general population.

II.　**A multi-path perspective of suicide.** Most discussions on the correlates of suicide seem to stress psychological, social, and sociocultural factors. But biological factors and the interplay of all four seem to be operating in determining suicides. Two sets of findings—from biochemistry and from genetics—suggest that suicide may have a strong biological component. There are many psychological factors that have been found to be significantly related to suicide. Findings have consistently revealed that a number of individuals who commit suicide suffer from a DSM-IV-TR disorder. One of the most consistently reported correlates of suicidal behavior is alcohol consumption. Social factors that operate to separate people or to make them somehow less connected to other people or to their families, religious institutions, or their community can increase susceptibility to suicide. Rates of suicide vary with age, gender, marital status, occupation, socioeconomic level, religion and ethnic group. Higher rates are associated with high- and low-status (as opposed to middle-status) occupations, urban living, middle-aged men, single or divorced status, and upper and lower socioeconomic classes.

III.　**Victims of suicide.** Suicide among the young is an unmentioned tragedy in our society. We have traditionally avoided the idea that some of our young people find life so painful that they consciously and deliberately take their own lives. Children and adolescents take their lives at an alarming rate. Those who attempt suicide tend to show clinical symptoms of psychological disturbance, to use drug overdose as the method, to make their attempt at home, and to come from families with high levels of stress as a result of economic instability, substance abuse, or other life events. Copycat suicides, in which adolescents imitate media portrayals of other adolescents' suicides, are less common than the media suggest and tend to occur among those already contemplating suicide. However, highly publicized suicides can increase the chances of attempts. The many stresses of life among the elderly place them at high risk for suicide. Suicide rates are particularly high for white males and first-generation Asian Americans. Native Americans and African Americans show low rates of suicide among older adults, although both groups are at high risk during young adulthood.

IV. **Preventing suicide.**
People who attempt suicide have a wish to live along with a wish to die. They usually leave verbal or behavioral clues of their intentions, although these may be subtle. A clinical approach to suicide intervention stresses that most individuals are ambivalent about ending their lives and that counselors must be comfortable discussing the subject. Crisis intervention strategies are used to assess lethality, and to abort suicide attempts by offering intensive counseling to the individual and stabilizing him or her, sometimes in a hospital environment, while clarifying ways to deal with the crisis. Suicide prevention centers usually use paraprofessionals to take telephone calls from potentially suicidal individuals. These paraprofessionals are trained to establish rapport with the caller, evaluate suicidal potential, clarify the nature of the problem and the caller's ability to cope, and recommend a plan of action. There is no conclusive evidence for the effectiveness of suicide prevention centers. Community prevention efforts can involve going into a school where a suicide has occurred and educating and providing counseling to survivors. Such an institutional response serves to minimize the mental health problems of survivors and can prevent future suicides

V.   **The right to suicide: Moral, ethical, and legal issues** The quality of life is a significant moral and ethical issue that has led to right-to-die legislation and "living wills" that are recognized in several states. Dr. Jack Kevorkian, a physician in Michigan, has assisted patients to commit suicide, an act that a new law states is illegal. Oregon voters passed a bill to allow physicians to help terminally ill patients die.

VI. **Implications.** There is a saying that goes like this: "We know much about suicide but we know very little about it." While this may sound contradictory, this chapter has been filled with an impressive array of facts, statistics, and information about many aspects of suicide. We are able to construct fairly accurate portraits of individuals most as risk, delineate protective factors, and even develop intervention strategies in working with suicidal individuals. We know that people commit suicide for many reasons. We know that biological, psychological, social, and sociocultural factors are related to suicides.

KEY TERMS REVIEW

1. A systematic examination of information in order to explain the behavior of a person prior to his or her death is called a(n) _____.

2. Thoughts about suicide are called _____.

3. The taking of one's own life is called _____.

4. The probability that a person will end his or her life is called _____.

FACTUAL MULTIPLE-CHOICE QUESTIONS

1. A psychological autopsy
    a. is difficult to perform because suicide notes provide little information.
    b. seeks to make psychological sense of a homicide or suicide.
    c. is the first step in treatment programs for people who are suicidal.
    d. is relatively easy to perform because more than 90 percent of suicides leave notes and other written explanations behind.

2. Which of the following statistics about suicide is *accurate?*
    a. Roughly two million people commit suicide in the United States each year.
    b. Men are six times as likely to attempt suicide as women.
    c. Suicides among people aged 15 to 24 have stayed about the same over the past ten years.
    d. The suicide rate for men is three times that for women.

3. Which of the following increases the risk of suicide?

    a. Being an American Indian adolescent or young adult
    b. Living in a country where the Catholic Church has strong influence
    c. Being married
    d. Living in a time of warfare or natural disaster

4. Abnormally low amounts of _____ have been found in the spinal fluid of patients who are at high risk for killing themselves.

    a. 5HIAA
    b. phenylalanine
    c. Thorazine
    d. dopamine

5. Research on adolescent suicide attempters indicates that

    a. they are unlikely to show any symptoms of psychological disturbance.
    b. most attempts occur at home.
    c. they represent fewer than 1 percent of all adolescents.
    d. almost all attempts occur during spring and summer.

6. Which statement about adolescent suicide attempters is *accurate?*

    a. They experience traumatic events in chaotic families.
    b. The majority are determined to end their lives.
    c. Most come from economically well-off families.
    d. Most use firearms or hanging.

7. Among the elderly in the United States, which group has the *highest* rate of suicide?

    a. Black females
    b. Black males
    c. First-generation Asian Americans
    d. Males of northern European backgrounds

8. Making or rewriting a will and giving away one's personal possessions are examples of

    a. verbal clues to suicide.
    b. lethality of suicide intent.
    c. learned helplessness.
    d. behavioral clues to suicide.

9. Studies of the effectiveness of suicide prevention centers have shown that

    a. callers feel that the service is far more helpful than discussions with friends.
    b. few suicidal people use the centers and those who do call only once.
    c. cities with centers have one-half the suicide rate of those without centers.
    d. approximately one-half of the callers do commit suicide.

CONCEPTUAL MULTIPLE-CHOICE QUESTIONS

1. What mental state seems to increase one's risk of suicide?

    a. Being in the depths of a severe depression
    b. Negative expectations about the future
    c. An inflated sense of self-importance
    d. Cognitive slippage

2.   When explaining suicidal behavior, Freud stresses _____ whereas Durkheim stresses _____.

   a.   lack of social support; economic influences
   b.   genetic factors; environmental factors
   c.   anger turned inward; economic influences
   d.   sexual symbolism; discrimination and prejudice

3.   Research on college student suicide, which category of student is most likely to take his or her own life?

   a.   Math and science majors
   b.   Black students
   c.   Students who commute to school
   d.   Very-high-achieving students at large universities

4.   Which of the following reasons for college student suicide is *most* plausible?

   a.   As final examinations approach, stress levels become unbearable.
   b.   Highly successful students are filled with doubt about their ability to succeed.
   c.   Men are confused about the new roles society has pressured them to adopt.
   d.   Foreign students are discriminated against by teachers and administrators.

5.   Which of the following is *not* characteristic of suicide?

   a.   A common emotion in suicide is hopelessness.
   b.   The cognitive state is one of ambivalence.
   c.   A common purpose of suicide is escape.
   d.   Threats of suicide are rarely genuine expressions of intent.

6.   Which of the following characterizes telephone crisis intervention efforts?

   a.   Paraprofessionals are rarely used.
   b.   Workers try to identify the client's stress and primary focal problems.
   c.   Most people who commit suicide have previously called a suicide prevention hotline.
   d.   Controlled evaluations show suicide hotlines are highly effective.

7.   Mental health professional are optimistic that suicide prevention is possible

   a.   because they assume that a wish to live coexists with a wish to die.
   b.   despite the fact that very few suicidal individuals give hints of their self-destructive intentions.
   c.   despite the knowledge that suicidal individuals are determined to die.
   d.   because suicide is such a rare event.

8.   The main difference between crisis intervention and suicide prevention centers is that

   a.   crisis intervention centers do not deal with suicidal people.
   b.   crisis intervention stresses the need to educate the whole community.
   c.   suicide prevention centers to not deal with distressed individuals.
   d.   suicide prevention centers are available around the clock through telephone hotlines.

9.   Community suicide prevention programs might include

   a.   suggestions that negative feelings be kept tightly controlled.
   b.   classroom discussions in which students are assured that another person's suicide is not their fault.
   c.   media portrayals that dramatize the suicides of celebrities.
   d.   discussions of the right to commit suicide.

10. Which of the following statements regarding health professionals and the law is *accurate*?
    a. Therapists have a responsibility to prevent suicide if they anticipate it.
    b. Lawsuits cannot be brought against a psychologist who fails to treat a person who threatens to commit suicide.
    c. "Living wills" are not recognized as valid in any state in the United States.
    d. The Constitution specifically states that professionals must save people's lives, even if the person wants to die.

APPLICATION MULTIPLE-CHOICE QUESTIONS

1. Dr. Ortman is interviewing the friends and family of a college student who committed suicide. She is also analyzing the student's suicide note and diary. Dr. Ortman is engaged in
    a. a form of treatment called "crisis intervention."
    b. a psychological autopsy.
    c. an assessment called "anomic evaluation."
    d. a medical autopsy

2. Rita committed suicide when she was very drunk. Research suggests that the alcohol
    a. produced an intensified depression that caused the suicide.
    b. counteracted her previous angry emotional state.
    c. made her thinking constricted and rigid.
    d. allowed her to see the future more clearly.

3. A psychologist who made use of Durkheim's explanation for suicide would stress the
    a. early childhood experiences that led to anger turned inward.
    b. genetics of neurotransmitter imbalance.
    c. social factors that influence individuals.
    d. attention-seeking nature of suicide.

4. Dr. Emory wants to replicate a recent Gallup Poll survey about teen suicide. If his survey does derive similar results, he is likely to find that
    a. most of the students have seriously considered suicide.
    b. many more of the students have inflicted self-harm than have come close to attempting suicide.
    c. almost 75 percent of them have engaged in self-harm behavior.
    d. 6 percent of the students admit to a suicide attempt, while another 15 percent say they have come close.

5. Dr. Wilton says, "The suicide rate for children under fourteen is rapidly decreasing, but it is increasing for those aged 14 to 25. Suicide is second only to automobile accidents as a cause of death among teens. Girls are three times as likely as boys to attempt it." What part of Dr. Wilson's statement is *accurate*?
    a. It is inaccurate to say that suicide is decreasing among those under 14.
    b. It is inaccurate to say that suicide is increasing among those 14 to 25.
    c. It is inaccurate to say that suicide is the second leading cause of death among teens.
    d. It is inaccurate to say that girls are more likely to attempt suicide.

6. Which adolescent is *most* likely to attempt suicide?
    a. George, whose parents are wealthy.
    b. Paula, whose parents are alcoholics.
    c. Jonathan, who is depressed during the summertime.
    d. Nathan, who shows little hostility or anger.

7. After a television news episode showing dramatic scenes of a tenth grader's suicide is broadcast, a second tenth grader at the same school kills herself. This kind of suicide is

    a.   much more common than the news media have suggested.

    b.   called an altruistic suicide.

    c.   especially unfortunate because such depictions influence well-adjusted teens to kill themselves.

    d.   called a copycat suicide.

8. Which of the following examples is most consistent with the results of research on college suicide at the University of California at Berkeley?

    a.   A graduate student with poor grades committed suicide.

    b.   An undergraduate with below-average grades committed suicide during final examinations.

    c.   A foreign student, younger than the average student, committed suicide.

    d.   A freshman, male, science major committed suicide at home.

9. Marlene attempted suicide but was rescued by her husband. She refused treatment. Her husband and psychiatrist agree that

    a.   danger is past.

    b.   her attempt wasn't serious.

    c.   Marlene was just feigning.

    d.   she should be involuntarily hospitalized.

10. A psychologist is on the phone with a person who is considering suicide. The psychologist asks, "What methods have you thought about using to kill yourself?" and "When do you plan to do this?" What is the psychologist doing?

    a.   a psychological autopsy

    b.   writing a behavioral contract

    c.   eliminating a copycat suicide

    d.   assessing lethality

ANSWER KEY: KEY TERMS REVIEW

1. psychological autopsy

2. suicidal ideation

3. suicide

4. lethality

ANSWER KEY: FACTUAL MULTIPLE-CHOICE QUESTIONS

1. b.   The purpose of the psychological autopsy is to understand the causes for suicide so that prevention of future suicides is possible.

    a.   Psychological autopsies rely on suicide notes, which provide important information into the thinking and emotions of the person before he or she took his or her life.

    c.   A psychological autopsy is done after a death has occurred; it is too late for treatment.

    d.   Suicide notes are provided by less than one-third of people who commit suicide; psychological autopsies are difficult because of the lack of firsthand information.

2.   d.   The completed suicide rate is three times greater among men, although women are three times as likely to, attempt suicide.

     a.   Although the figure of 31,000 cases per year is an underestimate, it is highly unlikely that the true incidence is forty times greater.

     b.   Women are three times as likely as men to attempt suicide.

     c.   The suicide rate among teens and young adults has risen dramatically.

3.   a.   Among ethnic groups, American, Indians have the highest suicide rate in the United States; among adolescents, 26 per 100,000 take their own lives compared with 14 per 100,000 in the general population.

     b.   Countries where the Catholic Church is influential have among the lowest suicide rates because the Catholic church considers suicide a sin.

     c.   Suicide is more likely when a person is divorced or single.

     d.   In times of warfare and natural disaster, suicide rates drop

4.   a.   5HIAA is a metabolite of the neurotransmitter serotonin, and it is abnormally low in people who commit suicide, even those who are not depressed.

     b.   Phenylalanine is an amino acid unrelated to suicide.

     c.   Thorazine is the brand name of a chemical used to treat schizophrenia.

     d.   Dopamine is a neurotransmitter; too much dopamine activity is associated with schizophrenia.

5.   b.   Suicide attempts tend to take place in the home.

     a.   Suicide attempters are likely to have a past history of psychological disturbance.

     c.   Recent polls indicate that 6 percent of teens admit to a suicide attempt; probably between 8 and 9 percent of teens engage in self-harmful behavior.

     d.   Winter is the most typical time for adolescents to make suicide attempts.

6.   a.   Suicidal adolescents frequently experience traumatic events prior to their suicide and live in unstable, chaotic families that can provide minimal support.

     b.   Most adolescents are not really sure they want to die.

     c.   Adolescents with economically stressed families are at higher risk.

     d.   Firearms and hanging, highly lethal methods, are rarely used in attempts.

7.   c.   First generation Asian Americans have a high rate of suicide, perhaps because of their cultural dislocation.

     a.   Black females have a relatively low suicide rate.

     b.   Elderly black males have a relatively low suicide rate.

     d.   White males have a suicide rate lower than that of Asian Americans.

8.   d.   Making a will is a physical action; therefore it is a behavioral clue.

     a.   An example of a verbal clue might be, "Everyone would be happier if I just shot myself."

     b.   Lethality is determined by a persons plan to take his or her life and his or her access to the means of doing it.

     c.   Learned helplessness has more to do with believing that one has no control over the consequences of one's actions.

9.   b.   Only 2 percent of suicidal individuals use suicide prevention hotlines; about 95 percent of those who call once never call again.

     a.   Unfortunately, callers who were included in such evaluation studies saw no more benefit from calling the center than from discussing the problem with friends.

     c.   No clear difference in community suicide rates has been found; those with hotlines can have higher, lower, and similar rates of suicide compared with communities not having hotlines.

     d.   Because there is no way to trace callers, we do not know how many actually commit suicide.

ANSWER KEY: CONCEPTUAL MULTIPLE-CHOICE QUESTIONS

1.   b.   Negative expectations—or hopelessness—seem to be even more predictive of suicide than depression is.

     a.   When people are in the depths of a severe depression, their motor behavior is so retarded and their thinking so impaired, that they are at low risk for suicide.

     c.   People contemplating suicide often have a reduced sense of self-worth.

     d.   Cognitive slippage is a characteristic of schizophrenia and is unrelated to suicide.

2.   c.   Freud sees suicide as a self-destructive act that originates in rage at another person; Durkheim emphasizes social conditions, including economic ones.

     a.   Although Durkheim is interested in economic conditions, Freud never discusses social supports.

     b.   Freud stresses unconscious conflicts, not genetics.

     d.   Freud's theory of suicide emphasizes the *thanatos* (death instinct) rather than the *libido* (sexual, id instinct).

3.   d.   High-achieving undergraduates were among the most likely suicide victims; suicide is more prevalent at large universities than at small colleges.

     a.   Language and literature majors are more prone to suicide than others.

     b.   Black students were not found to be at high risk.

     c.   Most suicides take place at campus residences.

4.   b.   Suicide risk is high for the strongest students because they appear to have unrealistically high standards of performance.

     a.   Suicidal behavior peaks at the beginning of semesters, not at final examination time.

     c.   Women may be more inclined to commit suicide because of role confusion.

     d.   Foreign students may be more inclined to commit suicide because of shame and fear of letting down their parents.

5. d. Verbal communication, indirect threats, and behavioral clues are all signs that predict suicide and should be treated seriously.

    a. Pessimism about the future and belief that nothing can be done may predispose a person to suicide.

    b. Most individuals have dual motivations—to live and to die.

    c. The goal is to escape a perceived intolerable situation.

6. b. Problem identification is critical before intervention can be made.

    a. Paraprofessionals are frequently used in suicide hotlines.

    c. It's estimated that 2 percent of suicides have contacted a hotline before committing suicide.

    d. Controlled studies are not available, since hotlines are anonymous.

7. a. Mental health professionals operate under the assumption that most (if not all) people who are suicidal also have a desire to live.

    b. Most suicidal people leave clues to their intentions, although some are rather subtle.

    c. Mental health professionals do not believe that suicidal people have shut the door on living

    d. Suicide is all too common.

8. d. Suicide prevention centers have paraprofessionals who take telephone calls twenty-four hours per day; crisis intervention involves direct care after the person presents himself or herself to the counseling center.

    a. Suicide is certainly a crisis and is a part of crisis intervention work.

    b. Crisis intervention focuses on direct care for the suicidal person rather than on community education.

    c. Suicide prevention centers take telephone calls from people in acute distress.

9. b. In one program described in the text, children were reassured that their teacher's decision to commit suicide was not their fault; children need to have unnecessary guilt removed.

    a. Interventions provide survivors with the opportunity to express strong negative feelings; bottling them up would be seen as impairing recovery.

    c. Media portrayals that dramatize the suicides of celebrities or others may foster copycat suicides.

    d. It would not be appropriate for students to consider suicide a personal right under the circumstances of a tragedy in the school.

10. a. Although laws are not clear on all points, therapists have an ethical duty to preserve life when they can.

    b. Therapists can be sued for refusing to offer life-protective treatment.

    c. "Living wills" are recognized as valid in fifteen states.

    d. The Constitution implies that people can refuse treatment that will save their lives (as in cases when those who believe in faith healing refuse medical treatment).

ANSWER KEY: APPLICATION MULTIPLE-CHOICE QUESTIONS

1. b.   A psychological autopsy involves looking at material about the suicide victim to help us understand the person's motives.

    a.   Crisis intervention involves assisting a person who may be contemplating suicide.

    c.   *Ahomic evaluation* is a made-up term.

    d.   Although medical autopsies are performed on suicide victims, they do not involve interviewing friends or family or analyzing suicide notes.

2. c.   Researchers believe alcohol foreshortens one's thinking (alcohol myopia), reducing the suicidal person's capacity to think of alternative solutions to problems.

    a.   Alcohol typically does not intensify depression; it may actually relieve it partially and provide the person with energy enough to commit suicide.

    b.   There is no reason to believe that alcohol will counteract anger.

    d.   If anything, alcohol intoxication prevents one from seeing the future clearly.

3. c.   Durkheim was a sociologist; his interests included social integration, economic change, and individuals' responses to these factors.

    a.   Durkheim was a sociologist, not a psychodynamic thinker.

    b.   Durkheim was a sociologist, not a physiological psychologist.

    d.   Attention seeking might be a behavioral conceptualization of suicidal behavior; Durkheim was not a behaviorist.

4. d.   The poll found that 6 percent of the students admit to a suicide attempt, while another 15 percent say they have come close.

    a.   Only 6 percent had attempted suicide, with another 15 percent coming close to trying it.

    b.   The poll found that somewhere between 8 and 9 percent of the teens indicated they engaged in self-harm behavior, which would actually be about half (not "many more") those who had come close to attempting suicide.

    c.   Only 8 to 9 percent indicated they had engaged in self-harm behavior, not 75 percent.

5. a.   The suicide rate has been increasing in the preteenage population.

    b.   The suicide rate among those aged 15 to 24 has tripled in the past thirty years.

    c.   Automobile accidents are the leading cause of death; suicide is second.

    d.   Girls are more likely to attempt suicide, although boys are more likely to be successful.

6. b.   Suicide among teens is higher when their parents suffer from alcohol or other chemical dependencies.

    a.   Children whose parents are in financial stress are more likely to commit suicide than those whose parents are well-off.

    c.   Suicide among teens tends to be most common during the winter months.

    d.   Hostility and aggressiveness are strongly associated with suicide.

7. d.   Copycat suicides are more likely to occur when media portrayals of suicide influence those with suicidal tendencies to take their own lives.

    a.   Copycat suicides are far less common than the media indicate.

    b.   In altruistic suicide, one kills oneself for the group's greater good, such as *kamikaze* pilots did in World War II.

    c.   Depictions of suicide do not seem to influence well-adjusted adolescents; they do have an impact on those with suicidal tendencies.

8. a.   That graduate students who were doing poorly were a high-risk group for suicide.

    b.   When undergraduates were superb students, the risk of suicide increased.

    c.   Foreign students were at high risk, but older students were far more likely to commit suicide than younger ones.

    d.   Older students were more likely to commit suicide; literature and language majors were more likely to do so than science majors.

9. d.   She should be involuntarily hospitalized.

    a.   She may be in great danger.

    b.   Any attempted suicide is serious.

    c.   Marlene's attempt may have been a cry for help, but that does not mean she was feigning.

10. d.   Questions about suicidal plans and the means to carry them out are ways of assessing the chances a person will take his or her own life—lethality.

    a.   A psychological autopsy occurs after suicide is completed; this person is very much alive.

    b.   A behavioral contract involves a written agreement that the person who is suicidal will not try to take their life, will rid themselves of the means to committing suicide, and will seek counseling.

    c.   To eliminate copycat suicides we would need to change how the media disseminate information about suicides in the community.

OBJECTIVES DEFINED

1. **1. What do we know about suicide?**

- Suicide is the intentional, direct, and conscious taking of one's own life. In the past, it has often been kept hidden, and relatives and friends of the victim did not speak of it. Mental health professionals now realize that understanding the causes of suicide is extremely important.

- Much is known about the *facts* of suicide, but little about the reasons is understood. Men are more likely to kill themselves than women, although the latter makes more attempts; the elderly are at high risk for suicides; religious affiliation, marital status, and ethnicity all influence suicides; and firearms are the most frequent method used.

2. **What are the major explanations of suicide?**

- In keeping with the multi-path model, suicides appear to be an interaction of biological, psychological, social, and sociocultural factors.

- More recent evidence has indicated that biological factors may be important: genetics and biochemical factors are implicated in suicides.

- Psychological factors include mental disturbance, depression, hopelessness, and excessive alcohol consumption; all are highly correlated with suicide,

- Lack of positive social relationships can lead to feelings of loneliness and disconnection. The elderly are prone to the loss of loved ones and friends, and divorce or lack of a life partner increases the chances of suicide.

- Sociocultural factors like race, culture, ethnicity, social class, gender, and other such demographic variables can either increase or decrease the risk of suicide.

- The complex relationship between these four dimensions and suicide is not simply one of cause and effect, but an interaction among them.

3. **Who are the victims of suicide?**

- In recent years, childhood and adolescent suicides have increased at an alarming rate. A lack of research has limited our understanding of why children take their own lives.

- Many people tend to become depressed about "feeling old" as they age, and depressed elderly people often think about suicide.

4. **How can we intervene or prevent suicides?**

- Perhaps the best way to prevent suicide is to recognize its signs and intervene before it occurs. People are more likely to commit suicide if they are older, male, have a history of attempts, describe in detail how the act will be accomplished, and give verbal hints that they are planning self-destruction.

- Crisis intervention concepts and techniques have been used successfully to treat clients who contemplate suicide. Intensive short-term therapy is used to stabilize the immediate crisis.

- Suicide prevention centers operate twenty-four hours a day to provide intervention services to all potential suicide, especially those not undergoing treatment. Telephone hot lines are staffed by well-trained paraprofessionals who will work with anyone who is contemplating suicide. In addition, these centers provide preventive education to the public.

5. **Are there times and situations in which suicide should be an option?**

- This question is difficult to answer, particularly when the person is terminally ill and wishes to end his or her suffering. Nevertheless, therapists, like physicians, have been trained to preserve life, and they have a legal obligation to do so.

MARGIN DEFINITIONS

lethality the probability that a person will choose to end his or her life

psychological autopsy the systematic examination of existing information for the purpose of understanding and explaining a person's behavior before his or her death

suicidal ideation thoughts about suicide

suicide the intentional, direct, and conscious taking of one's own life

CHAPTER 13

Schizophrenia: Diagnosis, Etiology, and Treatment

TABLE OF CONTENTS

LEARNING OBJECTIVES

1. Describe the symptoms of schizophrenia.

2. Discuss how the specific types of schizophrenia differ from one another.

3. Discuss the debate about whether or not there is much chance of recovery from schizophrenia.

4. Discuss what causes schizophrenia.

5. Discuss the treatments currently available for schizophrenia and how effective they are.

CHAPTER OUTLINE

I. **The symptoms of schizophrenia.** Schizophrenia is a group of disorders characterized by cognitive distortions, personality disintegration, affective disturbances, and social withdrawal. It receives a great deal of attention because it is so disabling, the prevalence rate is 1 percent (and therefore millions of people are affected), and its symptoms and causes are diverse. There appear to be three types of symptoms in schizophrenia: psychoticism (hallucinations and delusions) and disorganization, which are considered *positive symptoms*, and flat affect and other forms of social withdrawal, which are considered negative symptoms. Positive symptoms: People with schizophrenia often report delusions (false beliefs) that can take many forms, such as delusions of grandeur (believing one is a famous person), thought broadcasting (others can hear the schizophrenic's thoughts), or delusions of persecution. Unlike other people, individuals with schizophrenia reach delusional conclusions on the basis of little information; they can, however, be trained to challenge their delusions. Hallucinations are sensory perceptions not attributable to environmental stimuli. Hallucinations are not pathognomonic (distinctive) to schizophrenia. Auditory hallucinations are most common During times when symptoms are prominent, hallucinations and delusions are so strong that they are treated as real; in other situations, people with schizophrenia can ward them off. Schizophrenic individuals have difficulty concentrating and communicating. One symptom is called loosening of associations, or cognitive slippage. Thoughts shift from topic to topic, and communication can be vague or overly concrete. People with schizophrenia also show odd movements or postures; maintaining an unusual body position is characteristic of catatonic schizophrenia. *Negative symptoms* of schizophrenia are associated with an inability or decreased ability to initiate actions or speech, express emotions, or feel pleasure. Such symptoms include *avolition* (an inability to take action or become goal-oriented), *alogia* (a lack of meaningful speech), and *flat affect* (little or no emotion in situations in which strong reactions are expected). A delusional patient, for instance, might explain in detail how parts of his or her body are rotting away but show absolutely no concern or worry through voice tone or facial expression. Clinicians are careful to distinguish between *primary symptoms* (symptoms that arise from the disease itself) and *secondary symptoms* (symptoms that may develop as a response to medication, institutionalization, or as a result of a mood disorder such as depression). Cognitive symptoms of schizophrenia include problems with attention, memory, and difficulty in developing a plan of action. As compared with healthy controls, those with schizophrenia have severe to moderately severe cognitive impairments as evidenced by poor "executive functioning"—deficits in the ability to absorb and interpret information and make decisions based on that information, sustain attention, and retain recently learned information and use it right away. Culture may affect how symptoms of schizophrenia are displayed or interpreted. In Japan, for example, schizophrenia is highly stigmatized.

II.   **Types of schizophrenia.** *Paranoid schizophrenia* is the most common form of schizophrenia and is characterized by delusions or hallucinations, usually involving persecution or grandiosity. It is possible to differentiate this disorder from *delusional disorder* because delusional disorder involves less bizarre beliefs and is free from other dysfunctional behaviors. *Disorganized schizophrenia* features severe regression to a childish state without delusions. Behavior and speech tend to be bizarre. *Catatonic schizophrenia* is divided into an excited form marked by hyperactivity and a withdrawn form in which immobility and waxy flexibility are seen. Often patients swing from one state to the other. *Undifferentiated schizophrenia* is a form marked by a mix of symptoms; *residual schizophrenics* are those people whose symptoms are in remission. In DSM-IV-TR, the term *schizophrenia* is reserved for psychotic episodes lasting six months or more. *Brief psychotic disorder* is diagnosed when symptoms have lasted less than one month; the disorder in which symptoms last between one and six months is called *schizophreniform disorder*. DSM-IV-TR recommends these disorders be "provisional." About two-thirds of those diagnosed with schizophreniform disorder will later be diagnosed with schizophrenia or *schizoaffective disorder*. Other psychotic disorders include *shared psychotic disorder*, in which a person who has a close relationship with a delusional person accepts those beliefs, and schizoaffective disorder, a combination of mood disorder and psychotic symptoms that last at least two weeks.

III.   **The course of schizophrenia.** Most people with schizophrenia show poor premorbid personality before the onset of the disorder. The typical course of schizophrenia consists of three phases. The *prodromal phase* includes social withdrawal and peculiar speech or actions. In the *active phase,* symptoms are in full evidence, and by the *residual phase,* symptoms are no longer prominent. It is unclear what the long-term outcome of schizophrenia tends to be. Because diagnosis requires that symptoms be present for at least six months, it makes sense that someone with a diagnosis of schizophrenia has a more severe condition than someone who recovered sooner; thus schizophrenia is defined as a chronic condition. However, in one long-term study, 26 percent of the patients had complete remission, and about 50 percent had partial remission of symptoms. Differences in outcome may be due to criteria used to define schizophrenia. Most individuals with schizophrenia recover enough to lead relatively productive lives.

IV.   **Etiology of schizophrenia.** The causes of schizophrenia may involve genetic, physiological, psychological, and environmental factors. The biological dimension uses endophenotypes, neurostructures, and neurotransmitters to attempt to explain schizophrenia. The psychological dimension includes behaviors, attitudes, and attributes that contribute to the symptoms of schizophrenia by increasing the vulnerability of predisposed individuals. For example, having depression or negative self-evaluations can trigger or worsen psychotic symptoms. Social relationships have long been considered to have etiological importance in the development of schizophrenia. Until the 1900s, biological factors were not considered to be of etiological importance. Instead, it was believed that schizophrenia was the result of exposure to specific dysfunctional family patterns. Although the prevalence of schizophrenia is roughly equal between men and women, gender differences in the age of onset for the disorder have been found. The age of onset for schizophrenia occurs earlier in males than in females. The gender ratio shifts by the mid-forties and fifties, when the percentage of women receiving this diagnosis exceeds that of men.

V.   **The treatment of schizophrenia** Antipsychotic medication *(neuroleptics)*is the principal means of treating schizophrenia today. Clozapine, may be effective in cases not previously helped by neuroleptics. Although effective in many cases, medications can produce neurological conditions, including *tardive dyskinesia*, a disorder of involuntary movements for which there is no cure. Other side effects such as extrapyramidal symptoms have led to legal action to provide patients with the right to refuse such medical treatment. Clinicians often misinterpret or ignore the symptoms of drug side effects. Psychosocial therapy is now often paired with drug treatment. Patients reported deriving most help from practical advice therapists give; they value the therapist's friendship. In inpatient settings, *milieu therapy* and social learning treatment have been shown to be more effective than the traditional treatment. Milieu therapy allows patients to take more responsibility for decision-making. "Cognitive-behavioral approaches have been useful in reducing delusions and hallucinations, and improving social skills." Intervention to reduce expressed emotion in families has also proven useful in reducing relapse rates. Families are given information about the disorder and taught ways to alter communication patterns. Schizophrenic patients can also be taught to respond to their parents' emotions more appropriately. Combining various treatments gives hope for even more successful therapy for schizophrenia in the future.

VI. **Implications.** Research and treatment on schizophrenia is undergoing dramatic shifts. Genetic research has moved beyond attempting to identify a specific gene underlying the disorder to the recognition that schizophrenia is a result of dozens of genes and their interactions. Research has shifted to identifying the endophenotypes that underlie the characteristics of the disorder and the genes responsible. It is also increasingly acknowledged that environmental factors may alter neurodevelopment in a manner that increases the susceptibility to schizophrenia. New antipsychotic medications continued to be developed, although there is increasing pessimism about current medications because many cognitive characteristics are not improved with their use and the majority of individuals on antipsychotics do not follow the treatment regimen. Psychosocial therapies are also evolving with greater attention focused on treatments that address the specific deficits found in schizophrenia. The focus on "recovery" rather than cure offers a more optimistic philosophy in treatment.

KEY TERMS REVIEW

1.   A group of disorders characterized by severe impairment of cognitive processes, personality disintegration, and social withdrawal is collectively called ___schizophrenic___

2.   A schizophrenic disorder in which the individual regresses to a childlike state but does not exhibit delusions is called ___disorganized___.

3.   A schizophrenic disorder characterized by persistent and systematized delusions is called ___paranoid___.

4.   A schizophrenic disorder characterized by extreme excitement or extreme withdrawal is called ___catatonic___.

5.   A schizophrenic disorder characterized by a mix of symptoms that do not clearly fit any other type of the disorder is called ___undifferentiated___

6.   A disorder characterized by persistent but nonbizarre delusions not accompanied by any other unusual behaviors is called ___delusional disorder___

7. A category of schizophrenic disorder reserved for individuals who manifested symptoms in the past but who now no longer show prominent signs of the disorder is called *residual* .

8. Sensory perceptions not directly attributable to environmental stimuli are *hallucinations*

9. Continual shifting between topics without meaningful connections is called *loose associations* .

10. A psychotic disorder that lasts no longer than one month is called *brief psychotic d/o*

11. A psychotic disorder that lasts between one month and six months is called *schizophreniform* .

12. In schizophrenia, a symptom that is associated with problems with attention, memory, and difficulty in developing a plan of action is called *cognitive* symptoms

13 *schizoaffective d/o* is a disorder characterized by both a mood disorder (major depression or bipolar disorder) and the presence of psychotic symptoms "for at least two weeks in the absence of prominent mood symptoms."

14. Symptoms that are present during the active phase of schizophrenia and include hallucinations, delusions, and disorganized speech are called *positive* .

15. The suggestion that schizophrenia results from an excess of dopamine activity at certain brain synapses is called the *dopamine hypothesis* .

16. Antipsychotic medication that can produce symptoms that mimic neurological disorders are called *neuroleptics* .

17. The likelihood that both members of a twin pair will exhibit the same disorder is called the *concordance rate* .

18. A therapy program in which the hospital environment operates as a community, and patients have decision-making responsibilities is called *Milieu* .

19. A type of negative communication pattern found in some families with schizophrenic members, which involves hypercritical and overprotective parenting, is called *expressed emotion*

20. *shared psych d/o* in schizophrenia is when a person who has a close relationship with an individual with delusional or psychotic beliefs comes to accept those beliefs.

FACTUAL MULTIPLE-CHOICE QUESTIONS

1. The lifetime prevalence for schizophrenia is
   a. lower for African Americans than it is for the general population.
   b. much higher among males than females.
   c. roughly 10 percent.
   d. roughly 1 percent.

2. A false belief that others are plotting to embarrass or harm you is called a
   a. delusion of persecution.
   b. delusion of grandeur.
   c. psychomotor disturbance.
   d. neologism.

3. A person with schizophrenia begins a response with appropriate comments but then becomes incoherent and mentions things that are unrelated. This shifting from topic to topic is called

    a. anhedonia.
    b. delusions of reference.
    c. loosening of associations.
    d. lack of insight.

4. When the sole symptom is a delusion that does not affect functioning in other spheres of a person's life, the best diagnosis is

    a. paranoid schizophrenia.
    b. brief psychotic disorder.
    c. delusional disorder.
    d. paranoid schizophreniform disorder.

5. International research seems to show that recovery from schizophrenia is

    a. more rapid in developed countries such as the United States.
    b. more rapid in developing countries such as India.
    c. virtually impossible no matter where it occurs.
    d. more dependent on good diet than on good therapy.

6. Because phenothiazines reduce schizophrenic symptoms and amphetamine overdoses can mimic schizophrenic symptoms, it is believed that the neurotransmitter _____ is involved in schizophrenia.

    a. L-dopa
    b. 5HIAA
    c. dopamine
    d. acetylcholine

7. The most common flaws with earlier research on the families of schizophrenics were

    a. too few subjects and too narrow a definition of schizophrenia.
    b. analysis of interactions after one family member was diagnosed and a lack of control groups.
    c. a lack of control groups and overreliance on MZ and DZ twins.
    d. too few subjects and the use of a developmental method.

8. When a person's financial status goes down after a person is diagnosed with schizophrenia, a _____ explanation of the relationship between the two is supported.

    a. schizophrenogenic
    b. biochemical
    c. stressful life events
    d. downward drift

9. Which of the following claims regarding shared psychotic disorder is NOT true?

    a. It is relatively rare.
    b. It is more prevalent among those who are socially isolated.
    c. It occurs when a person who has a close relationship with an individual with psychotic or delusional beliefs comes to accept those beliefs.
    d. Identical twins have been found to be most susceptible.

10. Schizoaffective mood disorder is most common among

    a. women.
    b. men.
    c. adolescents.
    d. Asians.

CONCEPTUAL MULTIPLE-CHOICE QUESTIONS

1. Unchangeable false beliefs are to _____ as perceptions in the absence of stimuli are to _____.

    a.   paranoid schizophrenia; catatonic schizophrenia
    b.   delusions; hallucinations
    c.   hallucinations; loosening of associations
    d.   loosening of associations; hallucinations

2. People with schizophrenia have problems with attention. What problems, exactly?

    a.   They crave the attention of others but withdraw from social attention.
    b.   They focus their attention so narrowly that they are unaware of other people.
    c.   They choose to focus their attention on fantasy instead of reality.
    d.   They find it difficult to concentrate and organize incoming information.

3. Which form of schizophrenia is associated with poor prognosis and must be diagnosed with care because the symptoms may develop in response to medication and institutionalization?

    a.   Schizophrenia with negative symptoms
    b.   Paranoid schizophrenia
    c.   Schizophrenia with positive symptoms
    d.   Capgras's syndrome

4. _____ schizophrenia is the most common form of the disorder and is characterized by illogical and contradictory delusions.

    a.   Paranoid
    b.   Catatonic
    c.   Disorganized
    d.   Undifferentiated

5. In what kind of schizophrenia do patients stand in awkward positions for hours at a time?

    a.   Paranoid
    b.   Catatonic
    c.   Disorganized
    d.   Undifferentiated

6. In what way is schizophreniform disorder different from schizophrenia?

    a.   It involves thought disturbances that the patient can control; in schizophrenia, there is no control.
    b.   It begins at an early age; in schizophrenia, the onset is in middle age.
    c.   It involves no thought disturbances; in schizophrenia, thought disturbances are critical symptoms.
    d.   It has not lasted six months or more; in schizophrenia, psychosis must have lasted at least that long.

7. Research on the relationship between the risk of developing schizophrenia and the degree of blood relatedness indicates

    a.   completely inconsistent results.
    b.   that schizophrenia is clearly a genetically caused disorder.
    c.   that social class and stressors are more important than genetic factors.
    d.   the closer the blood relationship to a person with schizophrenia the higher the risk of the disorder.

8. The value of a high-risk population study of schizophrenia over an adoption study is that it
   a. separates the effects of genetic factors from those of the environment.
   b. includes a control group.
   c. allows for the use of concordance rates.
   d. allows the investigator to see how the disorder develops.
9. Which of the following is a reason to be cautious in using the results of high-risk population research studies to conclude that schizophrenia is biologically caused?
   a. There is no significant difference in the rate of schizophrenia in high-risk versus control subjects.
   b. Such studies rarely examine such nongenetic factors as pregnancy and birth complications
   c. Most people diagnosed with schizophrenia do not have a schizophrenic parent.
   d. "High-risk" is defined in terms of dopamine sensitivity, and other neurotransmitters may be involved in the disorder.
10. What is the effect of reducing expressed emotion in the families of schizophrenic individuals?
    a. the need for medication is increased
    b. relapse rates are reduced
    c. other affective disorders take the place of schizophrenic symptoms
    d. communication skills are weakened

APPLICATION MULTIPLE-CHOICE QUESTIONS

1. Kristin, a schizophrenic patient, believes that all events revolve around her. Whatever anyone says, it is about her. All news broadcasts contain hidden messages for her. Kristin's thinking illustrates
   a. a delusion of persecution.
   b. a delusion of grandeur.
   c. Capgras's syndrome.
   d. a delusion of reference.
2. Justin was diagnosed with schizophrenia. He shows little emotional expression and has no motivation. He seems unable to feel pleasure. Justin's form of schizophrenia
   a. involves positive symptoms.
   b. is usually considered disorganized schizophrenia.
   c. usually has a very good prognosis.
   d. involves negative symptoms.
3. Jonathan has shown thought disturbances since he was 8 years old. He is now 27 and still acts in bizarre and silly ways. When most people would laugh, he cries. He shows no consistent delusions. Jonathan would most likely receive a diagnosis of
   a. schizophreniform disorder.
   b. catatonic schizophrenia.
   c. undifferentiated schizophrenia.
   d. disorganized schizophrenia.
4. When Tina is totally withdrawn, she shows waxy flexibility. When she is out of that state, she is extremely active and hypertalkative. Tina would most likely receive a diagnosis of schizophrenia.
   a. paranoid
   b. catatonic
   c. undifferentiated
   d. residual

5. Barney believes that his office phone is monitored and that his boss is trying to poison the air in his office. Other than these unfounded suspicions, Barney shows no thought disturbance or functioning problems. Barney would most likely receive a diagnosis of

    a. paranoid schizophrenia.
    b. undifferentiated schizophrenia.
    c. brief psychotic disorder.
    d. delusional disorder.

6. Dr. Jenkins says, 'More than one-half of schizophrenics show moderate to complete recovery, although recovery rates differ depending on whether the country is developed or developing. Developing countries have very poor recovery rates." What part of Dr. Jenkins's statement is *inaccurate?*

    a. It is inaccurate to say that one-half of schizophrenics recover.
    b. It is inaccurate to say that recovery can be complete for any schizophrenic.
    c. It is inaccurate to say that the type of country affects recovery.
    d. It is inaccurate to say that developing countries have very poor recovery rates.

7. Don and Ron are identical twins. Tim and Harry are fraternal twins. Don and Tim are both diagnosed as schizophrenics. According to the results of most research studies on twins,

    a. Ron has a greater chance of being schizophrenic than Harry.
    b. Ron and Harry have equal chances of being schizophrenic.
    c. Harry has a greater chance of being schizophrenic than Ron.
    d. there is little chance that either Harry or Ron will have schizophrenia.

8. Based on the prospective, high-risk population research done in Israel on children with schizophrenic mothers, what policy might the government adopt?

    a. Refuse to allow children of schizophrenic mothers to live in a kibbutz.
    b. Ensure that children of schizophrenic mothers be given antidepressant medication.
    c. Provide therapy to children in school who seem overly involved in relationships.
    d. Make sure that children of schizophrenic mothers receive adequate parenting.

9. Cindy says, "I don't think that poverty causes schizophrenia; I think being so dysfunctional makes schizophrenics poor." Cindy's ideas illustrate the

    a. downward drift hypothesis.
    b. diathesis-stress model of schizophrenia.
    c. schizophrenogenic theory.
    d. breeder hypothesis.

10. An elderly schizophrenic patient who has been taking phenothiazines for twenty years shows involuntary thrusting of her tongue, lip smacking, and jerking movements of the neck. What is wrong with this patient?

    a. She has cerebral atrophy as a result of negative symptom schizophrenia.
    b. She has symptoms of the disorder that are still not controlled through medication.
    c. She has developed Parkinson's disease because of her medication.
    d. She has developed tardive dyskinesia because of her medication.

ANSWER KEY: KEY TERMS REVIEW

1. schizophrenia

2. disorganized schizophrenia

3. paranoid schizophrenia

4. catatonic schizophrenia

5. undifferentiated schizophrenia

6. delusional disorder
7. residual schizophrenia
8. hallucinations
9. loosening of associations
10. brief psychotic disorder
11. schizophreniform disorder
12. cognitive symptoms
13. schizoaffective disorder
14. positive symptoms
15. dopamine hypothesis
16. neuroleptics
17. concordance rate
18. milieu therapy
19. expressed emotion
20. shared psychotic disorder

ANSWER KEY: FACTUAL MULTIPLE-CHOICE QUESTIONS

1. d. The lifetime prevalence of schizophrenia in the United States is about 1 percent.

   a. The lifetime prevalence for African Americans is about 2 percent, twice that for the general population.

   b. Schizophrenia affects males and females equally.

   c. The lifetime prevalence is about 1 percent.

2. a. Delusions of persecution involve suspicions that others will harm or humiliate you.

   b. Delusions of grandeur involve a belief in self-importance (such as, "I am the king of the world").

   c. Psychomotor disturbances involve wild activity or extreme immobility.

   d. A neologism is a made-up word, not a false belief.

3. c. Loosening of associations (also called cognitive slippage) is the cognitive symptom of shifting from topic to topic therefore speaking an incoherent way.

   a. Anhedonia is a negative symptom meaning an inability to experience pleasure.

   b. Delusions of reference are mistaken beliefs that all events revolve around the person with the delusion.

   d. Lack of insight is the inability of psychotic people to know that their thinking is bizarre.

4. c. The term *delusional disorder* is reserved for highly compartmentalized delusions that do not have a broad effect on functioning.

    a. In paranoid schizophrenia, delusions and other thought disturbances affect a wide range of functioning; there is a deterioration in functioning in all the schizophrenias.

    b. Brief psychotic disorder is diagnosed if symptoms last one month or less.

    d. There is no such subtype.

5. b. Recovery, including return to employment, was quicker in developing countries.

    a. Recovery was slower in developed countries such as the United States and the former Soviet Union.

    c. Many studies indicate that moderation or elimination of symptoms is likely in one-half of cases.

    d. If diet were important, we would expect better recovery in developed countries than in developing ones, where food may be scarce.

6. c. Dopamine activity has been found to be excessive in certain areas of the brains of schizophrenics, and it is reduced by phenothiazines and increased by amphetamines.

    a. L-dopa is a drug used to treat Parkinson's disease because it is used by the body to manufacture dopamine.

    b. 5HIAA is a metabolite of the neurotransmitter serotonin and is involved in affective disorders.

    d. Acetylcholine is a neurotransmitter, but it is not implicated in schizophrenia.

7. b. Both of these problems characterized earlier work and made its results suspect.

    a. One of the problems with earlier research was that the definition of the disorder was too broad.

    c. MZ and DZ twins were never used in family studies.

    d. One of the problems with earlier research was the failure to use a developmental method.

8. d. Downward drift suggest that poverty is the effect of schizophrenia; people cannot work well and so become poorer.

    a. Genetic explanations are supported by high-risk population, twin, or adoption studies.

    b. Biochemical explanations are supported by neurotransmitter imbalances or drug effects.

    c. Schizophrenic mothers are believed by psychoanalysts to generate schizophrenia by acting toward their children in a cold and domineering manner.

9. d. Identical twins have not been found to be most susceptible to shared psychotic disorder.

    a. It is relatively rare.

    b. It does occur most frequently among those who are socially isolated.

    c. It does occur when a person who has a close relationship with an individual with delusional or psychotic beliefs comes to accept those beliefs.

10.   a.   Schizoaffective mood disorder is most common among women.

       b.   Schizoaffective mood disorder is not most common among men.

       c.   Schizoaffective mood disorder is not most common among adolescents.

       d.   Schizoaffective mood disorder is not most common among Asians.

ANSWER KEY: CONCEPTUAL MULTIPLE-CHOICE QUESTIONS

1.   b.   False beliefs are delusions; false sensory perceptions are hallucinations.

       a.   Although paranoid schizophrenia is characterized by false beliefs, catatonic schizophrenia involves motor disturbances, not hallucinations.

       c.   False sensory perceptions are hallucinations, not delusions.

       d.   Loose associations involve incoherent thoughts, not consistent ones that defy evidence (delusions)

2.   d.   People with schizophrenia are easily distracted, and their ability to organize incoming information is severely impaired.

       a.   People with schizophrenia are often socially withdrawn; they do not seek attention from others.

       b.   They have the opposite problem-they cannot focus their attention narrowly.

       c.   While people with schizophrenia have trouble distinguishing fantasy and reality, it is untrue that the problem of attention is a choice they make.

3.   a.   Schizophrenia with negative symptoms (apathy, remaining mute, showing little emotion) is associated with poor prognosis, but these symptoms may be brought on by medication or institutionalization.

       b.   Paranoid schizophrenia is marked by positive symptoms and does not necessarily warrant a poor prognosis.

       c.   Schizophrenia with positive symptoms (delusions and hallucinations) has a more promising prognosis than the disorder with negative symptoms.

       d.   Capgras's syndrome is a delusion (positive symptom) in which people think there. are doubles for oneself and others.

4.   a.   The hallmark of paranoid schizophrenia is delusions; it is the most common subtype of schizophrenia.

       b.   Catatonic schizophrenia is characterized by psychomotor disturbances.

       c.   Disorganized schizophrenia features very regressive behavior without delusions.

       d.   Undifferentiated schizophrenia has no particular symptom picture. It may include delusions, but it is not the most common subtype.

5.   b.   Psychomotor disturbances such as extreme activity and complete immobility are the fundamental signs of catatonic schizophrenia.

       a.   Paranoid schizophrenia features consistent delusions.

       c.   Disorganized schizophrenia is marked by extremely bizarre and childish behavior from an early age.

       d.   Undifferentiated schizophrenia is the label given when no particular symptom stands out.

6. d. Duration is the only accurate means of differentiating these disorders.

    a. Schizophrenic patients report being able to control or modify their symptoms.

    b. Schizophrenia does not usually begin in middle age; age of onset does not differentiate these disorders.

    c. There are thought disturbances in schizophreniform disorder.

7. d. The closer the blood relationship to a person with schizophrenia the higher the odds of developing schizophrenia.

    a. Results are not inconsistent: children run a 12- to 13-percent risk whereas for nieces or nephews the risk is about 2 to 3 percent.

    b. Because environmental influences are strong in family studies, such a statement is inaccurate.

    c. Family studies have not controlled for the effects of social class or other environmental effects.

8. d. High-risk population studies begin observations before the onset of symptoms in the members of the high-risk populations; such studies have the advantage of being developmental or prospective studies.

    a. High-risk children are raised by their biological parents, so such a separation is not possible.

    b. Control groups are a part of both research designs, so this does not represent a specific advantage of high-risk population studies.

    c. Concordance rates are used in any study that compares a proband and someone else; they are used in twin, adoption, and other genetic research designs.

9. c. The majority of people with schizophrenia do not, have a schizophrenic parent, so whatever genetic vulnerability there is less than that seen in high-risk population studies.

    a. High-risk population studies consistently find more cases of schizophrenia among those who are high-risk than among controls.

    b. Such studies do examine nongenetic biological factors; Mednick's work, for instance, found that high-risk children who develop schizophrenia have mothers who experienced pregnancy and birth complications.

    d. "High-risk" is defined by having a mother who was diagnosed with schizophrenia; it has nothing to do with dopamine sensitivity.

10. b. Reducing expressed emotion in the family has been found to be a better way to reduce risk of relapse than medication alone.

    a. Such training may actually reduce the need for medication since it improves the chances of staying symptom-free.

    c. There is no evidence that reducing expressed emotion has any negative effects.

    d. These interventions improve communication skills.

ANSWER KEY: APPLICATION MULTIPLE-CHOICE QUESTIONS

1.   d.   Delusions of reference involve beliefs that external events have personal meaning ("When police sirens are sounded, they are signaling me").

      a.   A delusion of persecution would involve threats of harm or humiliation.

      b.   Delusions of grandeur involve a belief in one's special status or ability ("I can see through walls").

      c.   Capgras's syndrome is a delusion that oneself and others have been replaced by identical doubles.

2.   d.   Negative symptoms such as the ones Justin shows are associated with poor prognosis.

      a.   Positive symptoms include activity such as bizarre. gestures, as well as delusions, hallucinations, and disorganized thought.

      b.   Disorganized schizophrenia is characterized by bizarre actions, fragmented thinking, and emotional expression that can include silly smiles or giggles.

      c.   Schizophrenia involving an absence of emotion and motivation involves negative symptoms; these are associated with poor prognosis.

3.   d.   Disorganized schizophrenia involves bizarre symptoms that have an early onset, as in Jonathan's case.

      a.   Schizophreniform disorder is diagnosed when symptoms last less than six months.

      b.   Catatonic schizophrenia is characterized by psychomotor disturbances, which Jonathan does not display.

      c.   In undifferentiated schizophrenia, symptoms are more diffuse than Jonathan's and are not so regressive.

4.   b.   Catatonic schizophrenia involves the psychomotor disturbances and social withdrawal seen in Tina's case.

      a.   Paranoid schizophrenia is characterized by delusions.

      c.   Undifferentiated schizophrenia does not involve such bizarre behaviors as are described in Tina's case.

      d.   Residual schizophrenia is diagnosed when a person has had an episode of full-blown schizophrenia and now shows some symptoms but not prominently enough to get another diagnosis.

5.   d.   In delusional disorder, paranoid ideas are highly organized, but no other thought disturbance is seen.

      a.   In paranoid schizophrenia, delusions are part of a more general cognitive impairment that leads to deteriorated functioning.

      b.   In undifferentiated schizophrenia, delusions are not predominant.

      c.   Brief psychotic disorder is an acute condition that impairs functioning; it lasts less than one month.

6.   d.   Although misdiagnosis may be the reason, higher recovery rates have been found in developing countries (Nigeria and India) than in developed countries (the United States and Great Britain).

     a.   Long-term outcomes show that one-half of schizophrenic patients make moderate or complete recoveries.

     b.   Some schizophrenics make complete recoveries.

     c.   Recovery seems to be more rapid in developing countries than in developed ones such as the United States.

7.   a.   Identical twins have a higher concordance rate than fraternal twins because all of their genes are the same.

     b.   Because there is one-half the similarity of genes in fraternal twins, compared to identical twins, there should be a reduced likelihood for Harry.

     c.   Being a fraternal twin, Harry's likelihood is lower.

     d.   It is true that schizophrenia is rare, but as Meehl points out, an identical twin has about a 50 percent chance of developing the disorder if the other twin is so diagnosed.

8.   d.   None of the high-risk children who received adequate parenting developed schizophrenia; the results of the study point to the importance of both genetics and family nurturing.

     a.   There was no significant difference in the likelihood of developing schizophrenia between high-risk children raised in a kibbutz or in a suburban town.

     b.   Although somewhat more high-risk children showed affective disorders than did controls, the overwhelming majority showed good adjustment.

     c.   The characteristic most associated with the development of schizophrenia was social withdrawal, not overinvolvement in relationships.

9.   a.   In downward drift theory, the fact that schizophrenics cannot be gainfully employed is the explanation for the correlation between low social class and the disorder.

     b.   Diathesis-stress theory states only that a combination of predisposition and environmental stress produces the disorder; it says nothing about social class.

     c.   Schizophrenogenic theory stresses the role of a dominating and rejecting mother; it says nothing about social class.

     d.   If Cindy believed that the stress of poverty causes the disorder, this would be the best answer.

10. d.   These are the classic signs of tardive dyskinesia, which is most likely in elderly individuals who have taken neuroleptic medications for some years.

     a.   The negative symptoms of schizophrenia are flat affect and passivity.

     b.   Although, in rare cases, lip smacking may be a psychotic behavior, it is far more commonly seen in tardive dyskinesia.

     c.   The symptoms of Parkinson's disease are a shuffling gait and flat affect; medication can produce only similar symptoms, not the disease itself.

OBJECTIVES DEFINED

1. **What are the symptoms of schizophrenia?**

- Positive symptoms of schizophrenia involve unusual thoughts or perceptions such as delusions, hallucinations, thought disorder (shifting and unrelated ideas that produce incoherent communication), and bizarre behavior.

- Negative symptoms of schizophrenia are associated with an inability or decreased ability to initiate actions or speech, express emotions, or feel pleasure. Such symptoms include *avolition* (an inability to take action or become goal-oriented), *alogia* (a lack of meaningful speech), and *flat affect* (little or no emotion in situations in which strong reactions are expected).

- Cognitive symptoms of schizophrenia include problems with attention, memory, and difficulty in developing a plan of action.

2. **How do the specific types of schizophrenia differ from one another?**

- Paranoid schizophrenia is characterized by one or more systematized delusions or auditory hallucinations and by the absence of such symptoms as disorganized speech and behavior or flat affect.

- Disorganized schizophrenia grossly disorganized behaviors manifested in disorganized speech and behavior and flat or grossly inappropriate affect.

- Catatonic schizophrenia's major feature is disturbance of motor activity. Patients show excessive excitement, agitation and hyperactivity or withdrawn behavior patterns.

- The undifferentiated type includes schizophrenic behavior that cannot be classified as one of the other types.

- Residual schizophrenia is a category for people who have had at least one episode of schizophrenia but are not now showing prominent symptoms. In addition, other severe disorders may include schizophrenic-like symptoms.

3. **Is there much chance of recovery from schizophrenia?**

- The degree of recovery from schizophrenia is difficult to evaluate, in part because of changing definitions. Although most people assume that the prognosis for individuals with schizophrenia is not good, research is beginning to show that that may not be the case. Many of these individuals experience minimal or no lasting impairment. Most individuals with schizophrenia recover enough to lead relatively productive lives.

4. **What causes schizophrenia?**

- The best conclusion is that genetics, along with environmental factors (physical, psychological, or social) combine to cause the disorder. Heredity is a major factor but not sufficient to cause schizophrenia; environmental factors are also involved. Certain negative family patterns involving parental characteristics or intrafamilial communication processes have been hypothesized to result in schizophrenia. There is little evidence that psychological factors in and of themselves can cause the condition.

5. **What treatments are currently available, and are they effective?**

- Schizophrenia seems to involve both biological and physiological factors, and treatment programs that combine drugs with psychotherapy appear to hold the most promise.

- Drug therapy usually involves conventional antipsychotics (the phenothiazines) or the newer atypical antipsychotics.

- The accompanying psychosocial therapy consists of either supportive counseling or behavior therapy, with an emphasis on social-skills training and changing communication patterns among patients and family members.

MARGIN DEFINITIONS

brief psychotic disorder psychotic disorder that lasts no longer than one month

catatonic schizophrenia a schizophrenic disorder characterized by marked disturbance in motor activity—either extreme excitement or motoric immobility; symptoms may include motoric immobility or stupor; excessive purposeless motor activity; extreme negativism or physical resistance; peculiar voluntary movements; or echolalia or echopraxia

cognitive symptoms in schizophrenia, a symptom that is associated with problems with attention, memory, and difficulty in developing a plan of action

concordance rate the likelihood that both members of a twin pair will show the same characteristic

delusion a false belief that is firmly and consistently held despite disconfirming evidence or logic

delusional disorder a disorder characterized by persistent, nonbizarre delusions that are not accompanied by other unusual or odd behaviors

disorganized schizophrenia a schizophrenic disorder characterized by grossly disorganized behaviors manifested in disorganized speech and behavior and flat or grossly inappropriate affect

dopamine hypothesis the suggestion that schizophrenia may result from excess dopamine activity at certain synaptic sites

expressed emotion (EE) a negative communication pattern that is found among some relatives of individuals with schizophrenia and which is associated with higher relapse rates

hallucination sensory perception that is not directly attributable to environmental stimuli

loosening of associations in schizophrenia, continual shifting from topic to topic without any apparent logical or meaningful connection between thoughts

milieu therapy a therapy program in which the hospital environment operates as a community and patients exercise a wide range of responsibility, helping to make decisions and to manage wards

negative symptom in schizophrenia, a symptom associated with an inability or decreased ability to initiate actions or speech, express emotions, or feel pleasure; includes avolition, alogia, and flat affect

neuroleptic antipsychotic drug that can help treat symptoms of schizophrenia but can produce undesirable side effects, such as symptoms that mimic neurological disorders

paranoid schizophrenia a schizophrenic disorder characterized by one or more systematized delusions or auditory hallucinations and by the absence of such symptoms as disorganized speech and behavior or flat affect

positive symptom symptom of schizophrenia that involves unusual thoughts or perceptions such as delusions, hallucinations, thought disorder (shifting and unrelated ideas that produce incoherent communication), and bizarre behavior

prospective study a long-term study of a group of people, beginning before the onset of a disorder, to allow investigators to see how the disorder develops

residual schizophrenia a category of schizophrenic disorder reserved for people who have had at least one previous schizophrenic episode but are now showing an absence of prominent psychotic features; there is continuing evidence of two or more symptoms, such as marked social isolation, peculiar behaviors, blunted affect, odd beliefs, or unusual perceptual experiences

schizoaffective disorder a disorder characterized by both a mood disorder (major depression or bipolar disorder) and the presence of psychotic symptoms "for at least two weeks in the absence of prominent mood symptoms"

schizophrenia a group of disorders characterized by severely impaired cognitive processes, personality disintegration, affective disturbances, and social withdrawal

schizophreniform disorder psychotic disorder that lasts more than one month but less than six months

shared psychotic disorder in schizophrenia, when a person who has a close relationship with an individual with delusional or psychotic beliefs comes to accept those beliefs

undifferentiated schizophrenia a schizophrenic disorder in which the person's behavior shows prominent psychotic symptoms that do not meet the criteria for paranoid, disorganized, or catatonic schizophrenia

CHAPTER 14

Cognitive Disorders

TABLE OF CONTENTS

LEARNING OBJECTIVES

1. Describe how we can determine whether someone has brain damage or a cognitive disorder.

2. Discuss the different types of cognitive disorders.

3. Explain why people develop cognitive disorders.

4. Describe the kinds of interventions that can be used to treat people with cognitive disorders.

CHAPTER OUTLINE

I.   **The assessment of brain damage.** Cognitive disorders are behavioral disturbances that result from transient or permanent damage to the brain and affect thinking, memory, consciousness, and perception and are affected by social and psychological factors, such as coping ability and stress. DSM-IV-TR differentiates delirium, dementia, amnestic disorders, and other cognitive disorders. Brain damage can be assessed through neuropsychological testing and neurological tests. The first uses behavioral responses from the patient on memory or manual dexterity tasks. The second directly monitors the brain through *electroencephalography (EEG), computerized axial tomography (CT) scans, positron emission tomography (PET), magnetic resonance imaging (MRI),* and *cerebral blood flow measurements.* Each has its strengths and weaknesses.

II.   **Types of cognitive disorders.** Within the types of cognitive disorders, clinicians categorize according to cause, such as psychoactive substance-induced or general medical condition. The most prominent features of *dementia* are memory impairment and cognitive disturbance, including language disturbance (aphasia, impairments in motor activities (apraxia), misidentification of faces or objects (agnosia), and problems with planning and abstractions. *Delirium* involves impairments in consciousness and changes in cognition (disorientation, incoherent speech, perceptual distortions), and it usually develops rapidly. *Amnestic disorders* entail an inability to retain new information or recall old information, or both, and may be caused by head trauma, stroke. While the three conditions have overlapping symptoms, dementias are usually accompanied by language problems such as aphasia and come on gradually (as opposed to delirium). Memory loss is the primary symptom of amnestic disorders.

III. **Etiology of cognitive disorders.** *Traumatic brain injury(TBI)*—a physical wound to the brain-is one cause of cognitive disorders. Head injuries include *concussions,* when blood vessels are damaged by a blow to the head; *contusions,* when blood vessels rupture because of the brain's impact against the skull; and *lacerations,* when tissue is torn or pierced by an object penetrating the skull. Personality changes as well as cognitive and motor impairments are common. Only one-third of closed-head injury patients return to gainful employment after traditional rehabilitation. The aging population of the United States is growing, due both to longer life expectancy and the large numbers. *Stroke*, the third major cause of death in the United States, is a common cognitive disorder in the elderly. Strokes (cerebrovascular accidents) occur when blood flow to an area of the brain is cut off, causing a loss of brain function. Causes of stroke include bursting of blood vessels and narrowing or blockage of blood vessels owing to the buildup of fatty material on interior walls (atherosclerosis), which results in cerebral infarction (death of the brain cells results). A series of small strokes is known as vascular dementia; it is characterized by uneven deterioration of physical and intellectual abilities. Risk factors include hypertension, heart disease, cigarette smoking, diabetes, and excessive alcohol consumption. Memory loss in the elderly may be due to brain cell deterioration, vascular dementia, and the normal aging process. A common cause is intoxication from prescribed medications. To assess age-related cognitive deficits, the individual's performance can be compared with general population norms, age-group norms, norms based on similarity in status or education, and the person's previous functioning. Alzheimer's disease, involving atrophy of cortical tissue, leads to intellectual and emotional deterioration, including memory loss, irritability, and social withdrawal. Autopsies show neurofibrillary tangles and senile plaques in the brains of people with the disease. The etiology of Alzheimer's are unknown, but heredity may play a role in some subtypes; infection, head injury, exposure to aluminum, and reduced neurotransmitter levels may be related to others. Protective factors include genetic endowment with the ApoE-e2 allele, higher education, use of non-steroidal anti-inflammatories or estrogen replacement, and vitamin E. Parkinson's disease has the following symptoms: muscle tremors, a stiff, shuffling gait, and an expressionless face. The disorder is associated with lesions in the motor area of the brain stem and insufficient dopamine levels. Treatment is generally L-dopa or a similar drug. The majority of AIDS patients also suffer from some form of dementia. It is not clear whether the AIIDS virus affects the brain; AIDS-related infections cause neuropsychological problems, or depression and anxiety about having AIDS cause cognitive symptoms. *Neurosyphilis (general paresis)* is brain damage caused by the delayed effect of a syphilis infection. It occurs in about 10 percent of syphilis cases. Symptoms include memory impairment, delusions, paralysis, and death within five years. *Encephalitis* (sleeping sickness) is a viral infection of the brain that produces long periods of sleep followed by agitation and seizures. *Meningitis,* an inflammation of the membrane around the brain, can be caused by bacteria, viruses, or fungi, and has a wide range of effects and potential residual disturbances. *Huntington's disease* is a genetically transmitted disorder that first shows in early middle age. Symptoms begin with twitches and progress to uncontrollable jerking movements, irritability, and confusion. Death comes within thirteen to sixteen years after onset. A gene has been identified that causes the disorder. It is frequently misdiagnosed as schizophrenia. A *cerebral tumor* is a mass of abnormal tissue growing in the brain. Fast-growing tumors in the brain produce severe mental symptoms, such as diminished attention, drowsiness, dementia, and mood changes, or may be severe enough to result in coma. Removal of tumors can result in dramatic improvement of functioning. *Epilepsy* is a set of symptoms, not a disorder. It involves brief periods of altered consciousness, often accompanied by seizures. About 2.7 million children and adults in the United States have epilepsy or some other seizure disorder. Causes are genetic a well as environmental. Although epilepsy cannot be cured, it can be controlled with medication.

IV. **Treatment/prevention considerations.** Treatment approaches include medical strategies such as surgery and medication (for the disorder itself or to control emotional problems accompanying the disorder), and psychological efforts such as skills acquisition, cognitive preparation, application training, and psychotherapy, such as behavior modification and biofeedback. How family and friends can assist those with cognitive disorders is an important issue. In preventing or reducing the effects of cognitive disorders, research suggests that lifestyle changes are important. For vascular dementia, health habits related to preventing stroke—e.g., avoiding smoking, obesity, and hypertension—are relevant to prevention. Some suggestions are preserving a sense of independence and control, maintaining interpersonal contacts that do not overwhelm, engaging in pleasant diversions, providing tasks that increase self-worth, and ensuring that caregivers obtain social support for themselves.

V. **Implications.** We have not directly focused on the multi-path model simply because cognitive disorders are usually classified by etiology. Because most cognitive disorders, including mental retardation, have underlying damage, deterioration, or abnormalities to the brain or its processes, biological factors are apparent. However, we have also noted the importance of psychological, social, and sociocultural factors in the disorders.

KEY TERMS REVIEW

1. A sudden stoppage of blood flow to a portion of the brain that leads to a loss of brain function is called a(n) _____.

2. The syndrome characterized by a continuous decline in intellectual ability and judgment and that often includes language problems and has a gradual onset is called _____.

3. Disorders involving impairments of thinking, memory, perception, or consciousness caused by brain damage are called _____.

4. The progressively worsening cognitive disorder characterized by muscle tremors, stiff and shuffling gait, lack of facial expression, and social withdrawal is called _____.

5. The cognitive disorder in which there is reduced ability to attend to stimuli, difficulty in shifting attention, and disorganized thinking, and which usually has a sudden onset, is called _____.

6. The cognitive disorder that involves atrophy of the brain and leads to marked deterioration in memory and emotional functioning is called _____.

7. Any disorder that is characterized by intermittent and brief periods of altered consciousness and is often accompanied by seizures is called _____.

8. The death of brain tissue resulting from a decrease in blood supply to that tissue is called a(n) _____.

9. A physical wound or injury to the brain is called a(n) _____.

10. Cognitive disorders in which the primary symptom is an inability to learn new information or a failure to retain old information are called _____.

11. The cognitive disorder characterized by uneven deterioration of intellectual abilities (dementia) that results from a number of cerebral infarctions, is called _____.

12. A neurological test that uses x-rays and computer technology to assess brain damage is called _____.

13. A neurological test for the assessment of brain damage that measures the electrical activity of the brain is called a(n) _____.

14. The technique that uses radio waves and a magnetic field to produce an image of the brain and to assess brain functioning is called _____.

15. The technique for assessing brain damage that involves the injection of radioactive glucose and the monitoring of glucose metabolism is called _____.

16. A cognitive disorder caused by viral infection that produces symptoms of lethargy, fever, delirium, and long periods of stupor and sleep is _____.

17. A rare degenerative disease characterized by involuntary twitching movements and eventual dementia is _____.

18. A medical condition in which there is inflammation of the membrane that surrounds the brain and spinal cord is _____.

19. A procedure used to assess brain damage in which radioactive gas is inhaled and then a gamma ray camera tracks the gas, and thus flow of blood through the brain, is _____.

20. A mass of abnormal tissue growing in the brain is a _____.

FACTUAL MULTIPLE-CHOICE QUESTIONS

1. A person showing behavioral disturbances that are caused by brain damage is considered to have a _____ disorder.
   a. cognitive
   b. general medical
   c. delirium
   d. psychotic

2. Treatment for cognitive disorders
   a. is always medical, never psychological.
   b. is always psychological, never medical.
   c. is often a combination of medical and psychological.
   d. is never psychological if the brain damage is irreversible.

3. When brain damage leads to permanent and irreversible loss of function, the disorder is considered
   a. chronic.
   b. diffuse.
   c. acute.
   d. endogenous.

4. Dementia is characterized by
   a. the inability to either comprehend or produce speech.
   b. fever, disorganized thinking, and an inability to concentrate on a particular stimulus.
   c. rapid onset and rapid recovery.
   d. slow-onset impairment of memory and judgment that interferes with functioning.

5. Difficulty in forming words and an inability to retain their meanings are central problems in
   a. aphasia.
   b. delirium.
   c. Parkinson's disease.
   d. strokes that affect the right side of the brain.

6. Young adults who survive severe head injuries typically
   a. make full recoveries.
   b. completely recover their mental functioning, but continue to have emotional disturbances.
   c. have continuing mental and emotional disturbances that make return to full employment unlikely.
   d. have continuing physical problems, but rarely emotional disturbances.

7. This organic mental disorder represents the third major cause of death in the United States. It can occur when blood vessels burst or when blocked blood flow causes brain tissue to die. What is this disorder?

    a. Aphasia
    b. Stroke (cerebrovascular accident)
    c. Senile dementia
    d. Alzheimer's disease

8. Which statement about Alzheimer's disease is *accurate*?

    a. Alzheimer's is usually caused by people taking too many prescription medications.
    b. Memory loss is the last symptom to appear in the disorder.
    c. Although a disabling disorder, Alzheimer's does not lead to early death.
    d. Alzheimer's accounts for almost 80 percent of dementia in older persons.

9. Which of the following is associated with Parkinson's disease?

    a. Stiff, shuffling walk
    b. Onset in adolescence
    c. Atrophy of large portions of the brain as a result of aging
    d. Excessive emotionality

10. Which statement concerning epilepsy is accurate?

    a. It is the third leading cause of death in the United States.
    b. It is most frequently diagnosed during childhood.
    c. It can be caused only by a genetic defect.
    d. It is an organic mental disorder that affects the limbic system.

CONCEPTUAL MULTIPLE-CHOICE QUESTIONS

1. Neuropsychological testing relies on

    a. electroencephalographs.
    b. CT scans.
    c. radioactive chemicals.
    d. assessments of cognitive and behavioral functioning, such as memory and manual dexterity.

2. Plasticity is one explanation of why it is difficult to identify specific areas of the brain and their function. Plasticity refers to the fact that

    a. undeveloped portions of the brain can take up the functions of damaged portions.
    b. lesions in one area of the brain can disrupt function in distant, undamaged areas.
    c. no two brains are identical.
    d. one hemisphere of the brain controls behavior on the opposite side of the body.

3. Why is it important to know that dementia can be caused by factors other than aging?

    a. Because it makes psychotherapy unnecessary
    b. Because other causative problems can be corrected
    c. Because nearly 50 percent of the elderly are demented
    d. Because it used to be thought of as a functional disorder

4. When the primary symptoms are an inability to learn new information or recall past events and the probable cause is a thiamine deficiency, the diagnosis should be

    a. delirium caused by substance use.
    b. amnestic disorder.
    c. dementia caused by nutrition deficit.
    d. aphasia.

5. When portions of the brain are torn or pierced, survivors may have very serious symptoms, including intellectual impairment and personality changes. The cause is a

    a. concussion.
    b. form of epilepsy.
    c. brain. laceration.
    d. cerebral tumor.

6. What one symptom is found in Alzheimer's disease, senile dementia, and vascular dementia?

    a. Brain trauma
    b. Brief periods of unconsciousness
    c. Restlessness and irritability followed by excessive sleep
    d. Memory loss

7. What do encephalitis, meningitis, and neurosyphilis have in common?

    a. They are all associated with aging.
    b. They are all caused by viral or bacterial infections.
    c. They are all incurable and caused by genetic factors.
    d. They are all effectively treated with the neurotransmitter L-dopa.

8. Family and friends who are caregivers for people with irreversible cognitive disorders are advised to

    a. prevent the patient from taking on tasks unless they can be completed perfectly.
    b. prevent the patient from making personal decisions.
    c. maintain social contacts that are brief and without pressure.
    d. keep their anxieties and concerns private, and refrain from using outside help.

APPLICATION MULTIPLE-CHOICE QUESTIONS

1. Based on epidemiological research, which person has the highest likelihood of having a severe form of cognitive disorder?

    a. A white male teenager
    b. An African American woman who is 76 years old
    c. A middle-aged Hispanic American man
    d. An African American male who is 26 years old

2. Dr. Elsberg says, "My patient has experienced specific brain damage in the frontal and parietal lobes of the right hemisphere. We can expect that she will experience motor impairments and, if the injury is of an acute nature, there is a chance the damage is reversible." What is *inaccurate* About Dr. Elsberg's statement?

    a. It is inaccurate to say that right frontal damage leads to motor impairment.
    b. It is inaccurate to say that right parietal damage leads to motor impairment.
    c. It is inaccurate to say that acute injuries are reversible.
    d. Nothing Dr. Elsberg said is inaccurate.

3. John was not wearing his seat belt, and his head struck the windshield when he was in a car accident. He was dazed and had a headache for several days after the accident, but soon he recovered completely. John's problem would most likely be diagnosed as a

    a. cerebrovascular accident.
    b. cerebral infarction.
    c. laceration.
    d. concussion.

4. Mrs. Lee is a 70-year-old woman whose children brought her to the doctor because she suddenly lost the ability to speak, was confused and had memory loss, and could not move the right side of her body. The doctors disagreed over Mrs. Lee's diagnosis. Dr. Chin believes that Mrs. Lee has a somatoform disorder, but Dr. Lau thinks that Mrs. Lee has a cognitive disorder. You are called in to give an opinion. What would you say?

    a. Agree with Dr. Chin that Mrs. Lee has a somatoform disorder, most probably conversion disorder.
    b. Agree with Dr. Lau that Mrs. Lee has a cognitive disorder.
    c. Disagree with both Drs. Lau and Chin, because Mrs. Lee shows signs of a dissociative disorder, most likely dissociative amnesia.
    d. Disagree with both Drs. Lau and Chin, because Mrs. Lee is showing signs of Korsakoff's syndrome.

5. An autopsy was done after George died. His memory problems were discovered to be the result of severe cortical atrophy; and, at a microscopic level, neurofibrillary tangles and senile plaques were discovered. These findings indicate that George suffered from

    a. Alzheimer's disease.
    b. vascular dementia.
    c. Huntington's disease.
    d. a stroke.

6. Glenn has AIDS. He has trouble remembering where he has put things, and occasionally is frightened when he cannot concentrate or keep track of simple conversations. Glenn's behavior illustrates

    a. early signs of delirium, a rare symptom in AIDS.
    b. Parkinson's disease, a common result of AIDS.
    c. dementia, a common symptom of AIDS.
    d. vascular dementia, a rare symptom in AIDS.

7. Roger shows increasing muscle tremors, a shuffling walk, and an expressionless face. He also has delusions that people are poisoning him, and he is frequently depressed. Which of Roger's symptoms are *uncommon* in cases of Parkinson's disease?

    a. The delusions of persecution
    b. The expressionless face
    c. The muscle tremors
    d. The shuffling walk

8. A doctor says, "It is caused by bacterial, viral, or sometimes fungal infectious agents that attack and inflame the membrane surrounding the brain and spinal cord." What is the doctor describing?

    a. Neurosyphilis (general paresis)
    b. Meningitis
    c. Cerebral tumor
    d. Cerebrovascular accident (stroke)

9. Brandon was recently in a car accident. Since the accident, Brandon has had difficulty concentrating and has been suffering from reoccurring headaches and fatigue. Brandon is likely suffering from

    a. a traumatic brain injury.
    b. schizoaffective disorder.
    c. the flu.
    d. bipolar disorder.

ANSWER KEY: KEY TERMS REVIEW

1. stroke (cerebrovascular accident)

2. dementia

3.   cognitive disorders

4.   Parkinson's disease

5.   delirium

6.   Alzheimer's disease

7.   epilepsy

8.   cerebral infarction

9.   traumatic brain injury (TBI)

10.   amnestic disorders

11.   vascular dementia

12.   computerized axial tomography (CT) scan

13.   electroencephalograph (EEG)

14.   magnetic resonance imaging (MRI)

15.   positron emission tomography (PET) scan

16.   encephalitis

17.   Huntington's disease

18.   meningitis

19.   cerebral blood flow measurement

20.   cerebral tumor

ANSWER KEY: FACTUAL MULTIPLE-CHOICE QUESTIONS

1.   a.   Cognitive disorders are ones that are caused by either temporary or permanent brain damage and that affect memory, behavior, and affect in a way that significantly impairs functioning.

b.   General medical conditions do not necessarily affect thinking or other psychological functions.

c.   Delirium is a form of cognitive disorder in which symptoms involving disorientation, disruptions of the sleep-wake cycle, and other effects have a rapid onset.

d.   Psychotic disorders are ones in which delusions, hallucinations, and other breaks with reality are common symptoms; they do not need to involve brain damage.

2.   c.   Medical treatments are often helpful for controlling symptoms; psychological treatments can help patients master their emotions and relearn functional behaviors.

a.   Social skills training and other psychological treatments are useful in the treatment of many cognitive disorders.

b.   Such medical procedures as surgery and medication can be very effective in treating many cognitive disorders.

d.   When brain damage is irreversible, social skills and other rehabilitative treatments that are psychological are often the only treatments available.

3. a.   *Chronic* means a continuing problem.

    b.   *Diffuse* means that damage occurs in a broad region of the brain.

    c.   *Acute* is the opposite of chronic; it means temporary.

    d.   *Endogenous* means that damage is caused from within.

4. d.   Dementia is a cognitive deterioration in memory and judgment that makes living difficult; it usually has a gradual onset.

    a.   An inability to comprehend or produce speech is a definition of aphasia.

    b.   Disorganized thinking and lack of concentration are characteristics of delirium.

    c.   Rapid onset and recovery are characteristics of delirium.

5. a.   Aphasia involves the loss of the ability to speak or to comprehend speech.

    b.   Delirium occurs when thinking is disorganized and attention and concentration cannot be maintained.

    c.   Parkinson's disease affects motor control, not language.

    d.   Strokes that affect the right hemisphere are less likely to produce language impairment (aphasia) than those that affect the left.

6. c.   In the majority of cases, recovery includes a combination of problems that make gainful employment quite difficult.

    a.   Full recoveries from severe head injury are fairly rare.

    b.   Continuing problems of memory loss, inattention, and speech are common in severe head injury.

    d   Those who recover from severe head injury often show irritability and depression, although they are unaware of it.

7. b.   Stroke is the third major cause of death (400,000 or more cases annually) and is defined as tissue death (infarction) caused by insufficient blood flow.

    a.   Aphasia is impairment of language comprehension or production; it is a symptom, not a disorder.

    c.   Senile dementia is caused by the aging process.

    d.   Alzheimer's disease is caused by a general atrophy of brain tissue and is unrelated to a sudden shutoff of blood.

8. d.   Alzheimer's accounts for about 80 percent of older people with dementias.

    a.   Excessive medication is a reason for misdiagnosing cognitive disorders, but Alzheimer's is not caused by medication.

    b.   Memory loss is the first symptom to appear.

    c.   Alzheimer's involves a prolonged deterioration that leads to death in an average of five years.

9. a. Together with muscle tremors and an expressionless face, a stiff, shuffling gait is a fundamental sign of Parkinson's disease.

   b. Parkinson's disease rarely develops until a person is in his or her forties or fifties.

   c. Atrophy of large brain areas as a result of aging is associated with senile dementia.

   d. Lack of emotional expression is a symptom of Parkinson's disease.

10. b. Epilepsy is usually diagnosed early in life.

   a. The third leading cause of death is stroke.

   c. Although there may be a genetic component in the cause of epilepsy, environmental factors such as drug use and head injury can cause the disorder as well.

   d. Epilepsy is not a disorder, but a symptom that involves uncontrolled electrical activity in many portions of the brain.

ANSWER KEY: CONCEPTUAL MULTIPLE-CHOICE QUESTIONS

1. d. Neuropsychological tests such as the Halstead-Reitan use measurements of memory, cognitive flexibility, and manual dexterity to determine organic damage.

   a. Electroencephalographs record brain activity and are neurological tests.

   b. CT scans are computer-composite pictures of the brain using x-rays; they are neurological tests.

   c. Radioactive chemicals are used in blood flow and positron emission tomography, both of which are neurological tests.

2. a. Plasticity is the brain's ability to use undeveloped portions as substitutes for damaged areas; children born without an entire hemisphere can have the remaining hemisphere perform functions usually found in the missing one.

   b. When damage in one portion of the brain disrupts functioning in other, intact portions, the phenomenon is called diaschisis.

   c. While it is true that no two brains are the same, this is unrelated to plasticity.

   d. That one hemisphere controls specific functions underscores structure-function specificity, the opposite of plasticity.

3. b. Not much can be done to treat aging, but brain tumors, for example, can be surgically removed.

   a. Dementia and most of the other organic mental syndromes produce emotional problems that can be helped through psychotherapy.

   c. Probably less than 15 percent of the elderly are demented.

   d. Dementia has always been seen as an organic symptom.

4.   b.   Amnestic cognitive disorder involves memory and learning problems and little else; Wernicke's encephalopathy, which is probably caused by thiamine deficiency, is the most common form of amnestic disorder.

    a.   Delirium involves disorganized thinking rather than failure to learn or recall; it is not associated with a thiamine deficiency.

    c.   Dementia is not caused by nutrition deficit: the leading causes are Alzheimer's disease, stroke, and hydrocephalus. Dementias have other symptoms besides amnesia—delusions, hallucinations, and speech problems.

    d.   Aphasias are speech impairments involving either the comprehension or expression of words and their meanings.

5.   c.   A laceration is defined as a cut or tear caused by an external object, such as a bullet.

    a.   Aphasia is impairment of language comprehension or production.

    b.   Epilepsy involves uncontrolled electrical activity in the brain.

    d.   Tumors are abnormal masses of tissue.

6.   d.   All three are forms of dementia, and the chief symptom of dementia is memory loss.

    a.   Brain traumas are sudden-onset causes and rarely produce dementias.

    b.   Brief periods of unconsciousness are characteristics of epilepsy and concussions, not dementias.

    c.   Restlessness and irritability followed by excessive sleep are prominent symptoms in encephalitis, not dementias.

7.   b.   All three are caused by infectious agents that produce damage to the brain or its surrounding membranes.

    a.   The disorders associated with aging are stroke, Alzheimer's disease, and senile dementia.

    c.   None of these disorders has a genetic link.

    d.   Parkinson's disease is treated with L-dopa, since that disorder is associated with reduced amounts of dopamine.

8.   c.   Social contacts that are brief and do not overwhelm the patient counteract the social withdrawal that often occurs in cognitive disorders.

    a.   If tasks must be performed to perfection, patients with cognitive disorders lose confidence and give up trying.

    b.   Allowing patients to have control in their lives increases their cognitive functioning and prolongs the quality of their lives.

    d.   Caregivers can become overwhelmed, emotionally drained, and physically ill; they need to vent their emotions and make use of such resources as self-help groups.

ANSWER KEY: APPLICATION MULTIPLE-CHOICE QUESTIONS

1. b.   The likelihood is much, greater for cognitive disorder among those over 75, and African Americans have a higher rate of severe disorders than whites or Hispanic Americans; there is no gender difference.

    a.   Teenagers and people up to the age of 34 have twenty-two times less likelihood of having a cognitive disorder as a person over 75.

    c.   Hispanic Americans have no greater likelihood of cognitive disorders than whites and a lower rate of severe disorders than African Americans; the older population has the highest prevalence of cognitive disorders.

    d.   Although African Americans have a higher rate of severe cognitive disorders than whites or Hispanic Americans, 26 is too young to be at high risk.

2. d.   Since right frontal and right parietal damage that is specific to those areas is associated with motor impairment (in fact, damage to any right hemisphere lobe is associated with motor problems), and acute disorders are ones that are temporary, nothing the doctor said is inaccurate.

    a.   Brain damage that is specific and in the right frontal area is associated with motor impairments.

    b.   Brain damage that is specific and in the right parietal area is associated with motor impairments.

    c.   The definition of *acute is* a nonpermanent condition; although recovery from central nervous system damage is difficult, acute conditions are relatively temporary.

3. d.   A concussion causes relatively minor problems and usually leads to a full recovery.

    a.   A cerebrovascular accident (stroke) is caused by internal problems such as atherosclerosis, not external ones like a car accident.

    b.   A cerebral infarction occurs when tissue dies because, for example, the blood supply for that area was cutoff

    c.   Such minor problems and rapid recovery would not be likely in a laceration, in which areas of the brain are cut or ripped.

4. b.   Agree with Dr. Lau that Mrs. Lee has a cognitive disorder.

    a.   Her age and the rapid onset would suggest that Mrs. Lee may have a vascular disease and has perhaps suffered a stroke.

    c.   Dissociative amnesia would not cause paralysis. The symptoms suggest a real physical problem.

    d.   No mention is made of alcohol use by Mrs. Lee.

5. a.   Alzheimer's disease causes memory loss and is diagnosed at autopsy by atrophy of the cerebral cortex and the presence of neurofibrillary tangles (abnormal fibers that are tangles of brain filaments) and senile plaques (patches of degenerated nerve endings).

    b.   Vascular dementia is associated with a series of small strokes, not cerebral atrophy.

    c.   Huntington's disease is a genetically caused degenerative disorder but is unassociated with tangles or plaques.

    d.   A stroke involves the, death of tissue owing to blood and oxygen deficit, not cortical atrophy, tangles, or plaques.

6. c. Memory loss is a key symptom of dementia, a problem that occurs frequently in people with AIDS.

    a. Memory loss is associated with dementia, not delirium.

    b. Parkinson's disease cannot be acquired from AIDS and does not involve memory loss.

    d. Multi-infarct dementia is caused by a series of small strokes, not by AIDS.

7. a. Delusions of persecution are more commonly found in Alzheimer's disease or Huntington's disease than in Parkinson's disease.

    b. An expressionless face is a symptom of Parkinson's disease.

    c. Muscle tremors are a fundamental symptom of Parkinson's disease.

    d. A stiff, shuffling walk is a central feature of Parkinson's disease.

8. b. Meningitis is an infection of the meninges (membrane around the brain and spinal cord) that can be caused by viruses, bacteria, or sometimes fungi.

    a. Neurosyphilis is caused by an infection, but damage is done to the cerebral cortex, not the membrane around the brain.

    c. Cerebral tumors are abnormal masses that are not due to infections.

    d. Cerebrovascular accidents (strokes) occur when brain tissue dies because of a blood vessel rupturing or because of a blockage in blood flow through a blood vessel.

9. a. Such symptoms following an accident make it likely that Brandon suffered a traumatic brain industry.

    b. The circumstances coupled with Brandon's symptoms do not make schizoaffective disorder the likely problem.

    c. The circumstances coupled with Brandon's symptoms do not make the flu the likely problem.

    d. The circumstances coupled with Brandon's symptoms do not make bipolar disorder the likely problem.

OBJECTIVES DEFINED

1. **How can we determine whether someone has brain damage or a cognitive disorder?**

*   Cognitive disorders are behavioral disturbances that result from transient or permanent damage to the brain. The effects of brain damage vary greatly.

*   The most common symptoms include impaired consciousness and memory, impaired judgment, orientation difficulties, and attentional deficits.

*   The assessment of brain damage is performed using interviews, psychological tests, brain scans and imaging, and other observational or biological measures.

2. **What are the different types of cognitive disorders?**

*   DSM-IV-TR lists four major types of cognitive disorders: dementia, delirium, amnestic disorders, and other cognitive disorders.

*   In dementia, memory is impaired and cognitive functioning declines, as revealed by aphasia (language disturbance), apraxia (inability to carry out motor activities despite intact

comprehension and motor function), agnosia (failure to recognize or identify objects despite intact sensory function), or disturbances in planning, organizing, and abstracting in thought processes.

- Delirium is characterized by disturbance of consciousness and changes in cognition (memory deficit, disorientation, and language and perceptual disturbances). These impairments and changes are not attributable to dementia.

- Amnestic disorders are characterized by memory impairment, as manifested by the inability to learn new information and the inability to recall previously learned knowledge or past events.

- Cognitive impairments that do not meet the criteria for the other three are classified as cognitive disorders not otherwise specified.

3. **Why do people develop cognitive disorders?**

- Many different agents can cause cognitive disorders; among these are physical wounds or injuries to the brain, processes of aging, diseases that destroy brain tissue (such as neurosyphilis and encephalitis), and brain tumors.

- As we age, the proportions of persons with memory problems and cognitive disorders increase. In fact, one of the best predictors of Alzheimer's disease is being elderly. However, many elderly do not suffer from any major cognitive decline.

- Epilepsy is characterized by intermittent and brief periods of altered consciousness, frequently accompanied by seizures, and excessive electrical discharge by neurons. Psychoactive substances can also cause cognitive disorders.

4. **What kinds of interventions can be used to treat people with cognitive disorders?**

- Treatment strategies include corrective surgery and cognitive and behavioral training. Medication is often used, either alone or with other therapies, to decrease or control the symptoms of the various cognitive disorders. Caregivers can learn to provide assistance to loved ones with cognitive disorders.

MARGIN DEFINITIONS

Alzheimer's disease (AD) a dementia in which brain tissue atrophies, leading to marked deterioration of intellectual and emotional functioning

amnestic disorder a disorder characterized by memory impairment as manifested by the inability to learn new information and the inability to recall previously learned knowledge or past events

cerebral blood flow measurement a technique for assessing brain damage in which the patient inhales radioactive gas and a gamma ray camera tracks the gas—and thus the flow of blood—as it moves throughout the brain

cerebral infarction the death of brain tissue resulting from a decrease in the supply of blood serving that tissue

cerebral tumor a mass of abnormal tissue growing within the brain

cognitive disorder disorder that affects thinking processes, memory, consciousness, and perception and that is caused by brain dysfunction

computerized axial tomography (CT) neurological test that assesses brain damage by means of x-rays and computer technology

delirium a syndrome in which there is disturbance of consciousness and changes in cognition, such as memory deficit, disorientation, and language and perceptual disturbances

dementia a syndrome characterized by memory impairment and cognitive disturbances, such as aphasia, apraxia, agnosia, or disturbances in planning or abstraction in thought processes

electroencephalograph (EEG) a neurological test that assesses brain damage by measuring the electrical activity of brain cells

encephalitis brain inflammation that is caused by a viral or bacterial infection and that produces symptoms of lethargy, drowsiness, fever, delirium, vomiting, and headaches

epilepsy any disorder characterized by intermittent and brief periods of altered consciousness, often accompanied by seizures, and excessive electrical discharge from brain cells

Huntington's disease a rare, genetically transmitted degenerative disease characterized by involuntary twitching movements and eventual dementia

magnetic resonance imaging (MRI) a technique to assess brain functioning using a magnetic field and radio waves to produce pictures of the brain

meningitis inflammation of the meninges, the membrane that surrounds the brain and spinal cord; can result in the localized destruction of brain tissue and seizures

Parkinson's disease a progressively worsening disorder characterized by four primary symptoms: tremor, or trembling in hands, arms, legs, jaw, and face; rigidity, or stiffness of the limbs and trunk; bradykinesia, or slowness of movement; and postural instability, or impaired balance and coordination

positron emission tomography (PET) a technique for assessing brain damage in which the patient is injected with radioactive glucose and the metabolism of the glucose in the brain is monitored

stroke (cerebrovascular accident) a sudden stoppage of blood flow to a portion of the brain, leading to a loss of brain function

traumatic brain injury a physical wound or injury to the brain

vascular dementia dementia characterized by uneven deterioration of intellectual abilities and resulting from a number of cerebral infarctions

CHAPTER 15

Disorders of Childhood and Adolescence

TABLE OF CONTENTS

LEARNING OBJECTIVES

1. Explain which disorders fall under the category of pervasive developmental disorders.

2. Discuss some of the characteristics of attention deficit/hyperactivity disorder, and explain the difference between conduct disorder and oppositional defiant disorder.

3. Define elimination disorders and their prognosis.

4. Discuss how common learning disorders are.

5. Define mental retardation and some of its causes and treatments.

CHAPTER OUTLINE

I.   **Pervasive developmental disorders.** *Pervasive developmental disorders* are severe disturbances affecting language, social relations, and emotions, distortions that would be abnormal at any developmental stage. Prevalence of autistic disorder is about 2 per 10,000 children; the other pervasive developmental disorders occur at a rate of about 6.7 in 1,000. *Autistic disorder* was first described by Leo Kanner in 1943 and is characterized by great impairment in social interaction and/or communication, stereotyped interests and activities, and delays or abnormal functioning in major areas before age 3. Autistic children interact with others as though people were unimportant objects. Half do not speak; the other half often show *echolalia*—echoing whatever was just said— or pronoun reversal (where "you" is said instead of "I"). Most autistic children are mentally retarded, although *splinter skills* (special abilities) are found, most dramatically in *autistic savants*. Misdiagnosis as mental retardation only or as a different disorder or condition is common. About 22 in 10,000 children show some, but not all, of the characteristics of autistic disorder along with severe social impairment and would be diagnosed with pervasive developmental disorders that do not meet the criteria for autistic disorders. These include *Asperger's disorder* (similar symptoms to autism, but more highly functional); *childhood disintegrative disorder* (at least two years of normal development), *Rett's disorder* (normal for at least five months, onset between age 5 and 48 months, and deceleration of head growth seen only in females), and *pervasive developmental disorder* not otherwise specified. Biological dimension evidence points to genetic factors playing a prominent role in the causes for autism spectrum disorders. Concordance rates for autism are much higher for MZ (monozygotic) than DZ (dizygotic) twins. Furthermore, the prevalence of autistic disorder among siblings of individuals with autistic disorder ranges from 2 to 14 percent. In terms of the psychological dimension some research suggests that autism may be a disorder involving cognitive impairments that affect perception, particularly in the recognition and response to others. Early psychodynamic theories that involve social relationships of autism stressed the importance of deviant parent-child interactions in producing this condition. Kanner (1943), who named the syndrome, concluded that cold and unresponsive parenting is responsible for the development of autism. In terms of the sociocultural dimension Autism appears to vary according to sociocultural and demographic characteristics. Studies have found higher or equal prevalence of the disorder among African American mothers and lower prevalence among Mexican-born mothers than among white, Asian, and U.S.-born Hispanic mothers. The prognosis for children with pervasive developmental disorders is mixed. Most children diagnosed with autism retain their diagnosis at 9 years of age. However, many, especially those with initial higher levels of functioning (e.g., those with Asperger's syndrome), improve. A minority have good outcomes. Because patients with these disorders have communication or social impairments, pervasive developmental disorders are very difficult to treat. Therapy with the parents, family therapy, drug therapy, and behavior modification techniques are all currently being used, with some success

II. **Attention deficit/hyperactivity disorder and disruptive behavior disorders.** *Attention deficit1hyperactive disorder (ADHD)* is characterized by attention problems and may involve heightened motor activity. There are three types: predominantly hyperactive impulsive, predominantly inattentive, and combined (showing both hyperactivity and inattentiveness). ADHD is a relatively common disorder, far more common in boys than in girls. In some cases, ADHD children continue to have antisocial or psychiatric problems as adults; those with attention problems but not hyperactivity have better outcome. Attention-deficit/hyperactivity disorder is an early-onset, highly prevalent neurobehavioral disorder, with genetic, biologic, and environmental etiologies, that persists into adolescence and adulthood in a sizable majority of afflicted children of both sexes. 75 to 90 percent of children with ADHD respond to stimulant medications. Children with ADHD are typically treated with stimulant medication, but there is considerable controversy about the overmedication of children and the poorly supervised prescription of drugs. *Oppositional defiant disorder* is characterized by negativistic and hostile behavior, but without serious violations of others' rights. DSM-IV-TR criteria include "significant impairment in social and academic functioning," a raising of the threshold for diagnosis. *Conduct disorder* involves a persistent pattern of antisocial behavior in which others' rights are violated. Etiology, many cases of conduct disorder begin in early childhood. Some infants who are especially "fussy" seem to be at risk for developing conduct disorder. The etiology of conduct disorder probably involves an interaction of genetic/constitutional, psychological, social-familial, and sociocultural factors. Although conduct disorders have resisted traditional forms of psychotherapy, training in social and cognitive skills appears promising. One program, for example, focused on helping aggressive boys develop verbal skills to enter groups, play cooperatively, and provide reinforcement for peers. The cognitive element included using problem-solving skills to identify behavior problems, generate solutions to them, and select alternative behaviors. In addition, the children learned positive social skills through viewing videotapes and role-playing with therapists and peers.

III. **Elimination disorders.** *Enuresis* (urination in inappropriate places that is usually involuntary) and *encopresis* (defecation in inappropriate places) may have biological and psychological origins. Treatment may include medication and behavior modification procedures.

IV. **Learning disorders.** Disorders of childhood and adolescence also include cognitive and academic functioning. Learning disorders are characterized by academic functioning that is substantially below that expected in terms of the person's chronological age, measured intelligence, and age-appropriate education. The disturbance significantly interferes with academic achievement or with activities of daily living. Learning disabilities are lifelong and cannot simply go away with treatment. However, persons with learning disabilities can adjust and adapt in order to function effectively in society. Severity of the disorder varies, and appropriate action involves the accurate assessment of the limitations of the disorder and individualized interventions. What has been helpful is to teach children with learning disabilities skills to capitalize on their abilities and strengths while correcting and compensating for disabilities and limitations.

V.   **Mental retardation**. Mental retardation (MR) is a disability characterized by significant limitations both in intellectual functioning and in adaptive behaviors as expressed in conceptual, social, and practical adaptive. Prevalence figures for the United States are 1 to 3 percent, depending primarily on the definition of adaptive functioning. Levels of Retardation DSM-IV-TR specifies four different levels of mental retardation, which are based on IQ score ranges, as measured on the revised Wechsler scales (WISC-R and WAIS-R): (1) mild (IQ score 50–55 to 70), (2) moderate (IQ score 35–40 to 50–55), (3) severe (IQ score 20–25 to 35–40), and (4) profound (IQ score below 20 or 25). In terms of Etiology mental retardation is thought to be produced by biological, psychological, social, and sociocultural factors. These factors are largely included into environmental conditions (such as poor living conditions), biological conditions, or some combination of the two. It can be caused by injury, disease, or a brain abnormality. The etiology is dependent to some extent on the level of mental retardation. Mild retardation is generally idiopathic (having no known cause) and familial, whereas severe retardation is typically related to genetic factors or to brain damage. Because mental retardation is a disability rather than a disease that can be "cured," the goal of intervention is to develop the person's potential to the fullest extent possible. Early intervention programs such as Head Start have not produced dramatic increases in intellectual ability among at-risk children (those from low-income families). School services received by children diagnosed with mental retardation can vary greatly between school districts. Employment programs for people with mental retardation can achieve more than was previously thought. Living arrangements, institutionalization of people with mental retardation is declining, as more individuals are placed in group homes or in situations in which they can live independently or semi-independently within the community.

VI.   **Implications**. In this chapter, we have discussed the symptoms, causes, and treatment/prevention of childhood disorders. Because we are dealing with a population (i.e., children and adolescents) and not a disorder (e.g., depression), many kinds of disorders are included. Thus, some such as autism spectrum disorders and mental retardation have a strong biological etiology. Heredity, conditions during pregnancy, and early infant factors are likely to play a strong role in these disorders. Nevertheless, even in these and other childhood disorders, we see that psychological, social, and sociocultural factors are implicated.

KEY TERMS REVIEW

1.   Disorders of childhood and adolescence that involve persistent patterns of antisocial behavior that violate the rights of others are called <u>conduct d/o</u>.

2.   _____ is a screening procedure in which a hollow needle is inserted through the pregnant woman's abdominal wall and amniotic fluid is withdrawn from the fetal sac; used during the fourteenth or fifteenth week of pregnancy to determine the presence of down syndrome and other fetal abnormalities.

3.   _____ is a condition produced by the presence of an extra chromosome (trisomy 21) and resulting in mental retardation and distinctive physical characteristics.

4.   _____ is a group of congenital physical and mental defects found in some children born to alcoholic mothers; symptoms include small body size and microcephaly, in which the brain is unusually small and mild retardation may occur.

5.   A severe childhood disorder characterized by early onset, an extreme lack of interest in interpersonal relationships, and impairment in verbal and nonverbal communication is called <u>Autism</u>.

6. A disorder of childhood and adolescence characterized by short attention span, impulsiveness, constant activity, and lack of self-control is called ___ADHD___ .

7. Severe disorders of childhood that affect language, social relationships, attention, and affect, and that include autistic disorder, are called _pervasive developmental d/o_.

8. A childhood disorder characterized by negativistic, argumentative, and hostile behavior that impairs social or academic functioning but does not usually involve serious violations of others' rights is called _oppositional defiance_

9. _Learning d/o_ are disorders characterized by academic functioning that is substantially below that expected in terms of the person's chronological age, measured intelligence, and age-appropriate education.

10. _Mental retardation_ is a disability characterized by significant limitations both in intellectual functioning and in adaptive behaviors as expressed in conceptual, social, and practical adaptive skills.

11. An elimination disorder in which the child defecates into his or her clothes or bed is called

    _____ .

12. An elimination disorder in which a child voids urine into his or her clothes or bed is called

    _____ .

FACTUAL MULTIPLE-CHOICE QUESTIONS

1. Pervasive developmental disorders are childhood disorders that

    a. are quite common, with four to five cases per 100 births.
    b. are presently considered forms of schizophrenia.
    c. usually have their onset after age 10.
    d. involve behavior that is abnormal for any developmental stage.

2. In the majority of cases, autistic children are

    a. autistic savants.
    b. mentally retarded.
    c. able to speak like normal children.
    d. overly attached to their parents.

3. Treatment of children with pervasive developmental disorders

    a. usually includes psychodynamic approaches.
    b. involves humanistic and family systems approaches.
    c. is, in general, very difficult.
    d. has excellent long-term outcomes.

4. Heightened motor activity, impulsiveness, and school problems because of distractibility are all symptoms of

    a. attention-deficit/hyperactivity disorder (ADHD).
    b. school phobia.
    c. conduct disorder.
    d. pervasive developmental disorder not otherwise specified.

5. The type of drug most often prescribed for attention deficit/hyperactivity disorder is

    a. the tranquilizer haloperidol.
    b. the antimanic drug lithium carbonate.
    c. a stimulant.
    d. an antidepressant.

6. Which type of treatment has been most effective with adolescents with conduct disorders?

    a. Tranquilizers and central nervous stimulants
    b. Psychotherapy and incarceration
    c. Negative practice and relaxation skills
    d. Cognitive social Skills and parent training

7. Which disorder is characterized by argumentativeness and negativistic and hostile behavior?

    a. Conduct disorder
    b. Antisocial personality disorder
    c. Oppositional defiant disorder
    d. Attention deficit/hyperactivity disorder

8. All of the following are disorders of childhood and adolescence *except*

    a. autism.
    b. Asperger's disorder.
    c. oppositional defiant disorder.
    d. antisocial personality disorder.

9. In the United States, fetal alcohol syndrome is most prevalent among

    a. Blacks.
    b. Whites.
    c. Asians.
    d. American Indians.

10. Approximately what percentage of students in U.S. public schools are identified as having a learning disorder?

    a. 5%
    b. 15%
    c. 25%
    d. 35%

CONCEPTUAL MULTIPLE-CHOICE QUESTIONS

1. Diagnosis of autism is deceptively difficult because

    a. symptoms are not noticeable until age 6 or later.
    b. most of the symptoms of autism are internalized and not observable.
    c. symptoms can vary widely among such children.
    d. parents are unwilling to accept that something is wrong with the child.

2. Parents have described their autistic children as being "embarrassingly honest," and "not really knowing what a joke is." These characteristics are interpreted as supporting the idea that autistic children

    a. view the world much more seriously than normal children.
    b. live in an inner world filled with auditory hallucinations and delusions.
    c. lack a "theory of mind" and so are unable to understand that others think.
    d. have brain damage in the left temporal lobe that causes language problems.

3. What do Rett's disorder and Asperger's disorder have in common?

    a. They are pervasive developmental disorders other than autistic disorder.
    b. Children with these disorders fail to develop any language skills.
    c. They are both successfully treated with antipsychotic medications.
    d. They are forms of anxiety disorder that have been eliminated from the list of DSM-IV childhood disorders.

4.   Which statement about the causes of autism is *most accurate*?

   a.   Recent research strengthens the belief that there is an underlying cause for all its forms.
   b.   The only research on genetic influence was weak methodologically and showed no difference in concordance rates for NU and DZ twins.
   c.   Nearly all autistic children have abnormally low levels of serotonin, a pathognomonic sign for the disorder.
   d.   Organic causes are likely, although research findings are inconsistent.

5.   Some clinical psychologists are quite upset with the childhood and adolescent section of DSM-IV-TR. Why?

   a.   Because significant categories of disorders, such as tic disorders and eating disorders, have been eliminated
   b.   Because conduct disorders have been separated from pervasive developmental disorders
   c.   Because bothersome childhood behaviors that may be normal are now considered disorders
   d.   Because all subjective judgments have been taken out of the diagnostic criteria

6.   Psychodynamic theory suggests that conduct disorder is caused by _____ whereas learning theory suggests it is caused by _____.

   a.   underlying anxiety and emotional deprivation; central nervous system damage
   b.   conflict over sexuality; parental reinforcement
   c.   double-bind communication patterns; inconsistent discipline
   d.   underlying anxiety and emotional deprivation; inconsistent discipline

7.   It is much more likely in children from broken homes and is particularly apparent in adolescent girls. It is associated with low self-esteem and self-blame. What is being described?

   a.   Childhood depression
   b.   Tic disorders
   c.   Separation anxiety disorder
   d.   Conduct disorders

8.   What behavior would differentiate between enuresis and encopresis?

   a.   Enuresis is a more advanced form of encopresis.
   b.   Encopresis is a more advanced form of enuresis.
   c.   Enuresis involves urination at inappropriate times or places, while encopresis involves defecation at inappropriate times or places.
   d.   Encopresis involves urination at inappropriate times or places, while enuresis involves defecation at inappropriate times or places.

9.   Dewayne, aged 9, was depressed. His doctor would probably prescribe

   a.   antidepressant medication.
   b.   no treatment because Dewayne is too young.
   c.   further observation until the real problem surfaced.
   d.   behavioral or cognitive therapy to prevent worsening of the condition.

10.   Which of the following statements regarding Down syndrome is NOT true?

   a.   The prevalence rate increases dramatically with the age at which the mother gives birth.
   b.   Most cases of Down syndrome are genetically inherited.
   c.   The condition is produced by the presence of an extra chromosome.
   d.   It occurs at a rate of about 1 in 800 to 1,000 births.

11.   Which of the following is NOT a primary factor for diagnosing mental retardation?

   a.   Significant subaverage general intellectual functioning
   b.   Concurrent deficiencies in adaptive behavior
   c.   Onset before age eighteen
   d.   Reoccurring headaches and difficulty concentrating

APPLICATION MULTIPLE-CHOICE QUESTIONS

1. Warren is mentally retarded and autistic, yet he can calculate, in his head, the square root of any number and give the answer to three decimal points. This remarkable feat illustrates

    a.   the autistic's superior ability to empathize.
    b.   the term *echolalia*.
    c.   the attention deficit that is found in autistics.
    d.   the abilities of rare cases of autistic savants.

2. An autistic child is in an inpatient treatment facility. What form of therapy is *most* likely to be offered?

    a.   Central nervous system stimulants such as Ritalin
    b.   Group therapy
    c.   Self-instructional procedures and role playing
    d.   Intensive behavior modification

3. Chuck was diagnosed with attention deficit *without* hyperactivity disorder when he was 7 years old. He has difficulty concentrating, so he does poorly in school. As an adolescent, he was frequently arrested for criminal activity. What aspect of Chuck's case is unusual?

    a.   It is unusual for boys to have attention deficits.
    b.   It is unusual for attention deficit to be diagnosed at seven.
    c.   It is unusual for attention deficit children to have school difficulties.
    d.   It is unusual for children without hyperactivity disorder to become criminals.

4. A child is being treated with stimulant medication while his parents get parent training. This child probably has the disorder called

    a.   attention deficit/hyperactivity disorder.
    b.   separation anxiety disorder.
    c.   Tourette's syndrome.
    d.   pervasive developmental disorder.

5. Terry is in outpatient treatment and is being taught relaxation skills and social skills so she is less dependent on her mother. What disorder is probably being treated?

    a.   Rett's disorder
    b.   Oppositional defiant disorder
    c.   School phobia
    d.   Autism

6. Kermit shrieks every day when his mother says it's time for him to go to school. He becomes nauseated, vomits, and develops a headache. His psychologist says this is due to Kermit's overdependence on his mother, which supports which view of school phobia?

    a.   psychodynamic
    b.   learning
    c.   cognitive
    d.   humanistic

7. Matthew's parents have found that waking Matthew up to go to the bathroom and using a bedtime alarm have been particularly effective to help Matthew overcome his

    a.   depression.
    b.   separation anxiety.
    c.   enuresis.
    d.   encopresis.

8.   Lawrence plans to give a speech to his abnormal psychology class about ADHD. Which of the following should Lawrence say *best* explains the causes of ADHD?

    a.   Anatomical brain differences caused by minimal brain dysfunction.

    b.   Allergic reactions caused by an oversensitivity to dietic factors, especially sugar sensitivity.

    c.   ADHD is probably caused by multiple pathways.

    d.   Reactions to lighting conditions, especially x-rays emitted from fluorescent lights.

9.   Lam, age 8, has severe anxiety attacks and depression. Lam refuses to go to school. A psychologist discussing the case of Lam would say that he suffers from

    a.   internalizing disorders.

    b.   externalizing disorders.

    c.   behavioral disorders.

    d.   undercontrolled disorders.

ANSWER KEY: KEY TERMS REVIEW

1.   conduct disorders

2.   Amniocentesis

3.   Down syndrome

4.   Fetal alcohol syndrome (FAS)

5.   autistic disorder

6.   attention deficit/hyperactive disorder (ADHD)

7.   pervasive developmental disorders

8.   oppositional defiant disorder (ODD))

9.   Learning disorders

10.   Mental retardation (MR)

11.   encopresis

12.   enuresis

ANSWER KEY: FACTUAL MULTIPLE-CHOICE QUESTIONS

1.   d.   Pervasive developmental disorders involve bizarre behaviors or severe deficits, such as an absence of language, that are abnormal at any developmental stage.

    a.   The prevalence rate of autistic disorder is closer to 2 to 20 per 10,000; the other pervasive developmental disorders are 22 per 10,000.

    b.   Pervasive developmental disorders are sufficiently different from schizophrenia to warrant their own category.

    c.   Pervasive developmental disorders are usually evident in the first several years of life.

2.   b.   Up to 75 percent of autistic children have IQs below 70.

    a.   Only about 10 percent of autistics show the savant phenomenon.

    c.   One of the key symptoms of autism is lack of speech or its dysfunctional quality.

    d.   Autistic children fail to show affection for anyone, even their parents.

3.   c.   Because there are such profound impairments, the treatment of children with these disorders has had limited success.

      a.   Psychoanalytic thinking about pervasive developmental disorders is largely discredited.

      b.   Humanistic approaches are both uncommon and unlikely to be successful.

      d.   Even high-functioning adults with autistic disorder display problem behaviors involving inappropriate communication and poor interpersonal skills.

4.   a.   ADHD is characterized by short attention span, high motor activity, impulsivity, and poor self-control.

      b.   School phobia is a subcategory of separation anxiety disorder and does not include these symptoms.

      c.   Conduct disorder overlaps somewhat with ADHD but is characterized by repeated violations of the rights of others.

      d.   This disorder is diagnosed when a child acts in a bizarre fashion at an early age, but this behavior does not match the criteria for autism.

5.   c.   Stimulants are frequently prescribed for children with ADHD.

      a.   Haloperidol is not used with ADHD; it has been somewhat effective with autistic children.

      b.   Mania is not a problem for ADHD children.

      d.   Antidepressants are not typically used to treat ADHD.

6.   d.   Cognitive social skills programs and Patterson's parent training groups have shown both short- and long-term effectiveness.

      a.   Psychoactive drugs have not been successful in treating conduct disorders.

      b.   These children are not motivated to use psychotherapy; incarceration does not effectively "treat" them.

      c.   Negative practice—the repetition of a behavior until it becomes aversive—is useful in eliminating tics; anxiety is not a problem for those with conduct disorders.

7.   c.   Individuals diagnosed with oppositional defiant disorder defy and refuse direction from authorities.

      a.   Conduct disorders are characterized by a persistent pattern of antisocial behaviors that violate the rights of others. It is a diagnosis reserved for children and adolescents, not adults.

      b.   The diagnosis of APD is not given to individuals under the age of 18.

      d.   The diagnosis of ADHD involves the presence of socially disruptive behavior such as attentional problems or hyperactivity.

8.   d.   Antisocial personality disorder is not diagnosed until age 18.

      a.   Autism is a disorder of childhood.

      b.   Asperger's disorder is a childhood disorder.

      c.   Oppositional defiant disorder is a childhood disorder.

9. d. Fetal alcohol syndrome is most prevalent among American Indians.

    a. Fetal alcohol syndrome is not most prevalent among Blacks, but rather American Indians.

    b. Fetal alcohol syndrome is not most prevalent among Whites, but rather American Indians.

    c. Fetal alcohol syndrome is not most prevalent among Asians, but rather American Indians.

10. a. Five percent of students are identified as having a learning disorder.

    b. Five percent of students are identified as having a learning disorder, not 15 percent.

    c. Five percent of students are identified as having a learning disorder, not 25 percent.

    d. Five percent of students are identified as having a learning disorder, not 35 percent.

ANSWER KEY: CONCEPTUAL MULTIPLE-CHOICE QUESTIONS

1. c. Symptoms can vary widely, particularly with regard to level of functioning and developmental delay.

    a. Autistic symptoms are noticeable at a very early age, even in infancy.

    b. Almost all autistic behaviors, from echolalia to wild tantrums to spectacular feats of memory, are observable.

    d. There is no reason to believe that parents of autistic children are dysfunctional.

2. c. Frith (1991) has suggested that autistic children lack a "theory of mind," and cannot appreciate the thoughts and beliefs of others. Lacking this level of cognitive empathy they do not understand the concepts of embarrassment, lying, or jokes.

    a. There is no evidence that autistic children view the world more seriously; they do not seem to take notice of many things in the world, particularly people.

    b. Autistic children do not have auditory hallucinations or delusions.

    d. No single area of the brain has been found to correlate with autistic disorder or, more specifically, the autistic person's inability to feel embarrassment or tell a joke.

3. a. Four new pervasive developmental disorders have been added to DSM-IV: Rett's disorder, Asperger's disorder, childhood disintegrative disorder, and pervasive developmental disorder not otherwise specified.

    b. Children with Asperger's disorder have major impairments but normal language.

    c. These disorders are too new for us to know what treatments are effective.

    d   The childhood anxiety disorders eliminated from DSM-IV are avoidant disorder and overanxious disorder.

4. d. Many central nervous system abnormalities have been found, but research results are inconsistent and inconclusive.

    a. Research shows a multitude of causal factors, so it is unlikely that a single cause exists.

    b. A very strong study found that 36 percent of MZ twins were concordant while 0 percent of DZ twins were concordant.

    c. There is no pathognomonic sign for autism; when serotonin levels are abnormal in the disorder, they are high.

5.   c.   Temper tantrums, argumentativeness, and problems doing arithmetic are now included as disorders; many clinicians see this as wrongly characterizing ordinary childhood difficulties as psychopathological.

     a.   Both tic and eating disorders remain in DSM-IV-TR.

     b.   Pervasive developmental disorders involve psychotic, thoroughly dysfunctional behaviors; conduct disorders involve neither psychosis nor interpersonal dysfunction. They deserve to be separated.

     d.   There are many subjective decisions, such as deciding if "often does not finish tasks" is abnormal given the child's developmental level and cultural norms.

6.   d.   Psychoanalysts believe such children are neglected and have underlying anxiety; behaviorists think they have learned to be antisocial because their parents failed to control them.

     a.   Learning theory does not speculate on central nervous system damage.

     b.   For this disorder, conflicts over sexuality are not important in the psychoanalytic explanation of cause.

     c.   Double-bind communications are important in explaining schizophrenic disorder.

7.   a.   Childhood depression is much more common when there is a broken home than when the family is intact, it is more prominent in adolescent girls, and as with adults, it involves cognitive distortions of self-blame.

     b.   Tic disorders are most common in childhood, not adolescence; they are unrelated to divorce.

     c.   Separation anxiety disorder is much more common in childhood than adolescence.

     d.   Conduct disorders are far more common in boys than girls and involve problems of blaming others.

8.   c.   Enuresis is a problem with appropriate time/place of urination; encopresis is a problem with defecation.

     a.   Enuresis is a problem with appropriate time/place of urination; encopresis is a problem with defecation.

     b.   Enuresis is a problem with appropriate time/place of urination; encopresis is a problem with defecation.

     d.   Enuresis is a problem with appropriate time/place of urination; encopresis is a problem with defecation.

9.   d.   Behavioral or cognitive therapy would be recommended to prevent worsening of the condition.

     a.   Most of the research on medication has been conducted with adults, not children, and many medications that work for adults do not work for children.

     b.   Dewayne needs help if the symptoms are to be prevented from worsening.

     c.   Dewayne has a real problem with depression that needs treatment.

10. b.   Down syndrome actually occurs most often as a random event that affects the genes during the formation of reproductive cells.

        a.   The prevalence rate does in fact increase dramatically with the age at which the mother gives birth.

        c.   It is in fact a condition produced by the presence of an extra chromosome.

        d.   The condition may in fact occur as often as once in every 800 to 1,000 live births.

11. d.   Reoccurring headaches and difficulty concentrating are not primary criteria in diagnosing mental retardation.

        a.   Significant subaverage general intellectual functioning is a primary factor in diagnosing mental retardation.

        b.   Deficiencies in adaptive behavior are a primary factor in diagnosing mental retardation.

        c.   Onset before age 18 is a primary factor in diagnosing mental retardation.

ANSWER KEY: APPLICATION MULTIPLE-CHOICE QUESTIONS

1. d.   Astounding memory and artistic feats performed by otherwise severely dysfunctional individuals characterize autistic savants, who are unusual or rare cases.

        a.   Frith (1991) suggests that autistic individuals have no "theory of mind" they are especially deficient at empathizing with others.

        b.   Echolalia is the meaningless repetition of phrases spoken by others.

        c.   Autistics do not have the attention deficits seen in children with ADHD.

2. d.   Intensive behavior modification for learning language and attending to others has had modest success in treating children with autistic disorder.

        a.   Stimulant medication is used for children with ADHD.

        b.   Because they do not attend to others and one-half do not speak, group therapy would be useless.

        c.   Self-instructional procedures and role playing are too advanced for autistics, many of whom do not speak.

3. d.   The prognosis for attention deficit without hyperactive disorder is quite good; criminal behavior is more likely if there is hyperactivity and sexual aggression.

        a.   Males outnumber females with ADHD by four or five to one.

        b.   ADHD is often detected in the preschool or early elementary school years.

        c.   Because of attention problems, most ADHD children have great difficulty completing academic work.

4. a.   Stimulant medication and parent training are typically used to treat attention deficit/hyperactivity disorder.

    b.   Separation anxiety disorder is best treated with psychotherapy; if any medication were used it would probably be antianxiety drugs.

    c.   Tourette's is believed to be triggered by stimulant medication in some cases, so those drugs would not be used in its treatment.

    d.   Pervasive developmental disorder has sometimes been treated with haloperidol and fenfluramine, neither of which are stimulants.

5. c.   School phobia is considered a problem of anxiety and poor social skills, but behaviorists would treat the disorder with relaxation and social skill training.

    a.   Rett's disorder is a pervasive developmental disorder in which there is marked deterioration of social and language skills after at least six months of normal development.

    b.   Oppositional defiant disorder involves defying parental rules and being hostile, not overly dependent.

    d.   Autism is a pervasive developmental disorder with impaired social interaction and/or communication, stereotyped behavior, and abnormal functioning in major areas before age 3.

6. a.   Psychodynamic explanations of school phobia stress the child's overdependence on the mother.

    b.   According to learning principles, parents reinforce the child's fears and seeks refuge away from school where the kind of reinforcement the child received earlier in life is available.

    c.   No cognitive etiology was discussed.

    d.   No humanistic etiology was discussed.

7. c.   The techniques of waking a child to go to the bathroom and using a bedtime alarm have been effective with enuresis.

    a.   The techniques of waking a child to go to the bathroom and using a bedtime alarm have been effective with enuresis; they do not apply to depression.

    b.   The techniques of waking a child to go to the bathroom and using a bedtime alarm have been effective with enuresis; they do not apply to separation anxiety.

    d.   The techniques of waking a child to go to the bathroom and using a bedtime alarm have been effective with enuresis; they do not apply to encopresis.

8. c.   Research findings on the causes of ADHD show inconsistent and conflicting results, suggesting that ADHD may consist of several types, probably caused by multiple pathways.

    a.   CAT scans do not reveal anatomical brain differences between persons with ADHD and normal individuals.

    b.   Sugar does not cause hyperactivity.

    d.   Lighting conditions have no effect on hyperactivity.

9.   a.   Internalizing disorders are those psychological difficulties that are considered inner-directed, and show core symptoms associated with overcontrolled behaviors such as anxiety and depression.

b.   Externalizing disorders are behavioral disorders that create problems for others.

c.   Behavioral disorders is another term for externalizing disorders.

d.   Undercontrolled disorders is another term for externalizing disorders.

OBJECTIVES DEFINED

1.   **Which disorders fall under the category of pervasive developmental disorders?**

- Pervasive developmental disorders include autistic disorder, Rett syndrome, childhood disintegrative disorder, Asperger's syndrome, and pervasive developmental disorder not otherwise specified.

2.   **What are some of the characteristics of attention deficit/hyperactivity disorder, and what is the difference between conduct disorder and oppositional defiant disorder?**

- Attention deficit/hyperactivity disorder, or ADHD, is characterized by overactivity, restlessness, distractibility, short attention span, and impulsiveness. Three types of ADHD are recognized: predominantly hyperactive-impulsive, predominantly inattentive, and combined.

- Oppositional defiant disorder (ODD) is characterized by a pattern of hostile, defiant behavior toward authority figures. Children with ODD do not display the more serious violations of others' rights that are symptomatic of conduct disorders. Conduct disorders, especially those that have an early onset, show a clear continuity with adult problems.

3.   **What are elimination disorders, and what is their prognosis?**

- Enuresis and encopresis are elimination disorders that are diagnosed when children pass an age in which bladder or bowel control should normally exist. Enuresis is the usually involuntary voiding of urine into one's own clothes or bed Encopresis is the usually involuntary expulsion of feces into one's own clothes or bed. Although they cause considerable distress to the child, both elimination disorders usually abate with increasing age.

4.   **How common are learning disorders?**

- Approximately 5 percent of students in public schools in the United States have learning disorders in which their academic functioning is substantially below that expected in terms of the person's chronological age, measured intelligence, and age-appropriate education.

5.   **What is mental retardation and what are some of its causes and treatments?**

- DSM-IV-TR identifies four different levels of mental retardation, which are based only on IQ scores: mild (IQ score 50 to 70), moderate (IQ score 35 to 49), severe (IQ score 20 to 34), and profound (IQ score below 20).

- Causes of retardation include environmental factors (psychological, social, and sociocultural factors), normal genetic processes, genetic anomalies, and other biological abnormalities such as physiological or anatomical defects. Most mental retardation does not have an identifiable organic cause and is associated with only mild intellectual impairment.

- The vast majority of those with mental retardation can become completely self-supporting with appropriate education and training. Public schools provide special programs for children and adolescents; even people with severe retardation are given instruction and training in practical self-help skills. Various approaches—behavioral therapy in particular—are used successfully to help people with mental retardation acquire needed "living" skills.

MARGIN DEFINITIONS

amniocentesis a screening procedure in which a hollow needle is inserted through the pregnant woman's abdominal wall and amniotic fluid is withdrawn from the fetal sac; used during the fourteenth or fifteenth week of pregnancy to determine the presence of down syndrome and other fetal abnormalities

attention deficit/hyperactivity disorder (ADHD) disorders of childhood and adolescence characterized by socially disruptive behaviors—either attentional problems or hyperactivity—that are present before age seven and persist for at least six months

autistic disorder a severe childhood disorder characterized by qualitative impairment in social interaction and/or communication; restricted, stereotyped interest and activities; and delays or abnormal functioning in a major area before the age of three

conduct disorder disorder of childhood and adolescence characterized by a persistent pattern of antisocial behaviors that violate the rights of others; repetitive and persistent behaviors include bullying, lying, cheating, fighting, temper tantrums, destruction of property, stealing, setting fires, cruelty to people and animals, assaults, rape, and truant behavior

Down syndrome a condition produced by the presence of an extra chromosome (trisomy 21) and resulting in mental retardation and distinctive physical characteristics

encopresis an elimination disorder in which a child who is at least four years old defecates in his or her clothes, on the floor, or other inappropriate places, at least once a month for three months

enuresis an elimination disorder in which a child who is at least five years old voids urine during the day or night into his or her clothes or bed or on the floor, at least twice weekly for at least three months

fetal alcohol syndrome (FAS) a group of congenital physical and mental defects found in some children born to alcoholic mothers; symptoms include small body size and microcephaly, in which the brain is unusually small and mild retardation may occur

learning disorders disorders characterized by academic functioning that is substantially below that expected in terms of the person's chronological age, measured intelligence, and age-appropriate education

mental retardation (MR) disability characterized by significant limitations both in intellectual functioning and in adaptive behaviors as expressed in conceptual, social, and practical adaptive skills

oppositional defiant disorder (ODD) a childhood disorder characterized by a pattern of negativistic, argumentative, and hostile behavior in which the child often loses his or her temper, argues with adults, and defies or refuses adult requests; refusal to take responsibility for actions, anger, resentment, blaming others, and spiteful and vindictive behavior are common, but serious violations of other's rights are not

pervasive developmental disorders disorders involving severe childhood impairment in areas such as social interaction and communication skills and the display of stereotyped interests and behaviors; includes autistic disorder, Rett syndrome, childhood disintegrative disorder, Asperger's syndrome, and pervasive developmental disorders not otherwise specified

CHAPTER 16

Eating Disorders

TABLE OF CONTENTS

LEARNING OBJECTIVES

1. Name the kinds of eating disorders..

2. Discuss some causes of eating disorders.

3. Describe some treatment options for eating disorders.

4. Explain what obesity is and if it should be included in DSM-V.

5. Discuss some causes of obesity.

6. Discuss some treatment options for obesity.

CHAPTER OUTLINE

I.   **Eating disorders.** Although nearly 42 percent of adolescent females and 25 percent of adolescent males report dieting to control their weight, the population of the United States is becoming heavier. Between 30 and 67 percent of normal-weight adolescent and college females believe they are overweight; their male age-peers also showed dissatisfaction with weight, wanting to be more muscular. Perceptions of ideal body weight and shape differed for males and females. *Anorexia nervosa* is characterized by a refusal to maintain a body weight above the minimum normal weight for one's age and height, an intense fear of becoming obese that does not diminish with weight loss, body image distortion, and (in females) the absence of at least three consecutive menstrual cycles otherwise expected to occur. Prevalence is estimated as ranging from 0.5 to 1 percent of the female population. The restricting type loses weight through dieting or exercising; the binge-eating/purging type loses weight through self-induced vomiting, laxatives, or diuretics. There are serious physical complications, such as cardiac arrhythmias, low blood pressure, lethargy, and irreversible osteoporosis. As evidenced by the Internet, many women believe it is their right to refuse treatment. Comorbid disorders include obsessive-compulsive behaviors and certain personality characteristics. *Bulimia nervosa* is characterized by recurrent episodes of binge eating high caloric foods at least twice a week for three months, during which the person loses control over eating. In the purging type, the individual regularly vomits or uses laxatives, diuretics, or enemas; in the nonpurging type, excessive exercise or fasting are used to compensate for binges. Prevalence rate is 1-2 percent of women in the Untied States; few males exhibit the disorder. Physical complications include erosion of tooth enamel, dehydration, swollen parotid glands, and lowered potassium, which can weaken the heart and cause arrhythmia and cardiac arrest. Comorbid mood disorders are common, as well as characteristics of borderline personality. Onset is generally later than for anorexia (late adolescence or early adulthood), and follow-up studies tend to find almost 70 percent remission. *Binge-eating disorder*, a diagnostic category "provided for further study" in DSM-IV-TR, involves consumption of large amounts of food over a short period of time, accompanying feeling of loss of control, and marked distress over the binges; but it lacks the compensatory behaviors of bulimia (e.g., vomiting). Females are one and one-half times more likely than males to have the disorder; prevalence rate estimates range from 0.7 to 4 percent. Comorbid features include major depression, obsessive-compulsive personality disorder, and avoidant personality disorder. Onset is typically in late adolescence or early adulthood; although most individuals make a full recovery even without treatment, weight is likely to remain high. DSM-IV-TR includes the category eating disorder not otherwise specified, for those that do not meet all the criteria for anorexia or bulimia nervosa.

II. **Etiology of eating disorders.** The etiology of eating disorders is believed to be determined by social, gender, psychological, familial, cultural, and biological factors. In the Biological dimension genetic influences may contribute to eating disorders since disordered eating appears to run in families, especially among female relatives. Strober and colleagues (2000) examined the lifetime rates of full or partial anorexia nervosa and bulimia nervosa among first-degree relatives of patients with these eating disorders. In the psychological dimension individuals with eating disorders often display excess concern regarding body image, fragile or low self-esteem, moderate levels of depression, and feelings of helplessness; they appear to use food or weight control as a means of handling stress or anxieties. In the social dimension interpersonal interaction patterns with parents and peers have also been put forth as explanations for eating disorders. In the sociocultural dimension by far, the greatest amount of research has been directed to sociocultural factors in the etiology of eating disorders and the influence of unrealistic standards of beauty that are derived from mass media portrayals. In the United States and most Western cultures, physical appearance is a very important attribute, especially for females. The average American woman is five feet four inches tall and weighs 162 pounds, but teenage girls describe their ideal body as five feet seven inches, weighing 110 pounds, and fitting into a size five dress.

III. **Treatment of eating disorders.** Prevention programs in schools are aimed at reducing the incidence of eating disorders and disordered eating patterns. Initial treatment for anorexia focuses on weight gain (by feeding tube, contingent reinforcement for weight gain, or both). Cognitive-behavioral and family therapy sessions are common after weight gain, but relapse and continued obsession with weight are common. Bulimia is initially assessed for conditions that may have resulted from purging, including cardiac and gastrointestinal problems. In bulimia nervosa, treatment goals include (1) reducing or eliminating binge eating and purging; (2) treating any physical complications; (3) motivating the client to participate in the restoration of healthy eating patterns; (4) providing psychoeducation regarding nutrition and eating; (5) identifying dysfunctional thoughts, moods, and conflicts that are associated with eating; (6) providing psychotherapy to deal with these issues; (7) obtaining family support and conduct family therapy, if needed; and (8) preventing relapse The disorder is treated with psychotherapy, cognitive-behavioral treatment, and antidepressant medications; the combination of cognitive-behavioral therapy and medications appears to be best, although even with these approaches, only about 50 percent of those with the disorder recover fully. Treatments for anorexia and bulimia both involve interdisciplinary teams that include physicians and psychotherapists. Treatments for binge-eating disorder are similar to those for bulimia, including weight reduction strategies, although there are fewer physical complications for BED.

IV. **Obesity.** Obesity is defined as a body mass index (BMI)—an estimate of body fat calculated on the basis of a person's height and weight—greater than 30. DSM-IV-TR acknowledges eating disorders such as anorexia and bulimia as mental disorders with serious adverse outcomes but does not recognize obesity despite its devastating medical and psychological consequences.

V.   **Etiology of obesity.** Obesity is a product of biological/genetic, psychological, social, and sociocultural influences. In the biological dimension estimates regarding genetic contributions to obesity generally are derived by determining the frequency of obesity among family members and twins. Others have investigated specific genetic variations among the obese. In the psychological dimension individuals who are obese report negative mood states and poor self-esteem. These responses are likely affected by the weight stigma that exists in society with the resultant harassment, teasing, and discrimination in school, work, and hiring practices. In the social dimension family environments have also been associated with overweight and obese children and adolescents, including reports of teasing by family members about weight issues. In the sociocultural dimension attitudes regarding food and weight normalcy are developed in the home and community. Rates of obesity tend to be highest among ethnic minorities. In many ethnic groups, there is less pressure to remain thin, and being overweight is not a big concern unless it is extreme.

VI. **Treatments for obesity.** Treatments for obesity have included dieting, lifestyle changes, medications, and surgery. In general, dieting in and of itself may produce short-term weight loss but tends to be ineffective long-term; some individuals gain back more weight than was lost. Mann and colleagues (2007) concluded that most would be better off not dieting because of the stress on the body as a result of weight cycling.

VII. **Implications.** Eating disorders and obesity are a heterogeneous group of disorders. Scientists are only recently focusing on how genetics influence neurochemistry. Most of the research has been done with anorexia nervosa and obesity with a focus on dopaminergic activity that affects both a lack of appetite and overeating. However, we must be aware that, in some cases, the behavior of overeating or not eating may, in fact, result in changes in the level of dopamine in certain areas of the brain. Also, some individuals may have an eating disorder or problem even without evidence of biological predisposition. Thus it is important to consider psychological, social, and sociocultural dimensions that may also be involved

KEY TERMS REVIEW

1.   An eating disorder in which the person is intensely fearful of becoming obese and engages in either self-starvation or purging after eating is called _____.

2.   An eating disorder characterized by the consumption of large quantities of food, usually followed by self-induced vomiting, is called _____.

3.   An eating disorder similar to bulimia, but without compensatory behaviors such as vomiting, excessive exercise, or fasting is called _____.

4.   _____ is an estimate of body fat calculated on the basis of a person's height and weight.

5.   _____ is a category for individuals with problematic eating patterns who do not fully meet the criteria for one of the eating disorders; currently includes binge eating disorder.

6.   _____ is a body mass index of greater than 30.

FACTUAL MULTIPLE-CHOICE QUESTIONS

1.   Which of the following is a myth concerning anorexia?
     a.   Females and males attempt to attain the body shape preferred by the group they are attracted to.
     b.   Female heterosexuals desire a thinner body than those preferred by heterosexual males.
     c.   Male heterosexuals desire to have a more muscular body than the ones chosen by heterosexual females.
     d.   Lesbian females appear to have less body image problems than heterosexual females.

2.   A person with anorexia nervosa is *most likely* to

  a.   have a complete recovery.
  b.   continue to be of low weight.
  c.   continue to meet diagnostic criteria ten years after treatment.
  d.   die.

3.   The two subtypes of anorexia are

  a.   conduct and attention-deficit.
  b.   binge-eating/purging and restricting.
  c.   binge-eating/purging and binge-eating alone.
  d.   anxious and depressive.

4.   African American and European American women's binge-eating disorders differ from each other in all of the following ways *except*

  a.   African American women are less likely to have been treated for eating problems.
  b.   African American women are more likely to be obese.
  c.   African American women are more likely to be show symptoms of psychiatric distress.
  d.   African American women appear to have fewer attitudinal concerns.

5.   Which of the following is *unlikely* to occur with bulimia nervosa?

  a.   schizoaffective disorder.
  b.   seasonal affective disorder.
  c.   borderline personality disorder.
  d.   depression.

6.   Approximately percent of women in weight-control programs have binge-eating disorder.

  a.   5-10 percent
  b.   10-20 percent
  c.   20-30 percent
  d.   20-40 percent

7.   What percent of American women are able to achieve the size required for fashion models?

  a.   5 percent
  b.   7 percent
  c.   9 percent
  d.   10 percent

8.   A medium-framed woman who is 5'6" should weigh between

  a.   111 and 124 pounds.
  b.   114 and 127 pounds.
  c.   121 and 135 pounds.
  d.   130 and 144 pounds.

9.   How effective is cognitive-behavioral therapy in treating binge-eating disorder?

  a.   It is very successful in getting most patients to stop bingeing and to lose weight.
  b.   It is successful in getting patients to stop bingeing, but not particularly successful in helping them lose weight.
  c.   It is successful in getting patients to lose weight, but not particularly successful in helping them to stop bingeing.
  d.   It has not been particularly successful in either helping patients stop bingeing or losing weight.

10.   The body mass index (BMI) is

  a.   an estimate of body fat calculated on the basis of a person's height and weight.
  b.   an estimate of muscle mass calculated on the basis of a person's height and weight.
  c.   an estimate of the amount of muscle that the human skeleton can hold calculated by a person's height and bone density.
  d.   an estimate of body fat calculated by the mass of a person's midriff.

CONCEPTUAL MULTIPLE-CHOICE QUESTIONS

1. A study that looked at attitudes about body weight in Germany, France, and the United States concluded that

    a. both men and women think that women prefer men who have muscular bodies.
    b. men think women prefer men with lean bodies, but women said they prefer muscular men.
    c. both men and women think that women prefer men to have a lean body.
    d. men think women prefer men with muscular bodies, and women prefer ordinary male bodies.

2. The eating disorder characterized by a refusal to maintain a body weight above the minimum normal weight for one's age and height, an intense fear of becoming obese, body image distortion, and amenorrhea in females is

    a. anorexia nervosa.
    b. bulimia nervosa.
    c. body dysmorphic disorder.
    d. binge eating disorder.

3. Anorexia nervosa is defined by all of the following *except*

    a. a total lack of concern for food.
    b. an intense fear of becoming obese.
    c. a distorted self-perception of body image.
    d. the cessation of menstruation in females.

4. What behaviors differentiate anorexia nervosa from bulimia nervosa?

    a. Only anorexics are afraid of gaining weight.
    b. Only bulimics occasionally binge and purge.
    c. Only anorexics look like skeletons.
    d. Only bulimics tend to be women.

5. The person with bulimia nervosa is *most likely* to be

    a. underweight.
    b. overweight.
    c. of normal weight.
    d. obese.

6. Common complications of bulimia nervosa include all of the following *except*

    a. erosion of tooth enamel.
    b. stomach cancer.
    c. dehydration.
    d. heart problems that may lead to cardiac arrest.

7. A common Axis II disorder that often accompanies bulimia nervosa is:

    a. bipolar disorder.
    b. schizophrenia.
    c. borderline personality disorder.
    d. paranoid personality disorder.

8. What is the primary difference between bulimia nervosa and binge eating disorder?

    a. Bulimics tend to be grossly underweight from their eating disorder.
    b. People with binge eating disorder are grossly underweight.
    c. Binge eating does not involve the compensatory behaviors that are typical of bulimia.
    d. Fewer people with binge eating disorder are able to be treated.

9. Which characteristic would not fit the DSM-IV-TR category of eating disorder not otherwise specified?

   a. Someone who meets all the criteria for anorexia nervosa but has regular menses.
   b. Someone who meets all the criteria for anorexia nervosa and has lost a significant amount of weight, and is 25 lbs below normal weight.
   c. Someone who engages in binge eating and compensatory activities less than twice a week.
   d. Someone who engages in binge-eating.

10. Societal emphasis on thinness is

   a. a major cause of eating disorders.
   b. related to an increase in eating disorders.
   c. a sufficient explanation of eating disorders.
   d. only mildly related to eating disorders.

APPLICATION MULTIPLE-CHOICE QUESTIONS

1. Dr. Martin told his students that the factors associated with eating pattern disorders include being overweight, low self-esteem, mania, and substance use. Which factor is *inaccurate*?

   a. being overweight
   b. low self-esteem
   c. mania
   d. substance use

2. Cheryl, a high school student, sometimes eats in binges. Should she be diagnosed as having an eating disorder?

   a. No, a large minority of women in the United States binge.
   b. Yes, it is a pathognomonic sign of anorexia nervosa.
   c. No, eating disorders are diagnosed on the basis of preoccupations about weight, not behavior.
   d. Yes, it is a pathognomonic sign of bulimia.

3. Diane, of an average weight, loved to eat and would fix huge meals, which she would devour in one sitting. She would then spend a long time in the bathroom, where she said she was "freshening up." In reality, she was vomiting. Diane did not gain or lose weight because she was

   a. bulimic.
   b. depressed.
   c. anorexic.
   d. always dieting.

4. In Jennifer's treatment program for eating disorders the therapist notes that she is more introverted than most of the other girls. Jennifer denies being hungry and tells her therapist that she does not have any psychological distress. Jennifer has:

   a. restricting anorexia.
   b. binge-eating/purging anorexia.
   c. bulimia nervosa.
   d. binge eating disorder.

5. C. J. has been diagnosed with anorexia, and also has osteoporosis, substance use disorder, and antisocial personality. C. J. is

   a. most likely a male.
   b. most likely a female.
   c. most likely homosexual.
   d. equally as likely to be male or female.

6. Esther consumes large amounts of high-calorie foods at least three times a week. She usually does this when she is alone or nervous. After binging, she makes herself vomit. Although she is of normal weight, she is constantly concerned about her appearance. Esther's diagnosis is
   a. anorexia nervosa.
   b. overanxious disorder.
   c. bulimia nervosa.
   d. binge-eating disorder.

7. In a lecture on eating disorders, Professor Roff told his students that binge-eating has been classified as an Axis I disorder characterized by consumption of large amounts of food over a short period of time, an accompanying feeling of loss of control, but unlike bulimia the episodes are not generally followed by use of compensatory behaviors like vomiting or fasting. Which of Professor Roff's statements is *inaccurate*?
   a. Binge-eating has been classified as an Axis I disorder.
   b. Binge-eating is characterized by consumption of large amounts of food over a short period of time.
   c. Binge-eating is characterized by a feeling of loss of control.
   d. Binge-eating is not characterized by use of compensatory behaviors like vomiting or fasting.

8. Since she was a little girl, Audrey's father and older brother have teased her about her "baby fat," saying she was born with "fat genes." She has now lost 10 lbs and all of her friends remark on it, saying she could be a model with a figure like that. Her father and brother still tease her, calling her "Chubs." This suggests which risk factor for eating disorders?
   a. societal influence
   b. cultural factors
   c. familial/peer influence
   d. genetic influence

9. Paul is in treatment for binge-eating disorder. We would expect all of the following phases to be involved in his treatment *except*
   a. determining the cognitive factors underlying the eating disorder.
   b. developing behavioral techniques to maintain good eating habits.
   c. employing cognitive strategies regarding his distorted beliefs about eating.
   d. using relapse prevention strategies to identify potential obstacles and setbacks.

10. Hanan is being treated for binge-eating disorder. Her therapist told her to prepare a list of "forbidden" foods and to rank them in order of "dangerousness." Which phase of her treatment program is Hanan in?
    a. first
    b. second
    c. third
    d. maintenance

ANSWER KEY: KEY TERMS REVIEW

1. anorexia nervosa
2. bulimia nervosa (or bulimia)
3. binge-eating disorder
4. BMI index
5. Eating disorder not otherwise specified (NOS)
6. Obesity

ANSWER KEY: FACTUAL MULTIPLE-CHOICE QUESTIONS

1. b.   Although some anorexics recover completely, the majority continue to be of low weight, and 10 percent continue to meet diagnostic criteria ten years after treatment.

   a.   Although some anorexics recover completely, the majority continue to be of low weight, and 10 percent continue to meet diagnostic criteria ten years after treatment.

   c.   Although some anorexics recover completely, the majority continue to be of low weight, and 10 percent continue to meet diagnostic criteria ten years after treatment.

   d.   Mortality primarily from cardiac arrest or suicide ranges from 5 to 20 percent.

2. a.   It is a myth that females and males attempt to attain the body shape preferred by the group they are attracted to.

   b.   Female heterosexuals tend to desire a thinner body than those actually preferred by heterosexual males.

   c.   Male heterosexuals tend to want a more muscular body than the bodies chosen by heterosexual females.

   d.   Lesbian females appear to have less body image problems than heterosexual females.

3. b.   The two subtypes of anorexia nervosa are restricting (accomplishes weight loss through dieting or exercising) and binge-eating/purging (loses weight through the use of self-induced vomiting, laxatives, or diuretics).

   a.   Conduct disorder and attention-deficit/hyperactivity disorder are two types of childhood disorders.

   c.   Binge-eating/purging and binge-eating alone are the two types of bulimia nervosa.

   d.   Anxious and depressive are symptoms of disorders seen in children, adolescents, and adults that may accompany eating disorders, but they are not subtypes.

4. c.   Research on binge-eating disorders finds that African American women are actually less likely to show symptoms of psychiatric distress.

   a.   Research on binge-eating disorders finds that African American women are, indeed, less likely to have been treated for eating problems.

   b.   Research generally finds that African American women are, indeed, more likely to be obese.

   d.   Research on eating disorders generally finds that African American women are much less likely than European American women to have attitudinal concerns about weight.

5. a.   Schizoaffective disorder is not one that has been noted to be comorbid with bulimia nervosa.

   b.   Mood disorders, including seasonal affective disorder, are often associated with bulimia nervosa.

   c.   Characteristics of borderline personality often associated with bulimia nervosa.

   d.   Mood disorders, including depression, are often associated with bulimia nervosa.

6.   d.   It is estimated that from 20 to 40 percent of individuals in weight-control programs have BED.

     a.   It is estimated that from 20 to 40 percent of individuals in weight-control programs have BED.

     b.   It is estimated that from 20 to 40 percent of individuals in weight-control programs have BED.

     c.   It is estimated that from 20 to 40 percent of individuals in weight-control programs have BED.

7.   a.   It is estimated that only about 5 percent of American women can achieve the size required for fashion models.

     b.   It is estimated that only about 5 percent of American women can achieve the size required for fashion models.

     c.   It is estimated that only about 5 percent of American women can achieve the size required for fashion models.

     d.   It is estimated that only about 5 percent of American women can achieve the size required for fashion models.

8.   d.   A medium-framed woman, 5'6", should weight between 130 and 144 lbs.

     a.   A small-framed woman, 5'3", should weight between 111 and 124 lbs.

     b.   A small-framed woman, 5'4", should weight between 114 and 127 lbs.

     c.   A medium-framed woman, 5'3", should weight between 121 and 135 lbs.

9.   b.   Cognitive-behavior therapy produces significant reductions in binge-eating, but is less successful in reducing weight.

     a.   Cognitive-behavior therapy produces significant reductions in binge eating, but is less successful in reducing weight.

     c.   Cognitive-behavior therapy produces significant reductions in binge-eating, but is less successful in reducing weight.

     d.   Cognitive-behavior therapy produces significant reductions in binge-eating, but is less successful in reducing weight.

10. a.   BMI is an estimate of body fat calculated on the basis of a person's height and weight.

     b.   BMI is an estimate of body fat calculated on the basis of a person's height and weight.

     c.   BMI is an estimate of body fat calculated on the basis of a person's height and weight.

     d.   BMI is an estimate of body fat calculated on the basis of a person's height and weight.

ANSWER KEY: CONCEPTUAL MULTIPLE-CHOICE QUESTIONS

1. a. The study of attitudes about body weight in Germany, France, and the U.S. found that men think women prefer men with muscular bodies, but in fact women prefer ordinary male bodies.

   b. The study of attitudes about body weight in Germany, France, and the U.S. found that men think women prefer men with muscular bodies, but in fact women prefer ordinary male bodies.

   c. The study of attitudes about body weight in Germany, France, and the U.S. found that men think women prefer men with muscular bodies, but in fact women prefer ordinary male bodies.

   d. The study of attitudes about body weight in Germany, France, and the U.S. found that men think women prefer men with muscular bodies, but in fact women prefer ordinary male bodies.

2. a. Anorexia nervosa is characterized by a refusal to maintain a body weight above the minimum normal weight for one's age and height; an intense fear of becoming obese that does not diminish with weight loss; body image distortion; and amenorrhea in females.

   b. Bulimia nervosa is characterized by recurrent episodes of binge eating high caloric foods at least twice a week for three months, during which the person loses control over eating.

   c. Although anorexics do have a distorted image of their bodies, body dysmorphic disorder is a different disorder unrelated to obsessive self-starvation.

   d. Binge-eating disorder involves consumption of large amounts of food over a short period of time, accompanying feeling of loss of control, and marked distress over the binges; but it lacks the compensatory behaviors of bulimia (e.g., vomiting).

3. a. Anorexics are actually obsessed with food.

   b. Anorexics do have an intense fear of becoming obese, no matter how skeletal they are.

   c. The distorted self-perception of body image can be seen in the skeletal woman who believes she is fat.

   d. A woman needs a sufficient amount of body fat in order to have regular menstrual cycles; when the body fat is depleted, as it is in anorexia, her menstrual periods will stop.

4. a. Both anorexics and bulimics are afraid of gaining weight.

   b. One form of anorexia involves binging and purging.

   c. Anorexics starve themselves and look that way; bulimia is unrelated to body size (most of are normal weight).

   d. Both forms of eating disorder are more common in women.

5. c. Although individuals with bulimia overestimate their body size, most are within the normal weight range.

   a. Although individuals with bulimia overestimate their body size, most are within the normal weight range.

   b. Although individuals with bulimia overestimate their body size, most are within the normal weight range.

   d. Although individuals with bulimia overestimate their body size, most are within the normal weight range.

6. b.   Stomach cancer is not one of the physical complications that is often seen with bulimia.

    a.   Erosion of tooth enamel is common in bulimics because of the excessive vomiting.

    c.   The effects of vomiting (and other methods of purging) lead to dehydration.

    d.   The lowered potassium levels from vomiting and purging can weaken the heart.

7. c.   Characteristics of borderline personality disorder are often seen concurrently with bulimia nervosa.

    a.   Bipolar disorder is an Axis I disorder.

    b.   Schizophrenia is an Axis I disorder and is not comorbid with bulimia.

    d.   Although an Axis II diagnosis, paranoid personality disorder is not comorbid with bulimia.

8. c.   Binge-eating disorder is very similar to bulimia, but it lacks the compensatory behaviors of bulimia (e.g., vomiting).

    a.   Bulimics tend to be of normal weight; binge-eaters are more likely to be obese.

    b.   People with binge-eating disorder are likely to be obese.

    d.   Both bulimia and binge-eating are difficult to treat, although binge-eating disorder actually has a better success rate.

9. b.   Someone who meets all the criteria for anorexia and is 25 lbs below normal weight would meet all the criteria for anorexia (therefore not eating disorders not-otherwise-specified).

    a.   Someone who meets all the criteria for anorexia but has regular menstrual periods would meet the not-otherwise-specified category of eating disorder.

    c.   The criteria for bulimia would binge-eating and compensatory activities at least twice a week, so this would be eating disorder not-otherwise-specified.

    d.   Someone who merely engages in binge-eating without other characteristics of eating disorders would be classified as having an eating disorder not-otherwise-specified.

10. b.   Societal emphasis on thinness is clearly related to an increase in eating disorders; other cultures that do not have that emphasis (including African Americans) do not exhibit the same problems with eating disorders.

    a.   While societal emphasis on thinness is a factor in eating disorders, it is not a major cause of this problem.

    c.   Eating disorders are a complex category of disorders and it would be too simplistic to say that societal emphasis on thinness is a sufficient explanation.

    d.   Although not the only cause of eating disorders, societal emphasis on thinness is strongly related to these disorders.

ANSWER KEY: APPLICATION MULTIPLE-CHOICE QUESTIONS

1. c.   Rather than mania, individuals with eating pattern disorders are more likely to be fatigued and depressed.

    a.   Being overweight is one of the factors associated with eating pattern disorders.

    b.   Low self-esteem is a major factor noted in connection with eating pattern disorders.

    d.   Comorbidity between eating pattern disorders and substance abuse is common.

2. a.   Approximately 35 percent of women report binging or overeating; a diagnosis of bulimia requires meeting other criteria.

    b.   Binging is not a specific sign of anorexia; bulimics also purge after binging.

    c.   Eating disorders are diagnosed on the basis of both preoccupations and observable behaviors.

    d.   Binging and purging is a fundamental sign of bulimia, but also occurs in anorexia.

3. a.   Bulimia nervosa involves the consumption of large quantities of food, usually followed by self-induced vomiting.

    b.   Depression is not the most salient feature reflected in the binging described in this case.

    c.   Anorexics often binge and purge, but their weight is drastically below normal minimum.

    d.   Bulimics are not always dieting, because they can use the binge-purge cycle to eat as much as they want without gaining weight.

4. a.   Anorexics with the restricting subtype are more introverted and tend to deny that they suffer hunger and psychological distress.

    b.   Anorexics with the binge-eating/purging type are more extroverted and report more anxiety, depression, and guilt.

    c.   Bulimics do not deny being hungry; they will binge, then purge to keep their weight down.

    d.   Individuals with binge-eating disorder do not deny being hungry.

5. a.   Males with the bulimic type of anorexia are prone to osteoporosis and are more likely than women to have comorbid substance use disorder and antisocial personality.

    b.   No, these are more likely to be symptoms of a male.

    c.   There were no distinctions made between heterosexual and homosexual males.

    d.   These symptoms are more likely to be seen in a male.

6. c.   Yes, bulimia nervosa is characterized by recurrent episodes of binge eating high caloric foods at least twice a week, during which the person loses control over eating, then typically compensates by purging (e.g., vomiting).

    a.   No, the anorexic would not be consuming large amounts of high-calorie foods.

    b.   While she may be overanxious, the symptoms characterize bulimia nervosa.

    d.   No, binge-eating disorder would not involve compensatory behaviors like vomiting.

7. a.   The DSM-IV-TR classifies binge-eating as a provisional disorder, not an Axis I disorder.

    b.   Binge-eating is, in fact, characterized by consumption of large amounts of food over a short period of time.

    c.   Binge-eating is, in fact, characterized by a feeling of loss of control.

    d.   Binge-eating is not characterized by use of compensatory behaviors like vomiting or fasting.

8. c. Stice and Bearman believe that socialization agents such as peers or family members can produce pressure to be thin and can help create an ideal of the thin body through criticism of weight, encouragement to diet, and glorification of slim models.

   a. Social influences would be things like the media (television, magazines, etc.)

   b. Cultural factors would be exposure to cultural attitudes, such as "you can never be too rich or too thin."

   d. Genetic influences would be seen by way of concordance rates with close relatives, and there is no evidence of that in this situation.

9. b. Although behavioral strategies will be used, this is not one of the three phases.

   a. Determining the cognitive factors underlying the eating disorder is the first phase.

   c. Employing cognitive strategies regarding distorted beliefs about eating is the second phase.

   d. Using relapse prevention strategies to identify potential obstacles and setbacks is the third phase.

10. b. Yes, it is during the second phase that cognitive strategies (such as preparing a list of "forbidden foods" is undertaken.

    a. During the first phase, cognitive factors that underlie the eating disorder are determined.

    c. No, the third phase deals with relapse prevention.

    d. No, maintenance is not one of the phases; it would be included in the third (relapse prevention) phase.

OBJECTIVES DEFINED

1. **What kinds of eating disorders are there?**

- Individuals with anorexia nervosa suffer from body image distortion. They weigh less than 85 percent of their expected weight and suffer from effects of starvation but are still deathly afraid of getting fat.

- An individual with bulimia nervosa is generally of normal weight, engages in binge eating, feels a loss of control over eating during these periods, and uses vomiting, exercise, or laxatives to attempt to control weight. Some people with anorexia nervosa also engage in binge/purge eating but weigh less than 85 percent of their expected weight.

- Although many people have engaged in binge eating, the diagnosis for the disorder is given only when the individual has regularly recurrent episodes in which she or he feels a loss of control over eating and shows marked distress about the activity.

- Individuals who show atypical patterns of severely disordered eating that do not fully meet the criteria for anorexia nervosa, bulimia nervosa, or binge-eating disorder are given the diagnosis of eating disorder not otherwise specified. Currently, binge-eating disorders are subsumed under this category.

2. **What are some causes of eating disorders?**

- Genetics and neurotransmitter abnormalities are implicated in eating disorders. Research currently is focusing on the role of dopamine in eating disorders.

- It is believed that the societal emphasis on thinness as being attractive may contribute to the increasing incidence of eating disorder. This is believed to lead to an internalized thin ideal that girls and women aspire to achieve.

- Parental attitudes regarding the importance of thinness are implicated in eating disorders, as is teasing regarding weight, especially among children with low self-esteem or with childhood trauma.

- Countries that are influenced by Western standards also report an increased incidence of eating disorders in women.

3. **What are some treatment options for eating disorders?**

- Many of the therapies attempt to teach clients to identify the impact of societal messages regarding thinness and encourage them to develop healthier goals and values.

- For individuals with anorexia nervosa, medical, as well as psychological, treatment is necessary because the body is in starvation mode. The goal is to help clients gain weight, normalize their eating patterns, understand and alter their thoughts related to body image, and develop more healthy methods of dealing with stress.

- With bulimia nervosa, medical assistance may also be required because of the physiological changes associated with purging.

- Because many people with binge-eating disorder are overweight or obese, weight reduction strategies are also included in treatment.

- With both bulimia nervosa and binge-eating disorder, the therapy involves normalizing eating patterns, developing a more positive body image, and dealing with stress in a healthier fashion.

4. **What is obesity and should it be included in DSM-V?**

- Obesity is defined as having a body mass index greater than 30. Some researchers believe that obesity should be included since it has characteristics of addictive behavior similar to that seen in substance abuse.

5. **What are some of the causes of obesity?**

- The cause of obesity varies from individual to individual and is often a combination of biological predispositions and psychological, social, and sociocultural influences.

6. **What are some treatment options for obesity?**

- In general dieting alone has been ineffective over the long term. Lifestyle changes that include reduced intake of high-calorie foods combined with exercise have proven more effective. In the case of severely obese individuals, surgery has produced some promising long-term results.

MARGIN DEFINITIONS

anorexia nervosa an eating disorder characterized by low body, an intense fear of becoming obese and body image distortion

binge-eating disorder (BED) an eating disorder that involves the consumption of large amounts of food over a short period of time, an accompanying feeling of loss of control, and distress over the excess eating

BMI index an estimate of body fat calculated on the basis of a person's height and weight

bulimia nervosa an eating disorder characterized by recurrent episodes of the rapid consumption of large quantities of food, a sense of loss of control over eating combined with purging (vomiting, use of laxatives, diuretics, or enemas), excessive exercise or fasting in an attempt to compensate for binges

eating disorder not otherwise specified (NOS) a category for individuals with problematic eating patterns who do not fully meet the criteria for one of the eating disorders; currently includes binge eating disorder

obesity a body mass index of greater than 30

CHAPTER 17

Legal and Ethical Issues in Abnormal Psychology

TABLE OF CONTENTS

LEARNING OBJECTIVES

1. Discuss the criteria used to judge insanity, and what the difference is between being insane and being incompetent to stand trial.

2. Describe under what conditions a person can be involuntarily committed to a mental institution.

3. Explain the rights mental patients have with respect to treatment and care.

4. Discuss deinstitutionalization.

5. Explain what legal and ethical issues govern the therapist-client relationship.

6. Discuss cultural competence in the mental health profession.

CHAPTER OUTLINE

I. **Criminal commitment.** Behaviors ranging from murder to public profanity to therapists touching their clients, all have legal and ethical implications. Mental health decisions involve legal issues when psychologists consider a client or defendant's claim of insanity, competence to stand trial, need for involuntary hospitalization, dangerousness to others, or rights as a patient. The Tarasoff case raises questions about therapists' responsibility to potential victims versus their obligation not to breach confidentiality. Ethical questions also relate to therapists' conduct with clients. Criminal commitment is the incarceration of an individual for having committed a crime is the consequence of criminal acts. The *insanity defense* recognizes that individuals may not always be held accountable for their criminal actions.. The *M'Naghten Rule* defines insanity as not knowing right from wrong. The *irresistible impulse test* says that insanity is also involved when a person could not control his or her actions. The *Durham standard* argues that insanity must be a product of mental disease. The *American Law Institute (ALI) code* combines earlier definitions. In some regions, the concept of diminished capacity has been added, allowing that a mental disease or defect may reduce a person's specific intent to commit a crime. After the successful insanity defense by John W. Hinckley, Jr., the man who attempted to assassinate President Ronald Reagan, the definition of insanity changed to the individual not understanding what he or she did. The plea of "guilty, but mentally ill" was developed as well by some states, to separate mental illness and criminal responsibility. *Competency to stand trial* assesses the individual's mental state at the time of the trial. There are several criteria for competence. If individuals are found incompetent, they are committed, but only for finite periods *(Jackson v. Indiana, 1972),* thereby protecting *due process.*

II. **Civil commitment.** Individuals can be hospitalized against their will, although this should be avoided if possible. The criteria for commitment include danger to self or others, inability to care for self, inability to make responsible decisions, and unmanageable level of panic. Assessment of dangerousness is very difficult because it is rare, is influenced by specific situations, is best predicted by evidence inadmissible by courts and is ill-defined. Despite the difficulties in defining dangerousness, once someone believes that a person is a threat to himself or herself or to others, civil commitment procedures may be instituted. The rationale for this action is that it (1) prevents harm to the person or to others, (2) provides appropriate treatment and care, and (3) ensures due process of law (that is, legal hearing). In most cases, people deemed in need of protective confinement can be persuaded to voluntarily commit themselves to a period of hospitalization. This process is fairly straightforward, and many believe that it is the preferred one. Involuntary commitment occurs when the client does not consent to hospitalization. .

III. **Rights of mental patients.** Many people in the United States are concerned about the balance of power among the state, our mental institutions, and our citizens. The U.S. Constitution guarantees certain "inalienable rights" such as trial by jury, legal representation, and protection against self-incrimination. The mental health profession has great power, which may be used wittingly or unwittingly to abridge individual freedom. In recent decades, some courts have ruled that commitment for any purpose constitutes a major deprivation of liberty that requires due process protection. Mental patients can be committed only with a level of proof that is "clear and convincing" (Addington v. Texas, 1979). Treatment should be provided in the least restrictive environment, confining people to hospitals only when they cannot care for themselves in less structured settings. Wyatt v. Stickney (1972) established the concept of right to treatment and stipulated minimal living conditions for care. O'Connor v. Donaldson (1975) also affirmed the right to treatment, although there is debate about who defines "treatment." Several cases including Ford vs. Wainwright (2002) have supported the patient's right to refuse treatment and to receive treatment that takes the least intrusive form possible

IV. **Deinstitutionalization.** *Deinstitutionalization is* a policy begun in the 1960s involving the discharge of patients from mental hospitals. Reasons for this movement include the belief that living in institutions is harmful, that *mainstreaming* (integrating) patients back into the community can be accomplished, and that insufficient public funds necessitate early discharge. Critics of deinstitutionalization point to the problem of "dumping" patients on city streets and to the related problem of homelessness. The lack of community resources for discharged patients is a primary reason for the problems with deinstitutionalization.

V. **Therapist-client relationship** Ethics prohibit therapists from divulging information given by clients, in much the same way that attorneys and doctors may not reveal information. However, there are a number of situations that call for breaking the ethical standard of *confidentiality.* A narrower legal concept is *privileged communication,* which prevents disclosure of information without the client's permission. There are at least five situations in which the therapist is obliged to disclose privileged communications. One of them is when a client is likely to carry out a threat to attack someone else. The *Tarasoff v. Board of Regents* case (1976) established the duty-to-warn principle. There are several criticisms of the duty-to-warn principle. Sexual misconduct by therapists is considered one of the most serious of all ethical violations and is condemned by virtually all professional organizations. Clients who become sexually involved with their therapists are adversely affected. Professional organizations process ethical complaints against therapists who engage in misconduct.

VI.   **Cultural competence and the mental health profession** The proportion of racial, cultural, and ethnic minorities in the population of the United States is increasing. Mental health professionals need to be aware of biases, have adequate training, and adjust their methods to provide culturally appropriate services. DSM-IV-TR includes information on culture specific symptom patterns; the American Psychological Association has published guidelines for professionals serving culturally diverse populations. In a historic move by the American Psychological Association, the council of representatives passed "Guidelines on multicultural education, training, research, practice and organizational change for psychologists".

VII.   **Implications.** It is clear that psychology is increasingly serving a larger and larger role in our legal system. From evaluating the mental state of people to aiding in decisions regarding the care and treatment of patients, psychological knowledge has informed and been informed by legal statutes that guide our behavior. More importantly, mental health professionals realize that they do not work in isolation from the broader society, and clinical decisions must take into consideration changing legal precedents and the law. Just as psychological science may produce new knowledge that will affect the legal system and change our roles (better prediction of dangerousness and violence), so too the legal landscape may change and affect the field of abnormal psychology as well.

KEY TERMS REVIEW

1.   The plea that defendants use if they have committed a crime but plead not guilty because of mental illness at the time of the crime is called the _____.

2.   The shift of responsibility for the care of mental patients from large hospitals to agencies in local communities is called _____.

3.   The form of involuntary protective confinement in which a person is judged to be dangerous to self or others, even though no crime has been committed, is called _____.

4.   The definition of insanity stating that a defendant is not responsible if he or she lacked the willpower to control his or her behavior is called the _____.

5.   The concept of judging whether a defendant's mental state at the time of trial is sufficient to enable the defendant to assist in his or her own defense is called _____.

6.   The principle that patients should be placed in an environment that gives maximum freedom considering the person's capacities is called the _____.

7.   The involuntarily committed mental patient's right to receive therapy to improve his or her emotional state is called the _____.

8.   The assessment of an individual's potential to harm self or others is the assessment of _____.

9.   The integration of mental patients back into the community as soon as possible after treatment is called _____.

10.   The legal checks and balances that guarantee the right to a fair trial, to face accusers, and to present evidence (among other things) is called _____.

11.   The legal principle that prevents clients' confidential communications with their therapists from being disclosed in court without their permission is called _____.

12.   The incarceration of an individual on the basis of the commission of a crime is called _____.

13.   The ethical standard that protects clients from the disclosure of information without their consent is called _____.

14. The test of legal insanity that combines both cognitive and motivational criteria is called the
    _____.

15. Commonly called the "duty-to-warn principle," the mental health professional's obligation to break confidentiality when a client poses a clear danger to another person is called the _____ ruling.

16. The test of legal insanity that asks whether the person was overcome by an irresistible impulse is called the _____ standard.

17. The test of legal insanity that asks whether the accused knew right from wrong at the time the crime was committed is called the _____ rule.

FACTUAL MULTIPLE-CHOICE QUESTIONS

1. As a result of the successful insanity defense by John W. Hinckley, Jr.,

   a. defendants claim insanity in more than 20 percent of criminal cases today.
   b. the insanity defense was abolished.
   c. some states adopted alternative pleas, such as "guilty, but mentally ill."
   d. the criteria for defining "dangerousness" were made more rigorous.

2. The *Jackson v. Indiana* ruling of 1972 protects committed patients in what way?

   a. It protects them from being committed indefinitely without review.
   b. It protects them from coercive or ineffective treatment.
   c. It protects them from inadequate living conditions.
   d. It assures that information about them will not be divulged by their therapists.

3. Which statement about dangerousness in mental patients is most *accurate?*

   a. Psychologists tend to underpredict dangerousness in patients.
   b. Dangerousness is rarely used as a criterion for civil commitment.
   c. Psychiatric patients' are no more dangerous to others than is the population at large.
   d. Among mental patients, the legal determination of dangerousness has little impact on whether or not violence will occur.

4. Which statement about involuntary civil commitment proceedings is *accurate?*

   a. Judges have sole discretion to decide whether the person needs to be in treatment.
   b. The person being examined can speak on his or her own behalf and is represented by counsel.
   c. In some states, a family physician can commit a person.
   d. A jury always decides whether a person needs to be committed.

5. *Addington v. Texas* (1979) has had its greatest impact on

   a. deinstitutionalization.
   b. the ethics of divulging confidential client information.
   c. the insanity defense.
   d. the standards used to determine civil commitment.

6. The principle of _____ argues that patients should be confined to hospitals only when they are unable to care for themselves.

   a. deinstitutionalization
   b. most intrusive treatment
   c. least restrictive environment
   d. privileged communication

7. The right of patients to receive adequate care in a satisfactory living environment was based on rulings in which cases?

    a. *Wyatt v. Stickney* and *O'Connor v. Donaldson*
    b. *Tarasoff v. Board of Regents* and *Rouse v. Cameron*
    c. *Jackson v. Indiana* and *Tarasoff v. Board of Regents*
    d. *Rogers v. Okin* and *United States v. Hinckley*

8. According to a recent court ruling, who decides what constitutes "therapy"?

    a. Mental health professionals
    b. A jury
    c. The patient and his or her family
    d. No one; this has not been legally determined.

9. Research on sexual relationships between therapists and clients indicates that

    a. more than one-third of male therapists admit to having had sexual intercourse with clients.
    b. complaints to state licensing boards about sexual misconduct have dropped dramatically in recent years.
    c. while sexual involvement with therapists is rather common, it rarely has a harmful effect.
    d. sexual intimacy has adverse effects on nearly all clients.

10. What changes have occurred in the DSM-IV-TR that relate to clinical work with individuals from culturally diverse backgrounds?

    a. It now points out the disorders that never or rarely occur in certain cultural groups.
    b. It now explains the genetic basis for disorders occurring in certain cultural groups.
    c. It now gives guidelines on how symptoms of disorders among cultural groups may vary.
    d. It now instructs clinicians how to treat clients from culturally diverse backgrounds so their behavior becomes more similar to those in the majority culture.

CONCEPTUAL MULTIPLE-CHOICE QUESTIONS

1. According to the M'Naghten Rule, defendants are insane if, at the time of

    a. their trial, they cannot assist in their own defense.
    b. the crime, they did not understand the wrongfulness of their actions.
    c. the crime, they were unable to control their actions.
    d. their trial, they are severely mentally ill.

2. When psychologists assess a defendant to determine his or her competency to stand trial, they are interested in the

    a. person's mental state at present.
    b. Person's dangerousness.
    c. availability and effectiveness of treatment alternatives.
    d. person's mental state at the time of the crime.

3. Being unable to care for oneself, being a dangerous threat to someone else, or being in a severe state of panic are

    a. ways of defining dangerousness.
    b. reasons for declaring someone insane.
    c. reasons for being allowed to refuse treatment.
    d. reasons for involuntary commitment.

4. If, in the future, the use of ECT and psychosurgery to treat mildly disturbed patients is not permitted, this can be attributed to the

   a. principle of duty to warn.
   b. need for patients to be competent before being tried.
   c. concept of deinstitutionalization.
   d. principle of least intrusive treatment.

5. Which statement about deinstitutionalization is *accurate*?

   a. Despite thirty years of efforts to reduce the number of mental patients in hospitals, no decrease has occurred.
   b. The goal of deinstitutionalization was to eliminate the insanity defense.
   c. Generally speaking, deinstitutionalization has led to the successful reintegration of mental patients into their home communities.
   d. Deinstitutionalization has been very successful in reducing the number of patients in state mental hospitals.

6. Which problem is most directly related to deinstitutionalization?

   a. Therapists unethically engaging mi sexual relations with their clients
   b. Large numbers of discharged patients becoming homeless
   c. A dramatic increase in the number of successful insanity defense cases
   d. Greater abuse and neglect of patients in mental hospitals

7. The need for trust and openness in psychotherapy is the reason for

   a. the principle of duty to warn.
   b. deinstitutionalization.
   c. confidentiality of client information.
   d. the principle of least restrictive environment.

8. The concept of privileged communication is

   a. a legal one, similar to the arrangement between husband and wife.
   b. an ethical one that involves no legal obligation.
   c. a recent "invention" stemming from the *Tarasoff v. Board of Regents* (1976) ruling.
   d. not as available to the therapist and client as it is to the attorney and client.

9. Which statement about privileged communication is *accurate?*

   a. It can be broken when the therapist feels it would be helpful for therapy.
   b. It is a legal concept and is held by the client, not the therapist.
   c. The only exemption from privileged communication occurs in criminal cases.
   d. It is defined as an ethical standard protecting clients from disclosure of information.

10. According to the American Psychological Association's ethical principles involving the treatment of culturally different clients,

    a. therapy is forbidden if the therapist and client come from different cultural backgrounds.
    b. therapists should have adequate training in multicultural psychology.
    c. it is the client's responsibility to conform to the cultural expectations of the therapist.
    d. therapists should focus on the symptoms of disorders, not the cultural or environmental influences of clients from culturally diverse backgrounds.

APPLICATION MULTIPLE-CHOICE QUESTIONS

1. The Kenneth Bianchi (Hillside Strangler) case illustrates the issue of

   a. competency to stand trial.
   b. deinstitutionalization.
   c. faking insanity.
   d. privileged communication between therapist and client.

2. David T. is a defendant in a murder case. He claims that a mental disorder prevented him from acting in any way other than the way he did. David T.'s insanity defense is based on

    a. the principle of least restrictive treatment.
    b. the notion of irresistible impulse.
    c. the M'Naghten Rule.
    d. the principle of competency to stand trial.

3. George is being examined by a psychiatrist to see whether he can assist his attorney in his own defense. In what kind of legal hearing is George engaged?

    a. Competency to stand trial
    b. Involuntary civil commitment
    c. Waiver of privileged communication
    d. An insanity defense trial

4. Judge Wallace says, "Thanks to *Jackson v. Indiana,* people are protected against the abuse of endless incarceration when they have committed no crime." The judge is talking about

    a. a ruling restricting deinstitutionalization.
    b. the new "guilty, but mentally ill" plea.
    c. the principle of least restrictive treatment environment.
    d. a ruling restricting confinement based solely on the grounds of incompetency.

5. Dr. Roland says, "When people are so mentally ill that they cannot control their actions and may harm others, we cannot wait until they have become violent. We must treat them involuntarily." Dr. Roland's comments argue

    a. against the insanity defense.
    b. against deinstitutionalization.
    c. for the concept of duty to warn.
    d. for civil commitment.

6. Mr. Birch, an attorney, says, "If this person is going to be involuntarily committed, the judge needs to have clear and convincing evidence that the person is mentally ill and potentially dangerous." Mr. Birch is using the ruling in

    a. T*arasoff. v. Board of Regents (1976).*
    b. *Addington v. Texas (1979).*
    c. *Wyatt v. Stickney (1972).*
    d. *United States v. Hinckley (1982).*

7. Dr. Poole, director of a state hospital, says, "Because of deinstitutionalization, we need to release patients quickly. Although treatment is not required after discharge, while they are here, they have the right to the treatment standards outlined in *Wyatt v. Stickney.*" What part of Dr. Poole's statement is *inaccurate?*

    a. The idea that deinstitutionalization might lead to quick discharge.
    b. The idea that *Wyatt v. Stickney is* linked to patients' rights.
    c. The idea that the right to treatment ends when a person is discharged.
    d. Nothing in Dr. Poole's statement is inaccurate.

8. Dr. Luborsky says, "It has reduced the number of patients in state hospitals by more than 50 percent but has led to the criminalization of the mentally ill and has increased the problem of homelessness in the United States." Dr. Luborsky is commenting on

    a. deinstitutionalization.
    b. the insanity defense.
    c. the right to refuse treatment.
    d. the principle of duty to warn.

9. Dr. Judd's patient, Mike V., is threatening to blow up his father-in-law's store. Dr. Judd thinks the threat is legitimate. According to _____ Dr. Judd must _____.

    a. *Rogers v. Okin (1979);* not divulge this information to the police
    b. *Wyatt v. Stickney (1972);* have Mike V. committed
    c. *Tarasoff v. Board of Regents (1976);* warn Mike's father-in-law
    d. *Youngberg v. Romeo (1982);* have Mike V. arrested

10. Vanessa saw a male psychotherapist for seven months. Toward the end of that time the therapist engaged in sexual intercourse with her. Vanessa can expect

    a. to find that none of the professional organizations for therapists will condemn sexual intimacies in therapist-client relationships.
    b. to suffer emotionally from this experience.
    c. to learn, unfortunately, that there are no ways to file ethical complaints against the therapist.
    d. to feel more and more independent of her therapist as a result of this behavior.

ANSWER KEY: KEY TERMS REVIEW

1. insanity defense

2. deinstitutionalization

3. civil commitment

4. irresistible impulse test

5. competency to stand trial

6. least restrictive environment

7. right to treatment

8. dangerousness

9. mainstreaming

10. due process

11. privileged communication

12. criminal commitment

13. confidentiality

14. American Law Institute (ALI) Model Penal Code

15. *Tarasoff* ruling

16. *Durham* standard

17. M'Naghten Rule

ANSWER KEY: FACTUAL MULTIPLE-CHOICE QUESTIONS

1. c.   The furor after the verdict led to the American Bar and Medical associations' requests for changes in the law, to the Insanity Reform Act of 1984, and to several states developing new pleas.

    a.   The insanity defense is used in less than 1 percent of criminal cases.

    b.   The insanity defense still exists but in a somewhat more restricted form.

    d.   Dangerousness is an issue in civil commitment cases, not in the insanity defense.

2. a. Because of this ruling, people who are committed because they are incompetent to stand trial cannot be confined indefinitely without review.

  b. Relevant right to treatment rulings include *Wyatt v. Stickney* and *O'Connor v. Donaldson.*

  c. The relevant ruling here is *Wyatt v. Stickney.*

  d. This ruling deals with indefinite confinement, not privileged communication.

3. c. Despite the popular myth, few psychotic patients are assaultive and psychotic patients have only slightly higher rates of violent behavior than the population at large.

  a. The error that psychologists make is overpredicting dangerousness.

  b. Dangerousness is the chief criterion for civil commitment.

  d. Just as with other people, violent behavior among those with mental disorders is the result of both personality and situational factors.

4. b. Civil commitment proceedings include due process; the person can speak on his or her own behalf and have legal counsel.

  a. Expert witnesses, such as psychologists and psychiatrists, testify to provide their assessments of the person's need for treatment.

  c. No longer can one person determine that another person should be committed; the legal proceedings provide greater protection of civil rights now.

  d. In most cases, commitment is decided by a judge, not a jury.

5. d. *Addington* raised the level of proof in civil commitment cases to "clear and convincing evidence" (75-percent certainty).

  a. Deinstitutionalization is most affected by rulings involving the least restrictive environment principle.

  b. *Addington* had nothing to do with confidentiality.

  c. *Addington* had nothing to do with the placement of mental patients.

6. c. To ensure civil liberties, the principle of least restrictive environment allows for hospitalization only as a last resort.

  a. Deinstitutionalization is a related, but much broader, idea that considers all the reasons for using community agencies rather than large institutions.

  b. The legal principle is *least* intrusive treatment.

  d. The principle of privileged communication is confined to therapist-client relationships.

7. a. The *Wyatt* ruling of Judge Frank Johnson set the standards for mental treatment in institutions; *O'Connor* supported the right-to-treatment principle.

  b. *Tarasoff* dealt with duty to warn; *Rouse* did involve right to treatment.

  c. *Jackson* limited the duration of confinement for people found incompetent; *Tarasoff* dealt with duty to warn.

  d. *Rogers* dealt with the right to refuse treatment; *Hinckley* was the insanity defense case involving the man who shot President Ronald Reagan.

8. a. The case is *Youngberg v. Romeo (1982),* and the decision was that. mental health professionals should define "therapy."

    b. *Youngberg* ruled that professionals decide.

    c. *Youngberg* ruled that professionals decide.

    d. Although the law in this area is new, the *Youngberg* case does give guidance.

9. d. In a survey of clients sexually involved with therapists, 90 percent reported being negatively affected.

    a. In a survey of 1,000 psychologists, 5.5 percent of the males admitted to sexual intercourse with clients.

    b. Complaints have increased significantly.

    c. In a survey of clients sexually involved with therapists, 90 percent reported being negatively affected.

10. c. A new section in DSM-IV-TR provides guidelines on how clinical presentation of disorders among cultural groups may vary.

    a. DSM-IV-TR lists disorders that may be culturally specific, but does not point out those that are absent in certain cultures.

    b. The DSM-IV-TR omits all discussion of cause, genetics or otherwise.

    d. Rather than expecting clients to conform to the behavior of the majority culture, DSM-IV-TR seeks to reduce clinicians' possible cultural bias.

ANSWER KEY: CONCEPTUAL MULTIPLE-CHOICE QUESTIONS

1. b. The M'Naghten Rule is a cognitive test that defines insanity in terms of the inability to know right from wrong when the crime was committed.

    a. The ability to assist in one's own defense is a criterion for competency to stand trial, not for insanity.

    c. Irresistible impulse is the definition of insanity as an incapacity to control one's actions.

    d. The insanity defense pertains only to the person's mental state when the crime was committed.

2. a. Competency to stand trial is based on the defendant's current ability to understand the proceedings and to assist in his or her own defense.

    b. Dangerousness is most closely related to civil commitment cases, not competency.

    c. The availability of treatment does not pertain to competency to stand trial.

    d. The person's mental state at the time of the crime influences the validity of an insanity defense.

3. d. Dangerousness, an inability to care for oneself, and an extreme attack of anxiety are reasons for committing people to treatment against their will.

    a. Although presenting a threat to someone else is a part of "dangerousness," the rest of the information suggests the broader category of concern, the need for commitment.

    b. Insanity is defined as being unable to appreciate the wrongfulness of an act or being incapable of resisting an impulse.

    c. Reasons for refusing treatment have more to do with delusional thinking than with dangerousness or a state of panic.

4. d. This principle suggests that ECT and surgery are more intrusive therapies than insight or behavioral therapies and thus should not be used with mildly disturbed patients.

    a. Duty to warn defines a situation in which therapists must break confidentiality.

    b. Competency is unrelated to treatment issues.

    c. Deinstitutionalization is concerned with *where* treatment occurs, not so much with the matching of patients and therapy methods.

5. d. The state hospital population of the United States dropped by more than 50 percent, and the average daily number of committed patients decreased by 75 percent.

    a. Deinstitutionalization has reduced hospital populations by more than one-half.

    b. The goal of deinstitutionalization was to dramatically reduce the reliance on hospitals for treatment.

    c. The great failure of deinstitutionalization is that discharged patients, lacking community support, return to the hospital.

6. b. In many cases, discharged patients have been "dumped" in urban areas, and have no homes or social supports.

    a. Deinstitutionalization is unrelated to therapist-client relationships.

    c. Deinstitutionalization is unrelated to criminal commitment.

    d. If anything, the reduced populations in mental hospitals have led to improvements in care.

7. c. Confidentiality in therapy is necessary if clients are to believe that they can be open without fearing that they may be hurt.

    a. The duty-to-warn principle puts greater emphasis on protecting victims than on assuring confidentiality; this reduces openness.

    b. Deinstitutionalization is unrelated to therapist-client relationships.

    d. This Principle considers only the location of treatment.

8. a. Privileged communication between therapist and client is a legal concept.

    b. It is the wider concept of confidentiality that is an ethical concept unprotected by the law.

    c. *Tarasoff* defined when privileged communication must be breached.

    d. Therapists and clients have the same legal privilege as attorneys and their clients.

9. b. Privileged communication is a legal concept; the privilege is the client's and only the client can waive it.

    a. The privilege is in the hands of the client, not the therapist.

    c. There are other exemptions for the privilege: civil cases, cases involving civil commitment, and cases in which the client is under sixteen and the victim of a crime or abuse.

    d. Confidentiality is an ethical standard that has broader reach than the legal concept of privileged communication.

10. b. Psychologists are expected to be aware of cultural differences and their own biases, to be able to identify situations in which specific therapeutic strategies must be modified to be culturally sensitive, and to obtain sufficient training to do these things.

    a. As long as therapists are aware of cultural differences and provide appropriate treatment, there is nothing to prohibit cross-cultural treatment.

    c. Ethical principles place responsibility for adjusting to cultural differences on the therapist, not the client.

    d. DSM-IV-TR has an appendix that presents culture-bound syndromes; the APA ethical guidelines require psychologists to adjust treatment to be culturally appropriate.

ANSWER KEY: APPLICATION MULTIPLE-CHOICE QUESTIONS

1. c. Until it was uncovered Bianchi's faking, it was believed that he was suffering from multiple personality (dissociative identity) disorder.

    a. Bianchi's lawyers considered using the insanity defense.

    b. Bianchi was on trial for a series of murders; he was not a mental patient.

    d. Bianchi was not in therapy, so there was no such issue.

2. b. Irresistible impulse is one definition of insanity; it is based on an inability to conform to the law because of a mental disease or defect.

    a. Treatment becomes an issue only after a person is found incompetent or insane.

    c. The M'Naghten Rule is a cognitive definition of insanity based on the lack of appreciation that what one did was wrong.

    d. Competency is defined as mental capacity at the time of the trial, not at the time of the crime.

3. a. Competency involves a defendant's capacity to understand the proceedings and to assist in his or her own defense.

    b. Such an assessment assumes that a crime was committed; in civil commitment, no crime is presumed.

    c. Waiver of privileged communication is not based on a person's ability to act in his or her own defense.

    d. Insanity is concerned with a defendant's mental state at the time of the crime, not at the time of the trial.

4. d. The *Jackson* ruling held that those who were committed because they were not competent to stand trial could not be "forgotten" and must either stand trial or be committed for treatment.

    a. *Jackson* protected people against indefinite confinement; the ruling supports deinstitutionalization.

    b. *Jackson (1972)* occurred some ten years before the Hinckley case, which led to calls for more stringent definitions of insanity.

    c. *Jackson* dealt only with how long a person could be confined, not where.

5. d. Civil commitment deals with confining people for treatment before they have committed any crime.

    a. The insanity defense is unrelated to treatment.

    b. Although these comments have relevance to deinstitutionalization, that concept is much broader and deals with the need for community-based treatment.

    c. Duty to warn involves therapist-client relationships, not criminal cases.

6. b. *Addington* determined necessary levels of proof in commitment cases.

    a. Tarasoff decided the therapist's role in protecting potential victims of his or her client.

    c. Wyatt established the right to treatment and the conditions under which treatment should be offered.

    d. *Hinckley* dealt with the insanity defense.

7. d. Because a, b, and c are all correct, there is nothing inaccurate in Dr. Poole's comments.

    a. Deinstitutionalization has led to earlier discharge.

    b. *Wyatt* was a major case supporting the patient's right to treatment.

    c. There is no court ruling that suggests hospitals must provide treatment after discharge.

8. a. Deinstitutionalization has led to a reduction in hospital populations, but discharged patients often do not receive support in urban communities and windup homeless or in jail.

    b. The insanity defense has nothing to do with state hospital populations.

    c. The right to refuse treatment may lead to more untreated mental patients, but it does not as clearly lead to homelessness.

    d. Duty to warn is related to therapist-client relationships, not to hospitalization.

9. c. *Tarasoff* is the case that established the principle of duty to warn; Dr. Judd would be negligent if she did not warn.

    a. *Rogers is* a case involving the right to refuse treatment.

    b. Wyatt is a case involving the right to adequate treatment.

    d. *Youngberg is* a involving case the definition of "treatment" for committed patients.

10. b.   In a survey of 559 clients who became sexually intimate with their therapists, 90 percent were adversely affected, many showing symptoms similar to those of rape and battered spouse syndrome.

    a.   Virtually every organization that represents psychotherapists condemns sexual intimacy between therapist and client as unethical, immoral, and antitherapeutic.

    c.   Most states and professional organizations have means for filing ethical complaints; civil suits charging malpractice are always a legal recourse.

    d.   Rather than become more independent, many clients become more dependent on their therapist following sexual intimacy.

OBJECTIVES DEFINED

1. **What are the criteria used to judge insanity, and what is the difference between being insane and being incompetent to stand trial?**

*   Insanity is a legal concept. Historically, several standards have been used.

*   The M'Naghten Rule holds that people can be acquitted of a crime if it can be shown that their reasoning was so defective that they were unaware of their actions or, if aware of their actions, were unable to comprehend the wrongness of them. The irresistible impulse test holds that people are innocent if they are unable to control their behavior. The *Durham* decision acquits people if their criminal actions were products of mental disease or defects. The American Law Institute guidelines state that people are not responsible for a crime if they lack substantial capacity to appreciate the criminality of their conduct or to conform their conduct to the requirements of the law.

*   The phrase "competency to stand trial" refers to defendants' mental state at the time they are being examined. It is a separate issue from criminal responsibility, which refers to past behavior at the time of the offense. Accused people are considered incompetent if they have difficulty understanding the trial proceedings or cannot rationally consult with attorneys in their defense. Although competency to stand trial is important in ensuring fair trials, being judged incompetent can have negative consequences, such as unfair and prolonged denial of civil liberties.

2. **Under what conditions can a person be involuntarily committed to a mental institution?**

*   People who have committed no crime can be confined against their will if it can be shown that (1) they present a clear and imminent danger to themselves or others, (2) they are unable to care for themselves, (3) they are unable to make responsible decisions about appropriate treatment and hospitalization, and (4) they are in an unmanageable state of fright or panic.

*   Courts have tightened criteria and rely more than ever on the concept of dangerousness. Mental health professionals have great difficulty in predicting dangerousness because dangerous acts depend as much on social situations as on personal attributes and because the definition is unclear.

3. **What rights do mental patients have with respect to treatment and care issues?**

*   Concern with patients' rights has become an issue because many practices and procedures seem to violate constitutional guarantees. As a result, court rulings have established several important precedents. Among these are the right to treatment and the right to refuse treatment.

4. **What is deinstitutionalization?**

*   During the 1960s and 1970s, the policy of deinstitutionalization became popular: the shifting of responsibility for the care of mental patients from large central institutions to agencies within the local community. Deinstitutionalization was considered a promising answer to the "least

restrictive environment" ruling and to monetary problems experienced by state governments. Critics, however, have accused the states of "dumping" former patients and avoiding their responsibilities under the guise of mental health innovations.

5. **What legal and ethical issues govern the therapist-client relationship?**

- Most mental health professionals believe that confidentiality is crucial to the therapist-client relationship. Exceptions to this privilege include situations that involve (1) civil or criminal commitment and competency to stand trial, (2) a client's initiation of a lawsuit for malpractice or a civil action in which the client's mental condition is introduced, (3) the belief that child or elder abuse has occurred, (4) a criminal action, or (5) the danger a client poses to himself or herself or to others.

- Although psychologists have always known that privileged communication is not an absolute right, the *Tarasoff* decision makes therapists responsible for warning a potential victim to avoid liability.

- Sexual misconduct of therapists is considered to be one of the most serious of all ethical violations by virtually all professional organizations.

6. **What is cultural competence in the mental health profession?**

- Major demographic changes are forcing mental health professionals to consider culture, ethnicity, gender, and socioeconomic status as powerful variables in (1) the manifestation of mental disorders and (2) the need to provide culturally appropriate intervention strategies for minority groups. Increasingly, mental health organizations are taking the position that it is unethical to treat members of marginalized groups without adequate training and expertise in multicultural psychology.

MARGIN DEFINITIONS

American Law Institute (ALI) Model Penal Code a test of legal insanity that combines both cognitive criteria (diminished capacity) and motivational criteria (specific intent); its purpose is to give jurors increased latitude in determining the sanity of the accused

civil commitment the involuntary confinement of a person judged to be a danger to himself or herself or to others, even though the person has not committed a crime

competency to stand trial a judgment that a defendant has a factual and rational understanding of the proceedings and can rationally consult with counsel in presenting his or her own defense; refers to the defendant's mental state at the time of the psychiatric examination

confidentiality an ethical standard that protects clients from disclosure of information without their consent; an ethical obligation of the therapist

criminal commitment incarceration of an individual for having committed a crime

dangerousness a person's potential for doing harm to himself or herself or to others

deinstitutionalization the shifting of responsibility for the care of mental patients from large central institutions to agencies within local communities

due process legal checks and balances that are guaranteed to everyone (the right to a fair trial, the right to face accusers, the right to present evidence, the right to counsel, and so on)

Durham standard a test of legal insanity known as the products test—an accused person is not responsible if the unlawful act was the product of mental disease or defect

insanity defense the legal argument used by defendants who admit they have committed a crime but plead not guilty because they were mentally disturbed at the time the crime was committed

irresistible impulse test one test of sanity, which states that a defendant is not criminally responsible if he or she lacked the will power to control his or her behavior

least restrictive environment a person's right to the least restrictive alternative to freedom that is appropriate to his or her condition

M'Naghten rule a cognitive test of legal insanity that inquires whether the accused knew right from wrong when he or she committed the crime

mainstreaming integrating mental patients as soon as possible back into the community

privileged communication a therapist's legal obligation to protect a client's privacy and to prevent the disclosure of confidential communications without a client's permission

right to treatment the concept that mental patients who have been involuntarily committed have a right to receive therapy that would improve their emotional state

Tarasoff **ruling** often referred to as the "duty-to-warn" principle; obligates mental health professionals to break confidentiality when their clients pose clear and imminent danger to another person